MW01492495

MISSOURI BAPTISTS

1 September 2021

Dear State Convention Leader:

It's my pleasure to enclose a complimentary copy of a new book just released by High Street Press, the publishing imprint of the Missouri Baptist Convention, and made possible through the generous Cooperative Program giving of MBC-affiliated churches.

What Every Christian Should Know about Satan by the MBC's Rob Phillips explores more than a dozen biblical names and titles that reveal the evil one's character, tactics, and ultimate destiny in hell.

This resource is designed for pastors and laypersons who desire a deeper study of Satan's doomed campaign against God and God's people. Each chapter ends with summaries, as well as questions for personal or group study.

The book features terrifying biblical accounts of Satan's power, and insights into his devious ways. Yet, Christians have no reason to fear the evil one, for he is a lion on God's leash and his destiny in the lake of fire is as certain as the sovereign hand of God.

I am so confident in the disciple-making value of this book that I will share the cost with you. Order at least 10 copies of *What Every Christian Should Know about Satan* and pay just $5 apiece plus shipping.

To place an order, please contact Christie Dowell of the MBC at 573.636.0400 ext. 303, or via email at cdowell@mobaptist.org.

For individual print or e-book copies, visit highstreet.press or Amazon.com.

May the Lord bless you in your service to Him in the days ahead.

Sincerely,

Dr. John Yeats
Executive Director – Treasurer

WHAT EVERY CHRISTIAN SHOULD KNOW ABOUT SATAN

BIBLICAL NAMES AND TITLES THAT REVEAL HIS
NATURE, ACTIVITIES, AND DESTINY

ROB PHILLIPS

high street press

Acknowledgements:

Executive editor: Dr. John Yeats
Cover design and graphics: Laura Schembre
Layout: Brianna Boes, Beyond Here Publishing
Production management: Leah England
Electronic production: Brianna Boes
Scripture verification: Christie Dowell
Proofreading: Christie Dowell, Nancy Phillips

High Street Press is the publishing arm of the Missouri Baptist Convention (MBC) and exists because of the generous support of Missouri Baptists through the Cooperative Program. To learn more about the MBC and the way 1,800 affiliated churches cooperate voluntarily for the sake of the gospel, visit mobaptist.org. To learn more about High Street Press, visit highstreet.press.

CONTENTS

FOREWORD

"Pleased to meet you! Hope you guessed my name!"

Mick Jagger, lead singer of The Rolling Stones, repeated this line in the 1968 hit song, *Sympathy for the Devil*. In the song, Jagger assumed the character of the Devil, outlining tragedy after tragedy in human history where Satan was present and actively engaged in destroying life and society. If you didn't catch who he was at the start of the song, you definitely figured it out by the end.

But who exactly is Satan?

From movies to commercials, from pop fiction to video games, Satan plays a significant role in the culture's broad imagination. He's a cute, red cherub representing the wrong choice. He's the one whispering in your ear to do wrong. He's that red beast with horns in the middle of hell.

The truth is, unless he is part of a horror movie, Western culture tends to dismiss Satan as a person. He is seen simply as the personification of all things evil or a force working to counter the movements of God. Rarely do we think of the Devil as a literal, created being who, along with his demons, is working destructively in the world today.

Prior generations did better. Consider the great reformer, Martin

Luther. In his hymn, *A Mighty Fortress is Our God* (1528), Luther extols the manner in which God protects us as believers. But Luther didn't mince words about Satan. In the first verse of the hymn, he states:

> *For still our ancient foe*
> *Doth seek to work us woe;*
> *His craft and power are great,*
> *And, armed with cruel hate,*
> *On earth is not his equal.*

While the song moves forward to uphold Jesus as the King and victor over Satan, there is no minimizing the threat. In verse 3, Luther paints a picture that could be frightening:

> *And though this world, with devils filled,*
> *Should threaten to undo us,*
> *We will not fear, for God hath willed*
> *His truth to triumph through us:*
> *The Prince of Darkness grim,*
> *We tremble not for him;*
> *His rage we can endure,*
> *For lo! his doom is sure,*
> *One little word shall fell him.*

The Bible is rather clear about the person of Satan, and the book you hold in your hands will help you cut through the noise of cultural portrayals. Rob Phillips takes you into the pages of Scripture to help you understand that the evil one is not a creature in a red suit with a pointy tail and a pitchfork; rather, he is one who stands as "the accuser of our brothers and sisters" (Rev. 12:10), one "looking for anyone he can devour" (1 Pet. 5:8). By the end of this study, you will have a clear understanding of why we, as Christians, have no need to fear Satan, but also why the Bible tells us we are engaged in spiritual warfare.

It is my prayer that as you read this volume and study the

Scriptures, you come away with a clear understanding of Satan – a *biblical* view of Satan and his work. Once equipped, you will walk with confidence, knowing that the evil one's end is already decreed because Jesus is King.

John Mark Yeats
Dean of Students and Student Success
Professor of Church History
Midwestern Baptist Theological Seminary

INTRODUCTION

What's in a name? Our parents may have named us after beloved ancestors, movie stars, heroic leaders, or even favorite songs. Our daughter Aubrey, for example, shares the name of the title character in a 1970s pop hit. Popular names in one generation may fade as trendy new names emerge, only to return later. Others seem timeless, like James and Mary, which have remained the most popular U.S. baby names for a century.[1] It's hard to know what on earth celebrity parents are thinking when they christen their kids "Moon Unit" or "Pilot Inspektor." But even lyricist Shel Silverstein revealed a motive behind the dad who named his son "Sue":

> But ya ought to thank me, before I die
> For the gravel in ya guts and the spit in ya eye[2]

Biblical names seem a bit more purposeful. God names the first human *Adam*, which generally denotes "human being" or "mankind" and links to the Hebrew *adama* to indicate the earth from which he is formed. Pharaoh's daughter names her adopted baby *Moses*, based on a Hebrew term that means "to draw out [of the water]." The LORD commands Hosea to name his sons *Jezreel* and *Lo-ammi*, and his daughter *Lo-ruhamah*, all of which signify pending judgment on Israel. Elizabeth and Zechariah insist on naming their child *John*, resisting all pressure to name him after his father, because that's what the angel Gabriel has instructed them to do.

And then, of course, there are nicknames and descriptive titles. The son of Elizabeth and Zechariah comes to be known as *John the Baptizer*. God changes the names of Abram and Sarai to *Abraham* and *Sarah,* who receive a portion of the divine name, *Yahweh*, as a sign of God's covenant with them. Disciples James and John are *the sons of thunder*. The apostle Thomas is called *Didymus*, which means "the twin." And Saul of Tarsus becomes *Paul*, who gives himself a scathing nickname, "the worst of them [sinners]."

So, what are we to make of Satan and his many names and titles? Curiously, the Hebrew *satan* means "accuser" and is not a title devoted solely to the evil one; even the angel of the LORD plays the role of *satan* on one occasion (Num. 22:22, 32). The Greek *diabolos*, from which we get "devil," is used in the Septuagint – the Greek translation of the Old Testament – to translate *satan* and thus bears essentially the same meaning.

However, there *are* biblical names that focus on a single fallen angel who reigns over a host of demonic followers. These names include *dragon, serpent, father of lies, murderer, tempter, deceiver, evil one, Beelzebul, Belial, ruler of this world*, and *destroyer*. In the following pages, we explore these and other names in an effort to learn more about the archenemy of God and his people.

Chapter 1 examines a single scriptural reference to an *anointed guardian cherub*. Could this be Satan prior to his rebellion and fall?

Chapters 2 and 3 reveal the *serpent*, or *dragon*, introduced in Genesis 3 and cast into the lake of fire and sulfur in Revelation 20.

Chapter 4 explores this creature's most common titles: *Satan* and *the devil*. But neither is used exclusively to depict the evil one.

Chapter 5 takes us to the words of Jesus, who describes the enemy as the *father of lies*. As such, he is the original liar and the instigator of all untruths – especially when set against Jesus, who *is* the truth.

Chapter 6 depicts Satan as a *murderer* – in fact, the first murderer.

First, he murders the human race through his successful temptation of Adam and Eve. Then he prompts Cain to kill his brother Abel. He has been the CEO of Murder Incorporated ever since.

Chapter 7 introduces us to the *tempter*, a role he plays from his first recorded encounter with human beings, and a role he relishes throughout human history.

Chapter 8 exposes the *deceiver*, one who often presents himself as an angel of light.

Chapter 9 describes Satan as the *evil one*, the archetype of everything opposed to God and God's people.

Chapter 10 explores the ancient name *Beelzebul*, tying Satan to idolatrous practices in ancient Israel. He is the well-known prince of evil spirits.

Chapter 11 briefly visits a single but important reference to the evil one as *Belial*.

Chapter 12 surveys Satan's role as the *ruler of this world*. We learn how he commands an ever-shrinking army in a kingdom destined for defeat.

Chapter 13 reviews Satan's frightening role as *the destroyer*, called *Abaddon* and *Apollyon* in the Book of Revelation.

Chapter 14 reveals the ultimate destiny of the evil one: *hell*, a place Jesus says has been prepared for Satan and his messengers.

Finally, Chapter 15 examines Paul's teaching on the armor of God, which enables all believers to stand firm in the face of Satan's relentless onslaught.

Each chapter concludes with questions for personal or group study. This study features terrifying tales of Satan's power, and frightening accounts of his devious ways. Yet, we have no reason to fear the evil one, for he is a lion on God's leash and his destiny in the lake of fire is as certain as the sovereign hand of God.

As we study the evil one, we do well to remember that our enemy is not the atheist, animist, Muslim, or Latter-day Saint. They truly are victims of the evil one, who takes them captive to do his will (2 Tim. 2:26). Our anger should be directed at Satan, for he is the true enemy of God and God's people. And our prayers should be for the deliverance of all people whom the evil one has blinded, bound, and taken captive.

No matter how dark this world may seem, Christians always should look up, for our redemption draws near (Luke 21:28). The day approaches when the archenemy is cast into the lake of fire (Rev. 20:10), and our Savior creates new heavens and a new earth (2 Pet. 3:10-13; Rev. 21-22).

ANOINTED GUARDIAN CHERUB

Marcus Licinius Crassus was one of the wealthiest and most powerful men in ancient Rome. Born in 115 BC, he amassed a fortune through various enterprises, which ranged from dealing in slaves to restoring fire-ravaged land and selling it at huge profits. His wealth enabled him to crush rivals and buy influence with Julius Caesar. In fact, he bankrolled the army sent out to quash the Spartacus-led slave rebellion.

In gratitude, Caesar named Crassus governor of Syria, a land rich in resources. It should have been one more step in Crassus' meteoric rise, but he flamed out like a falling star. He led a disastrous campaign against the Parthian Empire. After the battle of Carrhae, he parlayed for peace. But the Parthians poured liquid gold down his throat. One of the richest men who ever lived choked to death from a scalding dose of what he valued most in life. An exalted crony of Caesar, Crassus died in humiliation – a spectacle for the ancient world to behold.[1]

Curiously, we know more about Crassus' rise and fall than we do about Satan's. The Bible offers little insight into the evil one's exaltation and rebellion, although it does tell us something of his fall and ignominious destiny. We know the devil is a created being. We know he is powerful, clever, deceitful, rapacious, and deadly. We know he throws his full weight into a guerilla campaign against God and God's people. We know he has a vast army of evil spirits who engage holy angels and humans in spiritual warfare. We know he has a kingdom and great authority over those he has taken captive.

But we also know his limits. Satan is neither omniscient, omnipotent, nor omnipresent, for these attributes belong to God alone. Equally important, we know that no matter how highly exalted he once was, or makes himself appear today, he is on a steep downward trajectory. He has been cast out of God's throne room and banished from the heavenly realm. Today, he furiously bides his time prowling the earth. One day, the fires of hell – stoked particularly for him and his minions – are to be his everlasting place of torment (Matt. 25:41).

But when did Satan become the evil one? How did wickedness rise in his heart? How did he ever get the notion he could defeat his creator? And why does he insist on taking as many people to hell with him as possible?

The only answer that makes sense biblically is that Satan is a created being of great intelligence and power who rebelled against God. Scripture is clear that God created everything in the physical and spiritual realms (Gen. 1:1-2; John 1:3; Col. 1:16). This includes Satan. Further, God created everything good (Gen. 1:31; Ps. 104:24; 1 Tim. 4:4).

So, for a supernatural being like Satan to become the evil one, he must have rebelled against God and thus fallen from his original state of innocence. It also follows that God knew this would happen, allowed it, and leveraged it to accomplish greater good through the revelation of his Son, who identified with fallen humans and redeemed them through his sinless life, death, burial, and resurrection. A stunning defeat for the evil one; a triumph for God and his people.

That doesn't answer every question about the rise and fall of Satan, but it gives us a framework for exploring a creature the prophet Ezekiel may have called an *anointed guardian cherub*.

Old Testament Light

Isaiah 14

Two much-debated Old Testament passages give us glimpses into the evil one's heart. The first is Isaiah 14:3-21, which serves as a "taunt" (Heb. *mashal* – a song of contempt, or a comparative parable) against the king of Babylon. At the same time, it features words in verses 12-14 that seem too otherworldly for a human figure.

Isaiah 14 is a message of hope. Although Judah falls to the Babylonians in divine judgment, Babylon itself is destroyed. Exile in Babylon gives way to a joyous escort back to Jerusalem. And then the people sing their victory song against the humbled king of Babylon. The song begins:

> How the oppressor has quieted down, and how the raging has become quiet! The LORD has broken the staff of the wicked, the scepter of the rulers. It struck the peoples in anger with unceasing blows. It subdued the nations in rage with relentless persecution. The whole earth is calm and at rest; people shout with a ringing cry. Even the cypresses and the cedars of Lebanon rejoice over you: "Since you have been laid low, no lumberjack has come against us."
>
> Sheol below is eager to greet your coming, stirring up the spirits of the departed for you – all the rulers of the earth – making all the kings of the nations rise from their thrones. They all respond to you, saying, "You too have become as weak as we are; you have become like us! Your splendor has been brought down to Sheol, along with the music of your harps. Maggots are spread out under you, and worms cover you" (vv. 4-11).

Clearly, the song so far is directed toward a human being – the king of Babylon. While he is addressed as an individual, the lack of a specific name may mean the king represents "the apex of the imperialistic machine that oppressed the people of God."[2]

The king's staff represents his responsibility to shepherd the people. The scepter, an ornamented mace used as a weapon, symbolizes the king's power. Both are broken, demonstrating God's sovereignty. Even the trees of Lebanon rejoice in their reprieve from being cut down to build siege works.

Verse 9 introduces *sheol*, the abode of the dead. *Sheol* is personified and pictured as warmly welcoming the king. The spirits of departed rulers are there, marveling at the king's weakness and humiliation. Verse 11 speaks of maggots and worms that devour the king's body in the grave.

But verses 12-14 address the king in otherworldly terms:

Shining morning star, how you have fallen from the heavens! You destroyer of nations, you have been cut down to the ground. You said to yourself, "I will ascend to the heavens; I will set up my throne above the stars of God. I will sit on the mount of the gods' assembly, in the remotest parts of the North. I will ascend above the highest clouds; I will make myself like the Most High."

Is this still the king of Babylon? Or is this literary bridge a reference to a supernatural being? The King James Version renders verse 12: "How art thou fallen from heaven, O Lucifer, son of the morning! how art thou cut down to the ground, which didst weaken the nations!" Based on this translation, and the view that Satan is the subject of this verse, some conclude that Lucifer (taken from the Latin Vulgate and meaning "light-bringer") is one of the names of the devil. Origen is the first person in the early church period to make this claim.[3] Augustine later adopted it.

Many Bible commentators reject this view, however. "Shining morning star" may figuratively refer to a Canaanite deity whose story provides the pattern for Judah's taunt. This lesser god tries to usurp the position of the high God, resulting in a quick and horrible fall.[4]

As an alternative explanation, the king may be compared to the planet Venus, which in ancient days is considered the morning star that falls quickly through the sky. As for the gods' assembly in the remotest parts of the North, Canaanite mythology again may be in play. The throne of Baal, the chief god, is considered to be on Mount North (Heb. *Zaphon*).

Further evidence against *Lucifer* as a reference to Satan is the Hebrew word from which the name is drawn: *helel*. Rather than follow the insistence of some early church fathers that *helel* derives from *halal*, which can, in rare cases, be rendered "to shine," it makes more sense to translate it from another root word, *yalal*, meaning "to howl" or "to wail."

In fact, Jerome, who produced the Latin Vulgate featuring the name *Lucifer*, admits in his commentary on Isaiah that a better translation of the Hebrew *helel* in this passage is the Latin *ulula*, which means "howling."[5] So why go with *Lucifer*? Jerome is already convinced from his reading of Origen that Isaiah 14 refers to Satan, so his Latin translation bends to this view.[6]

That's not all. The use of *yalal* in Isaiah and other prophetic Old Testament books falls in the context of judgment and lament, making it a better fit for this passage. In fact, "the word only occurs in the prophets and is frequently parallel to other Hebrew words for crying out in sorrow and distress (*zaaq* and *sapad*)," according to scholar John Gilhooly. "Since this particular passage (Isaiah 14) contains admitted elements of lament, the natural translation for the term would be 'Wail!' or 'Howl!,' not 'light-bringer.'"[7]

Gilhooly thus renders the verse, "How you are fallen from heaven! Wail, son of the morning! How you are cut down to the earth who once weakened the nations."[8]

The song of contempt returns solidly to the earthly king in Isaiah 14:

> But you will be brought down to Sheol into the deepest regions of the Pit. Those who see you will stare at you; they will look closely at you: "Is this the man who caused the earth to tremble, who shook the kingdoms, who turned the world into a wilderness, who destroyed its cities and would not release the prisoners to return home?" All the kings of the nations lie in splendor, each in his own

tomb. But you are thrown out without a grave, like a worthless branch, covered by those slain with the sword and dumped into a rocky pit like a trampled corpse. You will not join them in burial, because you destroyed your land and slaughtered your own people. The offspring of evildoers will never be mentioned again. Prepare a place of slaughter for his sons, because of the iniquity of their fathers. They will never rise up to possess a land or fill the surface of the earth with cities (vv. 15-21).

In death, the once powerful king of Babylon is now weak and helpless. The nameless people in the abode of the dead marvel at his demise. Unlike the corpses of other earthly kings who receive majestic burials, the king's body is abandoned on the field of battle, covered by other dead bodies.

In summary, there is little doubt that Isaiah 14 addresses an earthly king, perhaps a composite of the wicked rulers who shake their fists at God and persecute his people. Maggots and worms consume his body, while departed spirits welcome him to *sheol*. Even so, verses 12-14 perhaps project a scriptural shadow – a veiled glimpse of the evil one whose rebellion against God casts the die for all forms of human revolt against their creator.

As Gilhooly acknowledges (and cautions):

Given that the prophetic works have an eschatological character, one could see in the specific historical judgment of the king of Babylon a motif in a pattern of divine judgment that repeats itself and will repeat itself finally in the judgment of the Devil and all his sons in the end time. However, there is a significant difference between recognizing a pattern in prophetic portrayals of judgment and holding that this specific text informs us about the moral fall of Satan. Our desire to fill in gaps in our theological stories should not cause us to read into the prophets what they do not intend to say.[9]

Ezekiel 28

A second much-debated Old Testament passage regarding Satan's origin and fall is found in Ezekiel 28, which details the overthrow of Tyre's ruler and a lament for Tyre's king – perhaps, some argue, two references to the same person. Although no specific king is mentioned, just as in Isaiah 14, the king who reigns during Ezekiel's ministry is Ethbaal III (585-573 BC). The opening verses of Ezekiel 28 clearly address an arrogant human ruler:

> The word of the LORD came to me: "Son of man, say to the ruler of Tyre, 'This is what the Lord GOD says: Your heart is proud, and you have said, "I am a god; I sit in the seat of gods in the heart of the sea." Yet you are a man and not a god, though you have regarded your heart as that of a god. Yes, you are wiser than Daniel; no secret is hidden from you! By your wisdom and understanding you have acquired wealth for yourself. You have acquired gold and silver for your treasuries. By your great skill in trading you have increased your wealth, but your heart has become proud because of your wealth.
>
> "'Therefore, this is what the Lord GOD says: Because you regard your heart as that of a god, I am about to bring strangers against you, ruthless men from the nations. They will draw their swords against your magnificent wisdom and will pierce your splendor. They will bring you down to the Pit, and you will die a violent death in the heart of the sea. Will you still say, "I am a god," in the presence of those who slay you? Yet you will be only a man, not a god, in the hands of those who kill you. You will die the death of the uncircumcised at the hands of strangers. For I have spoken. This is the declaration of the Lord GOD'" (vv. 1-10).

Although the ruler of Tyre fancies himself a god, the Lord clearly rebukes him as an arrogant man who has allowed human wisdom and great wealth to deceive him. He is to die in battle at the hands of strangers and go down to the Pit, the abode of the dead. The text then transitions to a lament for Tyre's king:

> The word of the LORD came to me: "Son of man, lament for the king of Tyre and say to him, 'This is what the Lord GOD says:
>
> You were the seal of perfection, full of wisdom and perfect in beauty. You were in Eden, the garden of God. Every kind of precious stone covered you: carnelian, topaz, and diamond, beryl, onyx, and jasper, lapis lazuli, turquoise and emerald. Your mountings and settings were crafted in gold; they were prepared on the day you were created. You were an *anointed guardian cherub*, for I had appointed you. You were on the holy mountain of God; you walked among the fiery stones. From the day you were created you were blameless in your ways until wickedness was found in you.
>
> Through the abundance of your trade, you were filled with violence, and you sinned. So I expelled you in disgrace from the mountain of God, and banished you, *guardian cherub*, from among the fiery stones. Your heart became proud because of your beauty; For the sake of your splendor you corrupted your wisdom. So I threw you down to the ground; I made you a spectacle before kings. You profaned your sanctuaries by the magnitude of your iniquities in your dishonest trade. So I made fire come from within you, and it consumed you. I reduced you to ashes on the ground in the sight of everyone watching you. All those who know you among the peoples are appalled at you. You have become an object of horror and will never exist again'" (vv. 12-19, emphasis added).

The extravagant descriptions of the king of Tyre – "the seal of perfection;" "in Eden, the garden of God;" "anointed guardian cherub;" "on the holy mountain of God;" "blameless in your ways" – could not literally apply to a human being. The prophet is comparing the king with someone in an exalted position who became corrupt and lost favor with God. The CSB Apologetics Study Bible summarizes two competing viewpoints:

Of twenty descriptive elements identifiable in this passage, at least sixteen can be seen to correlate with Isa. 14:12-17, written some 150 years earlier. The correspondence leads many conservative scholars to conclude that the passages are related and refer to the fall of Satan, the adversary of God and his people and the source of evil. On this view, Ezekiel was stating – in terms his audience would understand – that Satan was the mastermind behind the king of Tyre.

Other commentators, no less committed to the inerrancy of Scripture, find such a theory speculative, going "beyond what is written" (1 Cor. 4:6). If Ezekiel had meant to speak of Satan there is no reason why he would not have mentioned him by name, as occurs in other OT passages (1 Chron. 21:1; Job 1-2; Zech. 3:1-2). Ezekiel, like other prophets of Israel, is known for exaggerated speech; in this passage he magnified the king of Tyre as an exalted Edenic figure in order to amplify the "spectacle" (v. 17) of his disgrace, as one who "will never exist again" (v. 19).[10]

Perhaps we can begin to see why Isaiah 14 and Ezekiel 28 are much debated among evangelical scholars. Let's look again at the first passage – this time, in light of the second one.

Anointed Guardian Cherub

To begin, Isaiah 14 and Ezekiel 28 share several traits. First, they describe wicked earthly kings who aspire to deity. Second, God decrees their humiliation in dramatic fashion; though they seek to sit among, or even above, the gods, they are brought down to the underworld. Third, the prophets' portrayal of the kings' boasting seems to go beyond hyperbole, as if a powerful unseen being lurks behind these kings. Therefore, many commentators believe both Isaiah and Ezekiel present us with descriptions of the evil one – descriptions that provide at least some hint of Satan's former exalted position and subsequent fall.

Isaiah refers to this being as "shining morning star," which, as we already noted, could be an allusion to a Canaanite deity. But Ezekiel calls him an *anointed guardian cherub*. Cherubim are unique heavenly creatures who, like seraphim, are never called *angels* in the Bible. They look nothing like angels. Both cherubim and seraphim are said to have wings (angels do not), though the number of wings varies (Exod. 25:20; 37:9; Isa. 6:2). Cherubim at times are described as having four faces, along with human and bovine body parts (Ezek. 1; 10). The faces may represent strengths for which the animals are known: ox (power); lion (strength, majesty, danger); human (wisdom); eagle (mobility, speed).

In a sense, cherubim and seraphim are hybrid figures. That is, they possess human as well as animal features. We find such beings in Ancient Near East culture, especially as creatures who represent power or prevent evil. So, cherubim and seraphim are either welcome protectors or terrifying punishers, depending on who encounters them.

Note some distinguishing characteristics of cherubim:

First, as in the garden of Eden, cherubim are placed at the boundary between the sacred and the profane. For example, they keep Adam and Eve, who are expelled from Eden, from returning (Gen. 3:24).

Second, the word *cherub* probably means "gatekeeper" or "intercessor." The word is used ninety-one times in the Old Testament. Frequently, writers refer to God as sitting, or enthroned, among the cherubim (Num. 7:89; 2 Sam. 6:2; Ps. 80:1). In other words, cherubim enjoy a special place in God's presence.

Third, cherubim adorn the golden ark of the covenant, with their wings spread across the mercy seat (or cover of the ark) on which the high priest sprinkles sacrificial blood to atone for the people's sins. Their image also is woven into the veil of the tabernacle (Exod. 26:1). In the temple, two large olive-wood cherubim are placed next to the ark of the covenant in the holy of holies (1 Kings 6:23, 27).

Fourth, cherubim are similar in description to seraphim, who serve God as they proclaim his holiness (Isa. 6:1-3; Rev. 4:6-10).

So, for the Lord to call the king of Tyre an *anointed guardian cherub*, he must be pointing to some unique attribute in the king's past. But it's hard to discern whether this description is literal or a form of hyperbole. We have to dig deeper.

Three Interpretations

When considered together, Isaiah 14 and Ezekiel 28 invite different interpretations. Three rise to the top: (1) the authors are describing the depravity of earthly kings, using exaggeration and/or sarcasm; (2) the authors are describing both earthly kings and – in Ezekiel 28 in particular – the fall of Adam; and (3) the authors are describing both earthly kings and Satan, peeling back the curtain to expose a supernatural creature who pulls the strings of his marionette monarchs.

Trusted Bible scholars vigorously debate which interpretation best fits the text. So, let's briefly survey each view.

View 1: Earthly Kings

Many commentators see Isaiah 14 and Ezekiel 28 as graphic depictions of wicked earthly kings, with hyperbole and/or sarcasm employed to show the folly of the rulers' bloated self-esteem.

Kenneth Boa and Robert Bowman favor this view. In Isaiah 14, the prophet directly addresses the king of Babylon (v. 4) and specifically refers to him as a "man" (v. 16). But the prophecy also draws on pagan mythology to depict the king's fall from power. For example, in one Canaanite myth, a god named *Athtar* (meaning something like "son of Dawn" or "morning star") wanted to rule on Baal's throne from *Zaphon*, a sacred mountain to the north. Compare "the North" (CSB) with "Zaphon" (NRSV) in verse 13 and see the connection. So, according to this view, Isaiah likely is using religious imagery typical for his time to describe the humiliation of an arrogant earthly king.[11]

As for Ezekiel 28, Boa and Bowman argue that the two oracles – one against the *prince* of Tyre and the other against the *king* of Tyre – focus on the same human ruler. What leads some interpreters to equate the king with Satan, according to Boa and Bowman, is that the Hebrew text refers to him as a "cherub" (vv. 14, 16). However, the Septuagint, an ancient Greek translation of the Old Testament, says the king of Tyre was "*with* the cherub" (v. 14), and this cherub brought him out (v. 16). Modern English translations often note this distinction. The NRSV, for example, reads, "*With* an anointed cherub as guardian I placed you ... the guardian cherub drove you out from among the stones of fire" (emphasis added).

Boa and Bowman conclude:

> The bottom line is that neither Isaiah 14 nor Ezekiel 28 clearly refers to the fall of Satan from his original innocence. We can surmise that Satan fell for reasons similar to those of the kings of Tyre and Babylon – arrogance or pride, and in particular the desire to be a god himself. This makes sense when we note that the serpent's temptation of Eve and Adam in Eden was that they could become "like God" (Gen. 3:5).[12]

Other commentators follow the same line of reasoning, offering the following observations: (1) Satan is never portrayed as a cherub, or even *with* a cherub in the garden, in any other passage of Scripture; (2) ancient Israel's understanding of Satan was far more limited than that found in the New Testament; even in the Book of Job, *satan* is not a personal name but a function; (3) Satan is not identified as the chief of fallen angels until about the second century BC, and he does not take up his position as the source and cause of evil before the formulation of Christian doctrine. Therefore, in the context of Ezekiel 28:

> ... it is a metaphorical description of the high stewardship entrusted to the prince of Tyre (as significant as the cherub's role in the garden). Rather than treating this sacred trust with reverence and awe, he exploited it to his own benefit – as if the cherub of the garden had opened a roadside fruit stand. He was therefore

discharged from his position, relieved of his trust and publicly humiliated.[13]

View 2: Earthly Kings and the Fall of Adam

A second view, to which scholars like G. K. Beale hold, is that Isaiah 14 and Ezekiel 28 describe wicked earthly kings who get their comeuppance in a way that sheds light on the first human to fall: Adam.[14] While the kings of Babylon and Tyre wish to sit among the gods, Adam actually walks with the Most High and sits among the heavenly council. He is in Eden, the garden of God.

In reference to jewels listed in Ezekiel 28:13, some commentators say this language refers to a literal jewel-encrusted garment a prince would wear. They in turn argue that the prince of Eden is Adam. In addition, they note that many of the jewels listed here correspond to the jewels on the breastplate of the Israelite high priest (cf. Exod. 28:17-20; 39:10-13). Thus, we get a picture of Adam as priest-king of Eden.

Since Jesus is the second Adam and a priest-king, the analogy fits. The backdrop to the prince of Tyre's arrogance is the rebellious Adam, not Satan.[15] Adam is blameless in his ways from the day of his creation until he disobeys God in an effort to become like his creator.

So, the Lord expels Adam in disgrace from Eden (the mountain of God), throws him to the ground, and ultimately makes him an object of horror. This view embraces the Septuagint, which says the king of Tyre (or Adam, according to this view) was *with* an anointed cherub who brings him out. In other words, Adam is not an anointed cherub; rather, an anointed cherub who once was Adam's protector has banished him from Eden and now stands guard, blazing sword in hand, to keep Adam from returning and partaking of the tree of life.

View 3: Earthly Kings and the Fall of Satan

C. Fred Dickason is one theologian who sees a double reference in both Isaiah 14 and Ezekiel 28. That is, he sees two persons addressed in each passage. In Ezekiel 28, for example, verses 1-10 address a human leader (the prince of Tyre), while verses 11-19 describe a supernatural leader (the king of Tyre / Satan) behind him.

The first leader is described as a man (vv. 2, 9), while the second is called a cherub (vv. 14, 16). The second figure is superior to the first; he is "full of wisdom," "perfect in beauty," and "blameless." Dickason concludes, "For these reasons we take Ezekiel 28:12-19 to refer to Satan, not to a human."[16] Other commentators, dating back at least as far as Origen (AD 185-254), hold similar views.

As for Isaiah 14, Dickason sees a parallel with Ezekiel 28, with the author first describing a human leader, and then the supernatural power behind him. This especially becomes clear when the king of Babylon proclaims his five *I wills*, the last being, "I will make myself like the Most High." Graham Cole notes, "If Dickason is correct, then how ironic that a cherub, whose role is to guard the interests of God, began to attack those very interests."[17]

Charles Dyer writes that the change from "ruler" (Heb. *nagid*) in Ezekiel 28:2 to "king" (Heb. *melek*) in Ezekiel 28:11 is significant in light of these prophecies. In verses 1-10, Ezekiel rebukes the *ruler* for claiming to be a god though he is just a man. But in verses 11-19, Ezekiel describes the *king* in terms that could not apply to a mere mortal. Further, in response to those who contend that the king is Adam, Dyer notes, "When Adam sinned he was not cast from the mountain of God to earth, and no nations existed to be appalled at his fall." He summarizes:

> Ezekiel was not describing an ideal man or a false god in verses 11-26. But his switch from "ruler" to "king" and his allusions to the Garden of Eden do imply that the individual being described was more than human. The best explanation is that Ezekiel was describing Satan who was the true "king" of Tyre, the one motivating the human "ruler" of Tyre. Satan was in the Garden of Eden (Gen. 3:1-7), and his chief sin was pride (1 Tim. 3:6). He also had access to God's presence (cf. Job 1:6-12). Speaking of God's judging the human "ruler" of Tyre for his pride (Ezek. 28:1-10), the prophet

lamented the satanic "king" of Tyre who was also judged for his pride (vv. 11-19). Tyre was motivated by the same sin as Satan, and would suffer the same fate.[18]

One interesting parallel between the ruler of Tyre and the king of Tyre is Ezekiel's use of the word *trade*. In verse 5, "trading" speaks of the ruler's skill in commerce, which leads to great wealth. In verses 16 and 18, "trade" refers to the king's violent and dishonest activities. The word for "trade" comes from the Hebrew verb *rakal*, which means "to go about from one to another." Ezekiel uses this word, with its broad application, to compare the ruler's commercial activities with the king's spiritual schemes. Dyer notes of *rakal*:

> So Ezekiel used a word that could convey a broad meaning. Satan's position in heaven involved broad contact with many elements of God's creation much as the prince of Tyre's position enabled him to contact many nations.
>
> Though Ezekiel was describing the "ultimate" ruler of Tyre, Satan, the purpose of the lament was to speak of the city's destruction. So he began to blend the characteristics of the satanic king with the human ruler. Satan would be cast to the earth (v. 17), and the king of Tyre would be cast down before other kings, his enemies. Satan's ultimate destiny will be the lake of fire (cf. Rev. 20:10), and the defeat and death of the human ruler of Tyre was pictured as being consumed by fire (Ezek. 28:18). Both Satan's and Tyre's defeats would shock those nations who had followed them. They would be appalled because of Satan's and Tyre's horrible end (cf. 27:35-36).[19]

In his commentary on Ezekiel, Lamar Cooper asks, "Who, then, was the person whose character was like the king of Tyre that fulfilled the elements of [Ezekiel 28] vv. 12-17?" His reply:

> The serpent was known for his craftiness (Gen. 3:1), his deceit, and his anti-God attitude (3:4), leading humanity to sin (3:6-7). Elsewhere

he is presented as a deceiver (Rev. 12:9; 20:3), an instigator of evil (John 13:2, 27), one who seeks worship as a god (Luke 4:6-8; 2 Thess. 2:3-4), and one who seeks to get others to renounce God (Job 2:4-5). He appears as an angel of light (2 Cor. 11:14) and as the father of lies and violence (John 8:44), distorts Scripture (Matt. 4:6), opposes believers (2 Cor. 2:11), and finally is judged (Matt. 25:41; Rev. 19:20-21; 20:13-15). Therefore the conclusion that the figure behind the poetic symbol is the serpent (also known as the adversary, the devil, Satan; Rev. 12:9) is a logical one.... Ezekiel presented the king of Tyre as an evil tyrant who was animated and motivated by a more sinister, unseen tyrant, Satan. The picture presented by the prophet goes beyond what we know about the adversary in other passages. It tells us of his wisdom, beauty, appearance of perfection, appointment as a guardian and his expulsion from the presence of God.[20]

Michael Heiser is another scholar who ties Isaiah 14 and Ezekiel 28 to Satan, and he connects both passages to Genesis 3. The serpent's crime, according to Heiser, is that he freely chooses to reject God's authority. God has chosen to create humans and entrust them with the power to extend Eden on earth. But the enemy bristles at the plan and thus decides to put himself in the place of God. He says in his heart, "I will ascend to the heavens; I will set up my throne above the stars of God. I will sit on the mount of the gods' assembly, in the remotest parts of the North" (Isa. 14:13).

"He got a rude awakening," writes Heiser. "Since the Serpent's deception led to Adam and Eve's sin, he was expelled from God's home (Ezek. 28:14-16) and banished to earth – 'cut [or cast] down to the ground' in biblical language (Isa. 14:12 NLT) – the place where death reigns, where life is not everlasting."[21]

Instead of being lord of life, Satan becomes lord of the dead, according to Heiser. This means the enemy now has claim over humans since the events in Eden result in the loss of earthly immortality. Humanity now needs to be redeemed to have eternal life with God in a new Eden.[22]

As for the imagery of the kings of Babylon and Tyre being cast down to the ground (Isa. 14:11-12; Ezek. 28:17), the Hebrew word *erets* refers literally to the dirt and metaphorically to the underworld. This ties back to Genesis 3, with God cursing the serpent to eat the dust of the ground. Snakes don't eat dirt for nutrition. The point being made in all three passages is that the evil one is cast away from God, and from God's heavenly host, down to the earth, and even under the earth. In the underworld, the serpent is even lower than the beasts of the field. He is hidden from view and from life in God's world. Death is his domain.[23]

Other Views

There are other views of Isaiah 14 and Ezekiel 28 beyond these three perspectives, including the belief that Satan actually indwelt the kings of Babylon and Tyre, along with the view that Isaiah and Ezekiel draw from Ancient Near Eastern paganism and myth to magnify the wickedness of human rulers.

In any case, it seems biblically faithful to understand that Isaiah and Ezekiel are foretelling the hard fall of two wicked earthly kings. At the same time, it's possible these prophets are drawing back the curtain to give us a glimpse of the one pulling the strings of his puppet kings. This bizarre show may enjoy a long run, but it ends tragically for all. Though we cannot say with certainty, it seems *anointed guardian cherub* is a fitting term for the evil one.[24]

The Mystery of When and How Satan Falls

Scripture offers no clear answers as to when and how Satan originally falls – or even why a sovereign God permits the evil one's rebellion and all its horrific consequences. Genesis 3 does not introduce us to the origin of evil, but reveals the presence of unexplained evil in the serpent. Adam and Eve are created innocent, and shortly thereafter the already-fallen serpent shows up. John Piper's candid perplexity is a welcome perspective. In response to a listener's question about where Satan even got the desire to sin, Piper replies, in part:

> As far as I can see, no explanation is offered in the Bible for how Satan became evil.... How could a perfectly good being – with a perfectly good will and a perfectly good heart – ever experience any imperfect impulse that would cause the will to move in the direction of sin? The answer is that nobody knows ...

Piper goes on:

> Here is what I do know. God is sovereign. Nothing comes to pass apart from his plan, which includes things he more or less causes directly – things he more or less permits indirectly. There is no doubt in my mind that Satan's fall and all the redemptive plan of God for the glory of grace afterward were according to God's eternal plan....
>
> God can see to it that something comes to pass which he hates. This is what he did, for example, when he planned the crucifixion of Jesus, according to Acts 4:27-28. The murder of Jesus was sinful, and it was planned down to the detail by God.... I think the Bible leads us to believe that he is sovereign over all sin and that he never sins. That is what I believe the Bible teaches.[25]

For reasons beyond our current understanding – and outside God's revelation in Scripture – the Lord has chosen not to disclose the details of Satan's rebellion and fall. Maybe, as Colonel Nathan Jessup proclaims during court-martial proceedings in *A Few Good Men*, we can't handle the truth. Perhaps the Lord is saving this revelation for the day his adopted children see him face to face. Or, it's possible God doesn't want us dwelling so much on angelic rebellion as on our own sin – and our need of a Savior.

Even so, the Bible offers subtle clues about the evil one's rapacious nature and cosmic fall. These come in the form of simple truths, such as:

First, Satan is a created being. God declared everything he made "very good indeed" (Gen. 1:31; cf. John 1:3; Col. 1:15-16). The creature we know as the evil one wasn't always this way. He couldn't be. Whether God created Satan and other heavenly beings prior to the six days of creation, or during the six days, is uncertain. One writer notes:

> We can deduce that Satan was created during creation week; since he was blameless, he was under God's 'very good' proclamation at the end of day 6.... The logical inference [of Job 38 and Gen. 1] is that the angels were created on either day 1 or at least by day 3.[26]

Second, God gave Satan wide latitude in his activities and entrusted him with great freedom. The evil one, like all holy and fallen angels, was given an opportunity to choose – an opportunity fueled by greater power and knowledge than humans possess. In addition, these heavenly beings operated in a sinless environment with no history of rebellion against God. This made their leap into sin bolder and more consequential.

Third, Satan consciously and willfully rebelled. It appears that pride played a key role, although where pride originated in a sinless environment is a mystery. The very fact that human beings are tempted in the garden of Eden to "be like God" may be the greatest clue as to the original sin of the tempter himself.[27]

Paul lends credence to Satan's sin of pride as he warns Timothy against appointing an immature believer as an elder: "He must not be a new convert, or he might become conceited and incur the same condemnation as the devil" (1 Tim.3:6). The word "conceited" comes from the Greek verb *typhoo* and means "to possess with the fumes of conceit; to be demented with conceit, puffed up."[28]

Perhaps jealousy also stoked Satan's rebellion. Since God created the angelic host first, Satan may have bristled when God created Adam and Eve and entrusted them with expanding Eden across the face of the earth. When God placed limits on Adam and Eve's freedom in the garden – instructing Adam not to eat from the tree of the knowledge of good and evil, under penalty of death (Gen. 2:17) –

Satan saw his chance. If he could get the first humans to disobey God, they would suffer death, and that would be the end of humanity.

Fourth, it appears Satan rebelled *after* the creation of the physical universe. There is some indication the entire angelic host celebrated this cosmic event (Job 38:7). But it's certain that he rebelled *before* approaching Eve in the garden of Eden (Gen. 3:1).

Finally, while God stripped Satan of his exalted heavenly position, the Lord has allowed the evil one to keep his intelligence, power, and cunning to use against human beings made as God's imagers. At least for a while. Like the ancient Roman Crassus, who died from an overdose of liquid gold, the anointed guardian cherub one day chokes on the sulfurous smoke of the lake of fire, where he is tormented night and day forever. We may know little about the evil one's origin, and even less about the birth of sin, but God has numbered Satan's days and decreed the end of his rule a certainty (Matt. 25:41; Rev. 20:10).

Summary

Key takeaways about the *anointed guardian cherub*:

(1) Two much-debated Old Testament passages give us potential glimpses into the evil one's heart: Isaiah 14:3-21 and Ezekiel 28.

(2) Isaiah 14 addresses an earthly king – the king of Babylon, perhaps a composite of wicked rulers who shake their fists at God and persecute his people. Yet perhaps we also see a veiled glimpse of the evil one, whose rebellion against God casts the die for all forms of human revolt against their creator.

(3) Ezekiel 28 details the overthrow of Tyre's ruler and a lament for Tyre's king (perhaps two titles for the same person). Commentators view these figures in different ways: (a) as depraved earthly leaders; (b) as an earthly leader (Tyre's ruler) and, behind him, a fallen Adam (Tyre's king); or (c) as both an earthly ruler (Tyre's ruler) and a fallen Satan (Tyre's king), with Ezekiel peeling back the curtain to expose a supernatural creature who pulls the strings of his marionette monarchs.

(4) Though we cannot say with certainty, it seems *anointed guardian cherub* is a fitting title for the evil one (Ezek. 28:14).

(5) Scripture offers no clear answers as to when and how Satan originally fell – or even why a sovereign God permitted the evil one's rebellion and all its horrific consequences.

(6) Further, we know little about Satan's origin, and even less about the birth of sin. Yet God has numbered Satan's days and decreed the end of his rule a certainty (Matt. 25:41; Rev. 20:10).

Questions for Personal or Group Study

1. Why do you think God has chosen to reveal so little about the creation, rebellion, and fall of Satan?
2. Read the "song of contempt" about the king of Babylon (Isa. 14:3-21). Which verses clearly refer to a human king, and which verses seem to depict an other-worldly figure? What do you think is the best way to reconcile these contrasting descriptions?
3. English Bible translations render Isaiah 14:12 in various ways. For example, the king of Babylon is called "shining morning star" (CSB), "Lucifer" (KJV), "star of the morning" (NASB), and "morning star, son of the dawn" (NIV). Although popular, why is the name "Lucifer" likely not what Isaiah intended?
4. What are four distinguishing characteristics of cherubim?
5. When taken together, Isaiah 14:3-21 and Ezekiel 28:1-19 invite a range of possible interpretations. What are the three leading candidates, and which one seems to best explain the biblical text?

The dragon's floodwaters never rise above the Lord's levees.

2

SERPENT / DRAGON
PART 1

In Greek mythology, Medusa is a gorgeous woman who engages in a tryst with Poseidon in one of Athena's temples. As punishment, the virgin goddess Athena turns Medusa into a Gorgon, a race of snake-women whose gazes turn people into stone. Gorgons have serpents for hair, long claws, sharp teeth, and scales covering their bodies. Athena later helps the hero Perseus slay Medusa, giving him a shiny bronze shield that enables him to watch Medusa's reflection rather than look directly at her. After cutting off Medusa's head, Perseus mounts it on his shield, using it to paralyze his enemies in battle.[1]

Jump forward to a fifteenth century Polish yarn in which a fearsome dragon lives in a dark cave along the banks of the Vistula River. Day after day, this fire-breathing monster terrorizes civilians, pillaging their homes and devouring their livestock. King Krakus sends out his bravest knights to slay the dragon, but all fall prey to the winged beast's deadly talons and bone-crunching jaws. In desperation, the king promises his beautiful daughter in marriage to the man who vanquishes the dragon.

A poor cobbler's apprentice named Skuba takes up the challenge. He stuffs a roasted lamb with sulfur and sets it outside the dragon's cave. The dragon takes the bait, gulping down the poisoned lamb. Soon, the sulfur burns his stomach. He becomes so thirsty that he drinks half of the Vistula River, causing him to swell and, ultimately, explode. True to his promise, the king grants Skuba his daughter's hand in marriage and, of course, Skuba and his bride live happily ever after.[2]

Tales of serpents and dragons have regaled the pages of folklore for centuries. Modern-day films and television series often borrow from these myths and legends, or present new creatures altogether. For example, a giant anaconda slithers onto the big screen in a 1997 major motion picture, and he lives on in sequels spanning nearly two decades. Crafty and comical animated serpents – from Kaa in *The Jungle Book* to Rattlesnake Jake in *Rango* – entertain kids and their parents. That's not all. From Smaug, the last of Middle Earth's great dragons in J. R. R. Tolkien's *The Hobbit,* to the converted and cuddly Toothless in *How to Train Your Dragon,* to the fierce and sympathetic Drogon in *Game of Thrones,* dragons spark our imaginations and excite our senses.

So, it should come as no surprise to Christians today that secular eyes roll after reading Genesis 3, as well as Revelation 12 and 20, in which Satan is called *the serpent* and *the dragon.* Skeptical readers howl at the very notion of a real Satan, concluding that his identification with serpents and dragons only proves his mythical existence. After all, what's up with a talking snake in Genesis 3, anyway? And Revelation features such apocalyptic language that dragons, six-winged heavenly creatures, and a beast with seven heads and ten horns all make for great entertainment but are hardly worth taking seriously.

While it's true that slithery serpents and fire-breathing dragons lavish the pages of fairy tales, it is an injustice to Scripture to write off these accounts in Genesis and Revelation so quickly. In fact, when applied to the evil one, the names *serpent* and *dragon* more aptly describe what Satan is like rather than how he appears.

Serpent

The word *serpent* appears twenty-four times in twenty-three verses in the Christian Standard Bible (CSB).[3] Ten applications are clear references to Satan (Gen. 3:1, 2, 4, 13, 14; 2 Cor. 11:3; Rev. 12:9, 14, 15; 20:2). Three times *serpent* appears in the confrontation between Moses and the magicians of Pharaoh's court (Exod. 7:9, 10, 12).[4] Three references are to a sea serpent or Leviathan, a mystical deity over which the Lord has absolute power (Job 26:13; Isa. 27:1; Amos 9:3).

Twice, there are mentions of a "flying serpent," either an analogy of Assyria (Isa. 14:29) or a reference to one of the wild beasts in the Negev (Isa. 30:6). Singular references include: an analogy of an enemy's wine ("serpent's venom," Deut. 32:33); a place ("Serpent's Well," Neh. 2:13); predators who lie in wait (Ps. 91:13); animal food in the new creation ("the serpent's food will be dust!" Isa. 65:25); and Jesus' instructions to his disciples to take prudent action in light of coming persecution (Matt. 10:16; cf. 21-23).

Old Testament writers use three different Hebrew words translated "serpent" in these passages. The most common is *nachash*, meaning "serpent" or "snake." The word even makes a hissing sound when spoken.[5] The word *tanniyn* (used in Exod. 7; Deut. 32:33; Neh. 2:13; and Ps. 91:13) has a broader application and can mean "serpent, venomous snake," "sea or river monster," or "dragon or dinosaur." The third word, *saraph*, is used only once (Isa. 30:6) and may be translated "serpent," "fiery serpent," or "poisonous serpent." It's also the word from which we get *seraphim*, the six-winged heavenly creatures Isaiah sees above the throne in his vision of God (Isa. 6).

In the CSB New Testament, the Greek word *ophis* is used more than a dozen times and is translated "snake" or "serpent." It may refer to an actual snake (Matt. 7:10; John 3:14-15; cf. Num. 21:8-9), or it may be used figuratively to illustrate certain traits or qualities. For example, Jesus calls the scribes and Pharisees "snakes" because of their venomous hypocrisy (Matt. 23:33). After sending his disciples to proclaim the gospel, Jesus tells them to be "as shrewd as serpents and as innocent as doves" (Matt. 10:16).

Other references are directed more toward the demonic realm. Believers are promised authority over snakes, demonstrating their power over Satan and his agents (Luke 10:19). And Paul warns the Corinthians that the ancient serpent continues to strike with lethal intent: "But I fear that, as the serpent deceived Eve by his cunning, your minds may be seduced from a sincere and pure devotion to Christ" (2 Cor. 11:3).

As you can see, the writers of Scripture employ numerous Hebrew and Greek terms to depict a variety of creatures associated with serpents. Andrew Naselli notes that *serpent* is an umbrella term – a "big category" – that includes both snakes and dragons. Further, he writes that a serpent has two major strategies that become evident in Scripture: to *deceive* and *devour*:

> As a general rule, the form a serpent takes depends on its strategy. When a serpent in Scripture attempts to deceive, it's a snake. When a serpent attempts to devour, it's a dragon. Snakes deceive; dragons devour. Snakes tempt and lie; dragons attack and murder. Snakes backstab; dragons assault.[6]

For our purposes, we focus primarily on depictions of Satan as the serpent in Genesis and Revelation.

Snake in the Grass

Occasionally, serpents symbolize good rather than evil. The first reference to serpents in the Bible is positive: "So God created the large sea-creatures" (Heb. *tanniyn*) and declared them good (Gen. 1:21). The psalmists praise God for demonstrating his creative power in *Leviathan* and *sea monsters* (Ps. 104:26; 148:7). As we noted earlier, the seraphim above the throne in heaven draw their names from the Hebrew word *saraph*, which may be translated "fiery serpent." And when Jesus sends out the twelve apostles to proclaim the kingdom of heaven to the lost sheep of Israel, he implores them to be "as shrewd as serpents" (Matt. 10:16).

Mostly, however, serpents represent evil – and in the ultimate sense, the evil one. This is true in Satan's first appearance in Scripture as the *nachash* in Genesis 3. He is "the most cunning of all the wild animals that the LORD God had made" (v. 1). This seems to describe the serpent as a true animal, but one with the remarkable qualities of intelligence and speech. If so, this is an ideal creature for the evil one to manipulate.

We know that people and animals may be demon-possessed, such as a Gadarene man and a herd of pigs in Jesus' encounter across the Sea of Galilee (Mark 5:1-20). Therefore, many Bible commentators contend that Satan co-opted the serpent and manipulated its marvelous natural gifts to deceive Eve.[7] But there may be a more biblically faithful explanation.

We might begin by asking why Eve does not fear the serpent, or why she shows no surprise when he speaks. Talking animals are the exception, not the rule, in Scripture (cf. Num. 22:28-30). We have no record of other talking animals in Eden. To suggest that this encounter happens before the Fall and therefore should not be considered unusual does not really answer the question.

In ancient Near Eastern literature of the Old Testament world, animal speech is fairly common. However, the context for such speaking is magic, which is tied to the pagan worlds of the gods. No person in ancient Egypt, for example, would have expected his cattle to carry on a conversation with him. But when the gods or magical forces are invoked, animals often are the means of manifesting a divine presence or power in a story. The kind of animal that appears and speaks depends on traits associated with that animal, or on the status of that animal in a culture's religion.

So, perhaps it makes more sense to see the serpent in Genesis 3 as a divine being – a member of the heavenly host. He inhabits Eden along with God and other supernatural beings. In this case, the serpent's appearance and language would be nothing out of the ordinary to Eve. Just as angels often appear on earth in human likeness, the serpent may have been a physical manifestation of an anointed guardian cherub (see Chapter 1). The apostle Paul reminds the Corinthians that Satan masquerades as an angel of light (2 Cor. 11:14). So, why not as an attractive and persuasive creature? As Michael Heiser notes, "If we're thinking only in terms of a snake, we'll miss the messaging."[8]

That messaging, according to Heiser, is this:

> Genesis telegraphed simple but profound ideas to Israelite readers: The world you experience was created by an all-powerful God; human beings are his created representatives; Eden was his abode; he was accompanied by a supernatural host; one member of that divine entourage was not pleased by God's decisions to create humanity and give them dominion. All that leads to how humanity got into the mess it's in.
>
> In some respects, we know that the Genesis "serpent" wasn't really a member of the animal kingdom. We have other passages to help us grasp that point, particularly in the New Testament. We understand that, even though New Testament writers refer to the serpent back in Eden, they are really referring to a supernatural entity – not a mere member of the animal kingdom (2 Cor. 11:3; 1 Thess. 3:5; Rev. 12:9).[9]

We might summarize it this way: When Moses and other human authors of Scripture depict the evil one as *the serpent*, they are not describing his appearance; rather, they are describing his character. He is an alluring, intelligent, shrewd, and attractive creature whose entire being is poised to deliver lethal poison. His smooth-talking deception of Eve illustrates both his beauty and his vileness, which remain as twin attributes throughout Scripture until he is cast into the lake of fire (Rev. 20:10).

God's curse upon the serpent is revealing:

> So the LORD God said to the serpent: Because you have done this, you are cursed more than any livestock and more than any wild animal. You will move on your belly and eat dust all the days of your life. I will put hostility between you and the woman, and between

your offspring and her offspring. He will strike your head, and you will strike his heel (Gen. 3:14-15).

While acknowledging that many Bible commentators identify the serpent as an actual animal Satan co-opted to tempt Eve, we might benefit from seeing this passage in light of the evil one's role as a heavenly being – perhaps the anointed guardian cherub of Ezekiel 28. The Lord's curse of the serpent doesn't actually call him "livestock" or a "wild animal." God curses the serpent *more than* any livestock and *more than* any wild animal.

The whole creation, including the animal kingdom, groans beneath the weight of sin (Rom. 8:22), which began in the garden of Eden. But the serpent's curse is worse: he moves on his belly and eats dust. We know snakes don't eat dirt for nutrition. But as Donald Barnhouse notes, "To eat dust is to know defeat, and that is God's prophetic judgment upon the enemy. He will always reach for his desires and fall just short of them. There will be continuous aspiration, but never any attainment."[10]

Just as conquered kings are made to lie on the ground with the feet of their conquerors on their necks (Josh. 10:24), Satan is surely a defeated foe whom Paul says God promises to crush beneath *our* feet (Rom. 16:20). Cursed as the tempter, the evil one is cast away from God, and from God's heavenly host, down to earth, and even under the earth. In the underworld, the serpent is even lower than the beasts of the field. Striving constantly for attention, and for control, he is hidden away from life in the world God created. And while he succeeds in bruising the heel of the promised Messiah, he finds that the death of the Son of God – for which he labors so neurotically – brings a fatal blow to his own head.

The Bronze Serpent

Before moving on to the dragon, and on to an examination of passages in Revelation involving both the serpent and the dragon, we should note an incident during Israel's forty years of wandering in the wilderness. In Numbers 21, we find the people grumbling against God and Moses. "Why have you led us up from Egypt to die in the wilderness?" they complain to Moses. "There is no bread or water, and we detest this wretched food!" (v. 5). So, the Lord sends poisonous snakes (Heb. *saraph*) among the people, resulting in many deaths.

The people run to Moses, confess their sin of speaking against God and his servant, and ask Moses to intercede on their behalf. Moses obliges, and the Lord instructs Moses to fashion a bronze snake and mount it on a pole. Whenever people are snake bitten, they are to look at the bronze serpent for healing (vv. 6-9). Over time, the people come to worship the bronze snake and burn incense to it. King Hezekiah finally breaks it into pieces as part of his effort to remove idolatry from the land (2 Kings 18:4).

End of story – or so it seems – until Jesus revives the historical account in his nighttime conversation with Nicodemus:

> Just as Moses lifted up the snake (Gr. *ophis*) in the wilderness, so the Son of Man must be lifted up, so that everyone who believes in him may have eternal life. For God loved the world in this way: He gave his one and only Son, so that everyone who believes in him will not perish but have eternal life. For God did not send his Son into the world to condemn the world, but to save the world through him (John 3:14-17).

Jesus reminds Nicodemus that the bronze serpent in the wilderness symbolized the means of salvation: faith in God, who removes sin and its stain. No mere hunk of metal cures a snakebite. But the God who offers a cure through a simple glance at a bronze serpent is more than able to save us from our sins. When Jesus is lifted up on the cross, those who look to him in faith are restored to a right relationship with God. Just as Moses made a bronze serpent to replicate the real thing, God "made the one who did not know sin to be sin for us, so that in him we might become the righteousness of God" (2 Cor. 5:21).

Jesus is the definitive serpent crusher, who became so when he was "crushed because of our iniquities" (Isa. 53:5). All of this is according to the eternal plan of God, who "was pleased to crush him [Jesus] severely" (Isa. 53:10; cf. Acts 2:23-24; 4:27-28). As a result, followers of Jesus participate in the crushing of Satan (Rom. 16:20).

As D. A. Carson notes, "By going to the cross, Jesus will ultimately destroy this serpent, this devil, who holds people captive under sin, shame, and guilt. He will crush the serpent's head by taking their guilt and shame on himself."[11]

Dragon

The word dragon (*drakon* in Greek) appears fourteen times in thirteen verses in the CSB New Testament – all of them in the Book of Revelation. Other English translations, such as the English Standard Version and the New American Standard Bible, sometimes translate the Hebrew *tanniyn* as "dragon," "serpent," or "monster" (e.g., Neh. 2:13; Isa. 27:1; 51:9; Ezek. 29:3; 32:2). The CSB renders *tanniyn* "serpent" or "monster" in these same verses, but "dragon" never appears in the CSB Old Testament.

In the Septuagint, which includes various Greek translations of the Old Testament, *drakon* translates a number of Hebrew words for a variety of animals, including the lion (Job 4:10; 38:39), snake and asp (Job 26:13; Amos 9:3), and the jackal (Jer. 9:11; Lam. 4:3; Mic. 1:8). It is also used for the great monster Leviathan (Job 40:20; Ps. 74:14; 104:26; Isa. 27:1). In the Septuagint version of Esther, an apocalyptic battle between Mordecai and Haman is depicted as dragons locked in mortal combat. This is similar to the battle between Marduk and Tiamat in the *Enuma Elish*, the Babylonian creation story. According to Peter Bolt, the same myth may lie behind the Septuagint addition to Daniel, the story known as *Bel and the Dragon*.[12]

The apostle John uses *drakon* exclusively in Revelation as a symbolic representation of Satan. Further, he links "dragon" and "serpent" to identify this creature as the ancient tempter in the garden of Eden. The dragon is explicitly identified as "the ancient serpent, who is called the devil and Satan, the one who deceives the whole world" (Rev. 12:9; cf. Rev. 20:2).

This depiction also associates him with the Old Testament "sea monster" that represents the enemies of God's people. For example, in Psalm 74:13-14, Asaph uses the language of Canaanite myths – "you smashed the heads of the sea monsters in the water; you crushed the heads of Leviathan" – to affirm the sovereignty of God. The names "Leviathan" and "sea monsters" are a pagan way of deifying the uncontrollable forces of nature in the sea. "But God defeated the sea at the exodus (Ps. 114:3; Isa. 51:9-10), meaning he controlled the sea to destroy the Egyptian army. In defeating Egypt, and later Assyria and Babylon, he also defeated the gods they worshiped."[13]

In Revelation, the dragon is the chief enemy of Christ and his church. The dragon uses human and demonic forces to advance his purposes on earth. Let's briefly examine each reference to the dragon and the serpent in Revelation. We close this chapter with a look at the woman, the child, and the dragon (Rev. 12:1-6); the dragon thrown out of heaven (Rev. 12:7-12); and the dragon and the persecuted woman (Rev. 12:13-17).

In Chapter 3, we pick up with the dragon and the beast from the sea (Rev. 12:18 – 13:10); the dragon and the beast from the earth (Rev. 13:11-18); the dragon and the sixth bowl (Rev. 16:12-16); the dragon bound (Rev. 20:1-3); and the dragon defeated (Rev. 20:7-10).

The Woman, the Child, and the Dragon (Rev. 12:1-6)

A great sign appeared in heaven: a woman clothed with the sun, with the moon under her feet and a crown of twelve stars on her head. She was pregnant and cried out in labor and agony as she was about to give birth. Then another sign appeared in heaven: There was *a great fiery red dragon* having seven heads and ten horns, and on its heads were seven crowns. Its tail swept away a third of the stars in heaven and hurled them to the earth. And *the dragon* stood in front of the woman who was about to give birth, so that when she did give birth it might devour her child. She gave birth to a Son, a male who is going to rule all nations with an iron rod. Her child was caught up to God and to his throne. The woman fled into the wilderness, where she had a place prepared by God, to be nourished there for 1,260 days (emphasis added).

Evangelical commentators essentially agree about the elements in this vision: The woman clothed with the sun is the nation of Israel; the Son is Jesus; the fiery red dragon is Satan; and the wilderness is a place of protection for God's people during intense persecution.[14] There are other views, to be sure, especially with regard to the woman – some argue she is the virgin Mary; others, the church – and to the location of the wilderness into which the woman flees. Even so, there's little disagreement about the identity of the dragon. Since he is central to our study, let's focus on his place in this vision.

As we've already seen, the Jewish reader in John's day would be quite familiar with the dragon. Old Testament authors tell us about Leviathan, Rahab, and the dragon or sea monster, with an emphasis on God's power to conquer him (Job 26:12-13; Ps. 74:13-14; 89:9-10). Leviathan means "twisting one" and refers either to a sea serpent or dragon associated with the chaos of creation, according to ancient Near Eastern myths. Rahab means "boisterous one" and is used in the same sense that Leviathan is used.

Scripture sometimes uses *Rahab* to describe Egypt (Isa. 51:9-10). Ezekiel depicts Egypt and her pharaohs as monsters of the seas (Ezek. 29:3 5; 32:2-8). Jeremiah compares the king of Babylon to a sea monster (Jer. 51:34). But nowhere is the dragon image more fully developed than in Revelation. As one resource notes:

> The dragon represents evil, chaos, and ancient opposition to God. Revelation explicitly identifies the dragon with Satan, the archenemy of God and his people. As God defeated the beast from the sea in Daniel and the dragon of Egypt through the Exodus, so he will defeat Satan. In the new heaven and earth there will no longer be a sea or an ancient sea dragon to threaten God's new creation.[15]

Fiery Red Dragon

The dragon's color is red, which could refer to the bloodshed he brings to earth (compare the fiery red horse of Rev. 6:4), or more specifically to persecution he unleashes on the saints (Rev. 6:9-10; 17:3-6). He is, after all, "the accuser of our brothers and sisters" and "has come down ... with great fury" (Rev. 12:10, 12). The color red is associated with death (Rev. 6:4), and the murderous Satan always has had blood on his hands (John 8:44).

Seven Heads and Ten Horns

John describes the dragon as having seven heads and ten horns. On his heads are seven *diadema*, or kingly crowns, as opposed to *stephanos*, laurel wreaths that signify victory, honor, or a prize. The number seven appears nearly four hundred times in Scripture and often is associated with God. So, the seven heads and seven crowns may symbolize the dragon's boastful claims to divine sovereignty, especially when we note the many *diadema* upon the head of Jesus as he returns triumphantly in Revelation 19:12. Satan is the supreme counterfeit, and seven is the number of divine perfection.

The dragon's ten horns take us back to Daniel 7, where the prophet sees a terrifying beast with ten horns, which represent ten kings. In Revelation 13, a beast emerges from the sea with seven heads and ten horns. While commentators differ as to the meaning of all this, one truth is clear: Satan is in the midst of human affairs, a self-crowned monarch doing his best to keep a doomed kingdom intact.

In Matthew 12, Jesus refers to Satan as a king with a kingdom. Three times in the Gospel of John, our Lord refers to Satan as the prince of this world. In 2 Corinthians 4:4, Paul calls Satan the god of this age. And in Ephesians 2, Paul refers to him as the ruler of the power of the air. In the temptation of Jesus, Satan takes our Lord to a high mountain and shows him all the kingdoms of the world, claiming authority over them. And in 1 John 5:19, we are told the whole world is under the sway of the wicked one.

Worldly kings and kingdoms rise. Behind his puppet kings, the fiery red dragon pulls the strings. Earth is his kingdom until the sounding of the seventh trumpet, when the kingdom of the world becomes the kingdom of our Lord and of his Christ, who reigns forever and ever (Rev. 11:15).

A Tail That Sweeps Away

The dragon's tail sweeps away a third of the stars in heaven and hurls them to the earth. This activity is a source of much debate. Do the stars represent an apostate church, which Satan has inspired fallen men and angels to lead? Is John giving us a brief glimpse into Satan's original rebellion against God in which, it is assumed, he led countless other angels to cast their lots with him? Or is this simply a picture of Satan's broad powers, with his tail – that is, his influence and power – stretching from the gates of heaven to the depths of the sea?

Robert Utley offers a much-needed word of caution:

> At this point it may be helpful to remember that although this issue is interesting, it probably was not the author's intent in this context to discuss the origin of the demonic or the fall of Satan or an angelic rebellion in heaven. In apocalyptic literature the central theme of the vision is crucial, but the literalness of the presentation, the details and the images are dramatic, symbolic, fictional.... Be careful of pushing the details; apocalyptic literature is often true theology presented in an imaginative frame-work. It is true, but symbolically presented.[16]

At the very least, we may see the dragon's cosmic influence pictured in his tail. From his role as one-time accuser of the saints before the throne in heaven, to his battleground in the spiritual realm, to his prowling the earth like a roaring lion, the evil one's scope of influence is unmatched among God's creatures.

The Dragon Stood in Front of the Woman

Satan's long-running animosity toward Israel reaches its boiling point at the birth of Christ, the promised seed of woman who crushes the serpent's head (Gen. 3:15). The Messiah defeats Satan through his incarnation (John 1:14), sinless life (2 Cor. 5:21), and finished work on the cross (1 Cor. 15:3-4). Through all this, Jesus defeats the work of the evil one (1 John 3:8).

No doubt, in Old Testament times Satan tries to thwart God's plan and destroy God's people. Whether it is through Abraham's impatience in seeking Ishmael as his heir; Pharaoh's brutality against God's people and his stubborn resistance to their freedom; the Israelites' intermarriage with pagan peoples in and around the Promised Land; or Haman's scheming to exterminate the Jews – the evil one works aggressively to prevent the people of God from fulfilling their divine purpose.

All efforts having failed, Satan now positions himself in such a way that when Mary delivers Jesus – a vulnerable child in the hands of a poor Jewish couple – he might devour the Son of God as he takes his first breath. The most obvious act is his stirring of King Herod's heart to have all male children in and around Bethlehem killed. This "massacre of the innocents" is foretold in Jeremiah 31:15 and, as always, God is at least one step ahead of Satan. He dispatches an angel to warn Joseph of Herod's plot. Joseph escapes with Mary and Jesus to Egypt (Matt. 2:13-20).

Foiled but unbowed, Satan maintains his pursuit of the Savior – in the wilderness temptations, for example – but the Son of Man emerges victorious. The male child knows his purpose in coming to earth. He comes to seek and to save the lost (Luke 19:10); to die on the cross (John 12:27); and to give his life as a ransom for many (Matt. 20:28).

In essence, Jesus and Satan have diametrically opposed purposes, and yet they share a common means to these purposes: death. Satan seeks to kill Jesus and thus devour him. Jesus seeks to be killed in order to deliver sinful people from the wages of sin: death and hell. Jesus does in fact die. But he does so on his terms, in the Father's perfect timing, and by the Spirit's power.

The Dragon Thrown Out of Heaven (Rev. 12:7-12)

> Then war broke out in heaven: Michael and his angels fought against *the dragon. The dragon* and his angels also fought, but he could not prevail, and there was no place for them in heaven any longer. So *the great dragon* was thrown out – *the ancient serpent*, who is called *the devil* and *Satan, the one who deceives the whole world*. He was thrown to earth, and his angels with him.
>
> Then I heard a loud voice in heaven say, The salvation and the power and the kingdom of our God and the authority of his Christ have now come, because *the accuser of our brothers and sisters*, who accuses them before our God day and night, has been thrown down. They conquered him by the blood of the Lamb and by the word of their testimony; for they did not love their lives to the point of death. Therefore rejoice, you heavens, and you who dwell in them! Woe to the earth and the sea, because *the devil* has come down to you with great fury, because he knows his time is short (emphasis added).

We are spirited away from the pregnant woman and the fiery red dragon (vv. 1-6) to a cosmic battle between Michael and the dragon involving holy and evil angels. The conflict is severe. Michael and his angels prevail. Satan and his angels are cast down to earth. No longer does "the accuser of our brothers and sisters" have access to the throne in heaven. While the battle is won in the unseen spiritual realm, John is careful to record that it is the blood of the Lamb and the testimony of Christian martyrs that deliver the knock-out punches. The heavens rejoice, but the earth and sea brace themselves for a furious dragon onslaught.

We should note that Satan has been falling ever since he first opposed God. After successfully tempting Eve, the serpent is cursed to inhabit the underworld. He tries, unsuccessfully, to regain his footing. His persecution of Job fails to bring a curse against God (Job 2:10), and his accusations against the high priest Joshua are met with the Lord's rebuke (Zech. 3:2). With Christ's victory at Calvary, the dragon loses the last of his judicial ground against believers. After his battle with Michael, he is cast to earth. In the last days, he is confined to the abyss. And on the cusp of new heavens and a new earth, he is sent to the eternal fire prepared for him and his angels (Matt. 25:41; Rev. 20:10).

So, here we turn our attention to the names by which the evil one is called in this passage. John makes it clear that the dragon is a sign, or symbol, of Satan. The apostle is not given to pagan myths and legends. Rather, he uses the imagery of a vile, dangerous, and wicked beast to describe the one who so often appears to humans as an angel of light (2 Cor. 11:14). John rips away the evil one's mask and exposes him for who he is.

The Ancient Serpent

In Paul's second letter to the church in Corinth, he draws our attention back to the garden of Eden: "But I fear that, as the serpent deceived Eve by his cunning, your minds may be seduced from a sincere and pure devotion to Christ" (2 Cor. 11:3). Paul warns us about self-proclaimed "super apostles" who infiltrate an unsuspecting body of believers and lead them astray (v. 5; 12:11). These leaders are, in fact, "false apostles, deceitful workers, disguising themselves as apostles of Christ" (11:13). This should not astonish us, Paul writes, "For Satan disguises himself as an angel of light. So it is no great surprise if his servants also disguise themselves as servants of righteousness. Their end will be according to their works" (11:14-15).

In Revelation 20, John sees the serpent's future confinement in the *abyss*, which in this context likely refers to a deep and inescapable prison for evil spirits (cf. Luke 8:31). As the apostle describes it, an angel coming down from heaven "seized the dragon, that ancient serpent who is the devil and Satan, and bound him for a thousand years. He threw him into the abyss, closed it, and put a seal on it ..." (vv. 2-3).

It may help to keep in mind that the serpent is an unclean animal (Lev. 11:42), who often symbolizes God's enemies (e.g., Isa. 14:29). As *the serpent*, Satan is the Lord's arch-enemy, and the final destination in his quest to displace his creator is the eternal fire (Matt. 25:41). Just as the apostle Paul flicks a poisonous snake off his hand into the fire (Acts 28:5), Christ one day dispenses with the serpent in a similar manner (Rev. 20:10).

The Devil

The name comes from the Greek *diabolos*, meaning "accuser" or "slanderer." Translators of the Septuagint used *diabolos* to render the Hebrew *satan*. Matthew uses "the devil" to introduce us to Jesus' tempter in the wilderness, and Jesus calls him "the devil" to reveal that the evil one commands a demonic host for whom hell is created (Matt. 25:41).

This may be the same accuser (Heb. *satan*) who cries foul for the protective hedge God allegedly has placed around Job, and who slanders Job for a presumed motive behind his righteous deeds (Job 1-2). He also may be the prosecutor who points an accusing finger at the high priest Joshua before the angel of the LORD (Zech. 3:1-2). For more on *the devil*, see Chapter 4.

Satan

The Hebrew word *satan* means "accuser" or "adversary." While *satan* in the Old Testament may apply to people, angelic beings, or even God himself as individuals who bring accusations, the clearest reference to a supernatural evil being known by the name *Satan* appears in 1 Chronicles 21:1. Here, he incites King David to take a census, which results in God's divine retribution. The New Testament clearly depicts Satan as head of demons and as the chief opponent of God and humans, particularly those who belong to Christ.

"Satan has a two-fold mission: to oppose God and to destroy humanity," according to one Bible dictionary. "Just as Satan tempted Adam and Eve to sin (Gen. 3), so he tempted Jesus to sin in hopes of destroying God's rescue mission (Matt. 4). Satan is the source of sin and the chief tempter. He was a murderer and liar from the beginning (John 8:44)."[17] For more on Satan, see Chapter 4.

The One Who Deceives the Whole World

This describes a broad range of the dragon's destructive activities. He blinds the minds of unbelievers (2 Cor. 4:4); influences people's thinking (Matt. 16:23); tempts them to sin (Acts 5:3; 1 Cor. 7:5); deceives through false teaching (2 Cor. 11:4); disguises himself as an angel of light, thus setting the bar for counterfeit "servants of righteousness" (2 Cor. 11:14-15); attacks Christ's followers (Luke 22:31); hinders God's work (1 Thess. 2:18); and works through enemies of the gospel (John 8:44; 2 Thess. 2:9; Rev. 2:9, 13; 13:2).

The Accuser of Our Brothers and Sisters

The dragon has been an accuser from the beginning. His first recorded words to humans are intended to cast doubt on their understanding of God's commands, and then to charge the Lord with lying (Gen. 3:1, 4-5). It gets worse as we progress through Scripture. Today, while the dragon may accurately charge followers of Jesus with sin, we have an advocate in Jesus Christ, who stands at the Father's right hand to plead his shed blood as the reason for our justification (1 Tim. 2:5; Heb. 8:1-2; 1 John 2:1).

Through this litany of descriptive terms for the dragon, John steps forward as an eyewitness of Christ. In the process, John becomes an accuser himself. He rises on the witness stand, bears testimony of the dragon's destructive powers, and points a finger at the evil one, identifying him as the guilty party.

The Dragon and the Persecuted Woman (Rev. 12:13-17)

> When *the dragon* saw that he had been thrown down to the earth, he persecuted the woman who had given birth to the male child. The woman was given two wings of a great eagle, so that she could fly from *the serpent's* presence to her place in the wilderness, where she was nourished for a time, times, and half a time. From his mouth *the serpent* spewed water like a river flowing after the woman, to sweep her away with a flood. But the earth helped the woman. The earth opened its mouth and swallowed up the river that *the dragon* had spewed from his mouth. So *the dragon* was furious with the woman and went off to wage war against the rest of her offspring – those who keep the commands of God and hold firmly to the testimony about Jesus (emphasis added).

John uses *the dragon* and *the serpent* interchangeably in this passage to capture the evil one's tireless pursuit of God's people. We now see what happens when Satan is banished from heaven and cast down to earth. Furious, and well aware of his fleeting days as the "god of this age" (2 Cor. 4:4), the dragon relentlessly pursues the people from whom Messiah came: the Jews.

But God thwarts his efforts, extending protection and provision to Israel. Satan uses the elements of the earth in an effort to destroy God's people, but the earth   which is the Lord's, along with everything in it (Ps. 24:1) – protects them. Now even more frenzied, Satan lays aside his anti-Semitism and turns his attack on "the rest of" the woman's offspring.

We must note that anti-Semitism is rooted in the dragon and always has been a satanically inspired assault on God's people. It is true in the land of Goshen when a pharaoh comes to power who does not remember Joseph, and who sees the prosperous sons of Jacob as a threat requiring enslavement and population control via infanticide. It is true in the king's cabinet in the days of Queen Esther, whose bold intervention on behalf of fellow Jews staves off Haman's plot to exterminate them.

Further, it is true in the palaces of King Herod, who feels so threatened by news of a newly born Jewish king that he orders the murder of all infant boys in and around Bethlehem. It is true on the cross, where the King of the Jews hangs naked, bloody, beaten, and mocked. It is true in the Nazi concentration camps, where Hitler's dream of a master race necessitates the Holocaust. And it is true today in Islamic rhetoric that calls for Israel to be driven into the sea. But God does not permit anti-Semitism to stand or Satan to succeed.

If Satan were human, one might charge him with insanity, for he does the same thing over and over – persecute the people of God – while expecting different results. But in each case, God continues to direct the course of human history, in which Israel and the church play leading roles.

Bible commentators offer various views of the eagle's wings given to the woman, and by which she escapes the serpent's presence. For example, some see the wings as a symbol of a Christianized Roman Empire under Constantine. Others see the allusion to eagle's wings as prophetic language for a massive airlift of Jewish believers out of Israel and into a safe place, perhaps Petra in Jordan, in the last days; the U.S., whose emblem is the eagle, could lead this rescue mission.

Still other views abound. In any case, it appears John is drawing from the same imagery used of Israel escaping the Egyptian army. In Exodus 19:4, the Lord tells Moses, "You have seen what I did to the Egyptians and how I carried you on eagles' wings and brought you to myself." And in the song of Moses we read, "He watches over his nest like an eagle and hovers over his young; he spreads his wings, catches him, and carries him on his feathers" (Deut. 32:11).

As with the identity of the eagle, John does not reveal the location of the wilderness. However, Scripture often depicts the wilderness as a place of safety from pursuers. King David flees from Saul into the wilderness (1 Sam. 23:14-15). Elijah runs there as well to escape Jezebel (1 Kings 19:4).

Yahweh protects and provides for his people during forty years in the wilderness following their escape from Egypt. He preserves a remnant in Babylon – which in Isaiah 21 is called "the desert by the sea" – during seventy years of exile. And he sends angels to minister to Jesus after forty days in the wilderness.

The wilderness itself is not necessarily a place of comfort; it can be desolate and dangerous, with extreme temperatures, renegade thieves, and wild animals. But it is a place where frail people clearly seek the sovereign hand of God to meet their every need.

The "time, times, and half a time" generally are understood as a period of three and a half years (cf. Dan. 7:25; 12:7; Luke 4:25; Rev. 11:2-3; 13:5). Interpreters argue either that this is the span of Nero's persecution, which ended with his suicide (AD 64-68); or the length of the Jewish War (AD 66-70); or perhaps one-half of a future seven-year tribulation. Other commentators avoid specific time frames, positing that John simply means to assure Christians their trials are of finite length and end with the coming of the Lord.

Perhaps it's best not to be dogmatic about a particular view of these three and a half years. Rather, we should grasp the clear message in John's apocalyptic words: The Lord preserves a believing remnant. He makes sure there is a faithful testimony to counter the false prophets of the age. He limits Satan's power to deceive and persecute. And he provides for his own when times of hardship come; some are delivered *from* death, and some *through* death.

The serpent / dragon spews water like a river from his mouth, seeking to sweep the woman away with a flood. But the earth opens its mouth and swallows the river. While it's certainly possible that Satan aims to destroy a believing remnant with rapidly rising flood-waters, it seems more in keeping with the text to view this passage figuratively. But how, exactly, should we understand the symbolism?

Some interpreters see this river as Germanic tribes pouring into the Roman Empire to destroy Christianity.[18] Others view the river as a torrent of false teaching, featuring such heretics as Arius, Nestorius, and Pelagius.[19] Still others understand the floodwaters to be Satan's effort to exterminate Israel, or as an outpouring of hatred and anti-Semitic propaganda.[20] Perhaps there are parallels in all of these with

Psalm 124, in which the Lord saves Israel from attacking armies depicted as "the torrent" and "raging water."

Whichever view is correct – and there are plenty of others from which to choose – we can be confident the Lord always is ahead of the evil one, who attacks believers only with God's permission and within the divinely set bounds for his wicked works. Satan indeed inflicts damage on both Israel and the church, but he cannot destroy them or prevent the Lord's purposes in human history from being fulfilled. Put another way, the dragon's floodwaters never rise above the Lord's levees.

Finally in this passage, the dragon wages war against *the rest* of the woman's offspring – "those who keep the commands of God and hold firmly to the testimony about Jesus" (12:17). If the woman is Israel, the rest of her seed must be the church, or some portion of it, although there are at least three schools of thought concerning this.

One school sees the woman's offspring as the entire church, made up of Jewish and Gentile believers, as distinguished from the woman, or ethnic Israel. A second perspective sees the offspring as the Gentile church. According to this view, the Gentiles are Jesus' "other sheep that are not from this sheep pen" (John 10:16). A third camp sees both the woman and her offspring as Jews, with the woman being ethnic Israel and her offspring being Jewish Christians.

If the dragon wages war against *the rest* of the woman's offspring, who are the initial offspring? If ethnic Jews, then it makes sense either to see the rest of the woman's offspring as the church made up of Jewish and Gentile believers (first school of thought), or as Jewish Christians (third school of thought). If the initial offspring are Jewish Christians, then it follows that the rest of the woman's seed are Gentile followers of Christ (second school of thought).

However, it's possible to read the text with Jesus – the Son / male child of the woman – as the initial offspring. In Scripture's first messianic prophecy, we are promised that the offspring of woman will strike Satan's head (Gen. 3:15). And Paul clearly ties other Old Testament passages to Christ as Abraham's "seed" or "offspring" (e.g., Gal. 3:16). If Jesus is the woman's initial offspring in Revelation 12:17, then the rest of her offspring are Christians. This is a simple and straightforward reading of John's words and may be what the writer intended us to know.

In summary, God has given us victory over the dragon. The dragon has lost the war but continues to pursue a scorched-earth policy as he retreats. When we endure persecution, submit ourselves to God, and resist the devil, we share in the victory Christ won for us on the cross. Satan will leave us – for a time – and pursue lower-hanging fruit in his futile campaign against the Lord and his people.

Summary

Key takeaways about the *serpent* and the *dragon* (Part 1):

(1) While slithery serpents and fire-breathing dragons lavish the pages of fairy tales, it's an injustice to Scripture to write off its accounts of the *serpent* and the *dragon* so quickly. In fact, when applied to the evil one, the names *serpent* and *dragon* more aptly describe what Satan is like rather than how he appears.

(2) Occasionally in Scripture, serpents symbolize good rather than evil. Mostly, however, serpents represent evil – and in the ultimate sense, the evil one. This is true in Satan's first appearance in Scripture as the serpent (Heb. *nachash*) in Genesis 3.

(3) When writers of Scripture depict the evil one as *the serpent*, they are not describing his appearance; rather they are describing his character. He is an alluring, intelligent, shrewd, and attractive creature whose entire being is poised to deliver lethal poison. His smooth-talking deception of Eve illustrates both his beauty and his vileness, which remain as twin attributes throughout Scripture until he is cast into the lake of fire (Rev. 20:10).

(4) Just as conquered kings are made to lie on the ground with the feet of their conquerors on their necks (Josh. 10:24), Satan is surely a defeated foe whom Paul says God promises to crush beneath *our* feet (Rom. 16:20).

(5) Because Jesus has been lifted up on the cross, those who look to him in faith are restored to a right relationship with God. Just as

Moses made a bronze serpent to replicate the real thing (Num. 21:4-9), God "made the one who did not know sin to be sin for us, so that in him we might become the righteousness of God" (2 Cor. 5:21).

(6) In the Book of Revelation, the dragon is the chief enemy of Christ and his church. The dragon uses human and demonic forces to advance his purposes on earth.

(7) Jesus and Satan have diametrically opposed purposes, and yet they share a common means to these purposes: death. Satan seeks to kill Jesus and thus devour him. Jesus seeks to be killed in order to deliver sinful people from the wages of sin: death and hell. Jesus does in fact die. But he does so on his terms, in the Father's perfect timing, and by the Spirit's power.

(8) The Lord always preserves a believing remnant. He makes sure there is a faithful testimony to counter the false prophets of the age. He limits Satan's power to deceive and persecute. And he provides for his own when times of hardship come; some are delivered *from* death, and some *through* death.

Questions for Personal or Group Study

1. A skeptic opens your Bible to Genesis 3 and chides you for believing in "a talking snake." How might you respond?

2. Read Genesis 3:15. This is the so-called *protoevangelium*, or the first mention of the gospel in Scripture. In light of the rest of the Bible, what does this verse foreshadow about Satan, Jesus, and human beings?

3. The Hebrew and Greek words for *serpent* and *dragon* sometimes refer to animals, heavenly creatures, or even mythical figures. But when they are applied to Satan, how do they help us understand the type of being he is?

4. In Revelation 12:1-6, who are the woman, the child, and the dragon?

5. Read Revelation 12:7-12. What names does John use to describe Satan? What is the significance of each name?

3

SERPENT / DRAGON

PART 2

W e continue our examination of the dragon in the Book of Revelation.

The Dragon and the Beast from the Sea (Rev. 12:18 – 13:10)

The *dragon* stood on the sand of the sea. And I saw a beast coming up out of the sea. It had ten horns and seven heads. On its horns were ten crowns, and on its heads were blasphemous names. The beast I saw was like a leopard, its feet were like a bear's, and its mouth was like a lion's mouth. The *dragon* gave the beast his power, his throne, and great authority. One of its heads appeared to be fatally wounded, but its fatal wound was healed. The whole earth was amazed and followed the beast. They worshiped the *dragon* because he gave authority to the beast. And they worshiped the beast, saying, "Who is like the beast? Who is able to wage war against it?" (Rev. 12:18 – 13:4, emphasis added).

The word *dragon* in 12:18 does not appear in the Greek, so translators seek to identify the one standing on the sand of the sea either as "the dragon," "he" (meaning the dragon), or "I" (referring to John). In any case, John sees a frightening beast rise out of the sea in Revelation 13:1-10. In verses 11-18, he sees a second beast rise from the earth. The dragon empowers both beasts. This is explicitly stated of the first beast and implied with respect to the second beast.

The first beast is similar to the dragon in that he has ten horns and seven heads. Yet, he is a distinct – and lesser – creature than the dragon because the dragon is the source of the beast's power, throne, and authority. The Greek word used here for "beast" (*therion*) means "wild animal" and metaphorically signifies a brutal, savage, ferocious being. The dragon gives the beast power to act for forty-two months. The dragon also grants the beast a mouth to speak haughty and blasphemous words.

The beast miraculously recovers from an apparently fatal head wound, causing the whole earth to follow him. The people worship the dragon and the beast, perhaps out of fear rather than love, for they declare, "Who is like the beast? Who is able to wage war against it?" (Rev. 13:4).

The dragon empowers – and the Lord permits – the beast to wage war against the saints and to gain authority over the people. Those faithful to Christ suffer persecution and death, while unbelievers – "everyone whose name was not written from the foundation of the world in the book of life of the Lamb who was slaughtered" – survive only by continuing to worship the beast (v. 8).

So, who is this beast? And what does the dragon have to do with him? One view is that the beast represents a large realm, such as the Roman Empire. More prominent is the view that the beast is a man who operates a sinister global organization. Other passages of Scripture support the interpretation of the beast as a person.

In Revelation 19:20, for example, we are told that the beast is taken, along with a second beast, and cast into the lake of fire, where the dragon joins them sometime later (Rev. 20:10). While God ultimately puts down all competing kingdoms, there is no indication he casts anything other than Satan, evil spirits, and people into hell. In addition, Paul warns of a coming "man of sin" (2 Thess. 2:3), and

John affirms a teaching throughout the church of a future antichrist (1 John 2:18).

It appears this is the same beast that emerges from the abyss in Revelation 11:7. He makes war with two witnesses, conquering and killing them. The beast is mentioned several other times in Revelation (Rev. 14:9, 11; 15:2; 16:2; 17:3, 13; 19:20; 20:10). Some commentators conclude that the beast is ancient Rome, or the papal church, or anti-Christian powers seeking to silence the church's witness.

Some futurists contend that there are three beasts. The beast that comes out of the abyss is Satan (Rev. 11:7), the beast out of the sea is the antichrist (Rev. 13:1), and the beast out of the land is the false prophet (Rev. 13:11). Other futurists say the beast out of the abyss and the beast out of the sea are one and the same.

Whoever the beast is, it's important to remember, first, that he comes *out* of the abyss (compare Rev. 11:7 and Rev. 13:1-8), a special place where certain demons are confined until judgment day, and *out* of the sea, which symbolizes humanity. Whether the beast is a person, an institution, or both, demonic and worldly forces empower him.

Second, God is sovereign over the beast's power and influence. The beast can do nothing to the saints except what the Lord allows. Third, the beast hates God and God's people. His violence toward the saints exposes a deeper animosity toward Yahweh. Finally, his victory is hollow. The victims of his persecution go to be with the Lord, while he ultimately is cast into the lake of fire.

It is interesting to note how John describes the beast's abilities. The dragon gives him his power, throne, and authority. This dominating beast has the same flesh and bones as other humans and yet rises above them on the wings of the dragon.

The god of this age is not able to manifest himself in human flesh as the Son of God does, so he inhabits the flesh of a naturally born human and infuses him with power. The prince of the power of the air will never rule all human beings, so he shares his earthly authority with a willing beast who wields satanic power over every living unbeliever. And the evil one will never sit on the throne of David, so he places a puppet king on a worldly throne and pulls the strings.

Revelation 13:8 makes it clear that the world's unbelievers – not Christians – worship the dragon and the "resurrected" beast: "All those who live on the earth will worship it, everyone whose name was not written from the foundation of the world in the book of life of the Lamb who was slaughtered." This miraculous deception – a counterfeit resurrection of Jesus, and a demonic response to the resurrection of the two witnesses in Revelation 11 – is enough to convince the world's lost people that a savior has come.

While the beast from the sea commands our attention in these verses, the dragon behind the throne should intrigue us more. We might ask: Why doesn't the dragon (Satan) just rule the world? Isn't he the god of this age, anyway? What does he need with a human puppet? Several observations may prove helpful.

First, Satan acts only within God's permissive will. While the evil one strains against an exceptionally long leash, it appears God limits the dragon's ability to appear in the physical realm. He certainly does so as the serpent in Genesis 3, prior to the Fall. But his other appearances are confined (perhaps) to the heavenly council (Job 1-2; Zech. 3) or to John's visions.

One possible exception is the evil one's direct temptation of Jesus in the wilderness (Matt. 4:1-11; Luke 4:1-13), but even then, the Gospel writers say only that Satan tempts Jesus, not necessarily that he appears physically. Put another way, for Satan to break into the physical realm, he must use secondary means. Yes, he prowls the earth like a roaring lion, but when he appears, it must always be in a borrowed disguise.

Second, Satan successfully uses secondary means – evil spirits, willing persons, or even nature itself – to accomplish his purposes. He kills Job's children, destroys Job's wealth, and takes Job to the brink of physical death. He incites King David to number his troops – an arrogant and defiant act that results in the deaths of seventy thousand people. He gets Peter to oppose Jesus' plan of crucifixion.

He enters Judas Iscariot. And he fills the hearts of Ananias and Sapphira to lie to the Holy Spirit. So, while he might prefer to break through into the physical realm, he doesn't need to do so in order to wreak havoc on the earth.

Third, Satan's desire for worship is accomplished through the beast. As the dragon inspires and empowers this world leader, people seem to know there is a "divine" entity behind the miracles, and they eagerly worship him.

The Dragon's Play – in Eight Acts

Let's see how the dragon pulls the beast's strings to deceive the whole world. It seems the dragon carries out his work through the beast – more commonly known as the *antichrist* – in eight primary acts.

Act 1 – Granting Power, a Throne, and Authority (Rev. 13:2)

"Power" comes from the Greek *dynamis*, from which we get the English word "dynamite." It means inherent power residing in a person or object by virtue of its nature. Put another way, the dragon invests his brutish strength in the beast. "Throne" is from the Greek *thronos* and depicts a chair of state having a footstool. In this context, it means kingly stature and royalty. "Authority" is from the Greek *exousia* and describes the beast's power of choice, or liberty to exercise influence and privilege. This authority is a limited-time offer, however; as far as the beast is concerned, it's good for forty-two months (v. 5).

Just as Satan's days are numbered, the beast must make the most of his time in the limelight. So, while the beast rules supremely, he is more like a velvet glove, with the dragon's iron hand firmly inside.

Act 2 – Using Counterfeit Miracles (Rev. 13:3)

The beast suffers a head wound that *appears* to be fatal. When he is miraculously healed, the whole earth is amazed and follows the beast. John mentions the deadly wound three times (Rev. 13:3, 12, 14) and reveals it is a sword-inflicted wound.

It does not appear that Satan holds the power to raise the dead, although God *could* allow it. But in this case, the dragon may be granted the power to heal a serious, life-threatening wound. Or, more likely, he deceives people into thinking a true miracle has occurred. As the apostle Paul points out, "The coming of the lawless one [antichrist; beast] is based on Satan's working, with every kind of miracle, both signs and wonders serving the lie ..." (2 Thess. 2:9).

The beast from the sea appears to be a counterfeit Christ, whose resurrection on the third day after his crucifixion is the cornerstone of the Christian faith. How clever it is for the dragon to counterfeit the Lamb's crowning achievement with an apparent resurrection of the beast.

But it should come as no surprise to us. Jesus warns about false messiahs and false prophets in the last days (cf. Matt. 24:4-5, 11, 24). The world's unbelievers – those whose names are not written in the Lamb's book of life – pay lip service to the God who raises his two witnesses from the dead (Rev. 11), but they worship the devil who mocks the resurrection of Jesus with a counterfeit rebirth of the beast.

Act 3 – Receiving Worship for Himself (Rev. 13:4)

When the people marvel at the beast's apparent resurrection, they worship the dragon because they recognize he is the ultimate authority behind the beast. And they express amazement, or perhaps fear, toward the satanically inspired beast by asking rhetorically, "Who is like the beast? Who is able to wage war against it?"

Note that throughout Revelation 13, John refers to the beast as "it" rather than "he" or "him." This may lead us to think the beast is an institution, or perhaps a mechanical creation, or even a cyborg. But in light of other Scriptures foretelling a world ruler in the last days, it seems best to understand the beast as a true person, although one who is so under Satan's control that his own true humanity – as an imager of God – is greatly disfigured.

Act 4 – Employing a Boastful and Blasphemous Voice (Rev. 13:5-6)

John describes it this way: "The beast was given a mouth to utter boasts and blasphemies…. It began to speak blasphemies against God: to blaspheme his name and his dwelling – those who dwell in heaven." Satan invests his supernatural cleverness, arrogance, and eloquence in the beast, who plies these skills to blaspheme God. This includes God's name (which no devout Jew would dare to speak out loud), his dwelling (literally, his tabernacle, or the place his Shekinah glory dwells), and his people (the throne-encircled redeemed whose praises he inhabits).

In the Old Testament, the root meaning of the word "blasphemy" is an act of effrontery in which a person insults the honor of God, and for which he or she may be stoned to death (Lev. 24:10-23; 1 Kings 21:9ff). In the New Testament, the meaning is extended to include God's representatives. For example, Jews from the Freedman's Synagogue accuse Stephen of "speaking blasphemous words against Moses and God" (Acts 6:11).

But the charge of blasphemy rises to a crescendo around the words and deeds of Jesus. When he forgives the sins of a paralyzed man (Mark 2:5-7), confirms his identity as the Son of God (Mark 14:61-65), and receives insults as he hangs bloody and disfigured on the cross (Matt. 27:39), Jesus is reviled for demonstrating his deity. Yet when the beast exalts himself above all divine figures, he is worshiped rather than put to death.

Act 5 – Leveraging Limited Time

John records, "It [the beast] was allowed to exercise authority [wage war; rule] for forty-two months" (Rev. 13:5). Satan knows his time is short (Rev. 12:12). Whether Satan sets the clock ticking for the

beast, or whether God establishes this allotment of time, it is clear
the beast cannot exercise earthly sovereignty indefinitely.

The Lord always sets limits on those who oppose him. In
addition, he often provides warnings of impending judgment, along
with an invitation to repent. The Amorites are given more than four
hundred years. The Egyptians are given ten plagues. The Israelites
are given prophet after prophet to call them to repentance.

Even when God's people suffer persecution, he assures them
there is a limit to their hardship. Jesus encourages the church at
Smyrna this way: "Don't be afraid of what you are about to suffer.
Look, the devil is about to throw some of you into prison to test you,
and you will experience affliction for *ten days*. Be faithful to the point
of death, and I will give you the crown of life" (Rev. 2:10, emphasis
added).

Act 6 – Granting War Powers (Rev. 13:7)

The beast is permitted to wage war against the saints and to
conquer them. While the dragon assigns this authority to his puppet
king, it is all within the permissive will of God. Take special note of
the sinister will of the dragon and the permissive will of God. The
dragon gives the beast power, a throne, and authority (v. 2). The
dragon, presumably, heals the beast's fatal head wound (v. 3). The
dragon amazes the whole earth through a counterfeit miracle,
deceiving people into following the beast (v. 3). The *dragon* receives
worship (v. 4). The *dragon* gives the beast a mouth to utter boasts and
blasphemies (v. 5). And on it goes.

But we see a different perspective beginning in verse 7 as it
becomes clear God permits these evil events to unfold. For example,
the beast is *permitted* to wage war against the saints and to conquer
them (v. 7). The beast's authority over every people, tribe, language,
and nation happens by divine permission. And God allows the beast
to receive worldwide worship that rightly belongs only to the King of
kings.

We see the dual nature of God's will – what he decrees and what he allows – throughout Scripture. Yahweh decrees the hardening of Pharaoh's heart as he allows the Egyptian king to make his own decisions (Exod. 7-14). He sends a spirit to entice King David to take a census, while permitting that same spirit to volunteer for duty and allowing the king to make the rebellious decision (2 Sam. 24; 1 Chron. 21). And God sends his Son to die for our sins, while Jesus makes it clear that no one takes his life – he lays it down voluntarily (John 10:18).

Satan plots, possesses, empowers, amazes, destroys, and deceives – all the while attracting the worship of the world's lost. And the whole time Almighty God permits it, even the slaughter of the saints. Satan can do nothing without God's permission. He cannot take Job's possessions, wipe out his family, or afflict his body without the Lord removing his protective hedge (see Job 1-2). And Satan cannot sift Peter like wheat, causing him to deny Christ, without the Lord allowing it; even so, the evil one cannot snatch Peter from the hand of God, for Jesus assures Peter he will turn back to his master (see Luke 22:31-32).

It's impossible for the finite human mind to grasp the infinite sovereignty of God, who allows evil and, at times, seems a willing participant in it, yet cannot be tempted with evil. The holiness of God is as true as the reality of evil, and what God causes and permits are two sides of the same coin. With all things under his authority – even the evil of Satan and demons, and the rebellion of sinful people – God is somehow able to take the worst his creatures dish out and fashion it into the very best.

Act 7 – Conquering the Saints (Rev. 13:7)

While the Lord temporarily withdraws his divine hand of protection from his adopted family, it is the dragon who empowers the beast to persecute the saints with a vengeance. The church rises to its greatest stature when it is weak and broken. Devoid of religious, military, or political power, Christians in the first century turn the world upside down for Jesus (Acts 17:6).

Jesus has only commendation for the afflicted and poverty-stricken church in Smyrna, while reserving unvarnished condemnation for the church at Laodicea, which claims to be rich and in need of nothing, not realizing it is "wretched, pitiful, poor, blind, and naked" (Rev. 3:17). No doubt, the saints suffer horrible indignity at the hands of the beast, and those who are martyred cry out, "How long, Lord?" beneath the altar in heaven (Rev. 6:10). The Lord urges them to be patient; the day of their exaltation and the judgment of evil is coming soon.

Act 8 – Ruling the World (Rev. 13:7)

Satan rules his own kingdom – a realm in opposition to God. This includes his position as the god of this age, the ruler of this world. Even Jesus does not contest Satan's claim to have temporary authority over the kingdoms of the world. But Satan's rule has always been a shadow. He rules the hearts of people, and he often uses people to scorch the earth with enormous evil influence – Hitler, Stalin, Pol Pot, Castro, Mao, to name a few – but none of these leaders ruled the entire world or publicly recognized the personal power behind their thrones.

Now, as the beast rules over every tribe, people, language, and nation, the dragon at last receives the world's worship through his surrogate. The entire population – with the exception of those whose names are written in the Lamb's book of life – worships a single world leader who owes everything to the dragon.

Just as Jesus relied on God the Father for direction in his earthly ministry, and on the Holy Spirit for power to carry out his mission of redemption, so the counterfeit messiah, the beast, relies completely on the dragon for direction, strength, power, and purpose.

But some might ask: Because the beast's worshipers have never had their names written in the Lamb's book of life – and believers always have had their names written there – doesn't this smack of fatalism? In reply, some Christians may try to explain this by saying God merely foresees the faith of the righteous and the rebellion of the unrighteous, and confirms their free choices. Others contend that God has determined all things, including the "free" choices of individuals (without becoming the author of sin or the creator of a fixed game). It may not be this simple.

We do God a great disservice when we accuse him either of aimless foreknowledge or fatalistic sovereignty. Certainly, he knows all things. He is sovereign. He has all power and authority. And in the midst of this mind-boggling transcendence, he created people in his image and entrusted them with the ability to make choices for which he holds them responsible. Though the beast-worshiping unbelievers of Revelation 13 are excluded from the Lamb's book of life, they would never have signed their names anyway – even if the Son of God opened the pages himself and offered them a pen.

The Dragon and the Beast from the Earth (Rev. 13:11-18)

> Then I saw another beast coming up out of the earth; it had two horns like a lamb, but it spoke like a *dragon*. It exercises all the authority of the first beast on its behalf and compels the earth and those who live on it to worship the first beast, whose fatal wound was healed. It also performs great signs, even causing fire to come down from heaven to earth in front of people. It deceives those who live on the earth because of the signs that it is permitted to perform in the presence of the beast, telling those who live on the earth to make an image of the beast who was wounded by the sword and yet lived. It was permitted to give breath to the image of the beast, so that the image of the beast could both speak and cause whoever would not worship the image of the beast to be killed. And it makes everyone – small and great, rich and poor, free and slave – to receive a mark on his right hand or on his forehead, so that no one can buy or sell unless he has the mark: the beast's name or the number of its name.
>
> This calls for wisdom: Let the one who has understanding

calculate the number of the beast, because it is the number of a person. Its number is 666 (emphasis added).

We are now introduced to the second of two beasts: a beast from the earth, more often identified as the *false prophet*. He has two horns like a lamb but speaks like a dragon. Like the first beast, he is endowed with great authority and power, which he uses to compel people to worship the first beast while deceiving them with miraculous signs. He even gives life to an image of the first beast and causes those who refuse to worship the image to be killed. Finally, he restricts commerce so that only those who take a special mark on their right hands or foreheads, indicating their allegiance to the first beast, may buy and sell.

Like the identity of the first beast, the identity of the second beast is a source of much speculation. Is he Gessius Florus, the first-century governor of Judea who operates with great cruelty and forces Christians to pay homage to a large statue of Nero? Is he symbolic of the heretical brand of Judaism so prevalent in the first century? Or does he represent false religion in general – religion whose goal is to feed man's spiritual hunger with any food except the bread of life? Is he papal Rome or the Roman priesthood? Or is he a yet-future false prophet – an exalted and eloquent sidekick who performs miracles and compels the world to worship the beast from the sea?

Perhaps there is some connection between all of these views. But our focus remains on the dragon behind this beast. It may help to observe how the dragon and his two beasts parody the Trinity. They shun the creative intent of the triune God, plotting instead to take a kingdom for themselves and deceive the whole world into following them. Their work results in hardship, deception, distrust, and ultimately death. And their method of operation denies the truth that leads men and women to the light of the world: Jesus. Instead, it entices them to embrace the darkness of the evil kingdom.

This beast is "another" beast, with the Greek word *allos* meaning another of the same kind. Indeed, the first and second beasts have much in common. The main similarity is that both are described as beasts (Gr. *therion)*. They are dangerous, wild creatures. John uses this word to describe their character. They are ravenous, sinister, wicked, yet they often appear as tame as domesticated animals. They are eloquent, charismatic, and intelligent, wooing the world to follow them.

As with the first beast, the second beast operates on a full charge of the dragon's power. Notice how the second beast:

Speaks like a dragon (v. 11). Satan's words are smooth, beguiling, and convincing. They hold enough truth to gain an audience but are laced with a lethal dose of error. No doubt, this beast's soothing words lull unbelievers into a false sense of security as they receive the strong delusion God sends them (cf. 2 Thess. 2:11).

Exercises all the authority of the first beast on its behalf (v. 12). The dragon spares no power in using the second beast to compel people to worship the first beast (and thus the authority behind him).

Performs great signs (v. 13). The Greek word used here for "signs" is *semeion* and is the same word used to describe the miracles of Jesus and the apostles. These are supernatural deeds, to be sure, but their source is the dragon, and their purpose is to lead the entire world astray. These signs include counterfeiting the fire Elijah and the two witnesses call down from heaven. Like the magicians in Pharaoh's court who conjure up demonic power to mirror Moses' miracles, the beast from the earth is able to convince onlookers that he holds equally divine powers.

The beast from the earth is a miracle worker, but his purpose is deceitful. His goal is to cause all people to turn away from the one true and living God to a false god. What a contrast to Jesus, whose miracles confirm his deity, and to the apostles, whose signs and wonders establish them as Christ's anointed representatives. As Paul writes to the Corinthians, countering the deeds of the false "super apostles," "The signs of an apostle were performed with unfailing endurance among you, including signs and wonders and miracles" (2 Cor. 12:12).

Deceives those who live on the earth (v. 14). Through counterfeit miracles, the second beast gains enough trust to compel people to build an image of the first beast. The Greek word translated "deceives" is *planao*. It means to cause someone to roam from safety, truth, or virtue; to seduce. This deception is deliberate and without any hint that the second beast (also known as the false prophet) is a victim of deception himself. For his grave, willful sin, he bypasses the great white throne judgment and is cast directly into the lake of fire, along with the first beast (Rev. 19:20). In a similar manner, the dragon gets no day in court; he is cast into the lake of fire (Rev. 20:10).

Gives life to the image of the first beast (v. 15). The second beast is permitted to give "breath" or "life" to the image of the first beast. The dragon gives the second beast his power, as God permits. This image speaks and causes those who refuse to worship the image to be killed. The talking role of the image is a considerable enhancement over the pagan idols of Old Testament times, and of first-century Rome, for those idols can neither speak nor act (Ps. 115:4-8; Jer. 10:5; Hab. 2:18-19). Whether the speaking is a result of human sleight-of-hand tricks or demonic animation, the image of the beast inspires both wonder and terror in the hearts of people, for he pronounces death sentences on those who hold fast their allegiance to Christ.

Makes everyone receive a mark on the right hand or forehead (vv. 16-17). No one may buy or sell without the mark. Some interpreters believe this mark is an actual mark – a brand burned into the skin, or a tattoo. Others point to imperial coins that bear the image of the emperor. Futurists say it could be a microchip planted just beneath the skin. Others argue that John's language is figurative, referring to people's thoughts (forehead) and deeds (right hands) as they place their trust in the first beast and pledge allegiance to him.

The Greek word translated "mark" is *charagma* and denotes the official stamp of Caesar. This stamp is applied to documents to certify them. In whatever manner the mark is taken, it seems clear it is used to verify those who have submitted themselves to the first beast, and to separate themselves from those who withhold their worship from the antichrist.

For both beasts in Revelation 13, we see the supernatural power of the dragon at work behind the scenes. While he remains unseen, he manipulates willing human beings to counterfeit the things of God – authority, wisdom, order, institutions, language, worship – and thus corrupt them so people sincerely embrace "another Jesus ... a different Spirit ... a different gospel" (2 Cor. 11:4).

The Dragon and the Sixth Bowl (Rev. 16:12-19)

> The sixth [angel] poured out his bowl on the great river Euphrates, and its water was dried up to prepare the way for the kings from the east. Then I saw three unclean spirits like frogs coming from the *dragon's* mouth, from the beast's mouth, and from the mouth of the false prophet. For they are demonic spirits performing signs, who travel to the kings of the whole world to assemble them for the battle on the great day of God, the Almighty. "Look, I am coming like a thief. Blessed is the one who is alert and remains clothed so that he may not go around naked and people see his shame." So they assembled the kings at the place called in Hebrew, Armageddon (emphasis added).

We are introduced to two exceptional beasts in Revelation 13. In union with the beast from the sea and the beast from the earth, the dragon forges an unholy trinity that counterfeits the nature and work of the Father, Son, and Holy Spirit.

In the sixth bowl judgment, recorded in Revelation 16:12-19, John sees three unclean spirits like frogs coming from the mouths of the dragon, beast, and false prophet. The description is straightforward: these are demonic spirits who perform miracles, thus deceiving world leaders to assemble for a battle in which they are certain to lose their lives. While God cannot lie, Satan can do nothing but lie, and these demonic minions of the evil one are so efficient in their work that they convince the world's best and brightest to engage in a most foolish battle against Almighty God.

In comparing the demonic spirits to frogs, John perhaps alludes to the second Egyptian plague (Exod. 8:1-15). This agrees with the view that Jerusalem – prophetically called Sodom and Egypt in Revelation 11:8 – is under attack. God judges geographical Egypt with biological frogs; he sends spiritual frogs – evil spirits – to punish spiritual Egypt (Jerusalem).

The primary means by which these spirits deceive the nations' leaders is the performance of "signs," or pseudo miracles. Satan and his minions often counterfeit the supernatural works of God to entice unbelievers. Where clever words are sufficient, as in the garden of Eden, Satan plies his trade as the "father of lies" most effectively. But stunning displays of power are at times even more convincing.

While Christians have the indwelling Holy Spirit to help us discern the things of God, we are not immune to demonic deception. The apostle Paul, warning against "false apostles, deceitful workers," writes, "And no wonder! For Satan disguises himself as an angel of light. So, it is no great surprise if his servants also disguise themselves as servants of righteousness" (2 Cor. 11:14-15).

It appears the deception in this passage affects only unbelievers, however. Jesus warns of a time when false messiahs and false prophets arise and perform great signs and wonders to lead astray even the elect, *if possible* (Matt. 24:24, emphasis added). As Paul writes, "The coming of the lawless one is based on Satan's working, with all kinds of false miracles, signs, and wonders, and with every wicked deception among those who are perishing. They perish because they did not accept the love of the truth and so be saved" (2 Thess. 2:9-10).

The dragon speaks and evil spirits respond. In the power of a counterfeit trinity, Satan and the two beasts set out to lie, deceive, entice, and destroy, although their sins are turned back on them in a stunning defeat as the glorified Christ returns. With his voice – depicted as a sharp two-edged sword coming from his mouth – Jesus hacks the enemy to pieces and ultimately commits the defeated foes to the fires of hell (Rev. 19:15ff).

The Dragon Bound (Rev. 20:1-3)

> Then I saw an angel coming down from heaven holding the key to
> the abyss and a great chain in his hand. He seized the *dragon*, that
> *ancient serpent* who is the *devil* and *Satan*, and bound him for a
> thousand years. He threw him into the abyss, closed it, and put a
> seal on it so that he would no longer deceive the nations until the
> thousand years were completed. After that, he must be released for a
> short time (emphasis added).

In an echo of Revelation 12:9, John applies five descriptors to the
evil one. He is the *dragon*, *serpent*, *devil*, *Satan*, and *deceiver* of nations.
In Revelation 12, he is thrown to earth; in Revelation 20, he is thrown
into the abyss. When we encounter the dragon at the end of the
thousand years, he is thrown into the lake of fire – his final descent
into everlasting torment (Rev. 20:10).

The evil one's incarceration is a curious matter. It begins with a
nondescript angel – not a cherub or seraph, not Michael or Gabriel,
not even a mighty angel. This unnamed messenger descends from
heaven, holding the keys to the abyss and a great chain in his hand.
Jesus has defeated Satan through his finished work on the cross.
Michael has defeated the devil in a cosmic battle in the heavenlies.
And now God dispatches a humble, obedient, and nameless heavenly
messenger to lead the evil one unwillingly down his own green mile.

We have seen the abyss before. In Revelation 9, a "star that had
fallen from heaven to earth" is given the key to the abyss.
Commentators disagree whether this *star* is Satan, a demon, an angel,
a heretical Jewish or Christian leader, Islam's prophet Muhammad, or
even Wormwood (Rev. 8:11). In any case, the star releases demons who
inflict severe pain on the world's unbelievers. In Revelation 20,
however, the gates swing the other way. No evil spirits are released;
rather, the dragon is cast *into* the abyss and prevented from deceiving
the nations for a period of time.

The *abyss*, also known as the bottomless pit, is a place of temporary confinement. The word appears ten times in ten verses in the CSB. In a few Bible passages, the term appears to be a synonym for *sheol*, or the abode of the dead (Ps. 140:10; Rom. 10:7; c.f. Deut. 30:13). In Luke 8:31, demons that are cast out of a man called Legion beg Jesus not to banish them to the abyss; this appears to be a place of confinement for demons, but it's not hell (*gehenna*), which is their final destination. Throughout Revelation, the abyss is a place where evil spirits are confined and over which a figure known as Abaddon rules (Rev. 9:1, 2, 11; 11:7; 17:8; 20:1; see Chapter 13 for more on Abaddon / Apollyon / Destroyer).

It's also helpful to note 2 Peter 2:4, in which the apostle writes that God threw rebellious angels into *Tartarus* to be kept in chains (or pits) of darkness until judgment. *Tartarus*, used only here in the New Testament, describes a subterranean place of confinement lower than hades. Possibly, *Tartarus* and the abyss are the same place, or at least related (see also Jude 6).

But why is the dragon imprisoned and then released for a short time? Kendell Easley suggests his temporary confinement in the abyss portrays a parallel to the intermediate imprisonment of wicked dead humans in hades:

> Wicked humans experience death of their bodies, go temporarily to Hades, are released from Hades for a short season to be judged at Christ's white throne, and then are thrown into the fiery lake. By parallel, the wicked serpent, who as a spirit cannot die bodily, is sent temporarily to the Abyss, is released from the Abyss for a short season, will finally be judged, and then is thrown into the fiery lake.[1]

The angel God sends to confine the dragon is given the key to the abyss. The *key* in Scripture symbolizes authority. In Revelation 1:17-18, Jesus holds the keys of death and hades. Since he defeated Satan on the cross, it is quite likely Jesus now holds the key to the abyss as well. Therefore, he grants the release of demons to bring judgment upon those who trample his blood beneath their feet (Rev. 9:1-12). He also uses his authority to confine Satan in Revelation 20.

The angel sent in Revelation 20:1 wields not only a key, but a chain with which he binds the dragon. Since Satan is not a physical creature, the chain obviously is not like one we would imagine, with thick metal links and shackles. John uses the word figuratively to depict the restricted movement of the one who at present roams the earth like a lion (1 Pet. 5:8). The double binding of the dragon – in chains and kept inside the abyss – ensures that despite his cunning and power, he does not escape, although later he is released for a short time.

Think for a moment about the angel's boldness in seizing the dragon. In a dispute over the body of Moses, Michael the archangel dares not utter a slanderous accusation against Satan but says, "The Lord rebuke you!" (Jude 9). And the angel of the LORD – the preincarnate Christ – defers to "the LORD" in rebuking Satan before a heavenly tribunal involving Joshua the high priest (Zech. 3:1-2). But here in Revelation 20, a lowly angel snatches the dragon without hesitation.

The Greek word *krateo* means "to seize." It also means to use strength, to hold on, arrest, control, or keep. Interestingly, this word is used several times in Revelation 2 in different ways. Jesus "holds" the seven stars in his right hand (v. 1). The church at Pergamum is "holding on" to Jesus' name (v. 13), even though some in that church "hold to" the teaching of Balaam (v. 14), while others "hold to" the teaching of the Nicolaitans (v. 15). The word is used a few other places in Revelation as well, but in every case the emphasis is on holding someone or something securely. This unnamed holy messenger seizes the dragon, holds him securely, and confines him in the abyss.

Breaking the Dragon's Head

Throughout its chapters, the Book of Revelation offers a brief history of the dragon, or serpent. The dragon begins his war against God and those made in God's image in the garden of Eden; he is "the ancient serpent" (12:9). He wields great power in the heavens, having seven heads, ten horns, and a great sweeping tail (12:3). He fails in his quest to destroy Messiah at the Incarnation (12:4-5). He is thrown down to earth for a while and deceives the nations (12:7-12). He endows two beastly world leaders with deceptive powers (12:18 – 13:18). He and these two beasts, in an unholy trinity, unleash demonic spirits who work miracles and convince world leaders to gather for battle (16:12-16). He is thrown into the abyss for a thousand years (20:1-3).[2]

This is the last time in Scripture we see Satan depicted as the *dragon* or *serpent*, but it's not our final encounter with the evil one. Revelation 20:7-10 tells us Satan is released from the abyss after a lengthy incarceration. He is rankled but not reformed. He sets out immediately to "deceive the nations at the four corners of the earth" and rallies a great army. But the dragon is toothless. Fire comes down from heaven and consumes the evil one and his army. John captures Satan's destiny in a single verse: "The devil who deceived them was thrown into the lake of fire and sulfur where the beast and the false prophet are, and they will be tormented day and night forever and ever" (Rev. 20:10).

We explore the evil one's final home more fully in Chapter 14.

A Puritan prayer wisely captures the battle between Christ and the dragon, assuring us of victory now and throughout eternity:

> O LORD,
>
> I bless thee that the issue of the battle between thyself and Satan has never been uncertain, and will end in victory.
>
> Calvary broke the dragon's head, and I contend with a vanquished foe, who with all his subtlety and strength has already been overcome.
>
> When I feel the serpent at my heel may I remember him whose heel was bruised, but who, when bruised, broke the devil's head.[3]

Summary

Key takeaways about the *serpent* and *dragon* (Part 2):

(1) The dragon (Satan) is the source of power behind the beast from the sea (Rev. 12:18 – 13:10). This beast, most likely, is a human

being who rules a sinister global enterprise. The dragon empowers – and the Lord permits – the beast to wage war against the saints and to gain authority over the people. Those faithful to Christ suffer persecution and death, while unbelievers survive only by continuing to worship the beast.

(2) This dominating beast from the sea (also known as the antichrist) has the same flesh and bones as other humans, and yet he rises above them on the wings of the dragon. The god of this age is not able to manifest himself in human flesh as the Son of God does, so he inhabits the flesh of a naturally born human and infuses him with power. The evil one will never sit on the throne of David, so he places a puppet king on a worldly throne and pulls the strings.

(3) Why does the dragon need a human puppet? Consider: (a) While the evil one strains against an exceptionally long leash, it appears God limits the dragon's ability to appear in the physical realm; (b) Satan successfully uses secondary means – evil spirits, willing persons, or even nature itself – to accomplish his purposes; and (c) Satan's desire for worship is accomplished through the beast from the sea, or antichrist. As the dragon inspires and empowers this world leader, people seem to know there is a "divine" entity behind the miracles, and they eagerly worship him.

(4) The second beast – the beast from the earth, also known as the false prophet (Rev. 13:11-18) – speaks like a dragon; exercises all the authority of the first beast on his behalf; performs great signs; deceives those who live on the earth; gives life to the image of the first beast; and makes everyone receive a mark on the right hand or forehead.

(5) For both beasts in Revelation 13, we see the supernatural power of the dragon at work behind the scenes. While he remains unseen, the dragon manipulates willing human beings to counterfeit the things of God – authority, wisdom, order, institutions, language, worship – and thus corrupts them so people sincerely embrace "another Jesus ... a different Spirit ... a different gospel" (2 Cor. 11:4).

(6) The dragon forges an unholy trinity with the two beasts of Revelation 13. In the power of this counterfeit trinity, Satan and the

two beasts set out to lie, deceive, entice, and destroy (Rev. 16:12-19), although their sins are turned back on them in a stunning defeat as the glorified Christ returns. With his voice – depicted as a sharp two-edged sword coming from his mouth – Jesus hacks the enemy to pieces and ultimately commits the defeated foes to the fires of hell (Rev. 19:15ff).

(7) The Lord sends a nondescript angel to incarcerate the dragon in the abyss. The double binding of the dragon – in chains and kept inside the abyss – ensures that despite his cunning and power, he does not escape, although later he is released for a short time.

(8) Revelation 20:7-10 tells us Satan is released from the abyss after a lengthy incarceration. He is rankled but not reformed. He sets out immediately to "deceive the nations at the four corners of the earth" and rallies a great army. But the dragon is toothless. Fire comes down from heaven and consumes the evil one and his army.

Questions for Personal or Group Study

1. In what ways does the dragon work through the two beasts of Revelation 13 to capture the unbelieving world's attention and worship?
2. The apostle Peter likens Satan to a prowling, roaring lion (1 Pet. 5:8), yet God keeps the evil one on a leash. What are some specific ways the Lord limits Satan's activities on earth?
3. There are so many different opinions about the meaning of symbols in the Book of Revelation. In what ways might we be tempted to focus so strongly on the symbols that we miss the greater message behind them?
4. Read Revelation 12:18 – 13:4. How does the dragon carry out his work through the beast from the sea?
5. In Revelation 20:1-3, we see the dragon bound for a thousand years. Do you think Satan is imprisoned now (during the church age) or at some point in the future?

What are the strengths and weaknesses of each position?
What is the larger, and more important, truth that
transcends this debate?

Satan is a bloodthirsty tyrant. He aims to rule the world. He moves with the speed of Alexander the Great, dominates with the ruthlessness of Joseph Stalin, and exterminates with the seething bigotry of Adolf Hitler.

4

SATAN / THE DEVIL

Social-media platforms like Twitter, Facebook, and Instagram have made slander a quick and easy blood sport for anyone with a smart phone or an Internet connection. American singer-songwriter Lizzo found herself on the receiving end of a defamation suit after tweeting the name, workplace, and photo of a food delivery person she claimed stole her food.[1]

Billionaire Elon Musk engaged in an online spat with a British diver who helped rescue twelve boys and their coach from a cave in Thailand. Musk called the hero a "pedo guy" and allegedly referred to him as a "child rapist" in an off-the-record email to a journalist. The result of Musk's accusations? You guessed it: a lawsuit.[2]

And hip-hop star The Game chose to rant about his children's former nanny to the rapper's one million Instagram followers. In reply, the babysitter sued for an unspecified amount of money, claiming loss of employment, inability to work in her chosen field, and depression.[3]

And so it goes. Despite ramped-up filtering efforts by social-media platforms, a subscriber's flash of anger, or a simmering grudge, becomes public fodder in a matter of seconds. Equally troubling, the consequences of these viral accusations may be difficult, if not impossible, to arrest until they've run their course.

How did people become so adept at slander? Practice. And a supernatural role model.

The Arch-enemy

Scripture calls the evil one *Satan* and *the devil* in numerous places. Nineteen of the twenty-seven New Testament books refer to Satan. Every New Testament writer recognizes the evil one's existence. And of the twenty-nine references to Satan in the Gospels, Jesus makes twenty-five of them.[4]

The names *Satan* and *the devil* essentially mean the same thing: adversary, accuser, or slanderer. The Hebrew *satan* means "adversary." The term is used throughout the Old Testament to describe different antagonists – some human, some supernatural. Three Old Testament passages refer to a particular supernatural being as "Satan" (1 Chron. 21:1; Job 1-2; Zech. 3:1-2).

The verb *satan* appears only six times in the Old Testament. Based on the context, the word means either to accuse, slander, or be an adversary.

In the New Testament, the concept of a supernatural being called *Satan* (Greek *satanas*) is more clearly defined. The word signifies an adversary, "one who lies in wait for or sets himself in opposition to another."[5]

New Testament writers depict Satan as the ruler of a host of angels and the controller of this world; he especially governs unbelievers (Matt. 25:41; John 8:44; 2 Cor. 4:4). He opposes God and labors to alienate people from their creator. This includes followers of Jesus, who must be aware of his wiles and steadfastly resist him (Eph. 6:11; 1 Pet. 5:8). Satan works as an adversary by tempting persons (John 13:2; Acts 5:3), hindering God's servants (1 Thess. 2:18), accusing believers before God (Rev. 12:10), and controlling wicked persons who resist the gospel (2 Thess. 2:9).

In comparison, the word *devil* comes from the Greek *diabolos*, from which we get "diabolical." It means "slanderer," "accuser," or "disrupter." Slander represents the evil of human speech that the New Testament describes with terms such as "blaspheme" and "speak evil against." The verb implies acting with hostile intent, or setting two people at odds with one another.

The name *devil* is based on two Greek words: *dia*, meaning "through" or "among," and *ballo*, meaning "to throw." As James Boice explains, "The devil is the one who from the beginning has been attempting to throw a monkey wrench into the machinery of the universe."[6]

Ancient Jews used *diabolos* to translate the Hebrew *satan* in their Greek versions of the Old Testament. The New Testament uses both words – *satanas* and *diabolos* – to refer to the same creature. We often use *Satan* as a proper name and *the devil* as a title. But both terms are essentially synonymous, meaning "adversary," "accuser," or "slanderer." *Easton's Bible Dictionary* describes the devil as "the arch-enemy of man's spiritual interest."[7]

While *accuse* and *slander* may overlap in meaning, they are not strictly synonymous. To accuse means to find fault in another and to bring charges against that person. An accusation may be truthful, and thus valid, or untruthful, and thus invalid. On the other hand, slander always is false. A slanderer levels false accusations with malicious intent, designed to damage the reputation, and even the livelihood, of the one slandered. So, justice or malice may motivate an adversary. Context is key.

Three Types of *Satans*

In Scripture, we find three types of *satans*: human, angelic, and divine.

Human

David is the first human being called a *satan* in the Old Testament. In 1 Samuel 27, David flees from King Saul to the land of the Philistines. There, he and six hundred men, along with their families, endear themselves to Achish, king of Gath, who gives David the town of Ziklag.

David proves himself a mighty warrior – so much so that Achish appoints David his permanent bodyguard (1 Sam. 28:2). But as the Philistines gather their military units into a single army to fight against Israel, the Philistine commanders protest David's presence among them. They complain to Achish that David is not to be trusted, that in battle he would abandon his claim to be a Philistine ally and in fact become their "adversary" (*satan*) once the battle is engaged (1 Sam. 29:4). Reluctantly, Achish orders David and his men to withdraw.

Sometime later, Shimei, a Benjaminite who earlier had cursed and humiliated King David as the king fled Jerusalem (2 Sam. 16:5-14), now repents and seeks forgiveness (2 Sam. 19:18-20). But Abishai, a member of David's court, demands Shimei's execution for having dishonored the king. While legally permissible, execution of Shimei would undermine David's efforts to rally the Benjaminites around him, so he opts for mercy and labels Abishai an "adversary" (*satan*) for suggesting capital punishment (2 Sam. 19:22).

After King David's death, Solomon writes to Hiram, king of Tyre, remarking that David had been unable to build the temple because of his preoccupation with warfare. Now, however, Solomon explains he is free to take up this ambitious project because Israel is at peace, lacking any "enemy" (*satan*; 1 Kings 5:4).

In the New Testament, we see one example of a person called "a devil." In John 6, after many disciples desert Jesus, he addresses his twelve apostles, saying, "Didn't I choose you, the Twelve? Yet one of you is *a devil*" (v. 70, emphasis added). Of course, Jesus is referring to Judas Iscariot, who later betrays Jesus.

Angelic

Chapters 1 and 2 of Job record encounters between God and *the satan* (Heb. *hassatan*). This is the only instance in the Old Testament where God and Satan converse with each other. We explore this passage in more detail shortly.

In a vision recorded in Zechariah 3:1-2, the prophet Zechariah observes Joshua, the high priest, standing in front of the angel of the LORD, along with *the satan* (Heb. *hassatan*), who positions himself nearby to accuse Joshua. We're not told the nature of the accusation, although it appears *the satan* is challenging Joshua's fitness to serve. The Lord rebukes Joshua's accuser, and the angel of the LORD – likely the preincarnate Christ – removes Joshua's sin and promises to clothe him in clean garments.[8]

In one other Old Testament account of an angelic *satan*, we see a malevolent adversary incite David to take a census of Israel. Recorded in 1 Chronicles 21:1, Satan rises up against Israel and persuades David to number his troops. This is the only time in the Old Testament where the Hebrew word *satan*, when applied to a diabolical spirit, is used without the definite article ("the"), leading some commentators to identify this as a personal name depicting the evil one.[9]

In the New Testament, the names *Satan* and *the devil* are used interchangeably dozens of times to refer to the evil one. Because the New Testament features a more fully developed doctrine of a singular fallen angel, there is little question about the identity of this malevolent creature – and far more detail about his activities. See Appendix 1 for a listing of every New Testament reference to Satan / the devil.

Divine

There is one Old Testament instance of a celestial accuser sent from Yahweh; in fact, he may be Yahweh himself. In Numbers 22, the angel of the LORD – likely the preincarnate Christ, as in Zechariah 3:1-2 – appears in a most curious scene involving a cursing king, a prophet for hire, and a talking donkey. It is the story of Balaam, a mercenary prophet whom Moab's King Balak hires to curse the Israelites.

Balak sends two successive envoys to Balaam, offering the prophet a substantial prize. Balaam tells the king he can only say what Yahweh tells him, which gives us the feeling we are encountering a faithful spokesman for the Lord. Yet there is ample indication throughout the story – and in New Testament references to this series of events – that Balaam is seeking to hedge his bets in order to satisfy greedy desires.

Heading for Moab with the king's ambassadors, Balaam doesn't get far before the sword-wielding angel of the LORD steps into his path. In two places, the angel is depicted as an adversary, or *satan*. In Numbers 22:22, the angel of the LORD takes his stand on the path to *oppose* Balaam. And, in verse 32, after Yahweh opens Balaam's eyes to see the angel of the LORD, the angel tells Balaam he has come out to *oppose* the false prophet. In both cases, the Hebrew *satan* is translated "oppose."[10]

The New Testament makes no reference to a member of the Trinity as a *satan* or *devil*, although the religious leaders of Jesus' day accuse him of having a demon (Greek *daimonion*; John 8:48) and working in concert with Beelzebul, the prince of demons (Matt. 12:24; Luke 11:15).

Even so, New Testament writers have much to say about the Father, Son, and Holy Spirit rightly accusing, convicting, and judging people. For example, Jesus tells his followers the Holy Spirit is coming to *convict* the unbelieving world of sin, righteousness, and judgment (John 16:8). The Greek verb rendered "convict" is *elencho* and means rebuke, as in exposing sin or convincing someone of guilt.[11]

Further, Jesus is clear that the Father has granted him all judgment, "so that all people may honor the Son just as they honor the Father" (John 5:22-23). And the apostle Paul reveals that all believers must stand one day before the judgment seat of God / Christ (Rom. 14:10; 2 Cor. 5:10).

Wherever members of the Trinity are depicted as adversaries or accusers, they stand as holy and righteous judges – in stark contrast to the evil one. In revealing his equality with the Father, Jesus challenges his Jewish listeners, "Who among you can convict me of sin?" (John 8:46).

One final note before moving on: Using the name *Satan*, or *accuser*, to depict the evil one would have made an especially strong impact in the first century, for there was a well-known and much-hated figure called *the delator* – a paid informant who made his living by accusing people before the authorities. As one commentator points out, it is not a large step from *accuser* to *slanderer*, and thus Satan (the accuser) is often called *the devil* (slanderer).[12] Thus, people's loathsome view of *the delator* easily could be transferred to the ultimate accuser/slanderer in the unseen realm.

Three Curious Cases of Slander

Let's briefly examine three biblical events that illustrate Satan's slanderous nature.

Case No. 1: Job 1:6 – 2:10

Satan (literally *the satan*)[13] appears with the sons of God before the Lord. The sons of God are members of the divine council, an assembly of created spirit beings to whom the Lord has endowed authority for governing of the universe. *The satan* shows up as well, although it seems he may not be a member of the divine council. Rather than consult with God, as council members do, he reports to God he has been "roaming through the earth ... and walking around on it" (Job 1:7). You might say he relishes the role of divine ambulance chaser.

"Have you considered my servant Job?" says the Lord. "No one else on earth is like him, a man of perfect integrity, who fears God and turns away from evil" (1:8).

"Does Job fear God for nothing?" asks the accuser. "Haven't you placed a hedge around him, his household, and everything he owns? You have blessed the work of his hands, and his possessions have increased in the land. But stretch out your hand and strike everything he owns, and he will surely curse you to your face" (1:9-11).

"Very well," the Lord replies, "everything he owns is in your power. However, do not lay a hand on Job himself" (1:12).

So, Satan leaves God's presence and goes to work. He incites the Sabeans to swoop into town, stealing Job's oxen and donkeys, and killing his servants, save one who rushes to report the incident to Job.

Without delay, another lone survivor of a separate, simultaneous disaster comes breathlessly to Job and reports that "God's fire ... from heaven" fell on the shepherds and their sheep, consuming them all.

Before he is finished speaking, another messenger tells Job that three bands of Chaldeans raided the camels, taking them away and killing the servants.

Then comes the worst news of all. A messenger reports that all of Job's sons and daughters were gathered in the home of the oldest brother when a powerful wind swept in from the desert, collapsing the structure and killing everyone inside.

In a matter of minutes, Satan destroys what he believes is the very foundation of Job's faithfulness – his family and his wealth.

What happens next is remarkable and – at least to Job's accuser – completely unexpected:

> Then Job stood up, tore his robe, and shaved his head. He fell to the ground and worshiped, saying:
> Naked I came from my mother's womb, and naked I will leave this life. The LORD gives, and the LORD takes away. Blessed be the name of the LORD.
> Throughout all this Job did not sin or blame God for anything (1:20-22).

Job has prevailed, but Satan isn't finished. Chapter 2 begins with the sons of God again presenting themselves to the Lord and the accuser joining them. God asks Satan where he's been, and Satan replies he's been roaming the earth and walking around on it (v. 2).

The Lord once again challenges Satan to consider Job, adding,

"He still retains his integrity, even though you incited me against him, to destroy him for no good reason" (v. 3).

"Skin for skin!" Satan snaps back. "A man will give up everything he owns in exchange for his life. But stretch out your hand and strike his flesh and bones, and he will surely curse you to your face" (vv. 4-5).

"Very well," the Lord tells Satan, "he is in your power; only spare his life" (v. 6).

So, Satan afflicts Job with painful boils from the top of his head to the soles of his feet. As he sits in the ashes, scraping his running sores with a piece of broken pottery, Job's wife can stand it no more.

"Are you still holding on to your integrity?" she asks. "Curse God and die!" (v. 9).

"You speak as a foolish woman speaks," Job replies. "Should we accept only good from God and not adversity?" (v. 10). Through it all, Job refrains from sinning with his lips.

Satan evidently withdraws at this point because we don't hear from him again in the Book of Job. But what might we observe about this angelic slanderer from his encounter with God and man? Consider:

First, Satan roams the earth in search of plunder. Centuries later, Peter echoes the evil one's words to God in Job 1-2: "Your adversary the devil is prowling around like a roaring lion, looking for anyone he can devour" (1 Pet. 5:8). The evil one is a dangerous, prowling beast. Peter exhorts his readers, who are experiencing persecution, "Resist him, firm in the faith, knowing that the same kind of sufferings are being experienced by your fellow believers throughout the world" (1 Pet. 5:9).

Second, Satan has a particular appetite for God's faithful ones. Certainly, righteous Job is a prime target. But Satan also sets his eyes on a man after God's own heart, King David. We read in 1 Chronicles 21:1, "Satan [or *an adversary*] rose up against Israel and incited David to count the people of Israel."[14]

Satan doesn't stop with messianic figures like King David. He launches his most cunning attack against the Messiah himself during a time of testing in the wilderness (Matt. 4:1-11; Luke 4:1-13). As Peter Bolt puts it, "With deep-seated arrogance, the devil claims to be lord of the world, and he wants Jesus to be his underling.... The devil slanders God in order to appease his insatiable hunger to be God."[15]

On more than one occasion, the evil one attacks the apostle Peter. At Caesarea Philippi, having just declared Jesus the Christ, Son of the living God, Peter becomes a pawn in Satan's hands as the apostle tries to prevent Jesus from fulfilling his earthly mission on the cross. "Oh no, Lord!" Peter says. "This will never happen to you!" Jesus rebukes Peter as the devil himself, saying, "Get behind me, Satan (*satanas*)! You are a hindrance to me because you're not thinking about God's concerns but human concerns" (Matt. 16:22-23).

Later, Jesus informs Peter of an imminent personal failure. "Simon, Simon, look out," says Jesus. "Satan has asked to sift you like wheat. But I have prayed for you that your faith may not fail. And you, when you have turned back, strengthen your brothers" (Luke 22:31-32). Peter assures Jesus of his loyalty, even to the point of death, but Jesus knows better. "I tell you, Peter," he says, "the rooster will not crow today until you deny three times that you know me" (v. 34).

Third, Satan attacks God's people only with God's permission and under God's sovereignty. Twice, the Lord grants Satan an occasion to buffet Job. Each time, however, God sets boundaries for the evil one: Don't lay a hand on Job. Spare his life.

In the case of Peter's denial of Jesus, Satan successfully petitions God to sift the apostle like wheat. The Greek word translated "sift" is *siniazo*, which means to shake in a sieve. In this context, it refers to Satan's desire to cause Peter inward agitation, thus trying his faith.

Even so, Jesus steps forward as Peter's advocate, praying that his faith, though tested, does not ultimately fail, and assuring Peter there is a divine purpose in granting the evil one such latitude in the apostle's life. Yes, Peter fails, but later he repents and strengthens his brothers.

The apostle Paul assures all believers that God sets limits to Satan's tempting power:

No temptation has come upon you except what is common to humanity. But God is faithful; he will not allow you to be tempted beyond what you are able, but with the temptation he will also provide a way out so that you may be able to bear it (1 Cor. 10:13).

The phrase "way out" comes from the Greek *ekbasis*. It means an egress, or exit. The word may be used to depict a narrow pass between mountains. The imagery Paul offers is that of an army trapped in nearly impassable terrain, only to discover an escape route that delivers soldiers from enemy fire. This flight to safety on solid ground is God's provision – a way out for us, and a way forward with the gospel. It means Satan cannot ultimately trap us in temptation. It also means we are fully responsible when we choose to sin.

Even more comforting than a way out of temptation is God's inward provision through the indwelling Holy Spirit. Jesus tells his disciples:

If you love me, you will keep my commands. And I will ask the Father, and he will give you another Counselor to be with you forever. He is the Spirit of truth. The world is unable to receive him because it doesn't see him or know him. But you do know him, because he remains with you and will be in you (John 14:15-17).

The name *Counselor*, translated "Advocate" or "Helper" in other versions, comes from the Greek *parakletos*. It refers to one who pleads another's cause before a judge, serving as legal counsel. In the widest sense, *parakletos* means a helper, aide, or assistant. With reference to the Holy Spirit, Jesus promises to send this advocate after Jesus returns to the Father. In a sense, the Spirit takes the place of Christ to lead the apostles to a deeper knowledge of the gospel, and to give them divine strength needed to enable them to undergo trials and persecutions on behalf of their Savior and for the sake of his kingdom.

Finally, regarding God's permissive will in Satan's attacks, the Lord provides us with the "full armor of God" so we can stand against "the schemes of the devil" and "resist in the evil day" (Eph. 6:11, 13). This armor includes the belt of truth, the breastplate of righteousness, the sandals of readiness with the gospel of peace, the helmet of salvation, and the shield of faith with which we can "extinguish all the flaming arrows of the evil one" (vv. 14-17). In addition to this defensive armor, the Lord gives us "the sword of the Spirit – which is the word of God" (v. 17).

It does not appear the Lord restricts Satan's influence over unbelievers in the same way he sets boundaries for his own children. In fact, Scripture depicts those outside the kingdom of God as natural, or without the Spirit (1 Cor. 2:14); blind (2 Cor. 4:4); excluded from the life of God (Eph. 4:17-18); enemies of God (Rom. 5:6-11); condemned (John 3:18); in darkness (Acts 26:18; Eph. 5:8; Col. 1:13; 1 Pet. 2:9); and spiritually dead (Eph. 2:1). As such, Satan has ensnared them and "taken them captive to do his will" (2 Tim. 2:26).

Fourth, Satan cannot see the future. His predictions of Job's spiritual demise prove wrong. In fact, Satan is unable to foresee how God uses the evil one to discipline Job for relying too strongly on self-righteousness – "I will cling to *my righteousness* and never let it go," declares Job (Job 27:6) – rather than on the unfathomable righteousness of God (Job 38-41). Nor can Satan predict Job's repentance and the Lord's two-fold restoration of material blessing.

No doubt, the evil one is intelligent and powerful, but he is not all-knowing, all-powerful, or everywhere present. This gives the person who is "in Christ" a decided advantage against the accuser of the brethren. The Lord is our advocate, our shield, and our victory. As the apostle John assures followers of Jesus, "the one who is in you is greater than the one who is in the world" (1 John 4:4).

Case No. 2: Zechariah 3:1-10

In the fourth of eight visions, Zechariah observes Joshua, the high priest, standing in front of the angel of the LORD, along with *the satan,* who stands nearby to accuse Joshua. The setting closely resembles that of the divine council before whom *the satan* accuses Job (Job 1-2).

The key difference, however, is Joshua's crushing guilt versus Job's relative innocence.

Joshua serves as high priest on behalf of the nearly fifty thousand exiles who have returned from Babylonian captivity. His role is to represent all of God's people. As such, his filthy garments symbolize not only his sins, but the Israelites' sins, which have prompted Yahweh to vomit the people out of the Promised Land for violating terms of the Mosaic Covenant (Lev. 18:24-30). In fact, the word translated "filthy" (Zech. 3:3-4) is linked to the Hebrew term for human excrement. It is one of the strongest expressions in the Hebrew language for something vile.

To Joshua's right stands a prosecutor, identified in many English translations as Satan. The Hebrew word *satan* appears here with the definite article (*the*), which makes it clear this is not a personal name. Whether *the satan* in Zechariah's vision is the same accuser Jesus calls "the father of lies" (John 8:44), and the apostle John depicts as "the great dragon ... the ancient serpent, who is called the devil and Satan, the one who deceives the whole world" (Rev. 12:9), is a matter of debate. Yet there's little doubt this accuser seeks to halt the return of the Israelites, the rebuilding of the temple, and the restoration of the priesthood. Zechariah places less emphasis on the identity of Joshua's accuser than on the message of the vision.

Even though Zechariah records none of *the satan's* words, there is little doubt the accuser points to the high priest in his soiled garments and charges him unworthy. This is not an isolated incident, for Satan often levels accusations against God's people (Rev. 12:10).

As with the accuser's charges against Joshua, Satan's claims against us bear some truth. We are, indeed, unworthy. We sin with impunity because it is our nature to do so, and because we choose to sin. We run from God rather than toward him. Left to our own devices, we would live out our days independently of God and pass, justly, into outer darkness. There is no hope for us, and there is no answer to Satan's biting accusations, except for the merciful call of God to salvation and the cleansing blood of Jesus Christ, who rebukes the evil one on our behalf.

We see a similar rebuke in Zechariah 3:2: "The LORD said to Satan: 'The LORD rebuke you, Satan! May the LORD who has chosen Jerusalem rebuke you! Isn't this man a burning stick snatched from the fire?'"

It's likely the angel of the LORD is the one speaking here. In other Scriptures, the angel of the LORD and Yahweh both are called *LORD*; both share the divine nature of the eternal, transcendent God of the universe, yet they are distinguishable persons. So, the angel of the LORD comes to Joshua's defense with a brief but compelling argument.

But why does the angel of the LORD seem to defer Satan's rebuke to the LORD? Because the angel of the LORD *is* the Lord. He "speaks under the title of 'LORD' and yet distinguishes Himself from the LORD in addressing Satan. This identification is further supported in 3:4 where His action is virtually that of forgiving sins."[16]

Michael Butterworth explains it this way: "It seems strange for the Lord himself to say '*the LORD rebuke you*,' but its meaning is 'I, who am the LORD, rebuke you,' and it assures the reader that the Satan's accusations are completely set aside."[17]

Case No. 3: Revelation 12:7-12

In the two events just cited from the Old Testament (Job 1-2; Zech. 3:1-10), we see Satan first slandering a righteous man – although Job is guilty of pride, which appears to be the reason for his severe chastening – and then a guilty man, bearing the physical evidence of his guilt. In the first case, God employs the accuser as a refining fire. In the second case, the angel of the LORD steps in to rebuke Satan, and to forgive the sins of the high priest and his fellow Israelites. In both cases, Satan plays the role of adversary, accuser, and slanderer. And in both cases, God sets limits to what the evil one can say and do.

Now, let's turn our attention to one of many New Testament appearances of Satan / the devil. Revelation 12:9-12 reads:

Then war broke out in heaven: Michael and his angels fought against the dragon. The dragon and his angels also fought, but he could not prevail, and there was no place for them in heaven any longer. So the great dragon was thrown out – the ancient serpent, who is called the devil and Satan, the one who deceives the whole world. He was thrown to earth, and his angels with him. Then I heard a loud voice in heaven say,

The salvation and the power and the kingdom of our God and the authority of his Christ have now come, because the accuser of our brothers and sisters, who accuses them before our God day and night, has been thrown down. They conquered him by the blood of the Lamb and by the word of their testimony; for they did not love their lives to the point of death. Therefore rejoice, you heavens, and you who dwell in them! Woe to the earth and the sea, because the devil has come down to you with great fury, because he knows his time is short.

Bible commentators disagree as to when this epic battle takes place. One view is that this scene depicts the clash between Michael the archangel and Satan for the body of Moses (Jude 9). Another perspective points back to rebellious angels who cohabitated with humans (Jude 6; cf. Gen. 6:1-4). Futurists argue that this battle has yet to take place; in fact, Satan's banishment from heaven precipitates his furious persecution of Israel and the saints during the great tribulation. If these views are not sufficiently diverse, one commentator lists ten possible times this war could occur, ranging from before Genesis 1 to the very end of human history.[18]

While it's difficult to discern the exact timing of this battle, we should note that it's set in the context of Christ's ascension (12:5), followed by the declaration that "the kingdom of our God and the authority of his Christ has now come" (12:10). Equally important, we know the outcome. The day is fast approaching when the devil, his demons, and all those who oppose the Son of Man are cast into the lake of fire (Rev. 20:10, 14-15). And despite affliction, distress, and persecution, we may declare confidently that "in all these things we are more than conquerors through him who loved us" (Rom. 8:37).

Now, let's focus on the depictions of the evil one as *the devil, Satan,* and *the accuser* in Revelation 12:9-12.

Twice, the evil one is called *the devil* (*ho diabolos,* vv. 9, 12); once, *Satan* (*satanas,* v. 9); and once, *the accuser* (*ho kategor*) who accuses Christians day and night (v. 10). While these terms are related, there are subtle differences. In calling the evil one *the devil,* John focuses on his activity as a slanderer, a backbiter, and a gossiper, one engaged in malicious talk. By *Satan,* he is an adversary, one who opposes God and his people. And in calling him *the accuser* of the brethren, John says the evil one speaks against them, denounces them, and brings charges against them.

All of this exposes the malicious intent of the evil one. He is not merely a prosecutor seeking to bring valid charges before the heavenly bench; he is a vile, underhanded slanderer who seeks to separate Christians from their Heavenly Father. But this angelic ambulance chaser is about to be disbarred. Consider:

First, this war takes on cosmic proportions. Michael and his angels battle with Satan and his angels on a scale rarely seen in Scripture, although we get a glimpse into a raging three-week fracas in the heavenlies involving Michael in the Book of Daniel (Dan. 10:10-21).

Second, the battlefield is heaven. It appears we are not in the sky, or the atmospheric heaven, at this point. Nor are we in the "third heaven" (2 Cor. 12:2), which is the throne room of God. There is only peace, joy, reverence, and worship in the place where God sits enthroned.

In John's vision of heaven (Rev. 4-5), he reports nothing of the evil one, his angels, or sin. There is no whiff of rebellion against the Holy One. The four living creatures, the twenty-four elders, and the redeemed all join in perfect unity, proclaiming their allegiance to God. So, the heaven where this cosmic battle between Michael and Satan takes place cannot be our future state in the presence of the Almighty.[19]

We need to look elsewhere for the location of the heaven to which

John refers. The phrase *in the heavens* or *in the heavenlies* occurs five times in the New Testament, and only in the Book of Ephesians, where it's used two ways. First, Paul says our heavenly blessings depend on Christ's exalted position at the Father's right hand (Eph. 1:3, 20). Because we share a spiritual union with Christ, we are seated with him "in the heavens" (2:6). In the remaining two references, Paul writes of "the heavens" as the realm of spiritual powers, particularly holy angels, Satan, and demons (3:10; 6:12). It's this unseen world where an angel – perhaps Gabriel – fights demonic forces and prevails, thanks to help from Michael (Dan. 10:13).

So, it seems reasonable to see the war between Michael and the dragon taking place in *the heavens*, or the realm of spiritual powers, where angelic forces fight for supremacy on behalf of their leaders (God or Satan) and for their leaders' claim of sovereignty over the earth.

Third, Satan is thrown out and cast to earth. Satan's sphere of influence has been shrinking ever since he rebelled against his creator. No longer welcome in the throne room of heaven, he wages war against God's holy angels in the unseen spiritual realm. There, Satan is incapable of defeating Michael and his formidable host of angels, who send him to the earth, where he prowls like a lion, seeking people to devour (1 Pet. 5:8). There is little doubt demonic activity increases as the return of Christ and the final defeat of Satan draw nearer.

Fourth, this is cause for a heavenly celebration. "Therefore, rejoice you heavens, and you who dwell in them!" (Rev. 12:12). If there is rejoicing in God's throne room over one sinner who repents (Luke 15:7), there's also celebration in the unseen spiritual realm when the epic battles between God's holy angels and Satan's forces come to an end. The anticipation mounts as the day of Satan's sentencing approaches.

Fifth, this is cause for woe on the earth and sea: "Woe to the earth and the sea, because the devil has come down to you with great fury, because he knows his time is short" (Rev. 12:12). By "the earth," John may be referring to those who live on large land masses, and by "the sea," he may mean those who live on islands, as well as those who engage in commerce across the watery depths. Traveling the long corridor of time, Satan nears his ultimate destiny in the lake of fire (Rev. 20:10). He hears the clock ticking and sees the walls closing in on him. No wonder he is furious.

Finally, martyred believers in heaven "conquered him by the blood of the Lamb and by the word of their testimony; for they did not love their lives to the point of death" (Rev. 12:11). What an amazing reversal of fortune. The shed blood of Jesus pays our sin debt and erases any valid accusations the devil may throw at us. Further, the word of our testimony (Gr. *martyria* – evidence given judicially, from which we get the English word *martyr*) points to the one who is our advocate. Jesus takes up our case, defends us with great eloquence, and declares us innocent because he – the defender *and* judge – has paid the debt for us and thus declares us righteous (cf. 2 Cor. 5:21). The trial ends in a resounding defeat for the accuser of the brethren.

In summary, it seems that John's account of the battle in heaven between Michael and Satan is one that takes place in the unseen spiritual realm and results in the further shrinking of the evil one's domain. Thrown down to earth – and confined here – the accuser of our brothers and sisters prowls angrily like a newly caged lion.

The Devil and His Details

Let's close this chapter with a short summary of Satan's diabolical activities and his ultimate destiny as recorded in the New Testament. Appendix 1 lists every New Testament reference to *Satan* and *the devil*, so we offer a condensed version here. Of course, these are not the only names by which the evil one is identified, but they are unmistakable references to this vile creature.

Specifically, note seven key contrasts between what Satan does and what eventually becomes of him.

First, Satan binds, then he is bound. After Jesus heals a woman that an evil spirit has disabled, he explains to the synagogue leader who objects to the Sabbath-day miracle, "Satan has bound this woman, a daughter of Abraham, for eighteen years – shouldn't she be untied from this bondage on the Sabbath day?" (Luke 13:16). Other Scriptures speak of those in bondage to sin (John 8:34; Acts 8:23) or taken captive by Satan to do his will (2 Tim. 2:26).

Ultimately, however, the evil one finds himself bound in the abyss. Revelation 20 records an angel coming down from heaven, holding the key to the abyss and a great chain in his hand. He seizes "the dragon, that ancient serpent who is the devil and Satan," and binds him for a thousand years (vv. 1-2). Then, Satan is "released from his prison" for a time, only to be cast into the lake of fire forever (vv. 7, 10).

Second, Satan deceives, and he is duped. The apostle John describes war in heaven between Michael the archangel and Satan, "the great dragon ... who deceives the whole world" (Rev. 12:9). The devil is cast down to earth, only to be imprisoned later in the abyss. After a short release, he goes out to "deceive the nations at the four corners of the earth" (Rev. 20:8).

Although a master of deception, the evil one himself is duped in a case of divine misdirection. In Matthew 16, Jesus goads Satan and his demons into seeking his death. The Messiah has taken his disciples to Caesarea Philippi at the base of Mount Hermon – a place historically tied to paganism and considered the very gates of hades. There, Jesus confirms his identity as the Son of God. Then, he declares that on "this rock" – perhaps a reference to Mount Hermon, a place the underworld claims for itself – "I will build my church, and the gates of Hades will not overpower it" (vv. 16, 18).

Six days later he brings Peter, James, and John to a "high mountain" – likely Mount Hermon once again – and is transfigured before them (Matt. 17:1-7). Jesus then sets his sights on Jerusalem and the cross. He has come into the world to die, and Satan is a willing, but unknowing, party to the divine plan. As Michael Heiser summarizes:

> The Devil and those aligned with him are lots of things, but they aren't morons. They were duped into killing Jesus, just as God had

planned. They launched the series of events that would lead to their own demise. It was divinely designed misdirection.[20]

This is precisely what the apostle Paul says in his first letter to the Corinthians:

> We do, however, speak a wisdom among the mature, but not a wisdom of this age, or of the rulers of this age, who are coming to nothing. On the contrary, we speak God's hidden wisdom in a mystery, a wisdom God predestined before the ages for our glory. *None of the rulers of this age knew this wisdom, because if they had known it, they would not have crucified the Lord of glory* (1 Cor. 2:6-8, emphasis added).

By "rulers," Paul acknowledges human authorities like Pontius Pilate and the religious leaders of Israel. But he also has in mind demonic powers (cf. Eph. 2:2). In other words, the Lord kept his enemies – human and spirit beings – in the dark until the death and resurrection of Christ were accomplished works. Satan is deceptive, but he's not omniscient. He falls for a divine ruse that leads to his defeat and our victory in Jesus.

Third, Satan forages, and he flees. Peter describes Satan as a stalking predator: "Your adversary the devil is prowling around like a roaring lion, looking for anyone he can devour" (1 Pet. 5:8). The evil one excels in tracking his prey, but Jesus shows us how to escape.

Through forty days in the desert, Satan throws his best at Jesus, whom fasting has physically weakened. With each temptation, Jesus plies Scripture to fend off the evil one's attacks. At last, Jesus says, "Go away, Satan! For it is written: Worship the Lord your God, and serve only him." Matthew records, "Then the devil left him, and angels came and began to serve him" (Matt. 4:10-11). Luke writes, "After the devil had finished every temptation, he departed from him for a time" (Luke 4:13).

James instructs Christians to follow the example of Jesus: "Therefore, submit to God. Resist the devil, and he will flee from you"

(Jas. 4:7). And Paul urges us to remember that for every temptation, the Lord provides a way out (1 Cor. 10:13). That way is Scripture – reading it, meditating on it, quoting it to the tempter, and applying its truths to every circumstance.

Fourth, Satan enters, and finally he is evicted. While demon possession is mentioned often in the New Testament, it's rare when the evil one himself enters a human being. Judas Iscariot is a notable exception. Just before hatching a plot with the chief priests and temple police to betray Jesus, Judas is Satan-possessed.

Luke notes, "Then Satan entered Judas, called Iscariot, who was numbered among the Twelve" (Luke 22:3). And John records at the last supper, "After Judas ate the piece of bread [that Jesus offered him], Satan entered him. So Jesus told him, 'What you're doing, do quickly'" (John 13:27).

But just as Jesus and the apostles cast demons out of people, God's servants evict Satan from the throne room of heaven, and then from the heavenly realm, and finally from the earth itself. Revelation 12 records the eviction of Satan from the heavenlies at the hands of Michael the archangel (vv. 7, 12). Ultimately, the evil one is imprisoned in the abyss for a time (Rev. 20:1-3), then finally banished to hell (Rev. 20:10).

Fifth, Satan conquers, and then he is crushed. The evil one is a bloodthirsty tyrant. He aims to rule the world. He moves with the speed of Alexander the Great, dominates with the ruthlessness of Joseph Stalin, and exterminates with the seething bigotry of Adolf Hitler. In his sermon at the house of Cornelius, Peter summarizes Jesus' earthly ministry:

> You know the events that took place throughout all Judea, beginning from Galilee after the baptism that John preached: how God anointed Jesus of Nazareth with the Holy Spirit and with power, and how he went about doing good and healing all who were under *the tyranny of the devil*, because God was with him (Acts 10:37-38, emphasis added).

Satan's days as a vicious despot are drawing to a close. As Paul writes in his concluding remarks to the Romans, "The God of peace will soon crush Satan under your feet" (Rom. 16:20).

Sixth, Satan is crowned, and then he is cast out. The evil one directs a slandering, counterfeit body of believers in Smyrna – "a synagogue of Satan" (Rev. 2:9). He rules in Pergamum, "where Satan's throne is" (Rev. 2:13). He guards the "so-called secrets of Satan" in Thyatira (Rev. 2:24). And he enslaves the world in false worship after giving the beast power, a throne, and authority (Rev. 13:1-8).

But his reign is short-lived. After seventy disciples report miraculous results from their mission to fan out and proclaim the coming kingdom, Jesus tells them, "I watched Satan fall from heaven like lightning" (Luke 10:18). The Messiah has come to invade the strong man's house, tie him up, and plunder his goods (cf. Matt. 12:28-29).

From the moment rebellion rose in his heart, Satan has been a fugitive. He finds himself in an ever-shrinking field of freedom, with the hound of heaven in hot pursuit. Unable to return to the scene of the crime, he battles God's agents in the heavenlies and carries out a scorched-earth policy in the physical realm. Justice is closing in. Time is short. So the evil one rages against the inevitable day of his demise.

Seventh, Satan torments, and finally he is tormented. Christians are not immune from the evil one's physical, spiritual, and emotional attacks. In some cases, the Lord even uses Satan's weapons to set boundaries for his most-gifted servants. After sharing a brief account of his visit to heaven – but no details – Paul reports:

> But I will spare you, so that no one can credit me with something beyond what he sees in me or hears from me, especially because of the extraordinary revelations. Therefore, so that I would not exalt myself, a thorn in the flesh was given to me, *a messenger of Satan to torment me* so that I would not exalt myself. Concerning this, I pleaded with the Lord three times that it would leave me. But he said to me, "My grace is sufficient for you, for my power is perfected in weakness" (2 Cor. 12:6-9, emphasis added).

Bible commentators hold a variety of views as to who, or what, this "messenger of Satan" might be. Popular theories include severe temptation, a chronic eye problem, malaria, migraine headaches, epilepsy, and a speech impediment. Some even suggest Paul's thorn is a person, such as Alexander the coppersmith, who does Paul a great deal of harm (2 Tim. 4:14). In any case, the "thorn in the flesh" originates with the evil one, and the affliction drives Paul to his knees, seeking relief.

But Satan's torments return to him one day. Jesus ends his Olivet Discourse with the sobering truth of everlasting punishment for the wicked. He tells his listeners of an eternal fire to which the lost are banished, a place "prepared for the devil and his angels" (Matt. 25:41). This is a place of "eternal punishment" (v. 46). While unbelievers suffer in hell, the lake of fire was originally intended for Satan and his minions. Those who reject Christ share in Satan's judgment (cf. John 16:7-11).

We see that day coming with certainty, as John records: "The devil who deceived them was thrown into the lake of fire and sulfur where the beast and the false prophet are, and they will be tormented day and night forever and ever" (Rev. 20:10). Today, Satan may sow tares in Christ's wheat fields (cf. Matt. 13:24-30, 36-43), but one day he reaps a fruitless harvest in the fires of hell.

There is even better news for us. After the great white throne judgment, death and hades are cast into the lake of fire; there is no more physical death, and no more need for heaven to wait. God creates new heavens and a new earth – and inhabits them. And just as Jesus "tabernacles" with humans in the Incarnation (John 1:14), God dwells with the redeemed on a regenerated earth:

> Look, God's dwelling is with humanity, and he will live with them. They will be his peoples, and God himself will be with them and will be their God. He will wipe away every tear from their eyes. Death will be no more; grief, crying, and pain will be no more, because the previous things have passed away (Rev. 21:3-4).

Summary

Key takeaways about *Satan / the devil*:

(1) *Satan* and *the devil* essentially mean the same thing: adversary, accuser, or slanderer. The Hebrew *satan* means "adversary." The Greek *diabolos* means "slanderer," "accuser," or "disrupter."

(2) In Scripture, we find three types of *satans*: human, angelic, and divine. King David, Abishai, and Judas Iscariot are all accused of being *satans* or *devils* (adversaries / accusers). The books of Job and Zechariah record encounters between an angelic accuser (*the satan*) and the Lord, and in 1 Chronicles, Satan incites King David to take a census of Israel. Last, there is one Old Testament instance of a divine *satan*, when the angel of the Lord *opposes* the corrupt prophet-for-hire, Balaam.

(3) In Satan's attack on Job, we learn several biblical truths: (a) Satan roams the earth in search of plunder; (b) Satan has a particular appetite for God's faithful ones; (c) Satan attacks God's people only with God's permission and under God's sovereignty; and (d) Satan cannot see the future, for he is not omniscient.

(4) Satan justly accuses the high priest Joshua and the Israelites he represents of gross sin. Yet the angel of the Lord, who is the Lord himself, steps in to rebuke the accuser and to forgive Joshua's sins.

(5) Satan's battle with Michael the archangel takes place in the unseen spiritual realm and results in the further shrinking of the evil one's domain (Rev. 12:7-12). Thrown down to earth – and confined here – the accuser of our brothers and sisters prowls angrily like a newly caged lion.

(6) Note seven key contrasts between what Satan does and what eventually becomes of him: (a) Satan binds, and then he is bound; (b) Satan deceives, and he is duped; (c) Satan forages, and he flees; (d) Satan enters, and finally he is evicted; (e) Satan conquers, and then he is crushed; (f) Satan is crowned, and then he is cast out; and (g) Satan torments, and finally he is tormented.

(7) After the great white throne judgment, death and hades are cast into the lake of fire; there is no more physical death, and no more

need for heaven to wait. God creates new heavens and a new earth – and inhabits them. And just as Jesus "tabernacles" with humans in the Incarnation (John 1:14), God dwells with the redeemed on a regenerated earth.

Questions for Personal or Group Study

1. What do the names *Satan* and *the devil* mean? While we might use these terms interchangeably, how do they identify different aspects of the evil one's nature and activities?
2. What are three types of *satans* in Scripture? Provide at least one example of each.
3. Read Revelation 12:9-12. List several observations about John's depiction of the evil one as *the devil, Satan*, and *the accuser*.
4. We often feel that Satan has the upper hand – that he's winning in his battle against God and God's people. How do Matthew 25:41 and Revelation 20:10 offer us assurance that Satan's defeat is certain and our victory is secure?
5. Satan is a formidable adversary who often targets us with false accusations. Generate a short list of the evil one's most convincing accusations against you, then respond to each one with a promise from God's Word. Here's one example:

> *Satan's false charge:* God will never forgive you of *that* sin!

> *God's response in his Word:* "If we confess our sins, he is faithful and righteous to forgive us our sins and to cleanse us from *all* unrighteousness" (1 John 1:9, emphasis added).

The evil one possesses great knowledge of the truth, but he holds no affection for it. Making himself a beautiful friend, he is nevertheless a sworn enemy of the truth, and he wishes to make us his allies.

5

FATHER OF LIES

W hat do Satan and Fletcher Reede have in common? Haven't heard of Mr. Reede? He's the fast-talking lawyer whose habitual untruths built a remarkably successful career for himself – and ruined just about everything else, including a relationship with his young son, Max. Actor Jim Carrey plays the strangely loveable louse in the 1997 film *Liar Liar*.

Reede undergoes a miraculous transformation when Max makes a wish. As he's blowing out the candles on his birthday cake, Max wishes his dad would tell the truth – and nothing but the truth – for just twenty-four hours. Max's wish comes true, and the ensuing scenes take Reede through an agonizing journey of self-discovery and, ultimately, a restored relationship with his son.

Redemption rarely looks this sweet, or funny. Throughout the story, Reede realizes he is incapable of telling the truth. His pathological behavior suits him, and benefits him, until he realizes it destroys nearly everything he loves. Reede lies because he is a liar. It is his nature to lie. And it takes a miracle to set him free.

Fletcher Reede and Satan are incorrigible liars. But that's where the similarity ends, for the California lawyer finds redemption, while the evil one remains true to himself as the father of lies. Jesus uses that very term – *the father of lies* – to describe Satan during an encounter with the religious leaders of his day. Jesus exposes their plot to kill him, and then he contrasts his Father (God) with their father (Satan). While the scribes and Pharisees claim to be descendants of Abraham, Jesus tells them their father is the devil. A key passage in this exchange is John 8:42-47:

> Jesus said to them, "If God were your Father, you would love me, because I came from God and I am here. For I didn't come on my own, but he sent me. Why don't you understand what I say? Because you cannot listen to my word. You are of your father the devil, and you want to carry out your father's desires. He was a murderer from the beginning and does not stand in the truth, because there is no truth in him. When he tells a lie, he speaks from his own nature, because *he is a liar and the father of lies*. Yet because I tell the truth, you do not believe me. Who among you can convict me of sin? If I am telling the truth, why don't you believe me? The one who is from God listens to God's words. This is why you don't listen, because you are not from God" (emphasis added).

Jesus not only presents the truth; he *is* the truth (John 14:6). The eternal Son of God leaves the portals of heaven to redeem us. He declares the truth of the Father because he and the Father are one (John 10:30), and because the Father sent him (John 20:21). If Jesus' listeners believe in him, his Father would be their Father, too. But because they reject the truth, they prove they are neither the children of God nor the true sons of Abraham. Rather, they are children of the devil. As such, they seek to suppress the truth and kill the one who is truth incarnate. Murder and lies are their tactics – precisely the wiles of their father, the evil one.

The fact that Jesus refers to Satan as a murderer and a liar in the same context exposes the truth that Satan is a liar with a murderous intent. He targets the first humans in an effort to kill them. Then sin and death take the stage (Rom. 5:12; cf. Gen. 3:19, 24). The *beginning* of which Jesus speaks – "he was a murderer from the beginning" – likely is a reference to Satan's first appearance on the stage of human history: his temptation of Eve in the garden.

The Serpent's Subtlety

So, let's go back to the first recorded human encounter with the father of lies. God has finished his work of creation and declared everything "very good indeed" (Gen. 1:31). He has set Adam and Eve in the garden of Eden and given them the privilege of tending it. He has made available to them the garden's abundant produce, restricting only their access to the tree of the knowledge of good and evil. Genesis 2 ends with a depiction of innocence: "Both the man and his wife were naked, yet felt no shame" (v. 25).

We pick up the story in Genesis 3:

> Now the serpent was the most cunning of all the wild animals that the LORD God had made. He said to the woman, "Did God really say, 'You can't eat from any tree in the garden'?"
>
> The woman said to the serpent, "We may eat the fruit from the trees in the garden. But about the fruit of the tree in the middle of the garden, God said, 'You must not eat it or touch it, or you will die.'"
>
> "No! You will not die," the serpent said to the woman. "In fact, God knows that when you eat it your eyes will be opened and you will be like God, knowing good and evil." The woman saw that the tree was good for food and delightful to look at, and that it was desirable for obtaining wisdom. So she took some of its fruit and ate it; she also gave some to her husband, who was with her, and he ate it. Then the eyes of both of them were opened, and they knew they were naked; so they sewed fig leaves together and made coverings for themselves (Gen. 3:1-7).

Satan appears suddenly in the garden as *the serpent*. We addressed this in more detail in previous chapters, including the possibility that the evil one, a fallen spirit being, breaks into the physical realm as an anointed guardian cherub. This remarkably beautiful member of the divine council comes for the express purpose of deceiving Eve (2 Cor. 11:3). As we begin to explore Satan as the father of lies, let's look at several tactics that flow from his evil nature.

First, Satan comes disguised. The evil one is a beast, a dragon, an insidious monster who inhabits the spiritual realm. Yet when he breaks into the physical world, he wears seductive costumes that appeal to our flesh. This isn't lipstick on a pig; it is a transformative disguise that attracts us to him and masks his wiles. The evil one possesses great knowledge of the truth, but he holds no affection for it. Making himself a beautiful friend, he is nevertheless a sworn enemy of the truth, and he wishes to make us his allies.

Second, Satan catches us alone. Since God has yet to create Eve when he gives Adam the command not to eat of the tree of the knowledge of good and evil (Gen. 2:16-17), Adam likely relays this warning to his wife, for she is well aware of it. While Eve has no reason to doubt Adam's truthfulness, the serpent approaches her because she's in a more vulnerable position than her husband, having received the Lord's instructions second-hand. Further, the serpent catches Eve when she's by herself (Gen. 3:1).

Satan often lies to us when we are alone, away from the spiritual support of fellow believers. He tempts Jesus when the Savior is alone in the wilderness (Matt. 4:1-11; Mark 1:12-13; Luke 4:1-13). He privately stirs up David's heart to number his troops (1 Chron. 21:1). And – we all know this – he comes to us when we're alone, and especially when we're tired, hungry, or lonely. The Covid-19 pandemic of 2020-21 isolated many Christians and made them more vulnerable to the evil one's fiery darts.

Third, Satan casts doubt. Note the question he poses to Eve: "Did God really say, 'You can't eat from any tree in the garden'?" (Gen. 3:1). It's a misquote of Genesis 2:16-17: "And the LORD God commanded the man, 'You are free to eat from any tree of the garden, but you must not eat from the tree of the knowledge of good and evil, for on the day you eat from it, you will certainly die.'"

Satan's subtle turn of a phrase is sufficient to cast doubt in Eve's mind, for she replies, "We may eat the fruit from the trees in the garden. But about the fruit of the tree in the middle of the garden, God said, 'You must not eat it or touch it, or you will die'" (Gen. 3:2-3).

Eve responds correctly to the serpent, with one caveat: she tells the serpent she is forbidden to eat of the tree *or touch it*. Lois Tverberg offers insight into Eve's exaggeration of God's Word:

> Eve was probably trying to be faithful to God in her conversation with Satan, but when she told the serpent God's regulations regarding the tree, she overstated what God had said by saying that they must not even touch it or they will die. She was exaggerating for God's sake, by making his rule more strict than it really was....
>
> We must be ever mindful that our own zeal does not cause us to go beyond God, as we put words in God's mouth. We need to always speak to let God's truth be known.[1]

Eve's well-intended overstatement opens the door for Satan's next tactic.

Fourth, Satan caters to falsehood. When Eve stretches God's prohibition regarding the tree, and then truthfully reports the penalty of death, Satan pounces: "No! You will not die" (Gen. 3:4). The serpent craftily tells Eve she will not die for touching the tree. Eve knows this, but now she's caught in her exaggerated statement. If the serpent confirms she won't die for touching the tree, maybe she won't die for eating from it, either. "At that point, [Satan's] temptations gained credibility in her mind because he corrected her own misstatement."[2]

Fifth, Satan caricatures the truth. With a foothold in Eve's mind, the serpent convinces her there are no consequences for disobedience – at least not drastic ones. What's more, he sells her on the notion that rebellion holds great advantages. Look at what Satan says next about the fruit on the forbidden tree: "In fact, God knows that when you eat it your eyes will be opened and you will be like God, knowing good and evil" (Gen. 3:5).

God certainly knows Eve's eyes will be opened, and he knows she will gain the capacity to explore good and evil. The Lord is omniscient; that is, he knows all things perfectly. But God also is omnipotent and immutable. That means he is all-powerful and unchanging. He is beyond reproach, unable to sin, perfect in holiness, and, by his very nature, he remains this way forever. Eve, on the other hand, isn't God, and the knowledge of sin is bound to wreck her.

There is more truth than falsehood in the serpent's words. Yet the father of lies spins such a subtle web of deception that the first humans are about to plunge themselves, their descendants, and the whole world under a curse. It doesn't take long.

Eve sees that the tree is good for food, delightful to gaze upon, and desirable for obtaining wisdom. So, she takes some of its fruit and eats it. She also gives some to Adam, and he partakes. The consequences are immediate and dramatic: "Then the eyes of both of them were opened, and they knew they were naked; so they sewed fig leaves together and made coverings for themselves" (Gen. 3:7).

Truly, the eyes of Adam and Eve are opened, but their first vision is not divine omniscience. Rather, it's a revelation of their nakedness, which they find necessary to cover with fig leaves. They have lost the radiant perfection of glorified bodies and must look with shame on their corruptible flesh. It must have horrified them, for they sought to cover their bodies as if trying to deny the effects of the Fall.

As Kurt Strassner notes, "Adam and Eve were promised liberation, but instead they received shame. They were promised that they would become like God, but instead they found themselves hiding from God."[3]

The Lord confronts Adam and Eve, who are quick to confess – and equally swift to pass the buck. Adam blames Eve, and Eve pins it on the serpent. God then curses the serpent, as well as the ground, and he announces the consequences of human rebellion against their creator (Gen. 3:14, 16-19). But the Lord also comes in grace, delivering a message of doom (for the serpent) and hope (for mankind): "I will put hostility between you [the serpent] and the woman, and between your offspring and her offspring. He will strike your head, and you will strike his heel" (Gen. 3:15).

This is the first of more than four hundred messianic references in the Old Testament.[4] God promises that a future male descendant of Eve will "strike" – that is, crush, smite in pieces, greatly injure – the head of the serpent, while the serpent strikes the deliverer's heel. As John Ankerberg writes, "God is saying the male seed of woman will be victorious over Satan – because he (the serpent) will be mortally wounded."[5]

Many additional Old Testament prophecies paint a more complete picture of a virgin-born redeemer who is God in human flesh. Jesus of Nazareth is the fulfillment of these prophecies. In fact, Jesus makes it clear he has come to destroy the works of the devil (John 12:31; 16:11; 1 John 3:8). Because of Jesus' death on the cross and his resurrection, he delivers the fatal blow to Satan's dominion over mankind (Acts 10:38; 26:15-18; Eph. 4:8; Col. 2:15; Jas. 4:7). At his future return, Jesus permanently defeats the father of lies and casts him into hell, a place prepared for him and his angels (Matt. 25:41; Rev. 20:10).

A final thought before moving on: We might consider the sight of God, walking in the garden in Genesis 3:8, as the first recorded appearance of the angel of the LORD – also known as a *Christophany*, or a manifestation of Jesus prior to his virgin birth.[6] If this *is* the angel of the LORD, then the preincarnate Christ delivers the very first prophecy about his own future mission to earth to rescue fallen people from the ravages of sin.

He Will Give His Angels Orders Concerning You

One other example may help illustrate Satan's subtlety as the father of lies. In his temptation of Jesus in the wilderness, which we examine in more detail in Chapter 7, the evil one quotes Psalm 91 in an effort to get Jesus to take a header off the temple's pinnacle. We pick up the story in Matthew 4:

Then the devil took him to the holy city, had him stand on the pinnacle of the temple, and said to him, "If you are the Son of God, throw yourself down. For it is written: He will give his angels orders concerning you, and they will support you with their hands so that you will not strike your foot against a stone." Jesus told him, "It is also written: Do not test the Lord your God" (Matt. 4:5-7; see also Luke 4:9-12).

Satan quotes from Psalm 91:11-12 and applies it to Jesus. Psalm 91 ultimately *is* a messianic psalm, but not exclusively so. And it's certainly not an invitation to double-dog-dare the Son of God. Some understanding of this psalm's context may help.

David and other men write psalms while under the old covenant, God's binding relationship with Israel. The psalmists often express what God did and would do for Israel (e.g., Ps. 68; 78; 105; 106; 135; 136). Sometimes, these writings narrow the focus to God's work on behalf of Jerusalem, or David and his descendants (e.g., Ps. 2; 18; 22; 45; 48; 72; 79; 87; 89; 110; 122; 132; 147).

As Kenneth Boa and Robert Bowman point out:

The focus in these psalms is typically on the physical miracles God did for Israel and the physical blessings God gave to Jerusalem and to David. This focus was appropriate because the purpose of the old covenant was to create and sustain a physical nation from which the Messiah would come.[7]

So, in context, Psalm 91 generally lays out the physical protection Israelites enjoy when they trust completely in the Lord. We see this many times in God's deliverance of his people from a variety of dangers. It is not, however, a proof text that guarantees every Israelite a problem-free life.

More to the point, Psalm 91 seems to speak most directly of David, while alluding to the coming Messiah, as verse 13 notes: "You will tread on the lion and the cobra; you will trample the young lion and the serpent." This is a reference to Scripture's first messianic promise

(Gen. 3:15). After Adam and Eve succumb to temptation, the Lord promises to send one who will crush the serpent's head.

In addition, Isaiah offers prophetic visions of a future under the Messiah's reign in which the serpent is subdued (Isa. 11:8; 65:25). Isaiah also pictures a future world in which the lion is completely tamed (Isa. 11:6-7; 65:25).

Therefore, Psalm 91:13 offers a glimpse of the day when the Messiah is victorious over the devil and his minions. Jesus tells his disciples he is granting them authority over "snakes and scorpions" – a reference to evil spirits, whom the disciples cast out (Luke 10:19).

We know Jesus suffers and dies – and this is prophesied in other psalms, as well as in Isaiah 53 – so Psalm 91 does not guarantee the Messiah a care-free path to the kingdom. Rather, the psalm explains that God's protection over the Messiah ensures that no harm comes to him until his appointed hour of death arrives.

This is fairly easy to see. An angel protects Jesus from assassination attempts early in his life (Matt. 2:13, 19-20). Jesus evades death threats and murderous mobs throughout his earthly ministry (Luke 4:28-30; John 8:59; 10:31-39). And Jesus makes it clear that when the time of his death arrives, no one takes his life; he voluntarily lays it down, only to take it up again in resurrection (John 10:17-18).

Satan's choice of Psalm 91:11-12 is a calculated effort to short-circuit Jesus' role as the messianic Son of God. The father of lies quotes from the psalm but craftily misapplies it. Christ's purpose in the Incarnation is not to entertain audiences, compensate for his human frailties, or reign as a puppet king under the authority of the god of this age. No, Jesus comes to earth to die, and to rise again, in order to redeem sinful and fallen people. His role as Messiah is fulfilled only when he cries from the cross, "It is finished" (John 19:30). An angelic rescue from a death-defying plunge would no more convince hardened unbelievers of Christ's deity than would his resurrection from the dead (cf. Luke 16:31).

What does all this mean to us? Boa and Bowman summarize:

The message of [Psalm] 91:11 is that God has acted through Jesus Christ to deliver us from the Devil and all spiritual harm, and he promises us that in the resurrection we will enjoy an eternal life free from all harm of any kind. In the meantime, God can and does send his angels to protect people when and as he chooses, but only as a foretaste or glimpse of the perfect life to which we look forward.[8]

Horns and a Pitchfork

The subtlety of the father of lies is rooted in his character as the master of a million faces. And these faces are beautifully bathed in light. The grotesque images of the evil one as a fiery red beast with horns, a pointy tail, and a pitchfork come to us, not from Scripture, but from Middle-Age caricatures.

The medieval church believed firmly in the reality of Satan. It understood that the evil one was a fallen angel whose head swelled with pride. So, the church proposed attacking Satan at his point of weakness – his arrogance – and he would flee. As R. C. Sproul puts it, "What better way to attack Satan's pride than to depict him as a cloven-hoofed court jester in a red suit?"[9] Unfortunately, later generations, including ours, maintain these distortions as if they are intended to be the real thing.

The evil one's beautiful disguises and silver tongue are intended to woo people into sin. The serpent in the garden did not frighten Eve. He charmed her. Thousands of years later, the apostle Paul points back to that fateful day.

Paul has spent a year and a half in Corinth, planting a church and establishing its doctrinal roots. Then, after moving on in his itinerant role as the apostle to the Gentiles, a band of "super apostles" slips into the church and gains a following. Evidently, they claim spiritual gifts that exceed Paul's, especially prophetic gifts. But Paul warns the Corinthians that these self-proclaimed "super apostles" are nothing more than false apostles who preach "another Jesus ... a different spirit ... a different gospel" (2 Cor. 11:4).

Paul further cautions against the sly tactics of these prophets, reminding the Corinthians that Satan masquerades as an angel of light. Therefore, says Paul, it's no wonder that his servants – the "super apostles" – disguise themselves as ministers of righteousness (2 Cor. 11:14-15).

The best lies aren't whoppers. They're plausible fictions laced with truth. And Satan is the master bartender serving up lethal cocktails.

What does it mean that Satan is *the father of lies*? Consider the following:

First, Satan is the original liar. We have no record of lies in Scripture prior to the evil one's activities. We're not told how Satan fell into sin, but at some point after his creation, he bristled at God's sovereign governance. He likely employed lies and deception to entice other created spirit beings to revolt with him. And no sooner does God pronounce his creation "very good indeed" (Gen. 1:31) than Satan swoops in to ruin everything.

Augustine summarizes it well:

> It is not every one who tells a lie that is the father of his lie. For if thou hast got a lie from another, and uttered it, thou indeed has lied in giving utterance to the lie; but thou art not the father of that lie, because thou hast got it from another. But the devil was a liar of himself. He begat his own falsehood; he heard it from no one. As God the Father begat as His Son the Truth, so the devil, having fallen, begat falsehood as his son.[10]

Second, Satan is a liar by nature. Lies reveal his fallen being. As Jesus makes clear, Satan cannot tell the truth "because there is no truth in him" (John 8:44). His willing distortions of reality spring from a rebellious heart that hates the truth. His animosity toward Jesus, at least in part, is aimed at the one who not only knows the truth and tells the truth, but *is* the truth (John 14:6).

Jesus goes on to say that when the evil one tells a lie, "he speaks from his own nature" (John 8:44). The New International Version renders it this way: "When he lies, he speaks his native language."

Literally, the text reads, "he speaks out of his own [nature or essential characteristics]."[11]

Satan is known to fill people's hearts to lie (Acts 5:3). When we lie, we borrow from him. Yet, when he lies, "the *model* of it is of his own framing, the motives to it are from himself."[12]

Third, all lies link back to Satan. Every liar is the evil one's child and shares his fate in the lake of fire (Rev. 21:8). Every lie spreads his contagion. The serpent's falsehoods so infected humanity from the beginning that every person is a carrier, and every person is a victim.

Like mutated cells, our lies may have their own unique features, but they trace back to the host. The chief financial officer who cooks the books is only doing what Satan entices Jesus to do – turn stones into bread. The charlatan who engages in parlor tricks to fleece his flock is just mimicking Satan's plan for Jesus – take a swan dive off the pinnacle of the temple and amaze the crowds with an angelic rescue. And the celebrity who jettisons all morality in exchange for fleeting fame is only reading from the evil one's script when he offers Jesus a short cut to the kingdom. There truly is nothing new under the sun (Eccles. 1:9), including our manufactured lies built on a chassis of the evil one's design.

This is not to say Satan has the power to beget spiritual children in the same way God does. Truly, the evil one *is* powerful. He blinds unbelievers to the truth of the gospel and holds them captive to do his will (2 Cor. 4:4; 2 Tim. 2:26). But all unbelievers are willing slaves in his kingdom. All those who reject the revelation of God stand before him one day without excuse (Rom. 1:20). They cannot say the devil made them do it.

So, it is Christ who must invade Satan's kingdom, bind the strong man, and plunder his goods (Matt. 12:28-29). As the gospel is preached, the Holy Spirit regenerates sinners – making them spiritually alive – and the Father adopts them into his family, thus making them new creatures in Christ (2 Cor. 5:17).

Instead of the devil being the source of sin in some deterministic sense, he is the source of sin in a more general sense as the first sinner, according to Rodney Whitacre: "And he is father in terms of providing a type of being; that is, he provides the pattern of sin. So there is a spiritual relationship, a unity of mind, in that sinners ... imitate the devil."[13]

Put another way, calling the devil *the father of lies* suggests he originated lying. Further, when Jesus says the devil does not stand in the truth, he hints at a falling away from the truth – all of which points to the mystery of the Fall.

Satan is an enemy of truth, which makes him an enemy of Christ. As Matthew Henry observes, the evil one is a deserter from the truth: "he *abode not in the truth*, did not continue in the purity and rectitude of his nature wherein he was created, but left his first state; when he degenerated from goodness, he departed from truth, for his apostasy was founded in a lie."[14]

Satan is the source and founder of every lie, not only the lies he tells, but the lies we spread as his spokespersons. While all humans bear the image of God, our lies bear the image of the evil one. So, what are followers of Jesus to do?

We are exhorted to love the truth and to tell the truth. Paul urged the Ephesians, "Therefore, putting away lying, speak the truth, each one to his neighbor, because we are members of one another" (Eph. 4:25).

This is no different than the LORD of Armies' message to the Israelites: "These are the things you must do: Speak truth to one another; make true and sound decisions within your city gates. Do not plot evil in your hearts against your neighbor, and do not love perjury, for I hate all this" (Zech. 8:16-17).

As Peter Bolt writes, "Lies hurt and anger people. Rather than allowing anger to fester and give the devil opportunity to undo the work of Christ, truth-telling on the same day will thwart the devil's work."[15]

Summary

Key takeaways about *the father of lies*:

(1) Jesus refers to Satan as a murderer and a liar in the same

context (John 8:42-47). This exposes the truth that Satan is a liar with a murderous intent. He targets the first humans in an effort to kill them. Then sin and death take the stage. The *beginning* of which Jesus speaks – "he was a murderer from the beginning" – likely is a reference to Satan's first appearance on the stage of human history: his temptation of Eve in the garden.

(2) In the first recorded human encounter with the father of lies (Gen. 3), Satan employs a number of sinister tactics: (a) he comes disguised – a hideous dragon veiled in beauty and eloquence; (b) he catches Eve alone, as he often catches us; (c) he casts doubt on God's word and human confidence in God; (d) he caters to falsehood, mixing it with truth; and (e) he caricatures the truth.

(3) Tempting Jesus in the wilderness, Satan misapplies Old Testament passages like Psalm 91 in an effort to short-circuit Christ's mission to earth. Jesus' purpose in the Incarnation is not to entertain audiences, or reign as a puppet king under the authority of the god of this age. No, Jesus comes to earth to die, and to rise again, in order to redeem sinful and fallen people. An angelic rescue from a death-defying plunge from the temple would no more convince hardened unbelievers of Christ's deity than would his later resurrection from the dead.

(4) As Satan demonstrates in the garden of Eden, and through the "super apostles" in Corinth, the best lies aren't whoppers. They're plausible fictions laced with truth. Satan is the master bartender serving up lethal cocktails.

(5) The subtlety of the father of lies is rooted in his character as the master of a million faces. And these faces are beautifully bathed in light. The grotesque images of the evil one as a fiery red beast with horns, a pointy tail, and a pitchfork come to us, not from Scripture, but from Middle-Age caricatures.

(6) What does it mean that Satan is *the father of lies*? First, Satan is the original liar; we have no record of lies in Scripture prior to the evil one's activities. Second, Satan is a liar by nature; when he lies, he speaks his native language. Third, all lies link back to Satan; every liar is the evil one's child.

(7) What are followers of Jesus to do about the father of lies? We are exhorted to love the truth and tell the truth. As the LORD of Armies instructs the Israelites: "These are the things you must do: Speak truth to one another; make true and sound decisions within your city gates. Do not plot evil in your hearts against your neighbor, and do not love perjury, for I hate all this" (Zech. 8:16-17).

Questions for Personal or Group Study

1. How would you describe what Jesus means when he says Satan is "the father of lies" (John 8:44)?
2. Read the account of Satan's temptation and mankind's fall in Genesis 3:1-7. Identify several tactics that flow from Satan's evil nature.
3. Genesis 3:15 is widely regarded as the *protoevangelium* – the "first good news." What promises does God make in this verse? What additional messianic prophecies does the Lord provide in Old Testament passages such as Psalm 16:8-11; Psalm 22; Isaiah 7:14; Isaiah 9:6-7; Isaiah 53; and Micah 5:2?
4. When and how did the depiction of Satan as an ugly creature with horns, a tail, and a pitchfork originate?
5. As the father of lies, Satan is the originator of everything contrary to truth. In effect, every lie is the devil's child. Take a few minutes to create a personal list of the evil one's top ten lies. In other words, sketch the most cunning lies Satan has tried to pass off on you as truth. Here's a suggested start:

    1. You don't need God for every decision in life; don't sweat the small stuff.
    2. God just wants you to be happy.
    3. It's *your* truth that matters.

In a very real sense, Satan murdered the human race, for he enticed Adam and Eve to sin, thus bringing death into the world.

6

MURDERER

James Fairweather was only fifteen years old when he stabbed a drunken and helpless man 102 times during an encounter in Colchester, England. Three months later, Fairweather stabbed a second victim in both eyes as she walked along a nature trail in the same Essex community, resulting in her death. He was stalking a third victim when police arrested him. What made his capture particularly chilling was his admission that he wanted to kill at least fifteen more people.

When the judge handed down the teenager's sentence, Fairweather turned toward his parents and mouthed, "I don't give a s---."

Fairweather is one of the world's youngest serial killers. He's also one of the few who showed absolutely no remorse for his crimes. His mother branded him a "monster." His teachers heard him express a desire to be a murderer but didn't believe him, thinking him to be merely an "edgy teenager." He idolized Peter Sutcliffe, the "Yorkshire Ripper," and regarded American serial killer Ted Bundy as his favorite murderer. He claimed possession by the devil and said he heard voices in his head that compelled him to kill. Both killings showed elements of planning and sadism.[1]

How does a young person like Fairweather become so obsessed with killing? Granted, he was later diagnosed with autism. He played violent video games. He owned a stash of horror films and a book called *The World's Worst Crimes*. Not a healthy combination, to say the least.

At the same time, lots of teenagers suffer from disabilities and lead otherwise normal lives. And many young people indulge in violent fantasies without crossing the line into criminal activity. Fairweather's heinous crimes draw attention to the macabre thoughts and motives that lie beneath the surface in criminal minds. Even more chilling, they remind us of the depths of our common human depravity. We don't like to think about it, but we all know we have it in us to be another James Fairweather.

Scripture is filled with stories of violent, often premeditated, murders. Cain strikes down his brother Abel. Moses kills an Egyptian and buries him in the sand. King David sends Bathsheba's husband to certain death at the front lines of battle in order to hide his own adultery. And on it goes. Almost from the beginning, humans have been murdering one another.

Jesus puts an even finer point on the sixth commandment when he tells his listeners that murder begins in the heart (Matt. 5:21-22; 15:19).[2] And if senseless killing is a human trait nearly as old as mankind, Jesus makes a bold statement about an evil creature behind it all, a being Jesus describes as "a murderer from the beginning" (John 8:44).

The Murder of Humanity

In John 8, Jesus confronts Jews who are trying to put him to death. These self-proclaimed descendants of Abraham are, in fact, children of the devil. That is, from a moral and ethical point of view, they share the evil one's nature. They love neither God nor truth, and therefore they reject the one God sent to be Savior of the world. We pick up the story in verse 37 with Jesus speaking:

"I know you are descendants of Abraham, but you are trying to kill me because my word has no place among you. I speak what I have seen in the presence of the Father; so then, you do what you have heard from your father."

"Our father is Abraham," they replied.

"If you were Abraham's children," Jesus told them, "you would do what Abraham did. But now you are trying to kill me, a man who has told you the truth that I heard from God. Abraham did not do this. You're doing what your father does."

"We weren't born of sexual immorality," they said. "We have one Father – God."

Jesus said to them, "If God were your Father, you would love me, because I came from God and I am here. For I didn't come on my own, but he sent me. Why don't you understand what I say? Because you cannot listen to my word. You are of your father the devil, and you want to carry out your father's desires. *He was a murderer from the beginning* and does not stand in the truth, because there is no truth in him. When he tells a lie, he speaks from his own nature, because he is a liar and the father of lies" (John 8:37-44, emphasis added).

In what way is Satan "a murderer from the beginning"? Certainly, God did not create him this way. The Lord declared everything he made "very good indeed" (Gen. 1:31), and this would imply the angelic host as well as the physical universe. Further, as *The Westminster Confession* states, God "neither is nor can be the author or approver of sin."[3]

At some point – either prior to God's creation of the world or shortly thereafter – Satan rebelled and then became a murderer, adopting other evil character traits as well. Some commentators suggest Satan's murderous rampage began when he enticed Cain to kill Abel.[4] But it seems more biblically faithful to place the evil one's serial killing in an earlier and wider context.

Through his successful temptation of the first humans, Satan robbed Adam and Eve of spiritual and physical life. In a very real sense, Satan murdered the human race, for he enticed Adam and Eve to sin, thus bringing death into the world (cf. Rom. 5:12).

On the Day ...

The story begins in Genesis 2. The Lord places Adam in the garden of Eden to work it and watch over it. The command is clear: "You are free to eat from any tree of the garden, but you must not eat from the tree of the knowledge of good and evil, for *on the day* you eat from it, you will certainly *die*" (Gen. 2:16-17, emphasis added). The Hebrew verb for "die" is *muwth* and may be translated "to die (as a penalty)," "be put to death," or even "to die prematurely (by neglect of wise moral conduct)."[5] Adam is given joyful work and bountiful rewards as he tends the garden paradise that meets his every need and serves as the intersection between the dwelling places of God and humanity.

To further Adam's bliss, God delivers a parade of animals to the first man and entrusts Adam with naming them. Adam comes to realize something is lacking. The animals are diverse and beautiful, but they are unable to provide the degree of companionship and intimacy for which God created Adam. So, the Lord causes a deep sleep to fall over Adam, and from Adam's side God creates a woman, who complements the man. As Genesis 2 ends, we find the man and his wife naked, yet feeling no shame (v. 25).

There is no hint of trouble in the garden. Adam and Eve enjoy all the Lord has given them, including personal intimacy with their creator. But we all know this is not the end of the story. The very next verse introduces the serpent, and the verses that follow introduce death. Here, we pause to consider the death of humanity and Satan's role as a murderer.

Eve has yet to be created when God gives Adam the command not to eat from the tree of the knowledge of good and evil. Eve gets the message, however. She's aware of the limits of her human freedom, and she understands the consequences of disobedience. She tells the serpent, "God said, 'You must not eat it or touch it, or you will die'"

(Gen. 3:3). So, either God or Adam – or perhaps both – have taught Eve about the tree, although Eve wrongly adds "or touch it" to the prohibition.

The serpent pounces on Eve's statement and declares, "No! You will not die" (v. 4). This may be the focal point of Jesus' statement in John 8:44 when he calls Satan both a liar and a murderer. Just as lies flow from the evil one's nature, murder is Satan's ultimate thrill. And the death of humanity is his aim. Consider this: When the serpent falsely assures Eve she will not die for disobeying God, his goal is to murder her. In getting Eve to think God is withholding divine wisdom from his creatures, he entices her to distrust God, then to disobey God, which the serpent knows will result in death at the hands of God.

Eve listens to the serpent's enchanting voice and believes him to be her advocate. Like Haman, who gleefully erects gallows intended for his Jewish enemies, not knowing they are to serve as the instrument of his own death, Eve examines the tree, sees it is good for food, delightful to behold, and desirable for attaining wisdom (Gen. 3:6). So, she takes some of its fruit and eats it. She also gives some to Adam, who partakes as well. At the very moment they believe to be entering a more divine state of knowledge, they receive a sentence of death – a shocking reversal of fortune.

Their eyes *are* opened, as the serpent promised, but not in the way they expected. Immediately, they see their nakedness and are ashamed – the opposite of their innocent state in Genesis 2:25. They sew fig leaves together and make coverings for themselves (Gen. 3:7). Next, they hide from the Lord among the trees in the garden (3:8). And finally, they deflect responsibility for their sin (3:12-13). Adam tells the Lord, "The woman you gave to be with me – she gave me some fruit from the tree and I ate" (3:12). And Eve explains, "The serpent deceived me, and I ate" (3:13).

Three Kinds of Death

God warned Adam that if he disobeyed, he would die "on the day" he ate from the forbidden tree (Gen. 2:17). Yet Adam lived at least another eight hundred years, breathing his last at the age of 930 (Gen. 5:5). So, in what sense did Adam die *on the day* he sinned? A little background may prove helpful.

When the Bible says we are made in the image of God (Gen. 1:27), it means, at least in some respects, we are a trinity – not that we exist as three co-equal divine persons, but that we each possess a body, soul, and spirit.[6] This means we also die in three stages as a consequence of sin.

The Fall affects each part of human beings' threefold nature. As James Boice explains, "Specifically, his [man's] spirit died, for the fellowship that he had with God was broken; his soul began to die, for he began to lie and cheat and kill; his body died eventually, for as God said, 'Dust you are and to dust you will return'" (Gen. 3:19).[7]

Let's look briefly at these three deaths in reverse chronological order.

Physical Death

Although it is hundreds of years after his flagrant disobedience, Adam experiences *physical death*, and so has nearly everyone since then. At some point, we all stop breathing, our brains stop functioning, our skin grows cold, and our bodies become stiff. No doubt, this type of death is easy to understand. Only Enoch and Elijah are recorded in Scripture as having escaped this type of death. Not even Jesus gets a pass – although he comes into this world to die (John 12:27; 1 John 4:10), and his death secures our everlasting life. Physical death comes to all of us as a consequence of sin.

God did not create Adam and Eve to die. Had they remained faithful to their creator, they would have enjoyed the direct presence of God in the garden every day for all eternity. And their descendants would live forever as well, without the ravages of decline and ultimate death. It is fair to say that, being cast out of Eden, Adam and Eve live in a *state* of death. As Peter Bolt explains:

> Without access to the tree of life and its promised immortality, they were left to a life characterized only by their mortality. Paul confirms this where he affirms that with the sin came "death through sin," and from that moment on "death reigned" (Rom. 5:12, 14, 21).[8]

Physical death *does* come to Adam and Eve, but not before they witness the murder of their son, the difficulty of childbirth, the toils of growing food in a hostile environment, and the creeping decline of youthful vigor. This touches on the second type of death.

Death of the Soul

Immediately after rebelling against God, Adam and Eve note a marked difference in their perceptions, words, and deeds. Their souls are dying. They see their nakedness and experience shame. They sense fear and hide from God. They make excuses for their rebellion and push the blame toward others – even toward God.

The serpent is right about one thing concerning Adam and Eve: their eyes *are* opened, and they know evil as well as good. But it's not what they expected. Adam shifts the blame to his wife. Worse, he essentially tells God the Fall never would have happened if God were not so mistaken in his judgment as to create a woman. In a similar manner, Eve is quick to blame the serpent.

Shame, fearfulness, and lying are symptoms of a mind and will alienated from God. The Lord is the source of all good things (Jas. 1:17). But when we break fellowship with God, we descend into rebellion, cowardice, malice, jealousy, pride, hatred, and every other kind of evil. It spreads like a contagion. Sin immediately stresses Adam and Eve's harmonious relationship. Their sons find themselves at odds, with Cain striking down Abel in a premeditated act of jealousy (Gen. 4:8; cf. 1 John 3:12, 15). Lamech takes two wives – the first human act of bigamy – and brags to his wives about killing another man (Gen. 4:19, 23).

By Genesis 6, human wickedness is so widespread, the Lord decides to destroy mankind with a flood. Even though Noah and his family find favor with God and are delivered from judgment on an ark, they pick up where their evil contemporaries left off as soon as the flood waters recede.

We read about the Tower of Babylon (Gen. 11), Abram's deceit with Pharaoh in Egypt (Gen. 12), Abram and Sarai's impatience with God over a promised son (Gen. 16), the destruction of Sodom and Gomorrah (Gen. 19), incest between Lot and his daughters (Gen. 19), and the list goes on. The death of the soul is slow and steady – but it is certain. Conceived in sin and guilty at birth (Ps. 51:5), all people find themselves at the mercy of the sin nature.

Spiritual Death

But there is an even worse death – more destructive than the slow rotting of the soul and the eventual cessation of physical life. This is *spiritual death*. This death is instantaneous and total. The spirit is what sets humans apart from and above animals. It enables us to have communion with God. And the spirit died instantly when Adam and Eve sinned. "In contemporary language this is described as alienation – alienation from God – and it is the first result of that death that came into human experience as the result of sin."[9]

John Stott calls spiritual death "the most dreadful of all sin's consequences." He further writes:

> Man's highest destiny is to know God and to be in a personal relationship with God. Man's chief claim to nobility is that he was made in the image of God and is therefore capable of knowing Him. But this God whom we are meant to know and whom we ought to know is a moral Being ... our sins blot out God's face from us as effectively as the clouds of the sun.... We have no communication

with God. We are "dead through trespasses and sins" (Eph. 2:1) which we have committed.[10]

The so-called *natural man* (1 Cor. 2:14 KJV), or "person without the Spirit" (CSB, NIV), certainly is alive in body and soul, but is spiritually dead. That is, he can think, have emotions, and make decisions. But because he has rejected Christ, the Holy Spirit does not inhabit that sinner's human spirit. Therefore, his life is directed by what he experiences through his five senses, what he thinks about, and what he reasons from a mind that Satan has blinded and the Spirit has not renewed (Rom. 12:2; 2 Cor. 4:4).

This death is absolute, complete, and permanent. It requires the Holy Spirit's work of regeneration. In the New Testament, the Greek *palingenesia* – a compound of *palin* ("again") and *ginomai* ("to become") – is used only twice and means "regeneration," "renewal," or "recreation." In Matthew 19:28, it refers to God's ultimate renovation of the cosmos, and in Titus 3:5, it speaks of the work of the Holy Spirit, bringing back to life a dead human spirit – "a radical change of heart and mind resulting in renewed devotion to God and Christ."[11]

Put simply, regeneration is the work of the Holy Spirit that brings a sinner from spiritual death into spiritual life. Our spirits – our innermost beings created for intimacy with God – are dead in trespasses and sins (Eph. 2:1), and they remain so unless and until the Holy Spirit breathes new life into them. John Frame writes:

> The new birth brings life out of that [spiritual] death. Without this new birth, we cannot even see the kingdom of God, because our spiritual eyes are dead. Paul teaches in Romans 1 that sinners suppress the truth and exchange it for a lie. So the new birth marks the beginning of spiritual understanding, as well as the beginning of obedient discipleship.[12]

In summary, we see how God's warning of death "on that day" came true in Adam's life. He died spiritually in an instant. He began to die in his soul, and kept dying slowly for the next eight hundred years. And, finally, he died physically. This is the darkest of tragedies, except for one distant light: the promised seed of woman in Genesis 3:15. This coming redeemer crushes the head of Satan and completely reverses the effects of the Fall – not only in believing sinners, but in the fallen cosmos as well (2 Pet. 3:10-13; Rev. 21-22).

God's work of redemption, completed in the death, burial, and resurrection of Jesus, turns spiritual death into spiritual life; makes the darkened mind the mind of Christ; and guarantees the future glorification of the corruptible earthly body. Even the curse of this sinful and fallen world is reversed one day in creation of the new heavens and new earth.

Murder by Proxy

As a general observation, Satan does not appear to murder directly, although he could – with God's permission. Rather, the evil one carries out his murderous pursuits through various agents. We might say the evil one commits murder by proxy.

A few examples: When God permits Satan to test Job, the evil one uses the Sabeans and Chaldeans to kill Job's stock, as well as some of Job's servants (Job 1:15, 17). Satan then employs fire from heaven and a great whirlwind to kill more of Job's servants and all of his children (Job 1:16, 18-19). He incites David to take a census of Israel, resulting in the deaths of many people (2 Sam. 24; 1 Chron. 21). He uses Roman and Jewish authorities, along with a back-stabbing apostle, to bring about the death of Jesus (Luke 22:3; John 13:2, 27). And he fills the hearts of Ananias and Sapphira to lie against the Holy Spirit, resulting in their deaths (Acts 5:1-11).

And there's more. Consider a sampling of the recorded murders in Scripture and look for the evil one's long shadow behind them:

- Cain kills Abel out of envy (Gen. 4:8).
- Lamech kills a young man out of pride and revenge (Gen. 4:23).

- Simeon and Levi kill Hamor and Shechem for revenge (Gen. 34:26).
- Moses kills an Egyptian out of a false sense of justice (Exod. 2:12).
- Joab kills Abner to eliminate competition (2 Sam. 3:27).
- David has Uriah killed to conceal the king's adultery with Bathsheba (2 Sam. 12:9).
- Zimri kills Elah to steal his throne (1 Kings 16:10).
- Jezebel has Naboth killed to steal his land for Ahab (1 Kings 21:13).
- Servants kill Joash to avenge his cruelty (2 Kings 12:20-21).
- Ishmael kills Gedaliah as an act of anarchy (2 Kings 25:25).
- Israelites kill Zechariah the high priest because they can't stand his righteous preaching (2 Chron. 24:20-21).
- Nebuchadnezzar kills Zedekiah's sons to punish him for rebellion (Jer. 39:6).
- Herod kills Bethlehem's babies in an effort to kill Jesus (Matt. 2:16).
- Herodias has John the Baptist killed for speaking out against her adultery (Mark 6:25, 27).
- The Jewish elders kill Stephen for telling them the truth (Acts 7:58-59).
- Rebels in Pergamos kill Antipas because of his faithful testimony (Rev. 2:13).
- And the antichrist kills two miracle-working witnesses – although they come back to life (Rev. 11:7).

The vortex line of these murders – the center of swirling satanic and human violence – is a cross at the base of a hill called "Skull Place" outside Jerusalem, where two thousand years ago the Son of Man comes to earth to die, and the murderer from the beginning is all too eager to accommodate.

But who, exactly, murders the Savior of the world? Here, the plot thickens. Satan does not directly murder Jesus, but he has plenty of help – and divine permission. According to Scripture, the Jews murder Jesus (Acts 5:30; 1 Thess. 2:15). So do Judas (Mark 14:10-11), Pilate (Matt. 27:24-26), and Roman soldiers (Matt. 27:27-31). As sinners, you and I murder Jesus as well (Isa. 53:4-9). Yet, none of this occurs outside of God's sovereign decrees. The Father is pleased to crush Jesus severely (Isa. 53:10). Jesus gladly lays down his life (John 10:18; Heb. 12:2). And the Spirit raises him on the third day (Rom. 8:11).

The most heinous crime ever committed – the murder of God – becomes a glorious triumph: "For God made Christ, who never sinned, to be the offering for our sin, so that we could be made right with God through Christ" (2 Cor. 5:21 NLT).

Three Greek Words

Let's close this chapter with a look at three Greek words translated "murderer" in the New Testament. The first word, *phoneus*, is found six times and refers to homicide. In the parable of the wedding banquet, Jesus tells of an enraged king who sends out his troops to kill the *murderers* of his servants (Matt. 22:7). When the people of Malta see a venomous snake strike the apostle Paul, they assume he is a *murderer* who has failed to escape "Justice" (*Dikee*, the Greek goddess of justice; Acts 28:4). And twice in the Book of Revelation, Jesus includes *murderers* among those cast out of his presence (Rev. 21:8; 22:15).

Second, the apostle Paul applies the Greek *androphonos* to place murderers (or manslayers) among the "lawless and rebellious," for whom the law is intended (1 Tim. 1:9).

Third, the apostle John uses the word *anthropoktonos* twice in 1 John 3:15: "Everyone who hates his brother or sister is a *murderer*, and you know that no *murderer* has eternal life residing in him." In context, John equates those who hate with those who commit murder, linking this passage to Jesus' words of warning that murder begins in the heart (Matt. 5:21-22).

Jesus is the only other person in the New Testament to use *anthropoktonos*, and he does so in the very passage we've been studying:

You [Jews who oppose Jesus] are of your father the devil, and you want to carry out your father's desires. He was a *murderer* from the beginning and does not stand in the truth, because there is no truth in him. When he tells a lie, he speaks from his own nature, because he is a liar and the father of lies (John 8:44, emphasis added).

This Greek word – *anthropoktonos* – is similar to the other two in that it denotes a manslayer, or one who engages in homicide. Taken together, all three Greek words define individuals who knowingly, deliberately, and with premeditation take the lives of others.

In the case of Satan, his murder in the garden of Eden is more heinous than the rest and more widespread in its consequences, for the evil one murdered Adam – and thus he murdered the entire human race. While humans may receive God's forgiveness for murder – because Christ was murdered on the cross in our place – there is no clemency for Satan's murderous act. He is cast into the lake of fire, which God created for his everlasting torment (Matt. 25:41.)

Yes, Satan is a murderer from the very beginning. And yet, Christians need not fear him, for Jesus has placed our lives in the Father's hands (John 10:28-29), and he will raise us up on the last day (John 6:37-40, 44).

As followers of Jesus, we experience all three kinds of death – death of spirit, soul, and body – but the murder of Jesus ensures that all three deaths are reversed. He has made us spiritually alive through *regeneration*. He is making us alive in our souls as he conforms us to his image through *sanctification*. And one day, he raises us from the dead in *glorification*, clothing us in the immortality Adam and Eve lost to a lying murderer one fateful day long ago.

Summary

Key takeaways about the *murderer*:

(1) Jesus refers to Satan as "a murderer from the beginning" (John 8:44). Certainly, God did not create Satan this way. Nevertheless, at some point – either prior to God's creation of the world or shortly

thereafter – Satan rebelled and then became a murderer. Through his successful temptation of the first humans, Satan robbed Adam and Eve of life. In a very real sense, Satan murdered the human race, for he enticed Adam and Eve to sin, thus bringing death into the world.

(2) At the very moment Adam and Eve partake of the forbidden tree, they believe they're entering a more divine state of knowledge. But instead, they receive a sentence of death – a shocking reversal of fortune. Their eyes *are* opened, as the serpent promised, but not in the way they expected.

(3) When the Bible says we are made in the image of God, it means, at least in some respects, we are a trinity. That is, we each possess a body, soul, and spirit. But we also die in three stages as a consequence of sin. We die physically one day as our bodies cease functioning. Our souls are in a state of death as sin impairs our thoughts, emotions, and wills. And, worst of all, our spirits – the innermost parts of us made as God's dwelling places – are dead in sin, desperately needing the regenerating work of the Holy Spirit.

(4) The three-fold deaths of Adam and Eve constitute the darkest of tragedies, except for one distant light: the promised seed of woman in Genesis 3:15. This coming redeemer crushes the head of Satan and completely reverses the effects of the Fall – not only in believing sinners, but in the fallen cosmos as well (2 Pet. 3:10-13; Rev. 21-22).

(5) God's work of redemption, completed in the death, burial, and resurrection of Jesus, turns spiritual death into spiritual life; makes the darkened mind the mind of Christ; and guarantees the future glorification of the corruptible earthly body. Even the curse of this sinful and fallen world is reversed one day in creation of the new heavens and new earth.

(6) Satan does not appear to murder directly, although he could – with God's permission. Rather, the evil one carries out his murderous pursuits through various agents. We might say the evil one commits murder by proxy. This includes the death of Jesus, for which Satan employs religious leaders, Judas, Pilate, and Roman soldiers. Even you and I, as sinners, are complicit in the crucifixion. Yet, none of this

occurs outside of God's sovereign decrees. The Father is pleased to crush Jesus severely (Isa. 53:10). Jesus gladly lays down his life (John 10:18; Heb. 12:2). And the Holy Spirit raises him from the dead (Rom. 8:11).

(7) The most heinous crime ever committed – the murder of God – becomes a glorious triumph: "For God made Christ, who never sinned, to be the offering for our sin, so that we could be made right with God through Christ" (2 Cor. 5:21 NLT). As followers of Jesus, we experience all three kinds of death – death of spirit, soul, and body – but the murder of Jesus ensures that all three deaths are reversed.

Questions for Personal or Group Study

1. To what event does Jesus refer when he says Satan was "a murderer from the beginning" (John 8:44)?
2. In what way did Satan murder the entire human race?
3. Briefly describe three types of death revealed in Scripture:

   • Physical death
   • Death of the soul
   • Spiritual death

4. Who murdered Jesus on the cross? What happened to overturn Satan's premeditated plan for the Savior's death?
5. How does Satan use secondary means – for example, people or natural elements – to commit murder? Provide a few examples.

Satan's number one activity is temptation. His goal is to drive a wedge between God and human beings made in God's image.

TEMPTER

In Homer's *Odyssey*, the *sirens* are three mysterious women who live on an island. When ships pass, the sirens stand on the cliffs above and sing. Their hauntingly beautiful voices lure sailors to steer their vessels closer to shore until eventually they shipwreck on the rocky coast.

Odysseus is curious to hear the sirens' songs as well, yet he knows the dangers. He orders his men to tie him to the ship's mast as they approach the island. Then he instructs them to plug their own ears with beeswax.

As expected, when Odysseus hears the sirens' call, he demands to be untied, but his shipmates obey his earlier command and bind him more tightly to the mast. Finally, they release him when the sirens' song is no longer heard.

This ancient myth illustrates how the powerful pull of temptation is common to all people. We know all too well the perils of flirting with danger. Temptation is common to every human being. It was well-known to Jesus. Yet, despite being tempted in every way common to humanity, he emerged unscathed (Heb. 4:15).

Unlike the Son of God, we've all succumbed to temptation at various times and in different ways. Worse, we've all played the tempter, plying our seductive charms or clumsy threats – all to satisfy our selfish desires. It isn't pretty that we act like little Satans, but it doesn't bother him. Quite the contrary, he appears to see imitation as the highest form of flattery.

The evil one is the ultimate siren, captivating us with his counterfeit beauty and wooing us with empty promises. Satan is the father of lies (John 8:44) and the mother of all tempters.

The New Testament calls Satan *the tempter* in only two places (Matt. 4:3; 1 Thess. 3:5), while depicting him as a source of temptation elsewhere (e.g., 1 Cor. 7:5). But from Genesis through Revelation, the evil one marks his territory with unrelenting attacks on everyone from Adam to the second Adam (Jesus).

By far, Satan's number one activity is temptation. His goal is to drive a wedge between God and human beings made in God's image. He engineers the first recorded temptation in Scripture, enticing Eve to eat of the forbidden tree in the garden of Eden (Gen.3:1-7). He destroys Job's family, wealth, and health in an effort to get Job to curse God (Job 1:11; 2:5). He tempts King David to take a census of Israel so that David seeks security in a large potential army rather than in God (1 Chron. 21:1, 5). And he stands before a divine assembly in heaven to accuse the high priest Joshua of unrighteousness (Zech. 3:1).

At the dawn of his public ministry, Jesus encounters Satan in the desert and faces intense temptation (Matt. 4:1-11; Mark 1:12-13; Luke 4:1-13). The evil one seeks to defeat Jesus from the outset of his earthly mission, appealing to the lust of the flesh ("tell these stones to become bread"), the lust of the eyes ("He will give his angels orders concerning you"), and the pride of life ("I will give you all these things"). As Kenneth Boa and Robert Bowman frame it, "Satan tempted Jesus to seek universal power apart from God's purposes, which for Jesus included suffering and dying."[1] Later, Jesus attributes Peter's efforts to divert Jesus' destiny with death to none other than the evil one (Matt. 16:21-23).

The New Testament epistles and the Book of Revelation warn about the wiles of the devil (e.g., 1 Cor. 7:5; Rev. 2:10). Satan's counterfeit miracles aim to deceive people into believing a lie

(2 Thess. 2:9-10). The evil one's antics are so successful that the Book of Revelation describes him as one who deceives the whole world (Rev. 12:9; 20:10).

As Boa and Bowman summarize:

> Whatever the Devil does … his purpose is to deceive us. His game plan is to tempt us to abandon our trust in God and to disobey him. Whenever we are tempted to turn away from God, we are listening to a diabolical lie. This is something everyone needs to know about the Devil.[2]

The Tempter's Limitations

While Satan is a master of temptation, God limits what he can do to harm us. First, Satan operates under the sovereignty of God and may only attack God's people with God's permission. Remember that Satan petitioned God for the right to come after Job (Job 1:9-11; 2:4-5). He also asked Jesus for permission to sift Peter like wheat (Luke 22:31).

Second, Satan may only tempt us up to a point. The apostle Paul assures us:

> No temptation has come upon you except what is common to humanity. But God is faithful; he will not allow you to be tempted beyond what you are able, but with the temptation he will also provide a way out so that you may be able to bear it (1 Cor. 10:13).

Third, Satan can't make us do anything against our wills. As a result, his temptations, and the temptations of evil spirits, generally appeal to our own selfish desires. James writes:

> No one undergoing a trial should say, "I am being tempted by God," since God is not tempted by evil, and he himself doesn't tempt anyone. But each person is tempted when he is drawn away and enticed by his own evil desire. Then after desire has conceived, it

gives birth to sin, and when sin is fully grown, it gives birth to death (Jas. 1:13-15).

Fourth, Satan's nature as a created being restricts him. He is highly intelligent, extremely powerful, and he rules a vast world system. But he does not have the qualities of God – omniscience, omnipotence, omnipresence, transcendence, immutability, etc. In other words, Satan prowls the earth like a lion because he has to operate that way (1 Pet. 5:8). Further, because the evil one can't be in more than one place at a time, he must rely on an army of evil spirits, who tempt us on a regular basis.

Fifth, it's important to keep in mind that sin is not inevitable. Satan and evil spirits carefully observe us. They know our strengths and weaknesses – through observation, not omniscience. They understand our vulnerabilities. And they attack with savage intent. But neither Satan nor demons are omniscient. They simply *don't know* whether we're going to successfully resist temptation or give in to it – until we act.

Sixth, the Lord grants us the ability to successfully fend off temptation. He has equipped us with "the full armor of God," along with prayer (see Eph. 6:11-20). God also has granted us the indwelling Holy Spirit to comfort, protect, warn, and even chasten us when necessary for our own good. Satan and evil spirits can be defeated when we submit to God and then resist the evil one (Jas. 4:7).

Satan, the Tempter

Let's look more closely at the two New Testament passages in which Satan is called "the tempter" – Matthew 4:3, and 1 Thessalonians 3:5.

Matthew 4:3

All three synoptic Gospels record the account of Jesus' temptations in the wilderness.[3] Let's look at Matthew's record since it alone refers to Satan as *the tempter*, although Mark and Luke are clear that it is the evil one tempting Jesus during this encounter.

Matthew 4:1-11 reads:

> Then Jesus was led up by the Spirit into the wilderness to be tempted by the devil. After he had fasted forty days and forty nights, he was hungry. Then *the tempter* approached him and said, "If you are the Son of God, tell these stones to become bread."
>
> He answered, "It is written: Man must not live on bread alone but on every word that comes from the mouth of God."
>
> Then the devil took him to the holy city, had him stand on the pinnacle of the temple, and said to him, "If you are the Son of God, throw yourself down. For it is written: He will give his angels orders concerning you, and they will support you with their hands so that you will not strike your foot against a stone."
>
> Jesus told him, "It is also written: Do not test the Lord your God."
>
> Again, the devil took him to a very high mountain and showed him all the kingdoms of the world and their splendor. And he said to him, "I will give you all these things if you will fall down and worship me."
>
> Then Jesus told him, "Go away, Satan! For it is written: Worship the Lord your God, and serve only him."
>
> Then the devil left him, and angels came and began to serve him (emphasis added).

No sooner does the Holy Spirit descend on Jesus, empowering the incarnate Son of God for public ministry, than he leads Jesus into the wilderness for an extended time of temptation. While Matthew and Luke say the Spirit *leads* Jesus into the wilderness,[4] Mark uses a more emphatic verb: *ekballo*, which means to drive out, cast out, expel, or compel one to depart. The verb may imply violence, but it also may be used to denote drawing out, extracting, or leading one away with an irresistible force.

Likely, this is the sense in which Jesus is led into the wilderness. It is Jesus' first act of submission to the will of the Father after the

Spirit's descent. And there is no doubt the Spirit accompanies Jesus on this otherwise solitary mission.

We should keep in mind the similarities between Jesus' forty days of testing in the wilderness and the Israelites' forty years of testing after God delivers them from Egypt. In both cases, the divine presence of Yahweh accompanies them – the Shekinah glory in the pillar of cloud and fire for the Israelites, and the Holy Spirit for Jesus.

In both cases, God's law is revealed and available. In both cases, temptation comes in appeals to fleshly desires, false gods, and prideful possessions. But the outcomes are starkly different. The Israelites fail the test; Jesus passes with flying colors.

The first temptation. Satan appeals to Jesus' hunger, urging the Son of God to prove himself by turning stones into bread. This appeal is to the "lust of the flesh" (1 John 2:16). Will the incarnate Creator use his infinite power to save himself?

Three years later, a similar taunt is hurled Jesus' way. As he hangs naked and bloody on the cross, passersby yell insults and shake their heads, saying, "You who would destroy the temple and rebuild it in three days, save yourself! If you are the Son of God, come down from the cross!"

Similarly, the chief priests, scribes, and elders mock him: "He saved others, but he cannot save himself! He is the King of Israel! Let him come down now from the cross, and we will believe in him. He trusts in God; let God rescue him now – if he takes pleasure in him! For he said, 'I am the Son of God.'" Even the criminals crucified with Jesus can't resist chiming in (Matt. 27:39-44).

There is nothing inherently sinful about turning stones into bread. Later, on two occasions, Jesus multiplies loaves of bread and fish to feed thousands (Matt. 14:13-21; 15:32-39). So, it isn't the miracle itself that would prove sinful, but the abuse of divine power for personal gratification. As Sharon Beekmann notes, "In this regard, the devil's temptations are not always to do something inherently sinful, but to do something outside of the will of God. A miracle in the service of Satan is magic."[5]

No doubt, Jesus is famished. Perhaps for the first time, the eternal

Son of God is experiencing the extreme limits of human endurance. What harm would there be for the one who created all things (John 1:3; Col. 1:15) to conjure up a few morsels of bread? But Jesus understands his earthly role – to serve, not to be served – and he understands the subtlety of Satan's siren call. And so he responds, "It is written: Man must not live on bread alone but on every word that comes from the mouth of God" (Matt. 4:4).

In the wilderness, God provided manna on a daily basis to teach the Israelites to trust fully in him, but they were not to demand that he satisfy their hunger (Deut. 8:3). Of course, the Israelites failed the test. But Jesus' reply to Satan shows the priority of maintaining close fellowship with the Father, who sustains his Son throughout his earthly mission.

Later, Jesus declares: "I am the bread of life. No one who comes to me will ever be hungry, and no one who believes in me will ever be thirsty again" (John 6:35). Only a sinless God-man is able to sustain spiritually hungry people.

The second temptation. Next, the devil appeals to Jesus' sense of self-importance, or as John depicts it, "the lust of the eyes" (1 John 2:16). Satan takes Jesus to the precipice of the temple, a towering vantage point more than a hundred feet above the shimmering pavement below. No doubt, many religious leaders and earnest supplicants are busily going about their business and would make an ideal audience for a divine parlor trick. What better way to launch a public ministry than with an open display of supernatural power.

The devil tells Jesus not to worry about spilling his guts on the stones beneath him. The Father is sure to send angels to cushion the fall. Here, Satan cleverly misquotes Psalm 91:11-12: "He will give his angels orders concerning you, and they will support you with their hands so that you will not strike your foot against a stone." However, the evil one makes two deliberate errors. First, he leaves out part of verse 11: "to protect you in all your ways." Second, he lifts the psalm out of context.

We explored Psalm 91 in greater depth in Chapter 5. Generally, it lays out the physical protection Israelites enjoy when they trust completely in the Lord. We see this many times in God's deliverance of his people from a variety of dangers. It is not, however, a proof text that guarantees every Israelite a problem-free life. More to the point, Psalm 91 seems to speak directly of David, while alluding to the coming Messiah, as verse 13 notes: "You will tread on the lion and the cobra; you will trample the young lion and the serpent."

Satan's choice of Psalm 91:11-12 is a calculated effort to short-circuit Jesus' role as the messianic Son of God. The father of lies quotes from the psalm but craftily misapplies it. Christ's purpose in the Incarnation is not to entertain audiences, satisfy his human desires, or become a puppet king under the authority of the god of this age. No, Jesus comes to earth to die, and to rise again, to redeem sinful and fallen people.

So, how does Jesus respond to Satan's argument from Scripture? He replies, "It is also written: Do not test the Lord your God" (Matt. 4:7). This quotation comes from Deuteronomy 6:16: "Do not test the LORD your God as you tested him at Massah." Massah recalls the people's quarreling with God at Mount Horeb, where they questioned the Lord's wisdom in delivering them from Egypt (Exod. 17:1-7). After obediently striking a rock to provide water for the people and their livestock, Moses names the place *Massah*, which means "testing," and *Meribah*, which means "quarreling" (Exod. 17:7).

Just as the Israelites demanded instant gratification from Yahweh in the wilderness, Satan tempts Jesus to press the Father for a miracle that would theatrically introduce the Son of God and dazzle the crowds. It seems like a reasonable request *if* Jesus' primary purpose is to openly display his deity and thus revel in divine glory. Yet for much of the next three years, Jesus carefully cloaks his deity, as well as his identity as Messiah, until the proper time comes to reveal them both.

To launch his public ministry with a death-defying plunge from the temple's pinnacle does nothing to advance Jesus' mission to seek and to save the lost (Luke 19:10). Further, to engage in such antics at Satan's behest is to succumb to the same temptation the Israelites experienced at Massah.

The third temptation. The devil takes Jesus to "a very high mountain" and shows him all the kingdoms of the world and their splendor (Matt. 4:8). Perhaps this is Mount Hermon, the highest peak in Israel, where Jesus likely is transfigured before Peter, James, and John (Matt. 17:1-9). It is a significant mountain in Israelite history. The headwaters of the Jordan River gush from its base. But also, in the foothills of Mount Hermon lies Caesarea Philippi, a place noted for idolatry, featuring caves believed to be the gates of hades. In any case, Satan gives Jesus a clear view of all the world has to offer, appealing to "the pride in one's possessions" (1 John 2:16).

Further, Satan makes it clear these kingdoms are his to give: "I will give you their splendor and all this authority, because it has been given over to me, and I can give it to anyone I want" (Luke 4:6). Now, Satan's true intentions are revealed. He wants Jesus to worship him, to acknowledge him as sovereign lord of the earth.

If only Jesus grants Satan's request, the world Jesus came to redeem would be his – without the cross. No contentious debates with Israel's religious leaders. No walking the dusty roads of Judea, Galilee, and Samaria. No escaping the plots to kill him, or to make him king. No betrayal at the hand of a close friend. No kangaroo court in Pilate's presence. No brutal beatings. No agonizing crucifixion. Just bend the knee to Satan and everything Jesus came for is granted, no questions asked.

But Jesus sees through Satan's lies. Satan is a usurper. He may well be "the ruler of this world" (see Chapter 12), but he occupies a realm that already belongs to God. He took it through deception and plunged it beneath a curse (Gen. 3). Jesus has not come to barter for the world. He has come to storm the strong man's house and plunder his goods (Matt. 12:29). Further, anything Satan owns or controls is by God's divine permission. The evil one may prowl the earth, but he is a lion on a leash.

Further, Satan has no rightful claim to worship; that is for God alone. That's why Jesus responds to Satan's invitation with these words: "Go away, Satan! For it is written: Worship the Lord your God, and serve only him" (Matt. 4:10). Jesus quotes from Deuteronomy 6:13, which follows the most well-known portion of the *Shema*, the centerpiece of daily morning prayer services, and considered by some the most essential prayer in all of Judaism: "Listen, Israel: The LORD our God, the LORD is one. Love the LORD your God with all your heart, with all your soul, and with all your strength" (Deut. 6:4-5).

Jesus would come to reign over the kingdoms of this world, but not through a deal with the devil, the worship of a false god, or by any other means than the way of the cross. Jesus commands Satan to go away, and the devil departs. Interestingly, the angels Satan promised to be a safety net for Jesus beneath the pinnacle of the temple now come and serve him (Matt. 4:11).

Lessons from the Wilderness

What may we learn from Jesus' victorious encounter over the evil one? A few observations may prove instructive. First, maintaining relational harmony with the Father is key to resisting the devil. Jesus came to do the Father's will. Jesus' conversations with the Father, and his proclamation of the Father's will, punctuate his earthly ministry.

Second, the indwelling Holy Spirit enables us to successfully resist temptation. While the Spirit steers Jesus into the wilderness, the Spirit does not abandon him there. Rather, he is present with Jesus the entire time. The Spirit, too, helps followers of Jesus pray, proclaim, and persevere. He has sealed us and is the guarantee of our future glorification. In the meantime, he indwells our human spirits, residing in the holy of holies of our bodily temples (1 Cor. 3:16; 6:19).

Third, the Word of God is our best defense. Paul calls God's Word the sword of the Spirit (Eph. 6:17). With the inspired, inerrant, infallible, and authoritative Word of God, we extinguish Satan's flaming arrows of temptation. Scripture memorization is the best way to carry the sword of the Spirit in our sheath, ready to be drawn at a moment's notice.

Fourth, we should realize that the devil's temptations of Jesus are designed specifically for him as the Son of God. They are not necessarily the model of how the evil one lures us into sin. Further, since Satan may only be in one place at a time, it's more likely that he sends evil spirits to tempt us, although he certainly may choose to buffet us himself.

Fifth, Satan and evil spirits often employ common tools, which Satan uses to tempt Jesus. Demons tempt us with physical cravings, the delights of the world, and our desire for personal prestige and power.[6] These are the things of the world, which John outlines in 1 John 2:15-16. The lust of the flesh, the lust of the eyes, and the sinful pride of life are common human vulnerabilities.

We experience the physical world with our five senses. Satan desires that we delight in sensual pleasures in ways God never intended. We dream the possible – or perhaps the impossible – with our imaginations. And while thinking about and planning for the future is no sin, we may be drawn into sin if we allow the cares of this world to consume us (Matt. 13:22; Jas. 1:14-15).

We should fear no human being or consider ourselves less worthy to display the *imago dei* – the image of God. But when thoughts of our own selves take us to imagined heights above others, we violate the very example of Christ, who, being equal with the Father, humbled himself and became obedient unto the point of death on a cross (Phil. 2:5-11).

Sixth, as in his wilderness encounter with Jesus, Satan does not always tempt us to do something inherently evil. In fact, he often woos us to take something God created for good – an activity related to food, sex, relationships, possessions, authority – and experience it in ways that run counter to God's design. The apostle Paul offers a fairly comprehensive list of sins the devil makes irresistible: sexual immorality, moral impurity, promiscuity, idolatry, sorcery, hatreds, strife, jealousy, outbursts of anger, selfish ambitions, dissensions, factions, envy, drunkenness, carousing, and anything similar (Gal. 5:19-21).

Seventh, Satan tempts in ways that make us think we are part of something divine. In some of his sneakier work, the devil tempts us through false signs, wonders, and other miracles, counterfeiting the true supernatural work of God (Mark 13:22; 2 Cor. 11-12; Rev. 13:13-14).

We are wonderfully created beings who bear the image of God.

Our creator values us and desires an intimate, everlasting relationship with us. We are built to live forever, and we are invited to a glorified eternity. But our flesh is weak (Mark 14:38), we have feet of clay, and we are easily lured away from complete dependence upon God (Jas. 1:14).

Even so, in the end, we are responsible for the choices we make, and we bear the penalty of our own sins, unless we take part in the great exchange – in which our sins are imputed to Jesus, and his righteousness is imputed to us.

We should always keep in mind the words of the writer of Hebrews about Jesus:

> For we do not have a high priest who is unable to sympathize with our weaknesses, but one who has been tempted in every way as we are, yet without sin. Therefore, let us approach the throne of grace with boldness, so that we may receive mercy and find grace to help us in time of need (Heb. 4:15-16).

1 Thessalonians 3:5

The apostle Paul is deeply concerned about the Thessalonians. Not that long ago, he and Silas led a missionary team westward out of Philippi on the Roman road known as the *Via Egnatia*. They came to Thessalonica, the strategic capital city of the Roman province of Macedonia. This large port city on the Aegean Sea was populated with idol worshipers, as well as those devoted to emperor worship.

In typical fashion, Paul and his comrades located the city's synagogue and began reasoning from the Scriptures with the Jews, many of whom believed Paul's bold declaration, "This Jesus I am proclaiming to you is the Messiah" (Acts 17:3). Some devout Greeks who worshiped at the synagogue also were persuaded, along with several prominent women. The church at Thessalonica was established.

But many Jews in the city rejected Paul's message and became jealous of Paul and Silas. They stirred up an angry crowd that invaded the home where the missionaries resided. Unable to find Paul, they dragged the homeowner (Jason) and other new believers before city authorities, who demanded a security payment to ensure against further disturbances. That night, the Thessalonian believers sent Paul and Silas to Berea, where they continued their missionary work (Acts 17:1-10).

From Berea, Paul went to Athens, but he longed to see the Thessalonians again. When his sorrow became nearly too intense to bear, he sent Timothy to encourage the Thessalonians and report on their progress (1 Thess. 3:2). Timothy returned with positive news: Although the church suffered persecution, the people held fast to the faith and served the Lord out of love and eagerness for their Savior's return. At the same time, they exposed certain doctrinal misunderstandings in the church.

Now in Corinth, Paul writes to his Thessalonian brothers and sisters in response to Timothy's report. The third chapter of Paul's first letter to the Thessalonians begins with these words:

> Therefore, when we could no longer stand it, we thought it was better to be left alone in Athens. And we sent Timothy, our brother and God's coworker in the gospel of Christ, to strengthen and encourage you concerning your faith, so that no one will be shaken by these afflictions. For you yourselves know that we are appointed to this. In fact, when we were with you, we told you in advance that we were going to experience affliction, and as you know, it happened. For this reason, when I could no longer stand it, I also sent him to find out about your faith, fearing that *the tempter* had tempted you and that our labor might be for nothing (1 Thess. 3:1-5, emphasis added).

Like Matthew, Paul calls the evil one *the tempter*. In a city of strong demonic influence, played out in the worship of idols and Caesar, along with strong Jewish opposition to the gospel, Paul worries aloud that Satan might lure these new believers away from their foundational faith and godly lifestyle. As Gene Green notes, Paul's focus is on the fruit of his labor, which is in danger because "this young church, bereft of leadership and struggling without full Christian instruction, faced Satan-inspired persecution that was designed to lead them to give up and abandon their alliance with the living God."[7]

Paul is not concerned that they have lost their salvation, for Paul is a champion of God's covenant promises with respect to redemption. However, he must wonder: Would the Thessalonians return to idol worship to avoid persecution? Would they allow unbiblical pagan and Jewish practices to water down their faith, which is still in its infancy? Would they forsake their fervent love of Jesus if they felt Paul had abandoned them?

Paul is concerned that the tempter may have wreaked havoc on his brothers and sisters in Thessalonica. There is no guarantee that believers who start strongly in the Christian faith won't finish with a whimper. Paul knows this, and he sees his encouragement of fellow believers as a vital part of his ministry. On occasion, the apostle acknowledges the possibility that his labors are in vain (Phil. 2:16), his running of the race is in vain (Gal. 2:2), or his ministry is in vain (1 Cor. 15:10; 2 Cor. 6:1). Even so, he expresses confidence that his work among the Thessalonians "was not without result" (1 Thess. 2:1).

Notice how Paul gives us insight into the evil one's nature and activities. For starters, the tempter loves a vacuum. When leaders like Paul move on to new places of ministry, especially when little time has been devoted to raising up new leaders, Satan moves in with a vengeance. Paul knows this about Satan and fears the evil one has ridden the slipstream of the apostle's departure from Thessalonica.

Second, the tempter always exacts a price. He stirs up persecution in Thessalonica, mostly at the hands of Jewish leaders who reject Jesus as Messiah, but also from idol worshipers and members of the cult of Caesar. This persecution is meant to discourage new or immature believers, leading them to wrongly assume faithfulness to God must be grounded in circumstances rather than in the Lord's covenant promises.

Third, the tempter always sows tares in Christ's wheat fields. Jesus makes this clear in the parable of the wheat and weeds (Matt. 13:24-30, 36-43). Wherever a work of God takes root, Satan is there to sow discord, doubt, and dissension. Just as tares in Jesus' parable intertwine their roots with those of the wheat, and even look similar to wheat as the two grow together, false teachers in the church often use persuasive words and charismatic personalities to make them virtually indistinguishable from genuine leaders. And as the farmer allows wheat and tares to grow together until harvest time, so Jesus allows false teachers to spring up in the church until the Son of Man returns in judgment.

Fourth, the tempter makes the status quo attractive. Surely, there was no persecution when the Thessalonians gathered in the synagogue or at the idol's temple. But when they entrusted their lives to Jesus, they necessarily moved outside their comfort zones. As Satan keeps turning up the pressure, these new followers of Jesus are now forced to examine their hearts and ask whether the pain is really worth it.

Fifth, the tempter generates doubt. If Jesus fed the crowds, turned water into wine, healed the sick, cast out demons, and even raised the dead, why doesn't he protect his followers from persecution and doctrinal doubts? Why are Jews in the synagogue resisting the gospel so strongly? Why do idol worshipers reject the story of Jesus? The Jews and idol worshipers aren't facing persecution, and they defend their beliefs with great vigor. Maybe they have a point. Further, if Paul really *is* for the Thessalonians, why isn't he there suffering beside them?

Sixth, the tempter twists the truth. Thankfully, Paul discovers that the Thessalonians are staying the course, serving God faithfully. Even so, they are yet babes in Christ, and they reveal a number of misunderstandings about doctrinal issues. If Satan can turn these questions into open debates, perhaps he can drive a wedge between those whom Paul has urged to be united in Christ. Thessalonica is a key city. If the church's influence there can be tainted, the gospel they spread might be sullied as well.

Tim Shenton writes:

> The devil's main object is to stop people from believing, but when he fails his next aim is to destroy their faith. He may use intellectual arguments to cause us to doubt the Bible and its message; he may use ridicule and verbal abuse to shame us into turning from Christ; he may tempt us into sin and then declare that God has abandoned us because of our unfaithfulness; or he may appear as an angel of light to persuade us that there is a better way. But whatever his method, true faith withstands persecution and deception.[8]

Unlike Satan's personal, direct challenges to Jesus in the wilderness, the evil one works through secondary agents in Thessalonica – unbelieving Jews, idolaters, and persecution – to entice immature followers of Jesus to abandon their faith. Unlike his bold appeals to Jesus for miraculous proofs of divinity, the evil one sows doubts in the minds of Thessalonian believers, perhaps causing them to wonder why Jesus doesn't miraculously deliver them from their time of testing. And unlike his blasphemous plea for Jesus' worship, the devil entices the Thessalonians to consider returning to Judaism, idolatry, or the cult of Caesar in exchange for a more comfortable life.

While the tempter's tactics may change, his strategies remain the same. He calls us to love the world – that is, the world order alienated from and in rebellion against God, and condemned for its godlessness. He appeals to "the lust of the flesh, the lust of the eyes, and the pride in one's possessions" (1 John 2:16). He calls us to focus on the here and now so we take our eyes off the eternal, forgetting that Satan's domain has an expiration date but God's kingdom does not (1 John 2:17).

In addition, Satan promises us instant gratification, while glossing over the damning consequences. And he delights in our worship of anyone or anything other than the only one to whom true worship is due. He is the tempter, and our only hope of defeating him is to rest in the finished work of the one who rebuffed the devil's taunts in the wilderness and destroyed the evil one on the cross.

Temptation, Testing, Trial

What's the difference between a temptation, a test, and a trial? It may help to briefly examine these English words as they appear in Scripture. New Testament writers use the Greek verb *peirazo* and the noun *peirasmos* nearly sixty times in a variety of ways. English translators render these words "tempt / temptation," "test / testing," or "try / trial," based on the context.

For example, *peirazo* may refer to a temptation to think or do something contrary to God's will (Gal. 6:1; Jas. 1:13). Both times Satan is called *the tempter* in the New Testament, that's the meaning we should take away (Matt. 4:3; 1 Thess. 3:5). Because he is the father of lies, a murderer from the beginning, and the unbowed enemy of God, Satan always tempts people to sin. However, God has armed us with everything we need for life and godliness, as Peter writes:

> His divine power has given us everything required for life and godliness through the knowledge of him who called us by his own glory and goodness. By these he has given us very great and precious promises, so that through them you may share in the divine nature, escaping the corruption that is in the world because of evil desire (2 Pet. 1:3-4; cf. 2 Tim. 3:16-17).

In addition, *peirazo* may mean testing, such as testing to discover the genuineness of one's faith (2 Cor. 13:5; Rev. 2:2). On occasion, Jesus puts his disciples to the test (John 6:6). These divine tests are designed to strengthen our faith and lead us to rely more fully on the Lord.

However, there are times human beings put God to the test, revealing a lack of trust in him (Acts 5:9; 15:10; 1 Cor. 10:9; Heb. 3:8-9). And then, there are times the opponents of Jesus test him by seeking to entrap him with trick questions (Matt. 16:1; 19:3; 22:18, 35; Mark 10:2; 12:15; John 8:6). Their motives reveal the evil nature of the test.

Next, the noun *peirasmos* sometimes is translated "trial." It may refer to a testing for our own good, even if the trial comes from opponents of Jesus and his followers. Or, it may mean a different kind of trial: a temptation to sin.

New Testament writers often use a different verb, *dokimazo*, to convey the idea of testing, approving, or critically examining something to determine its genuineness.[9] When God tests us, it's for our own good. He seeks to strengthen us spiritually, to rely on him more fully, and to become more fit to thrive in a sinful and fallen world. Followers of Jesus are exhorted to "test," or examine, ourselves regarding our own faithfulness (1 Cor. 11:28; 2 Cor. 13:5), as well as our own work (Gal. 6:4).

Paul encourages us to know the will of God and "approve" it (Rom. 2:18), and to "test" or "discern" what pleases the Lord (Eph. 5:10; Phil. 1:10). Peter writes of the testing of our faith by fire, resulting in praise and glory at the revelation of Jesus (1 Pet. 1:7). John tells us to "test" the spirits – those who claim divine gifting for service – to see if they are of God (1 John 4:1). Finally, Paul gives us a good general rule: "Test everything" (1 Thess. 5:21).

Considering these terms together, Christians should not be surprised when testing or trials come, any more than we should let temptation catch us off guard. Rather, we should rejoice in trials and testing because we are sharing the sufferings of Christ (1 Pet. 4:12-13).

There are abundant examples of trials, or testing, throughout Scripture. The Israelites endure a time of testing during their forty years in the desert, to see if they remain faithful to God (Heb. 3:8). The disciples stay with Jesus during his trials (Luke 22:28). Trials punctuate Paul's ministry (Acts 20:19). Peter urges his readers to look beyond the present trials to their heavenly status in Christ (1 Pet. 1:6), and later he reminds them that God knows how to rescue the godly from trials (2 Pet. 2:9). Jesus promises to spare his followers in Philadelphia from "the hour of trial that is going to come on the whole world to test the inhabitants of the earth" (Rev. 3:10 NIV).

While it may run contrary to our thinking, we should count it all joy when we experience times of testing, knowing they are producing endurance (Jas. 1:2-3; cf. 1 Pet. 1:7).

As William Mounce notes, "God does indeed sometimes put our faith to the test (Heb. 11:17) and at other times allows us to be tested (1 Cor. 10:13), but it is important to note that God himself never tempts us with evil (Jas. 1:13)."[10]

In summary, when we use the words *tempt* and *temptation* with respect to Scripture, we should keep in mind that they refer to the work of Satan, evil spirits, and even human beings to entice us to sin. The purpose of temptation is to bring out the worst in us. However, God never tempts anyone to sin, nor can he be tempted to sin.

The words *try* or *trial* may refer to temptations to sin, or to testing for our own good. As Roger Barrier notes, "the purpose of trials is to refine our lives and leave us with a purer, stronger faith, as well as a character that God can bless and use."[11]

And the words *test* or *testing* convey the idea of approving or critically examining something to determine its genuineness. The purpose of testing is to learn and apply biblical truths so we become consistently more like Jesus. Juli Camarin writes:

> Testing ... is God trusting us to make the right choice.... He entrusts us with kingdom principles, watching how we respond and act. Faithfulness in these tests [is] the road to promotion in His kingdom because He knows He can trust us to do what He has instructed.[12]

The best way to establish the correct application of these terms is to consider the context. Or, as Sharon Beekmann points out, "the motive of the agent determines whether one is tested, tempted, or on trial."[13]

Lead Us Not ...

Before moving on, we should wrestle with a hard saying in the Lord's Prayer: "And lead us not into temptation" (Matt. 6:13 KJV). We know

God cannot be tempted with sin, nor does he tempt us to sin. So why would he ever *lead* us into temptation?

Craig Blomberg notes that "these words seem best taken as 'don't let us succumb to temptation' (cf. Mark 14:38) or 'don't abandon us to temptation.'"[14] Of course, we do at times surrender to temptation, but never because God has failed to provide an alternative (1 Cor. 10:13).

Leon Morris adds this observation: "God tempts no one. But the worshiper knows his own weakness and in this prayer seeks to be kept far from anything that may bring him to sin."[15]

Finally, William Mounce offers this insight:

> One way of handling the biblical data is to draw a sharp distinction between trials and temptations. God does not induce anyone to sin, and in fact we are to admit our dependence on God as we pray for protection from temptation. However, trials and sufferings will occur so that our faith can be purified, shown to be true – all of which enables us to grow up into Christian maturity.[16]

So, it appears biblically faithful to understand Jesus' hard saying – "And lead us not into temptation" – as a model for us in prayer. We may come to the Father in full assurance of his love because we are his adopted children. We may plead our case before his holy bench because we are clothed in the righteousness of Christ. And we may escape the fiery darts of the tempter because the Spirit of God indwells us and arms us with his word.

Therefore, we may rightly appeal to the Father for deliverance from the tempter, fully aware of our human vulnerabilities, yet wholly resting in the triune God's sovereign work of redemption. The tempter may win many battles between now and the return of Christ, but ultimately, he is a defeated foe.

Summary

Key takeaways about *the tempter*:

(1) The New Testament calls Satan *the tempter* in only two places

(Matt. 4:3; 1 Thess. 3:5), while depicting him as a source of temptation elsewhere. But from Genesis through Revelation, the evil one marks his territory with unrelenting attacks on everyone from Adam to the second Adam (Jesus).

(2) By far, Satan's number one activity is temptation. His goal is to drive a wedge between God and human beings made in God's image.

(3) While Satan is a master of temptation, God limits what he can do to harm us. For example, Satan operates under the sovereignty of God; therefore, the evil one must have God's permission to attack us. Satan also lacks God's divine attributes, such as omniscience, omnipotence, and omnipresence. Further, God prevents Satan from tempting us beyond our ability to resist sin. The Lord even provides a way of escape and equips us for spiritual warfare with the "full armor of God."

(4) Satan's temptations of Jesus in the wilderness mirror the evil one's attacks on us. Clearly, the devil appeals to "the lust of the flesh, the lust of the eyes, and the pride in one's possessions" (1 John 2:16). Jesus' victory over temptation offers us important lessons. We are to: (a) maintain relational harmony with the Father; (b) trust the indwelling Holy Spirit; (c) rely on the Word of God; (d) realize the special intensity of Satan's attacks on the Son of God; (e) understand Satan's tactics; (f) understand that Satan often woos us to take something God created for good and experience it in ways that run counter to God's design; and (g) beware of Satan's ability to counterfeit the work of God.

(5) Paul's first letter to the Thessalonians offers insight into the tempter's activities. For example, Satan often rushes into the void left by departing leaders in the church. He uses persecution to exact a hefty price for faithfulness. He sows seeds of discord, doubt, and dissension. He twists the truth in ways that magnify the need for discernment and maturity in the body of Christ. And he calls us to focus on the here and now so we take our eyes off the eternal, forgetting that Satan's domain has an expiration date but God's kingdom does not.

(6) We should not confuse temptation with trials or testing.

Temptation refers to the work of Satan, evil spirits, and even human beings to entice us to sin. The purpose of temptation is to bring out the worst in us. However, God never tempts anyone to sin, nor can he be tempted to sin. Further, the Lord often uses trials and testing to strengthen our faith and deepen our trust in him.

Questions for Personal or Group Study

1. Why is temptation Satan's number one activity?
2. In what ways does God limit Satan's ability to tempt us?
3. Read Matthew 4:1-11, which records Satan's temptations of Jesus in the wilderness. To what human frailty does the evil one appeal in each of the three temptations (consider 1 John 2:16)? How does Jesus respond to each temptation?
4. What lessons may we learn from Jesus' victorious encounter with Satan in the wilderness?
5. Read 1 Thessalonians 3:1-5. What does Paul teach us about Satan's nature and activities in these verses?

DECEIVER

He was known as *The Great Impostor* and inspired a 1961 film by the same name. Ferdinand Waldo Demara began his nefarious career during World War II. He borrowed an Army buddy's name, went AWOL, and then faked his own suicide. A string of pseudo careers followed in which Demara portrayed a sheriff's deputy, a doctor of applied psychology, and a child-care expert.

But Demara reached the pinnacle of his quest for fame during the Korean War, when he masqueraded as a surgeon aboard a Canadian Navy destroyer. There, he successfully completed a string of major surgeries before it was discovered that he was no more qualified to gut a fish than to cut open a human. Drummed out of the military but undeterred, Demara moved on to other mock roles. His final gig: a Baptist minister.

Demara's life is a fascinating tale of one man's hunt for genuine status in a make-believe world of his own creation. His success as a deceiver also exposes the soft underbelly of a society whose people are easily duped by one who talks smoothly and claims to serve the greater good.

For Christians, Demara's story is a teachable moment. We are to guard against those who disguise themselves as "servants of righteousness" and infiltrate the church (2 Cor. 11:15). Even more important, we are to be ever vigilant concerning the greatest impostor of all: Satan.

There is no ultimate sense in which society regards deceivers positively. Consider just a few synonyms for *deceiver*: fraud, impostor, charlatan, double-dealer, faker, counterfeiter, bluffer, hypocrite, sham, fabricator, liar.[1] So, when we call people *deceivers*, we are making negative statements about their character. They don't commit isolated acts of duplicity; they habitually engage in deception.

To borrow a biblical example: When Abraham, on two occasions, deceives kings by telling them his wife, Sarah, is in fact his sister, he commits acts of treachery. But when we read the entire story of Abraham's life, we understand that his acts of deception are isolated sins, not true reflections of his character.

But what about the creature Scripture describes as the archetypal deceiver? Is deception an occasional work Satan employs to get his way? Or is he, by his very nature, a deceiver? In this chapter, we see that Satan is so cunning, he entices people to sin, often making us think we are doing something good, when in fact we are ruining ourselves and others.

The First and Last Deceiver

The words *deceive, deceived, deception,* and *deceiver* appear dozens of times in Scripture and refer to many different individuals. Not surprisingly, Satan is the first and last deceiver the Bible portrays.

In Genesis 3:13, Eve complains to God that the serpent *deceived* her; thus, she ate from the forbidden tree. This is the first account of deception in human history. The Hebrew word rendered "deceived" in this verse is *nasha* and means "to beguile, deceive ... lead astray, (mentally) to delude, or (morally) to seduce."[2] Referring back to this event, the apostle Paul uses the Greek *apatao*, which means "to beguile, deceive" or "seduce wholly" (1 Tim. 2:14).[3]

Now, jump to Revelation 20:10, and we're told that the devil who *deceived* the nations is thrown into the lake of fire and sulfur, where the beast and false prophet are. This is the last mention of deception in Scripture.

Between these crucial events, we may trace an arc of the evil one's atrocities, in which he often inspires human beings to deceive one another. Consider these examples:

Genesis 27:12 – Rebekah partners with her son, Jacob, to trick Isaac and thus steal Esau's birthright. Jacob fears being exposed as a deceiver who brings a curse, rather than a blessing, on his head.

Genesis 29:23-25; 31:20-21 – Laban sends Leah, rather than Rachel, to Jacob's honeymoon suite, thus deceiving Jacob. Jacob returns the favor, taking his wives and family away without notifying Laban, a move that invites a charge of deception.

Joshua 7:11 – God accuses the Israelites of deceiving him – or at least trying to deceive him – leading to their humiliating defeat at Ai.

Joshua 9:3-15, 22 – The Gibeonites deceive Joshua into making a treaty with them.

1 Samuel 28:7-12 – King Saul disguises himself in order to deceive the medium at Endor in an effort to recall the departed spirit of Samuel from the abode of the dead.

Ezekiel 14:9-11 – The Lord gets into the act, but in a very different way. He deceives a false prophet in order to expose him and punish him.

Matthew 24:4-5, 11 – Jesus warns against false prophets and false teachers who deceive the people.

Matthew 27:63; John 7:12 – The religious leaders falsely accuse Jesus of being a deceiver.

Romans 16:18 – Divisive people in the church at Rome use smooth talk and flattering words to deceive followers of Jesus.

1 Corinthians 3:18-20; 6:9; 15:33 – Paul warns the Corinthians against falling into deception – including self-deception.

Ephesians 4:14 – Mature believers are no longer "tossed by the waves and blown around by every wind of teaching, by human cunning with cleverness in the techniques of deceit."

Ephesians 5:6; Colossians 2:4 – False teachers use empty but persuasive arguments to deceive Christians.

Revelation 19:20 – The false prophet of the last days deceives people.

But in the end, the deceived and the deceiver belong to God (Job 12:16).

Satan's fiercest work of deception occurs at the beginning and end of Scripture. He deceives Eve in the garden of Eden (Gen. 3:1-7), which leads to Adam's fall and initiates an unbroken string of liars, frauds, charlatans, and shams until the evil one is finally cast into the lake of fire (Rev. 20:10). The apostle Paul reminds us of Satan's subtlety in the garden. He does this to brace us for the unyielding onslaught of deception the evil one commits through false prophets, false teachers, and false messiahs (2 Cor. 11:3; 1 Tim. 2:14).

By the time we get to Revelation, Satan has deceived the whole world (Rev. 12:9). He is imprisoned for a thousand years, a time during which he is prevented from leading the nations astray (Rev. 20:3). Then, released from the abyss for a short time, he picks up where he left off. And he succeeds famously – until Jesus casts him into the place prepared for him: the lake of fire, where he is tormented night and day forever (Rev. 20:8, 10; cf. Matt. 25:41).

From "Trifling with" to "Betray"

The verb *deceive* and its variants come from a number of Hebrew and Greek words. They range in meaning from "trifle with" to "mock," and from "entertain false hopes" to "betray." In the first appearance of the word, Eve complains to God that the serpent "deceived" her (Heb. *nasha*, Gen. 3:13). Citing this tragic event, Paul reminds Timothy that Adam was not "deceived," but the woman was "deceived" and transgressed (Gr. *apatao*, 1 Tim. 2:14).

Other Greek words are applied elsewhere in the New Testament. For example, the noun *dolos* means "deceit." Jesus, Paul, and Peter include deceit among the vices (Mark 7:22; Rom. 1:29; 1 Pet. 2:1), yet Peter makes it clear that Jesus is free of any deceitfulness (1 Pet. 2:22; cf. Isa. 53:9).

The verb *empaizo* denotes mocking or making sport of someone.

Used only in the Gospels, it sometimes carries the meaning of being tricked. For example, the Magi succeed in outwitting King Herod (Matt. 2:16).

The noun *plane* and the verb *planao* include the concept of error or wandering. James writes of those who wander from the truth (Jas. 5:19), while John identifies those who try to deceive others (1 John 2:26). The devil is the prime deceiver (Rev. 12:9), but there are many who hope to deceive others (1 Cor. 6:9; 15:33; Gal. 6:7). However, the one seeking to deceive others often finds himself or herself a victim (2 Tim. 3:13).

Finally, the noun *pseudos* typically is translated "lie," but it also may indicate falsehood, deception, or anything counterfeit (e.g., 1 John 2:27).[4]

It's evident from the Hebrew and Greek words used in Scripture that deception originates in Satan, and he has proven himself a very fine teacher.

The Deceiver's Quiver

The Book of Revelation identifies Satan as "the deceiver," or "the one who leads astray" (*ho planon*; see Rev. 12:9; 20:10; cf. 20:3, 8). The idea behind this term is to entice someone to wander, like the sheep in Jesus' parable (Matt. 18:12-13) or the saints of old forced to wander through a world not worthy of them (Heb. 11:38). As Peter Bolt writes, "The title 'deceiver' reflects Satan's endeavors to lead people away from the love and security of our holy God."[5]

Satan's role as deceiver is grounded in his character as the father of lies (John 8:44; see Chapter 5). His nature – his every tendency – is to distort the truth so that people made as God's imagers miss the very purpose for which God designed them. But how, exactly, does the evil one accomplish this? He sports a quiver of fiery darts and launches them strategically. Let's briefly examine eight arrows the evil one hurls to deceive us.

1. **The well-placed question.** We see this in the garden of Eden, where the serpent challenges Eve's understanding of God's clear

command not to eat of the tree of the knowledge of good and evil: "Did God really say, 'You can't eat from any tree in the garden'?" (Gen. 3:1). This question subtly misquotes God – who made every tree in the garden available to Adam and Eve, except one – and leads Eve to wonder about God's transparency. Did the Lord speak too hastily? Overstate his intentions? Or maybe try to keep Adam and Eve from enjoying the one thing that would truly make them God's imagers?

We see the well-placed question in contemporary society. How often do we hear these questions: Doesn't God just want me to be happy? Is Jesus really the only way to eternal life? How can my desires be wrong since God made me this way? Hasn't society advanced beyond outdated biblical commands? Why shouldn't I live my truth and let other people live theirs? And on it goes.

Often, the first step to wandering away from God is questioning his word. When Eve allows herself to question the Lord, she ends up fallen and then banished.

As Jared Wilson writes:

> The trap is subtle. What Satan continues to do today is what he originally did in the garden: substituting a version of rival facts in place of the real thing. Every sinful decision you and I make begins with the satanic question, "Did God really say …?"[6]

2. The outright lie. Jesus makes it clear that Satan "does not stand in the truth, because there is no truth in him. When he tells a lie, he speaks from his own nature, because he is a liar and the father of lies" (John 8:44). After his well-placed question to Eve, the serpent slings his barefaced lie: "No! You will not die" (Gen. 3:4).

When told forcefully and often enough, a lie may become an acquired truth. An unborn child becomes an expendable blob of tissue. The aged and infirm become pitiable objects of euthanizing in the name of "quality of life." Gender becomes fluid. The covenant of marriage becomes an open-ended agreement. And sexual immorality becomes a liberating right that all enlightened people must celebrate. The outright lie shocks us at first. But over time, we become desensitized and, finally, accepting. The evil one wields blunt-force lies to wear us down.

3. The blinded mind. This is especially true with regard to unbelievers, about whom Paul writes:

> But if our gospel is veiled, it is veiled to those who are perishing. In their case, the god of this age has blinded the minds of the unbelievers to keep them from seeing the light of the gospel of the glory of Christ, who is the image of God (2 Cor. 4:3-4).

Jesus describes this tactic in the parable of the sower. Like birds who swoop down to pluck seeds from a footpath, Satan snatches the word of God's kingdom from unbelievers' hearts before the truth can take hold (Matt. 13:1-9, 18-23).

As John Piper notes, Satan "not only speaks what is false. He hides what is true. He keeps us from seeing the treasure of the gospel. He lets us see facts, even proofs, but not preciousness."[7]

While the evil one keeps unbelievers in the dark, he also strives to obscure our thinking. In this way, we fail to be effective witnesses for Christ. For example, Paul's letter to the Galatians shows how Satan uses false teachers in the church to enslave Christians in a counterfeit works-based form of salvation. He expresses amazement that the Galatians have turned so quickly to "a different gospel" (Gal. 1:6). He uses harsh words to shock them out of their stupor: "You foolish Galatians! Who has cast a spell on you ...?" (3:1).

Further, Paul calls the Galatians to return to the true gospel of salvation by grace (5:1-6). He reminds them that they were running well, but then wonders, "Who prevented you from being persuaded regarding the truth?" (5:7). And he assures them, "But whoever it is that is confusing you will pay the penalty" (5:10). Followers of Jesus must always be on guard against satanically inspired thinking. Indeed, we must "take every thought captive to obey Christ" (2 Cor. 10:5).

4. The masquerade. Writing to the Corinthians, Paul must embrace the "foolishness" of defending his apostleship in light of the "super apostles" who have infiltrated the church (2 Cor. 11:1, 5). These "false apostles" and "deceitful workers," who disguise themselves as apostles of Christ, proclaim "another Jesus," "a different spirit," and "a different gospel" (11:4, 13).

Paul writes that such attacks on the body of Christ should not shock us: "And no wonder! For Satan disguises himself as an angel of light. So it is no great surprise if his servants also disguise themselves as servants of righteousness. Their end will be according to their works" (11:14-15).

Just as the evil one masquerades as the good guy, false teachers ride the Trojan Horse of eloquent persuasion to gain entrance into the church, and then proceed to destroy it. Satan employs not only evil spirits to do his bidding, but willing unbelievers. Professing themselves to be Christians, they weasel their way into unsuspecting churches and, from the inside, teach what Paul describes as "teachings of demons" (1 Tim. 4:1). Jesus also warns about these false prophets, likening them to ravaging wolves in sheep's clothing (Matt. 7:15).

In his farewell address to the Ephesian elders, Paul urges them to vigilance against false teachers: "I know that after my departure savage wolves will come in among you, not sparing the flock. Men will rise up even from your own number and distort the truth to lure the disciples into following them" (Acts 20:29-30). Discernment is key to identifying and countering these minions of the evil one (Phil. 1:9).

5. Lying signs and wonders. Paul describes the last days with these words: "The coming of the lawless one is based on Satan's working, with every kind of miracle, both signs and wonders serving the lie, and with every wicked deception among those who are perishing ..." (2 Thess. 2:9-10).

Jesus also addresses this subject in the Olivet Discourse: "For false messiahs and false prophets will arise and perform great signs and wonders to lead astray, if possible, even the elect" (Matt. 24:24).

At final judgment, some unbelievers protest Christ's sentence of hell, arguing, "Lord, Lord, didn't we prophesy in your name, drive out demons in your name, and do many miracles in your name?"

Unmoved, Jesus responds, "I never knew you. Depart from me, you lawbreakers!" (Matt. 7:22-23).

There's little doubt Satan and his servants use miracles to deceive people – including Christians. Bible commentators disagree as to whether Satan, demons, and false prophets actually perform miracles or merely produce highly persuasive counterfeits. Those who argue in favor of genuine miracles acknowledge that Satan operates under the sovereignty of God and is prohibited from performing such divine acts as raising the dead. Even so, God has granted the devil great leeway as a mighty spirit being, and the evil one may use his powers at will.

Other commentators challenge this view, arguing that the Lord only grants true miracles to his servants to demonstrate God has sent them.[8] That's why we tend to see miracles confined to prophets such as Moses and Elijah, to Jesus, and to the apostles; the signs and wonders are authenticating works (cf. Exod. 4:1-9; Heb. 2:1-4). R. C. Sproul writes, "If the devil could perform miracles, he would be a teacher from the Lord. He can perform lying signs and wonders, but not true miracles, for he is not a teacher from God."[9]

Whether Satan and his servants perform true miracles, or cunning slight-of-hand tricks, the purpose behind these lying signs and wonders is the same: to lead people astray. That's one reason the apostle John urges us not to believe "every spirit" – that is, every person who claims divine gifting for service. Rather, we are to "test the spirits" to see if they are from God (1 John 4:1).

Those who confess biblical truth about the person and work of Christ may be trusted. Those who deny the full deity and full humanity of Jesus – like first-century Docetics, who claimed Jesus only *appeared* to be human – are to be rejected. As one commentary puts it:

> Any time we are in doubt, we are to make sure that what is being taught lines up with what Scripture says. If the miracle worker is teaching something contrary to God's Word, then his miracles, no matter how convincing they seem, are a demonic delusion.[10]

6. Enticement. The previous chapter was devoted to Satan as *the tempter*. As we saw, he is a most persuasive antagonist. He is not omniscient, but he is a highly skilled observer who discovers our human frailties and sinful vulnerabilities – and exploits them all. He strikes hard and low at Jesus in the wilderness, although he fails to entice the Son of God to abandon the path of suffering and death (Matt. 4:1-11). He proves more successful in his pursuit of Judas Iscariot in the hours leading up to the apostle's betrayal of Jesus (Luke 22:3-6).

Paul worries aloud for the Corinthians, admitting, "But I fear that, as the serpent deceived Eve by his cunning, your minds may be seduced from a sincere and pure devotion to Christ" (2 Cor. 11:3). Sure enough, the local church Paul had planted in Corinth a few years earlier is now embracing false teachings about Jesus, the Holy Spirit, and the gospel (2 Cor. 11:4).

James warns how subtly and pervasively sin overtakes us. God cannot be tempted to sin, and he never tempts us. But the evil one sows seeds in our thought processes and – unless we immediately take these thoughts captive – we start down a slippery slope that ends in sin: "But each person is tempted when he is drawn away and enticed by his own evil desire. Then after desire has conceived, it gives birth to sin, and when sin is fully grown, it gives birth to death" (Jas. 1:14-15).

7. Accusation. In the first recorded encounter with humans, the evil one accuses God of denying Adam and Eve what's rightfully theirs: to become like God (Gen. 3:5). We see Satan again in the Book of Job, alleging that Job's loyalty to Yahweh hinges on the hedge of safety God has built around his servant (Job 1:9-11). When the Lord allows Satan to kill Job's children and destroy his property, Job maintains his integrity.

So, Satan returns to Yahweh to seek permission to strike Job's flesh and bones, certain that Job will curse God to his face (Job 2:5). Job endures painful sores from head to toe, along with self-righteous moralizing from his friends, before experiencing a humbling encounter with God, who restores Job's wealth two-fold and grants him seven sons and three daughters – a number equal to those who had perished.

Satan appears again in Zechariah 3 to accuse the high priest, Joshua. This time, the angel of the LORD comes to the rescue, rebuking Satan, forgiving Joshua's sin, and clothing the high priest in fresh garments.

The evil one's accusations continue today. His ultimate defeat is certain, however, and his days of finger-pointing are numbered. In Revelation 12:10, the apostle John writes:

> Then I heard a loud voice in heaven say, The salvation and the power and the kingdom of our God and the authority of his Christ have now come, because the accuser of our brothers and sisters, who accuses them before our God day and night, has been thrown down.

Until that day, the evil one continues prosecuting the people of God. But, just as the high priest, Joshua, had an advocate – the angel of the LORD, or the preincarnate Christ – so we have an advocate, the Lord Jesus, who "is able to save completely those who come to God through him, since he always lives to intercede for them" (Heb. 7:25).

8. Institutional leverage. Satan leads the world astray through false religions, as well as cultural, political, and economic institutions (cf. Rev. 13). For example, major world religions like Islam, Hinduism, and Buddhism express a high regard for Jesus. Yet their Jesus is strictly human, or mysteriously divine, and totally unable to address mankind's greatest need of redemption. Even more damaging are today's counterfeit forms of Christianity, most notably the Church of Jesus Christ of Latter-day Saints (Mormonism) and the Watchtower Bible and Tract Society (Jehovah's Witnesses).

In the former, Jesus is the first eternally existing intelligence to be born into the premortal spirit realm via sexual relations between Elohim (the god of this world) and a heavenly mother. After taking on flesh in mortal probation, Jesus dies on the cross and rises from the dead to reclaim the immortality Adam lost in the garden, thus making it possible for all humans to attain divinity.

In the latter, Jehovah's Witnesses grant Jesus the status of "mighty god," a created archangel who later is refashioned as Jesus the man. Then, after dying on a first-century torture stake to pay for Adam's sin (but not ours), he is spiritually reborn as an exalted archangel.

While there is no reason to question the sincerity of Latter-day Saints and Jehovah's Witnesses, it's clear they proclaim "another Jesus" (2 Cor. 11:4). And their hierarchical organizations enslave millions around the world with the shackles of works-based salvation. The LDS Church claims to be restored Christianity and thus the only true path to salvation. Meanwhile, the Watchtower claims its Governing Body to be God's "faithful and discreet slave" (Matt. 24:45-47), which alone dispenses spiritual food on earth.[11]

Both institutions make exclusive claims, yet neither biblically acknowledges Jesus as "the way, the truth, and the life" (John 14:6).

The Deceiver in the New Testament

Now, let's briefly survey key New Testament passages that describe *the deceiver*. He is:

The Consummate Schemer (2 Cor. 2:11; Eph. 6:11)

> Anyone you forgive, I do too. For what I have forgiven – if I have forgiven anything – it is for your benefit in the presence of Christ, so that we may not be taken advantage of by Satan. For we are not ignorant of his *schemes* (2 Cor. 2:10-11, emphasis added).

> Put on the full armor of God so that you can stand against the *schemes* of the devil (Eph. 6:11, emphasis added).

In each of these passages, Paul points to the evil one's *schemes*. First, as believers, we are to educate ourselves about Satan's plots so we may prevent him from gaining an advantage over us. The Greek word translated "schemes" in 2 Corinthians 2:11 is *noemata* and basically means "thoughts," "purposes," or "designs." No doubt, these are malicious schemes intended to cause harm.

Second, we are to wear God's protective armor, which enables us to stand tall in the face of the devil's blistering attacks. Paul employs a different Greek word for "schemes" in Ephesians 6:11 – *methodeias*, from which we get the English word "methods." The evil one hatches plans and devises great strategies to bring us down in his never-ending spiritual assault.

In 2 Corinthians 2, Paul may be referring to his first epistle, in which he offered instructions concerning a church member having sexual relations with his stepmother (1 Cor. 5:1-5). The apostle had urged the Corinthians to exercise church discipline against this man. Evidently, they followed Paul's command to "hand that one over to Satan for the destruction of the flesh" (1 Cor. 5:5).

Now, however, the church seems reluctant to forgive the repentant sinner and restore him to fellowship, which is the goal of church discipline in the first place. The Corinthians' unforgiving spirit unwittingly grants Satan an opportunity to gain advantage over them, or defraud them of the warm fellowship that is graciously theirs.

This story illustrates how important it is for the Christian community to balance church discipline and charity. One without the other plays into the evil one's hands. Satan can ruin a church that fails to rebuke sinners. At the same time, he can just as easily triumph when a church refuses to forgive chastened sinners who repent. As David Garland notes, "Paul reveals that showing forgiveness is one way for the church to close the door on Satan's evil designs to destroy it.... Satan is powerless before a united community filled with love and humble forgiveness."[12]

In Ephesians 6, Paul stresses the necessity of spiritual armor – truth, righteousness, readiness with the gospel, faith, salvation, and the Word of God – by which we take our stand in the struggle against Satan and his armies (Eph. 6:11-17). We explore the armor of God more fully in Chapter 15.

Until then, it's important to remember that Paul is under no delusions about the Christian life. It is an ongoing battle against a ruthless foe who is well-armed, wily, and relentless. Satan is a brilliant military strategist. Nevertheless, Paul exhorts us to study the devil's ways so he won't outfox us, and to leverage the armor and weapons the Lord supplies so the evil one won't retake sacred ground.

A Cunning Seducer (2 Cor. 11:3-4)

> But I fear that, as the serpent deceived Eve by his *cunning*, your minds may be *seduced* from a sincere and pure devotion to Christ. For if a person comes and preaches another Jesus, whom we did not preach, or you receive a different spirit, which you had not received, or a different gospel, which you had not accepted, you put up with it splendidly (2 Cor. 11:3-4, emphasis added).

In his first letter to the Corinthians, Paul depicted Christ as the *last Adam* and *second man* in order to show how Jesus' death and resurrection reversed the effects of the Fall and secured a glorious future for us (1 Cor. 15:45-49). Borrowing from that analogy in his second letter, Paul now likens the church to a second Eve. As Adam and Eve became one flesh (Gen. 2:24), Christ and the church are joined in a covenant relationship.

The image of salvation as betrothal between Christ and his followers is consistent with first-century Jewish marriage customs involving two separate ceremonies: the betrothal, and the nuptial ceremony that consummates the marriage. Usually, a year separates the two events, yet the betrothed young woman legally is regarded as the man's wife and obligates herself to remain a virgin. The contract is binding; only death or a formal bill of divorce may end it. If the betrothed woman cheats on her husband, she is considered an adulteress. She may be banished under Roman rule or stoned under Old Testament law (Deut. 22:23-27).

Since Paul spent considerable time planting the church in Corinth, he feels a personal responsibility, as spiritual father, to ensure the church's faithfulness to the Lord. But in his absence, Corinthian believers have welcomed seducers into the church – self-proclaimed "super apostles" who teach "another Jesus," "a different spirit," and "a different gospel" (2 Cor. 11:4-5).

Paul worries that the church at Corinth – Christ's betrothed bride – is falling prey to Satan's deception in the same way Eve allowed the serpent to seduce her. Some segments of Jewish tradition hold that Satan, masquerading as a good angel, sexually seduced Eve.[13] But Paul has spiritual debauchery in mind, and the text of Genesis 3 in no way suggests a sexual encounter between the serpent and Eve.

Rather, as the serpent enticed Eve to disobey God, the "super apostles" at Corinth beguile Christ's followers to embrace counterfeit doctrines. As David Garland notes, "Paul sounds the alarm that the same tempter who flattered and deceived Eve has ensnared them. Satan always lies coiled, ready to strike at the first sign of weakness and to exchange sugarcoated lies for the unvarnished truth."[14]

It's worth noting another similarity between Eve and the church at Corinth. The Lord does not exonerate Eve because she fell into seduction; neither will he pardon the Corinthians. The reason is straightforward: Both Eve and the church invite deception with eyes wide open. Eve is deceived "by exciting the unholy feelings in her heart."[15] The Corinthians show a strong leaning toward willful error, believing themselves to be kings who already reign (1 Cor. 4:8). Such arrogance makes them easy marks for the master of deception.

Paul writes that the serpent deceived Eve by his cunning. The Greek word rendered "deceived" is *exapatao* and means "to seduce wholly." It is stronger than mere temptation, for it results in both a victor and a victim. Eve does not struggle to a standoff; she succumbs. Satan emerges victorious and then vanishes from the scene. The serpent employs *cunning* to triumph over Eve. The Greek word here is *panourgia*. It means "craftiness," "a specious or false wisdom," "trickiness or sophistry."[16] In other words, Satan offers honey-laced poison to Eve, and she swallows it whole.

Thus, Eve's story serves as a backdrop for the danger the Corinthians face – a danger of wanton deception. Like Eve, the

Corinthians welcome their tempters and listen to their seductive arguments. And like Eve, the Corinthians have opened their minds to the crafty manipulator behind the "super apostles."

In fact, Paul states his concern that their *minds,* like Eve's, may be seduced from a sincere and pure devotion to Christ. Satan works on our thoughts to dislodge us from a firm spiritual footing. He raises doubts, entices us with what-if questions, whispers half-truths into our cupped ears, stuns us with pain and sorrow, and slowly dulls our consciences so that resistance is futile and sin becomes inevitable.

The word Paul uses for "minds" here is *noemata* and means "mental perceptions," "thoughts and purposes."[17] That's why Paul urges us to "take every thought captive to obey Christ" (2 Cor. 10:5). The serpent's seductive power over Eve is his persuasive words. The cunning of the "super apostles" is their attractive but counterfeit gospel and their charismatic charm. As Paul Barnett writes, "A sincere devotion to Christ is possible only where the true and authentic gospel of Christ is taught and heard."[18]

A Master of Disguise (2 Cor. 11:13-15)

> For such people are false apostles, deceitful workers, *disguising* themselves as apostles of Christ. And no wonder! For Satan *disguises* himself as an angel of light. So it is no great surprise if his servants also *disguise* themselves as servants of righteousness. Their end will be according to their works (2 Cor. 11:13-15, emphasis added).

Paul continues to expose the "super apostles" in Corinth for what they are: deceitful workers who disguise themselves as apostles of Christ. They present a triple threat to the church as they proclaim "another Jesus," "a different spirit," and "a different gospel" (2 Cor. 11:4). And yet, the church welcomes them with open arms. That's because the "super apostles" successfully disguise themselves as true apostles. They don't necessarily oppose the apostle Paul, but they claim to have eclipsed him in spiritual gifts and public ministry.

For example, their speaking skills are far superior – or so they say

– and their boldness in the church projects a contagious confidence that Paul seems to lack, as evidenced by his humility and self-inflicted poverty (2 Cor. 10:10; 11:5-10). If that isn't enough, Paul's physical presence is "weak" (2 Cor. 10:10), no doubt in part from the beatings, stoning, shipwrecks, and other hardships he faced as he carried on his apostolic ministry. The "super apostles" likely are physically fit and attractive, while Paul, if alive on earth today, would never make it on Christian television. In all of this, the false apostles are rotten to the core but come wrapped in the clever disguise of eloquent purveyors of the gospel.

This shouldn't take us by surprise, writes Paul. The "super apostles" are simply following the lead of Satan, who masquerades as an angel of light. Three times in 2 Corinthians 11:13-15, Paul uses a form of the word rendered "disguise" in English. The "super apostles" are *disguising* themselves as apostles of Christ. Satan *disguises* himself as an angel of light. And the false apostles, whom Paul identifies as Satan's servants, *disguise* themselves as servants of righteousness.

The Greek verb *metaschematizo* means "to change in fashion or appearance."[19] This is not a change of character but of clothing, an outward transformation for the purpose of hiding one's true nature and intentions. Various English translations seek to capture this meaning, rendering the word as "masquerade" (NIV), "disguise" (NASB, ESV), and "transformed" (KJV). The Message uses "posing," "dressing up," and "masquerade."

Paul's reference to Satan disguising himself as "an angel of light" perhaps draws more from popular Jewish tradition than from Scripture, although the serpent who appears to Eve in Genesis 3 may be a dazzling heavenly being. In the Jewish apocryphal *Life of Adam and Eve*, Satan transforms himself into the brightness of angels and pretends to grieve with Eve, who sits weeping by the Tigris River (9:1). In the *Apocalypse of Moses*, Eve recalls her seduction: "Satan appeared in the form of an angel and sang hymns like the angels. And I bent over the wall and saw him, like an angel" (17:1-2).

In any case, the evil one is a master of disguise. When he appears, people don't fall at his feet as dead men, the way they respond in holy fear of Christ (cf. Rev. 1:17). Rather, he is alluring, attractive, seductive, and glamorous. He approaches with beauty and flattery. He offers special knowledge, or unique privilege, or exalted position. His minions feed on the same human frailties.

Corinthian believers, who want to become rich and reign like kings (1 Cor. 4:8), "are particularly susceptible to a false gospel dispensed by jaunty, diamond-studded apostles that appeals to their innate human pride and desire to be special. Swollen with pride themselves, these rivals gull [take advantage of] the Corinthians by stoking their vanity."[20]

Satan's attacks on the church are seldom frontal. They don't need to be. The evil one is contented with false apostles, who gain a foothold in a community of believers and destroy them with flattery and false doctrine from the inside out. Paul's description of these "deceitful workers" employs the adjective *dolios*, which means someone who deals dishonestly or treacherously with others. The false apostles' misrepresentation of their missionary work does not result from self-deception or even prideful exaggeration. The masquerade is quite deliberate.

That's why Paul concludes these verses with the assurance that the false teachers' end "will be according to their works" (2 Cor. 11:15). Just as Corinthian believers stand one day before the judgment seat of Christ, resulting in varying degrees of rewards (Rom. 14:10; 1 Cor. 3:11-15; 2 Cor. 5:10), the "super apostles" are to be summoned before the great white throne and punished for their evil deeds. Not surprisingly, their role model also is banished to the lake of fire (Rev. 20:11-15; cf. Matt. 25:41).

The Original Usurper (1 Tim. 2:12-14)

> I do not allow a woman to teach or to have authority over a man; instead, she is to remain quiet. For Adam was formed first, then Eve. And Adam was not deceived, but the woman was deceived and transgressed (1 Tim. 2:12-14).

Satan is a usurper by nature. That is, he seizes authority not rightfully his. He rises up against God in an effort to displace his creator as the object of worship (see Chapter 1). He's also a usurper by proxy, acting through intermediate means to attack God and God's people. For example, he incites David to number his troops (1 Chron. 21:1; cf. 2 Sam. 24:1).[21] He fills the hearts of Ananias and Sapphira to seek undue credit for an otherwise good deed (Acts 5:1-11). He takes control of Judas Iscariot, inspiring him to betray Jesus (Luke 22:3; John 13:27). And he gives the antichrist his power, throne, and authority in the last days (Rev. 13:2).

But the earliest example of Satan operating as a usurper by proxy is his temptation of Eve in the garden. Paul alludes to this tragic event in his instructions to Timothy, urging the young pastor not to grant women authority over men in the local church. Paul is not prohibiting women from speaking or praying publicly in the church, for we see women like Phoebe, Priscilla, and the virgin daughters of Philip taking active roles in the community of faith.

This is not a question of value, for Paul is clear that all people – men and women alike – are equally guilty before God as sinners and equally welcome in his kingdom (Rom. 3:10, 23; Gal. 3:27-29). Nor is this a matter of giftedness for service, as if God has somehow endowed men with superior spiritual gifts, for Paul is clear that the Holy Spirit assigns these gifts to all, and all gifts are essential to a healthy community of faith (1 Cor. 12). Finally, this is not an issue of favoritism, for God is no respecter of persons (Acts 10:34 KJV).

For Paul, this is an issue of authority. God has reserved the role of pastor (elder, overseer) for men (1 Tim. 3:1-7; Tit. 1:5-9). And now, Paul offers two reasons why this is so: the order of creation and the order of the Fall. God forms Adam first, and then creates Eve as a helper for him. Both are commanded to "subdue" the earth and "rule" over its creatures (Gen. 1:28), but Adam clearly has primary responsibility as the first-created and the first one entrusted with God's revelation.

We should note that chronological order is not the sole factor. Animals are created before Adam, and yet he is granted dominion over them. The point here is that mankind consists of a pair (Adam and Eve). Eve is intended as a companion to Adam. Their relationship is designed to be complementary, not competitive.[22]

Second, Paul writes, "Adam was not deceived, but the woman was deceived and transgressed" (1 Tim. 2:14). For reasons not fully revealed in Scripture, Satan approaches Eve rather than Adam as his proxy to usurp God's authority. Perhaps this is because Eve is not fully acquainted with the nature of the prohibited tree and therefore is at a disadvantage.[23]

In any case, the evil one successfully entices Eve to transgress, and Eve, in turn, convinces Adam to disobey God's direct command not to partake of the tree of the knowledge of good and evil. All of this results in the Fall – and in the subsequent curse, which continues to poison God's good creation today.

Our choices have consequences. Just as Adam's willful rebellion against God leads to disastrous results for all humanity, Eve's deception is a precursor to the Fall. While more could be written about Paul's instructions to Timothy, along with the many sexist abuses in the professing church today, the main purpose of this passage is to illustrate that Satan deceives Eve and, by proxy, overturns God's order of authority.

Paul ends this section of 1 Timothy with a curious message for women: "But she will be saved through childbearing, if they continue in faith, love, and holiness, with good sense" (1 Tim. 2:15). This is a difficult statement that invites various interpretations. But the most likely meaning is that, rather than demand authoritative positions in the church, women may find true fulfillment through childbearing. This is in keeping with God's command before the Fall to be fruitful and multiply (Gen. 1:28).

In both 1 Timothy 2 and Titus 2, Paul declares that wives have a God-ordained role to play in caring for children and the home. As Denny Burk notes:

> This is not claiming that a woman must have children in order to be
> saved. It is not even teaching that a woman must be married to be

saved. But for those women who are married, God assigns a special responsibility to care for the home.[24]

While this view is not without its difficulties, it seems to harmonize best with Paul's teaching throughout the New Testament.

Chief of a Global Enterprise (Rev. 12:9)

> So the great dragon was thrown out – the ancient serpent, who is called the devil and Satan, the one who deceives the whole world. He was thrown to earth, and his angels with him (Rev. 12:9).

Finally, we see the scope of Satan's work as deceiver. John watches the cosmic battle between Michael the archangel and the great dragon. Michael prevails, and the dragon and his angels are cast down to earth (Rev. 12:7-12). We addressed this passage in greater detail in Chapter 2. For our purposes now, however, we focus on Satan's role as chief executive of a sinister global enterprise. John writes that the evil one "deceives the whole world." But what does the apostle mean by this?

As we explore in Chapter 12, the Greek word often translated "world" (*kosmos*) may be interpreted in a number of ways, from the planet Earth to the world system under Satan's control. But John uses a different Greek word here: *oikoumene*, which occurs fifteen times in the New Testament and, for the most part, refers to the entire inhabited earth.[25]

In this sense, the gospel is to be proclaimed to all the world (Matt. 24:14; Rom. 10:18). Christ is to judge the world at the end of time (Acts 17:31). Other general references to the world as the inhabited earth include: Luke 2:1 (Caesar's whole empire); Luke 4:5 (kingdoms of the world Satan shows Jesus); Acts 19:27 (the world that worships the goddess Artemis); Hebrews 1:6 (the inhabited world into which Christ is born); and Revelation 3:10 (the whole world that faces a time of testing).

So, John sees the great dragon as one seeking to deceive the entire human race. As William Barclay puts it, "Satan ... stands for the sleepless vigilance of evil against good."[26] The same serpent who accuses the saints in heaven also deceives the nations on earth. His global enterprise pursues an ambitious vision: to convince everyone he is the rightful ruler of the created order. There is much subterfuge in the way the evil one and his minions carry out this plan. Direct opposition to God is futile and counter-productive. Satan cannot play by God's rules and win. So, he cheats in a variety of ways. For example:

He stalks. Peter likens him to a prowling lion, selectively picking off stragglers. That's why the apostle urges his readers to be sober-minded and alert, resisting the evil one as we endure his attacks (1 Pet. 5:8-9).

He dilutes. Satan is the inspiration behind every spiritual thought in opposition to God. Countless world religions promote the common ideas of a deity (or deities), a universal human problem, and a divine solution. For the sake of harmony, we're told there are many paths to God – all of them equally valid. We're encouraged to believe we all worship the same God, although we may see him differently. We're urged to find our own truth, which may be different than someone else's truth. But in the end, it really doesn't matter, and the apparently vast doctrinal differences are mere trifles.

This is why Paul writes about demolishing arguments "and every proud thing that is raised up against the knowledge of God," as he exhorts us to "take every thought captive to obey Christ" (2 Cor. 10:4-5).

He divides. The adversary persecutes Christ's sheep in an effort to scatter the flock. He goads prideful people to start their own forms of counterfeit Christianity, or their own highly exclusive sects, from hyper-Calvinism to the prosperity gospel. He incites bitter debates on secondary and tertiary doctrines, while the non-negotiables of the Christian faith – such as the authority of Scripture, the Trinity, and justification by faith – suffer neglect.

With thirty-three thousand distinct Christian denominations in two hundred thirty-eight countries,[27] the professing church is so fractured that the gospel is unappealing or irrelevant to many people. That's why Jude tells followers of Jesus to "contend for the faith that was delivered to the saints once for all" (Jude 3).

He opposes. One of Satan's strategies is to lie about the church. Warren Wiersbe writes:

> He deceives the nations into thinking that the people of God are dangerous, deluded, even destructive. It is through Satan's deception that the leaders of the nations band together against Christ and His people (Ps. 2; Acts 4:23-30). God's people in every age must expect the world's opposition, but the church can always defeat the enemy by being faithful to Christ.[28]

The evil one plies many other tactics in his pursuit of global domination. It's clear that his ultimate goals are chaos, not order; confusion, not clarity; and damnation, not redemption. In stark contrast to God, who loves the entire human race (John 3:16), the evil one foments a global hatred for all mankind. While he loathes all beings created in the image of God, he has particular avarice for God's people – from the Israelites to the church.

As the apostle John notes, Satan successfully cons unbelievers worldwide. As the great deceiver, he has successfully infiltrated every nation, every culture, and every human institution. Some nations officially sanction a counterfeit God. Others settle for a watered-down version of state Christianity that bears little distinction from humanism. Still others promote attractive but spiritually fatal philosophies.

The great experiment with the Israelites, in which they joyfully declare their loyalty to the one true God – "We will do all that the Lord has spoken" (Exod. 19:8) – falls quickly into spiritual adultery and then rank idolatry. God's new covenant with the church has fared no better. Counterfeit forms of Christianity emerged as early as the first century and have blossomed into global apostate organizations that embrace a counterfeit Jesus and a forged gospel (2 Cor. 11:4).

God sends prophets to the Israelites under the Old Covenant to warn them against false prophets who wrongly foretell future events (Deut. 18:21-22), perform lying signs and wonders to lead the people astray (Deut. 13:1-4), and lull them into a false sense of security when they descend into deep and dangerous sin (Jer. 23:16-17, 31-32; Ezek. 13:21-22; 2 Tim. 4:3-4).

Jesus and the New Testament writers consistently warn Christians about false teachers, false prophets, and false messiahs. All of this makes it clear that the evil one has sowed tares in God's wheat fields from the very beginning. Satan's global enterprise, in opposition to God's kingdom, often looks the same, just as tares resemble wheat as they grow together. But the Lord ultimately reaps the harvest, gathering those who are his into his barns and burning the tares in the fires of hell. Satan's enterprise is indeed global, but it's a house of cards.

Summary

Key takeaways about *the deceiver*:

(1) Satan is the archetypal deceiver. He is so cunning that he often makes us think we are doing something good, when in fact we are ruining ourselves and others.

(2) Satan's fiercest work of deception occurs at the beginning and end of Scripture. He deceives Eve in the garden of Eden (Gen. 3:1-7), which leads to Adam's fall and initiates an unbroken string of liars, frauds, charlatans, and shams. By the time we get to Revelation, Satan has deceived the whole world (Rev. 12:9).

(3) Satan's role as deceiver is grounded in his character as the father of lies (John 8:44). His nature – his every tendency – is to distort the truth so that people made as God's imagers miss the very purpose for which God designed them.

(4) Satan fires many darts to deceive us, among them: (a) the well-placed question; (b) the outright lie; (c) the blinded mind; (d) the masquerade; (e) lying signs and wonders; (f) enticement; (g) accusation; and (h) institutional leverage.

(5) Several key New Testament passages shed light on the nature and activities of the deceiver. He is:

- The consummate schemer, a brilliant military strategist in the battle for our minds and wills (2 Cor. 2:11; Eph. 6:11)
- A cunning seducer, courting us with soothing words and false promises (2 Cor. 11:3-4)
- A master of disguise, appearing as an angel of light (2 Cor. 11:13-15)
- The original usurper, seizing authority not rightfully his (1 Tim. 2:12-14)
- Chief of a global enterprise that markets in deception (Rev. 12:9)

(6) Jesus and the New Testament writers consistently warn Christians about false teachers, false prophets, and false messiahs. Satan's global enterprise, in opposition to God's kingdom, often looks the same, just as tares resemble wheat as they grow together. But the Lord ultimately reaps the harvest, gathering those who are his into his barns and burning the tares in the fires of hell. Satan's enterprise is indeed global, but it's a house of cards.

Questions for Personal or Group Study

1. As we noted in this chapter, Satan is the first and last deceiver the Bible portrays. Recall Genesis 3:13 and Revelation 20:10. How does the devil operate as a deceiver in these two passages of Scripture?
2. The evil one sports a quiver of fiery darts and launches them strategically. What are the eight "arrows" he fires at us in order to deceive us?
3. Why do you think the apostle Paul describes Satan as a cunning seducer in 2 Corinthians 11:3-4?

4. In what ways is Satan a master of disguise? Consider 2 Corinthians 11:13-15.

5. Satan is the chief executive officer of a global enterprise in opposition to God and God's people. He can't play by God's rules and win, so he cheats. Briefly describe several ways the evil one bends or breaks the rules.

EVIL ONE

Who would you say is the most evil person in history? Leading candidates include:

Adolf Hitler, Germany's chancellor from 1933 to 1945 and Fuhrer of the Nazi Party. Intelligent and creative, this talented young artist became the figurehead of a brutal regime whose actions, including the Holocaust, resulted in the deaths of more than fifty million people.

Joseph Stalin, dictator of the Soviet Union from 1922 to 1953. The former robber and assassin reigned with terror and violence, killing friends and enemies with impunity. He once said, "One death is a tragedy, a million deaths is simply a statistic." Even so, he was twice nominated for a Nobel Peace Prize.

Vlad the Impaler, also known as Vlad Dracula. He reigned as prince in Wallachia three times between 1448 and 1462, and he managed to kill one in every five persons he was sworn to protect, mostly through sadistic means that ended with impaling.

Ivan the Terrible, the first tsar of Russia, a brilliant but mentally ill ruler in the sixteenth century. As a child, he was known to throw animals from the top of tall structures, but his preferred acts of

178 | ROB PHILLIPS

brutality included impaling, beheading, burning, strangling, frying, blinding, and disemboweling people.

Maximilien Robespierre, architect of the French Revolution, whose role as an advocate for a better life for the French people morphed into a sadistic obsession with the guillotine. His ten-month reign of terror resulted in forty thousand heads lost and cemented his belief that killing is always better than forgiveness.

We could mention others: Genghis Khan, emperor of Mongolia from 1206 to 1227, whose expansionist campaigns led to at least twenty million deaths; Mao Zedong, China's brutal dictator from 1943 to 1976; Emperor Nero of first-century Rome; the family of Kim Il Sung, Kim Jong-il, and Kim Jong-un, which continues to brainwash, starve, and terrorize the people of North Korea after seventy years in power; Leopold of Belgium, who killed half the population of the Congo Free State; and Iraq's Saddam Hussein, who liked to video his tortures and watch the replays.[1]

Not to leave out women, we could include: Mary I of England, also known as Bloody Mary, whose efforts to restore Catholicism to England resulted in the burning of more than three hundred Protestants accused of heresy; and Hungarian Countess Elizabeth Bathory, whom *Guinness World Records* considers the most prolific female serial killer of all time, accused of torturing, mutilating, and killing an estimated six hundred fifty women between 1585 and 1610.[2]

These examples illustrate that certain men and women have used their intelligence, creativity, and persuasive gifts to unleash terror in their corners of the world. Some of these human monsters died horrific deaths – Robespierre lost his head in the guillotine he so freely used on others – while others died of natural causes. Few are known to have recanted or repented. Some went defiantly to their deaths, like Saddam Hussein, who was hanged in front of video cameras. In every case, these people emerged as monuments to unrestrained evil.

The Bible records the names and deeds of many evil people – from Cain to Queen Jezebel to the antichrist of the last days. But behind them all is a personality who birthed evil and who inspires it in all people, especially those who willingly become his instruments of malice. Of course, we're talking about Satan, whom Scripture often calls *the evil one*. While all humans are responsible for their actions, and stand in final judgment one day before Jesus, the evil one holds the top spot on the list of the world's most evil beings.

What Is Evil?

We may be hard-pressed to come up with a universally accepted definition of evil, but most of us know evil when we see it – or at least we think we do. For example, most (but not all) would say the gas chambers of Auschwitz were evil, as were the U.S. institution of chattel slavery, the serial murders of Ted Bundy, the packaged explosives of "Unabomber" Ted Kaczynski, and the domestic terror of Oklahoma City bomber Timothy McVeigh.

God has placed in every human heart a conscience, which not only helps us discern right from wrong but universally testifies of a divine moral law giver (Rom. 2:14-16). And so, we know intuitively what evil is, and therefore we know who ultimately judges us for it. Or we should. The problem is, sin has knocked every human being's moral compass off magnetic north.

Evil is not so much the opposite of good as it is the *absence* of good, or the perversion of good. Just as darkness may only be described in contrast to light, evil is only understood in relation to good. And that's the rub, because all human beings, though made in the image of God, are evil. We all sin, and our sin separates us from an eternally and unequivocally good creator (Rom. 3:10, 23; 6:23).

As a result, we often call evil good, and good evil (Isa. 5:20). We willingly descend the long spiral of godlessness, rejecting the God who reveals himself to all people in creation and conscience (Rom. 1:18-20; 2:14-16). Incrementally, God delivers us over to the depravities of our hearts until we live in open rebellion against him, celebrating the very deeds for which we stand condemned (Rom. 1:28-32).

Put simply, *we* are evil. And although we may gloss over our wickedness, or compare ourselves positively with those we deem far worse than we are, it is a fool's game. God is holy. We are not. And apart from God's grace, we all share a common destination in the lake of fire.

When it comes to the character the Bible identifies as *the evil one*, our ability to discern between good and evil is even more precarious. In part, that's because Satan is the embodiment of evil, so much so that he comes to us as an angel of light and makes wrong seem right, wickedness seem righteous, and evil seem good. He places a veil over our eyes, whispers soothing words into our deepest depravities, and makes a lie sound like the greatest version of our own personal truth.

Let's look at several Greek words the New Testament employs to convey the concept of evil. Then, let's turn our attention to several passages of Scripture that tell us more about the evil one.

Adikia. The noun *adikia* appears about two dozen times in the New Testament and is translated variously as "iniquity," "evil," "wickedness," and "wrongdoing." *Adikia* specifically denotes anything at odds with divine or human law. For example, Paul says the wrath of God is being revealed from heaven against the godlessness and *wickedness* of people (Rom. 1:18). He further writes that all who do not believe the truth but delight in *wickedness* are condemned (2 Thess. 2:12 NIV). We are urged to confess our sins so that the Lord, who is faithful and just, forgives our sins and purifies us from all *unrighteousness* (1 John 1:9).

Kakia. The noun *kakia* means "malice" and appears in nearly a dozen passages. New Testament writers view *kakia* as a force that breaks or destroys fellowship. For example, Paul urges his readers to engage in good works, reminding them that they were once "foolish, disobedient, deceived, enslaved by various passions and pleasures, living in *malice* and envy, hateful, detesting one another" (Tit. 3:3). Christians are to put away *malice* (Eph. 4:31; Col. 3:8; 1 Pet. 2:1).

Akathartos. The adjective *akathartos* essentially means "unclean" and pertains to that which may not be brought into contact with the holy. Impurity often is associated with fornication and idolatry (Eph. 5:5; Rev. 17:4). Those afflicted with demons often are described as having an *unclean* or *evil* spirit (e.g., Matt. 10:1; 12:43; Mark 1:23, 26).

This Greek adjective appears more than thirty times in the New Testament.

Kakos. Another adjective, *kakos*, shows up about fifty times in the Greek text and conveys the idea of something "evil," "bad," or "wrong," with a view toward something good that has been perverted. The use of *kakos* may be loosely divided into what is morally or ethically evil and what is destructive, damaging, or harmful. For example, people are morally or ethically evil (Matt. 21:41; Phil. 3:2; Rev. 2:2), and so are emotions and deeds (Rom. 3:8; 7:19, 21; 1 Thess. 5:15; 1 Pet. 3:9). Meanwhile, objects, events, and actions may be evil in destructive or damaging ways (Luke 16:25; Acts 16:28; 28:5).

Poneros. The Greek term often used to describe Satan is *ho poneros* – the evil one. The adjective *poneros* basically means "bad," "wicked," or "evil." It may be used in a purely physical sense to mean sick or in bad condition (e.g., Matt. 6:23; Rev. 16:2). Most commonly, however, *poneros* holds a strong ethical meaning relating to someone or something wicked. Jesus calls the Israelites who oppose him an *evil* generation (Matt. 12:39; 16:4; Luke 11:29). In his common grace, God sends sunshine on both the *evil* and the good (Matt. 5:45). Thoughts and works may be evil as well (Matt. 15:19; Col. 1:21; 2 Tim. 4:18).

When used as a noun, *poneros* may refer to evildoers (Matt. 5:39), evil actions (Luke 6:45), or to the preeminently *evil one*, the devil (e.g., Matt. 6:13; 13:19; John 17:15; Eph. 6:16; 1 John 5:18). It is these passages – the ones focusing on Satan as the evil one – to which we now turn our attention.

Evil One

Consider the following New Testament passages that depict Satan as *the evil one*:

Matthew 5:37

"But let your 'yes' mean 'yes,' and your 'no' mean 'no.' Anything more than this is from the evil one."

In this part of the Sermon on the Mount, Jesus addresses the issue of oath-taking, which plays a significant role in first-century Judaism. Jesus begins with an Old Testament reference: "Again, you have heard that it was said to our ancestors, You must not break your oath, but you must keep your oaths to the Lord" (Matt. 5:33; cf. Lev. 19:12; Num. 30:2; Deut. 23:21-23). Then, Jesus follows with:

> "But I tell you, don't take an oath at all: either by heaven, because it is God's throne; or by the earth, because it is his footstool; or by Jerusalem, because it is the city of the great King. Do not swear by your head, because you cannot make a single hair white or black" (Matt. 5:34-36).

Jesus does not forbid the taking of an oath in a court of law or a similar setting. In fact, he offers a response when the high priest puts him under oath (Matt. 26:63-64). But taking oaths has become so commonplace in Jesus' day as to become meaningless. People have come to think that a lie between two individuals doesn't concern God unless they invoke the divine name. In this case, they risk perjury for false statements, not to mention undermining God's dignity.

Jesus' command not to take an oath, then, is meant to tell his followers, in the strongest terms, that those who follow him must speak the truth. One must never take the approach that he or she is *only* telling the truth when they make an oath – a solemn statement affirmed to be true before God.

Leon Morris explains:

> The Jews held that unless the name of God was specifically mentioned the oath was not binding; there were lengthy discussions about when an oath is or is not binding, and people would sometimes swear by heaven or earth or a similar oath and later claim that they were not bound by that oath because God was not mentioned. Jesus rejects such casuistry [an elaborate hierarchy of laws]. People should not swear oaths at all, certainly not by heaven, for that is the throne of God; to substitute heaven for God

does not in fact avoid a reference to the deity, for heaven is his throne.[3]

If heaven is God's throne, then earth is his footstool (Isa. 66:1), so a person may not circumvent a direct reference to God by invoking earth. Nor should an oath be sworn by Jerusalem, God's elect city (Ps 48:1-2; Lam. 2:1). Many Israelites in Jesus' day believed swearing by heaven, earth, Jerusalem, or one's own head was less binding than swearing by God. But Jesus makes it clear that each of these belongs to God in its own way. Therefore, arbitrary distinctions are wrong.

Finally, Jesus says not to swear by our heads. To swear means to make a solemn declaration with an appeal to God, a divine being, or some sacred object in confirmation of what is said. To swear by the head means the swearer offers his head (that is, his life) if he is not speaking the truth. Jesus moves from the greatness of God to the smallness of people. We cannot change the color of even one hair on our heads (Matt. 5:36). So, why should we invoke God's name – or our puny selves – to support our claims?

Followers of Jesus are not to split hairs to escape truthful conversations. No oath is necessary for the truthful person, and Jesus commands truthfulness from his followers. Jesus simply says to let our "yes" and "no" speak for themselves as reliable statements. James similarly writes, "Above all, my brothers and sisters, do not swear, either by heaven or by earth or with any other oath. But let your 'yes' mean 'yes,' and your 'no' mean 'no,' so that you won't fall under judgment" (Jas. 5:12).

Jesus closes this section of his sermon by saying, "Anything more than this [a truthful yes or no] is from the evil one" (Matt. 5:37). Satan is the father of lies (John 8:44). His lies come in all shades: twisted truths, compromises, complete fabrications, and so on. But a half truth is a full lie. And any compromise with the truth results in a victory for the evil one.

It doesn't help to take an oath because that suggests we are only truthful when it really matters. Worse, it puts the reputation of God on the line. Since we are fallen creatures, swearing by our heads doesn't enhance the truth. We are known to fashion our own brand of truth – and then fully believe it.

For those who carry the name of Jesus, the message is simple: we are to be truthful at all times. While oaths have their proper place – in a court of law, for example – our conversations should reflect the character of Christ, who *is* the truth (John 14:6). People should not find it necessary to demand that we invoke God's name to verify the truthfulness of our statements. If they do, it could be that our words more accurately mirror those of the evil one than of our Lord.

Craig Keener remarks, "All oaths implicitly call God to witness, because everything that exists was made by him. For Jesus, no aspect of life except sin is purely secular."[4]

Matthew 6:13

> "And do not bring us into temptation, but deliver us from the evil one."

This request comes at the close of the Lord's Prayer, perhaps better called the *Disciples' Prayer*.[5] Several English translations render the final phrase "deliver us from evil" rather than "deliver us from the evil one."[6] The Greek could mean either. While it's possible that deliverance from evil in general is Jesus' primary meaning, protection from the author of evil is a suitable request for disciples learning to pray.

"Do not bring us into temptation" does not imply "don't bring us to the place of temptation," or even "don't allow us to be tempted." Jesus already endured temptation at the hands of the evil one after the Holy Spirit drove him into the wilderness following his baptism (Matt. 4:1). It cannot mean "don't tempt us," either, for God does not tempt us with evil (Jas. 1:13). Rather, as Craig Blomberg points out, these words seem best taken as "don't let us succumb to temptation" or "don't abandon us to temptation."[7] At times, of course, we *do* give in to temptation, but it's not God's fault, for he always provides us with an avenue of escape (1 Cor. 10:13).

This leads naturally to our request that God deliver us from the evil one, from whom all evil ultimately proceeds. The emphasis in this verse is on our human vulnerability and, thus, our utter dependence upon God, who is the only one capable of conquering Satan, sin, and death through Jesus' finished work on the cross. Only "the Holy One of God" breaks the curse of the evil one (Mark 1:24).

Matthew 13:19

> "When anyone hears the word about the kingdom and doesn't understand it, the evil one comes and snatches away what was sown in his heart. This is the one sown along the path."

Jesus is explaining the parable of the sower (Matt. 13:3-9) to his disciples. In this familiar story, the Lord prepares his disciples for opposition to the gospel. Further, he encourages them to persevere in sowing the message of God's kingdom wherever they go, for a harvest is certain (cf. Matt. 13:24-30; 28:19-20). Clearly, Jesus is the sower, the seed is "the word about the kingdom" (13:18), and the various types of soil are those who hear the message. By extension, Jesus' followers are sowers who are to experience a wide range of responses to the gospel.

Jesus describes four different types of soil, depicting four different states of human readiness to receive the message of God's kingdom. The sower scatters his seed indiscriminately, just as the gospel message goes out to the entire world. Some seeds fall on hard-packed footpaths, where birds snatch them away. Some seeds fall on shallow, rocky soil, where the sun scorches them as soon as they sprout. Some seeds fall on thorny ground, where weeds smother the tender shoots and prevent maturity. Finally, some seeds fall on fertile ground, resulting in varying degrees of fruitfulness.

Jesus ties these four types of soil to four conditions of the human heart. In the first case, he likens the footpath to persons who don't "understand" the word of the kingdom. These are careless hearers. They are not necessarily hostile to the message. In fact, they may recognize the truth in it. But they don't act. The Greek verb rendered "understand" is *syniemi*. It means "to put together;" that is, mentally, "to comprehend." By implication, it means "to act piously: consider, understand, be wise."[8]

While this type of understanding sometimes is depicted as a gift from God, such as the understanding Jesus' disciples receive from him (Matt. 16:12; 17:13; Luke 24:45), *syniemi* also may be used to describe a lack of understanding due to sin or hard-heartedness (Mark 6:52). That's the meaning in Jesus' parable. "The failure to attend to the message and to find out what it means results in total loss, first of the message and ultimately of the hearer."[9]

Hard-heartedness makes hearers of the gospel easy pickings for the evil one. Like a bird swooping down from the sky to pluck seeds on the ground, Satan snatches away what is sown in unbelieving hearts. Jesus clearly has Satan in mind here, for the Gospel writers who record this parable identify him as "the evil one" (Matt. 13:19), "Satan" (Mark 4:15), and "the devil" (Luke 8:12).

Jesus graphically describes Satan's work as "snatching away" the word. The verb *harpazo* generally connotes a forceful or violent seizing. The word is used of burglary (Matt. 12:29); mob action (John 6:15); animal attacks (John 10:12); and arrests (Acts 23:10). However, *harpazo* also appears as the forceful proclamation of sound doctrine (Jude 23); Paul's visit to heaven (2 Cor. 12:2); and the catching up of believers to meet the Lord in the air (1 Thess. 4:17).

In the case of this parable, of course, Jesus has in mind a sudden and violent ripping out of what has been sown – the saving message of Christ and his kingdom. We should note that Satan's work runs concurrently with the work of Jesus and his followers. Just as birds don't wait for the farmer to leave his field before snatching seeds from the footpaths, the evil one descends immediately on hardened hearts to keep them from truly hearing and thus being saved.

Jesus goes on to describe three other types of listeners. And make no mistake: the evil one actively pursues them. The "rocky ground" represents those who enthusiastically receive the message. However, because their faith is shallow, they abandon the gospel when "distress or persecution ... because of the word" confronts them (13:21). In essence, they succumb to Satan's convincing argument, "You didn't sign up for this."

The thorny soil depicts those who hang on a little longer, but eventually "the worries of this age and the deceitfulness of wealth choke the word" (13:22). Their loyalties are divided, and the devil succeeds in wooing them into legitimate worldly concerns, which morph into various forms of idolatry. "You have to take care of yourself first," he whispers. "Just think of all the good you can do if you rise in the ranks of your organization." "Think of the noble causes you can advance if you pursue those financial opportunities." "Remember how gifted God made you; you can't limit what he's given you to this small rural church." And on it goes.

Lastly, however, there is great hope. The message of the kingdom takes root in the "good ground," those who hear and understand the word and yield a hundred, sixty, or thirty times what is sown (13:23). The evil one is present here as well. He viciously attacks God's people, and Jesus has another parable to illustrate that: the parable of the wheat and weeds, which follows immediately (Matt. 13:24-30; 36-43).

Even so, as followers of Jesus invest their spiritual gifts, time, talents, and other resources in the kingdom of God, the Lord of the harvest produces much fruit through them and rewards them for their faithfulness (Matt. 24:45-51; 25:14-30; Luke 19:11-27).

Craig Blomberg writes:

> This parable provides a sober reminder that even the most enthusiastic outward response to the gospel offers no guarantee that one is a true disciple. Only the tests of time, perseverance under difficult circumstances, the avoidance of the idolatries of wealth and anxiety over earthly concerns, and above all the presence of appropriate fruit (consistent obedience to God's will) can prove a profession genuine.[10]

Matthew 13:38

"... the field is the world; and the good seed – these are the children of the kingdom. The weeds are the children of the evil one ..."

Here, Jesus reveals the spiritual truths behind the parable of the wheat and weeds (Matt. 13:24-30). As in the parable of the sower, the Lord presents a farmer who has sown good seed in his field. But an enemy invades at night and plants weeds among the wheat. When the wheat matures and begins sprouting heads of grain, the weeds appear as well.

The hired hands report their discovery to the farmer and ask whether they should pull out the weeds, but the farmer tells them:

"No. When you pull up the weeds, you might also uproot the wheat with them. Let both grow together until the harvest. At harvest time I'll tell the reapers: Gather the weeds first and tie them in bundles to burn them, but collect the wheat in my barn" (Matt. 13:29-30).

After sharing this story, Jesus leaves the crowds and retreats to the home in which he is staying. The disciples come to him and ask him to interpret the parable. Jesus obliges:

"The one who sows the good seed is the Son of Man; the field is the world; and the good seed – these are the children of the kingdom. The weeds are the children of *the evil one*, and *the enemy* who sowed them is *the devil*. The harvest is the end of the age, and the harvesters are angels. Therefore, just as the weeds are gathered and burned in the fire, so it will be at the end of the age. The Son of Man will send out his angels, and they will gather from his kingdom all who cause sin and those guilty of lawlessness. They will throw them into the blazing furnace where there will be weeping and gnashing of teeth. Then the righteous will shine like the sun in their Father's kingdom. Let anyone who has ears listen" (Matt. 13:37-43, emphasis added).

This parable differs from the parable of the sower. It features distinctive characters and a unique central message: the kingdom of heaven and Satan's kingdom exist simultaneously during this "present evil age" (Gal. 1:4). Jesus paints a sweeping portrait of time with this story. The Son of Man – Jesus' favorite name for himself, using it some eighty times in the Gospels – plants true believers in the world. These are adopted sons of the Father to whom Jesus sends another advocate – the Holy Spirit. These "children of the kingdom" are called to bear much fruit in a hostile world of unbelievers whom "the evil one," "the enemy," and "the devil" has planted.

Until Jesus returns, the children of God and the offspring of the evil one contend with one another. At last, there is a harvest and a great separation. Unbelievers are rooted out and cast into hell, while true followers of Jesus remain and bask in the glow of the Son of Man's glorious presence.

Jesus refers to Satan in three ways in this parable. First, he is *an / the enemy* (vv. 28, 39). Primarily, he is an enemy of the Son of Man, seeking to render Jesus' earthly ministry fallow. As the father of lies, Satan is the archenemy of truth incarnate. As ruler of the kingdom of darkness, he seeks to smother the light of the world. And as one who masquerades as an angel of light, he parodies Christ's servants and distorts their gospel message. Satan is the enemy of the church in general, and of individual believers in particular. His chief aim is to defeat his creator and to ruin those made as God's image-bearers.

Second, Satan is *the evil one* (v. 38). Demons recognize Jesus as "the Holy One of God" (Mark 1:24). Jesus stands in stark contrast to the demons' master, the evil one. Jesus is the author of life; Satan, the agent of death. Jesus is the light of the world; Satan, the prince of darkness, ruling over a vast, loyal, and mobile army of evil spirits. As one who sows opponents of Christ's kingdom in the world, the evil one produces a bountiful crop of counterfeit wheat, which springs up and looks a great deal like Jesus' yield but produces a poisonous substitute.

The weeds – or *tares*, as they are sometimes called – are unbelievers who are "holding to the form of godliness but denying its power" (2 Tim. 3:5). A brief look at tares gives us a clearer image of these false professors of the faith. The Arabic name for tares is *zawan*, and they grow abundantly in the Middle East. The grain is small, emerging at the upper part of the stalk, which stands perfectly erect. It bears a bitter taste and, when eaten by itself or used in ordinary bread, causes dizziness and provokes vomiting. It is a strong, sleep-inducing poison that must be carefully winnowed, grain by grain, before grinding. Once mixed with healthy wheat, it is almost impossible to exterminate.[11]

In a similar manner, false professors of the Christian faith look and act a great deal like genuine Christians. They attend the same churches, mingle with the same congregations, and project a form of piety. They are religious. They talk freely about God but more guardedly about his Son. They engage in vibrant spiritual conversations. They may even present themselves as "super apostles" (2 Cor. 11:5; 12:11).

But they proclaim "another Jesus," "a different Spirit," and "a different gospel" (2 Cor. 11:4). Like tares, they stand tall in their self-righteousness. They entangle themselves with the children of the kingdom. And when the fruit of their false doctrine reaches full maturity, it produces a noxious crop that, if consumed, leads to spiritual death. They are, as Paul declares, "savage wolves" bent on destroying the flock (Acts 20:29-31).

Satan is indeed the evil one. Nothing he does is good. He only lies. He only deceives. He only murders. He only destroys. He only plants tares in Jesus' wheat fields. He only brings death. And he does all this with such alacrity that people willingly swallow his poison before they realize their peril.

Third, Satan is *the devil*. We examined this name in more detail in Chapter 4. The word *devil* comes from the Greek *diabolos*, from which we get "diabolical." It means "slanderer," "accuser," or "disrupter." Slander represents the evil of human speech. New Testament writers use verbs such as "blaspheme" and "speak evil against" to describe it. To slander implies acting with hostile intent, or setting two people against each other, thus placing them at odds with one another.

The name *devil* is based on two Greek words: *dia*, meaning "through" or "among," and *ballo*, meaning "to throw." As James Boice explains, "The devil is the one who from the beginning has been attempting to throw a monkey wrench into the machinery of the universe."[12]

No doubt, in his explanation of the parable of the wheat and weeds, Jesus calls Satan "the devil" to shed light on the enemy's diabolical nature and devious activities. He is the consummate disrupter. He sneaks in under the cover of darkness, sows false prophets and false teachers in the church, arms them with poisonous doctrines that lead unsuspecting people astray, and – perhaps most surprisingly – succeeds in deceiving the false prophets and teachers themselves so they profess their innocence at the final judgment (Matt. 7:21-23).

The devil's work is not confined to the church, of course, for Jesus says Satan plants tares in "the world." But if the devil can make the church look like the world – tares look very much like wheat until harvest time – then the world does not hunger for the healthy life-giving gospel message.

The day of harvest and gathering is coming, says Jesus. This refers to the resurrection and final judgment that separate believers and unbelievers (John 5:28-29). Just as tares are gathered and burned, those who reject Christ receive the same judgment pronounced on the evil one: everlasting separation from God in hell (Matt. 25:41; Rev. 20:10-15).

Believers, however, receive glorified bodies similar to Christ's resurrected body. They are rewarded for their faithfulness. And they spend eternity with their Savior in the new heavens and new earth (John 14:1-3; Rom. 14:10; 1 Cor. 3:11-15; 15:51-57; 1 Thess. 4:13-17; Rev. 21:1-7).

John 17:15

"I am not praying that you take them out of the world but that you protect them from the evil one."

John 17 features the longest-recorded prayer of Jesus in the Gospels. This comes after Jesus delivers final instructions to his disciples and before he is betrayed, arrested, and crucified. First, Jesus prays for himself (vv. 1-5), then for his disciples (vv. 6-19), and finally for all believers (vv. 20-26). This intercessory prayer is best known as Jesus' *high priestly prayer*.

Jesus confirms he has finished his heaven-sent task with the disciples. He has revealed the Father's name – that is, the very presence of God – to them (v. 6; cf. John 14:9). He has spoken to them the Father's words (v. 8). And he has ensured that they received the words, understood them, and believed the Father sent Jesus (v. 8).

Next, Jesus prays specifically for his followers. The apostles belong to the Father. The Father gives them to Jesus. Finally, Jesus cares for them throughout his earthly ministry. Jesus is glorified in the disciples (v. 10). He protects and guards them (v. 12). He completes his joy in them (v. 13). He gives them the Father's word (v. 14). He sends them into the world as the Father has sent him (v. 18). And he sanctifies himself for them, so the truth may sanctify them (v. 19).

But Jesus is about to leave his disciples and return to the Father (v. 11). In a matter of days, the Savior is to be crucified, buried, resurrected, and ascended. He has promised his followers another Counselor like himself – the Holy Spirit, who is to be with them and in them (John 14:16-17, 26; 16:7, 13). And now, he prays to the Father on his disciples' behalf. Specifically, he prays for their protection, unity, and sanctification:

> "Holy Father, *protect* them by your name that you have given me, so that they may be *one* as we are one. While I was with them, I was *protecting* them by your name that you have given me. I *guarded* them and not one of them is lost, except the son of destruction, so that the Scripture may be fulfilled.... I am not praying that you take them out of the world but that you *protect* them from the evil one. They are not of the world, just as I am not of the world. *Sanctify* them by the truth; your word is truth" (vv. 11-12, 15-17, emphasis added).

First, Jesus prays for *protection*. He has protected (Gr. *tareo*: attended carefully; kept from loss or injury) and guarded (Gr. *phylasso*: had an eye upon lest someone escape) his followers throughout his earthly ministry. But now, returning to the Father, Jesus entrusts the disciples' care to the Father, who is sending the Holy Spirit. We see the Trinity at work here. The Father, Son, and Holy Spirit carry out different roles in redemption, yet they are remarkably united in being and purpose.

The phrase "protect them from the evil one" (*ek tou ponerou*) could be taken in an abstract sense – that is, "protect them from evil" – or as a reference to the devil. The latter is almost certainly what is meant. As D. A. Carson notes, "The death/exaltation of the Master spells the principal defeat of the ruler of this world, but that does not rob him of all power to inflict terrible damage on the Lord's followers, if they are left without succor."[13]

Until Christ's return in glory to set things right, when the last enemy is destroyed, the whole world remains "under the sway of the evil one" (1 John 5:19). The Christian's task, then, according to Carson, is not to be withdrawn from the world, nor to be confused with the world, "but to remain in the world, maintaining the witness to the truth by the help of the Paraclete, and absorbing all the malice the world can muster, finally protected by the Father himself, in response to the prayer of Jesus."[14]

Second, Jesus prays for *unity*. Just as the Father and Son are one in being and purpose – "Everything I have is yours, and everything you have is mine" (v. 10) – Jesus prays for this same unity among his followers. This unity consists in a love like the Father and Son have for one another. In fact, Jesus tells his disciples the unbelieving world will know they are followers of Jesus if they love one another (John 13:35).

And yet this unity is not automatic, for the disciples are men of flesh who live in a sinful and fallen world. It is Satan's domain, and he rules it with great power. It is a world hostile to Christ and his followers. So, Jesus asks the Father to protect his followers from the evil one. Jesus makes it clear he is not asking the Father to remove his disciples from the world, for just as the Father sends Jesus into the world on a mission, so Jesus sends his disciples. Rather, Jesus implores the Father to protect the disciples from the evil one.

Jesus knows that the one who was lost – Judas Iscariot – is an instrument of Satan. In fact, Satan seems to have taken complete control of Judas, who is about to betray Jesus in a most cowardly way – with the kiss of a friend. Jesus also knows Satan is working in the lives of the high priest, members of the Sanhedrin, the temple police, the Roman soldiers and governors, and even in the fickle hearts of the countrymen he came to save.

All of this is about to play out in the garden of Gethsemane, in the home of Israel's highest religious authority, and in the courts of a provincial Roman governor. When blackness descends on noon that Friday, as Jesus hangs on a cross, the prince of darkness exults in apparent victory.

Even the blinded religious leaders are inclined to see the thunderheads and earthquakes as cosmic signs of a deity satisfied with the death of an impostor. In fact, the darkness and shaken earth harken back to Mount Sinai, when God came down in fearful power to deliver the very law that the expiring Son of God now fulfilled. This is not the end; it's the beginning of a great reversal. The prince of darkness now has his fate sealed in outer darkness – a truth he is about to realize come Sunday morning.

And just as the unbelieving world is hostile toward Jesus in a most remarkable way, the world is about to hate the eyewitnesses of Jesus' sacrificial and substitutionary work on the cross. "If the world hates you, understand that it hated me before it hated you," Jesus tells his followers (John 15:18). Jesus does not ask that his followers be given a pass on persecution. In fact, he prepares them for such a dark reception. More importantly, though, he asks the Father to protect them from the evil one – that is, to protect their souls, their salvation, and their testimony.

As with Shadrach, Meshach, and Abednego, the Lord does not necessarily prevent his faithful witnesses from walking in fire, but he walks through the fire with them. Satan cannot possess the ones who have always belonged to the Father and whom Jesus has preserved. But he can harass them, discourage them, distract them, and keep them from joyfully carrying out the work God has given them to do.

So, in requesting protection of his disciples from the evil one, Jesus asks the Father to ensure that they complete the course as faithful eyewitnesses, just as Jesus is about to complete his earthly ministry as the faithful Son of God. Like Daniel in Babylon (Dan. 1-2; 4-6) and the saints in Caesar's household (Phil. 4:22), Christ's followers are to be witnesses to truth in the midst of satanic falsehood.

Finally, Jesus prays for his disciples' *sanctification*. Specifically, he asks that the truth of God's Word set his followers apart for ministry. The Greek verb translated "sanctify" is *hagiazo*. It means "to make holy" or "to set apart for God's use." In the New Testament, this verb expresses the action of including a person or a thing in the sphere of what is holy. Verses 17-19 of Jesus' prayer provide additional details: "Sanctify (*hagiason*) them by the truth; your word is truth. As you sent me into the world, I also have sent them into the world. I sanctify (*hagiazo*) myself for them, so that they also may be sanctified (*hagiasmenoi*) by the truth."

Sanctification is the work of God making followers of Jesus more like him. In sanctification, the Holy Spirit produces holiness, which means bearing an actual likeness of God in our thoughts, words, and deeds. Sanctification may be understood in two ways, both of which relate to holiness. First, there is *positional sanctification*, the state of being separate, set apart from the common, and dedicated to a higher purpose.

Positional sanctification finds its place in the New Testament as a work of God occurring at conversion. Robert Morey describes this initial step of sanctification:

> There is a radical break with the total dominion and tyranny of sin,
> so that the believer now struggles with remaining sin instead of
> reigning sin.... sin is dethroned, the believer dies to sin, the old self
> is crucified and there is a new principle of holiness implanted in the

heart of the believer which will not allow sin to ultimately and permanently regain dominion over the believer.[15]

Second, there is *practical sanctification*, the lifelong process by which the Spirit makes us more like Jesus. This requires our ongoing submission to Christ and our obedience to the voice of the indwelling Spirit. Practical sanctification means not only that believers are set apart, thus belonging to Christ, but that our conduct naturally aligns with the revealed Word of God and the indwelling Spirit of God.

In Jesus' prayer for the disciples' sanctification, he may have both positional and practical sanctification in mind. In a sense, Jesus' disciples already are sanctified. That is, they are given to Jesus by the Father (v. 6); they have believed the Father sent Jesus (v. 8); they belong to the Father (v. 9); they are guarded and kept – none is lost except "the son of destruction" (v. 12); and they are not of the world, just as Jesus is not of the world (vv. 14, 16). These are qualities of persons belonging to God and set apart for his service. And yet, Jesus prays, "Sanctify them by the truth." What does that mean?

Matthew Henry paraphrases Jesus' prayer:

> Confirm the work of sanctification in them, strengthen their faith, inflame their good affections, rivet their good resolutions. Carry on that good work in them, and continue it; let the light shine more and more. Complete it, crown it with the perfection of holiness; sanctify them throughout and to the end.... The great thing to be asked of God for gospel ministries is that they may be sanctified, effectually separated from the world, entirely devoted to God, and experimentally acquainted with the influence of that word upon their own hearts which they preach to others. Let them have the *Urim* and *Thummim*, *light* and *integrity*.[16]

The truth that sanctifies followers of Jesus requires the Word of God (John 17:17), the Son of God (John 14:6), and the Spirit of God (1 John 5:6). The disciples needed all three to experience true sanctification. And so do we.

Ephesians 6:16

> In every situation take up the shield of faith with which you can
> extinguish all the flaming arrows of the evil one.

We explore this passage more fully in Chapter 15. However, a few
observations here may prove helpful.

First, the evil one wields a quiver full of "flaming arrows." In New
Testament times, soldiers often covered the tips of their arrows in
coarse fibers dipped in pitch and then set on fire. These flaming
arrows were shot at different trajectories toward enemy lines,
presenting the double threat of piercing iron and scattering flames.

In a similar way, Satan hurls a seemingly endless volley of
temptations at us: thoughts of pride, selfishness, fear, doubt,
disappointment, greed, anger, vengeance, lust, and judgmentalism.
They strike at different times and in different ways, but they all are
deadly in their intent.

What's more, the evil one fires these temptations from a distance.
They seem harmless at first – even alluring, like the sparks of a
welder's torch, or the glowing debris of a volcanic eruption – until
they descend on us, too close and too late. "Satan attacks by
indirection – through good things from which no evil is expected,"
writes Marvin Vincent. "There is a hint of its propagating power: one
sin draws another in its track: the flame of the fire-tipped dart
spreads."[17]

When good things like beauty, comfort, and morality enter our
line of sight, we often embrace them in self-centered and satanically
inspired ways. Then, beauty catches fire and becomes lust; comfort
bursts into greed; and morality morphs into self-righteousness. The
evil one's fiery darts are an awe-inspiring sight to behold, but they are
deadly if not quenched.

Second, believers are urged to take up the shield of faith, which
successfully douses the fire and absorbs the piercing arrowheads of
satanic assaults. The shield described here is the Roman *scutum*, a
heavy, oblong piece of armor four feet high and two and a half feet

wide, often curved on the inner side and designed to connect with other shields for maximum protection of the whole infantry. Soldiers fashioned the shields from two layers of wood glued together and covered, first, with linen, and then with hide, which could be soaked in water to extinguish fiery darts. Finally, soldiers bound the shields with iron above and below. Francis Foulkes writes:

> The apostle knew that only faith's reliance on God could *quench* and deflect such weapons whenever they were hurled at the Christian. It is of interest also to recall that the Romans had a system of locking these large shields together for their corporate defense against their enemies and for attack.[18]

Faith does away with dependence on self and holds fast to the Lord, our shield and protector. As King David writes, "My shield is God Most High, who saves the upright in heart" (Ps. 7:10 NIV). Further, the Lord is "my shield and the horn of my salvation" (Ps. 18:2). And the writer of Proverbs notes, God is "a shield to those who take refuge in him" (Prov. 30:5). When we rely fully on the Lord as our shield, we rob Satan's fiery darts of their necessary oxygen.

Third, Paul addresses this message to Christians, whom the evil one besieges. Followers of Jesus are encouraged to put on the full armor of God so that we may stand against the devil's schemes (Eph. 6:11). Satan's tactics are many and varied, and we must always wear the full armor God supplies.

No doubt, Satan assaults unbelievers as well. But they already are in his grasp and under his power, and they willingly follow the evil one's lead. Therefore, it is less necessary for the evil one to continuously bombard them with temptations; their flesh is naturally inclined to evil. Christians, however, have been delivered from sin's bondage. So, Satan engages in warfare because, as citizens of Christ's kingdom, we are the evil one's true enemies.

William Gurnall, a seventeenth-century Puritan minister, wrote a three-volume treatise on the armor of God, titling his 1,472-page exposition *The Christian in Complete Armour*. Here is a snippet: "In heaven we shall appear not in armour but in robes of glory; but here they [the pieces of armor Paul specifies in Eph. 6:11-17] are to be worn night and day; we must walk, work and sleep in them, or else we are not true soldiers of Christ." In this armor we are to stand and watch, for "the saint's sleeping time is Satan's tempting time; every fly dares venture to creep on a sleeping lion."[19]

In this passage, Paul refers to Satan as "the evil one" (or "wicked one") to draw attention to the nature from which his malicious actions flow. Matthew Henry notes:

> Our enemy the devil is here called *the wicked one*. He is wicked himself, and he endeavours to make us wicked. His temptations are called *darts*, because of their swift and undiscerned flight, and the deep wounds that they give to the soul; *fiery darts*, by way of allusion to the poisonous darts which were wont to inflame the parts which were wounded with them, and therefore were so called, as the serpents with poisonous stings are called fiery serpents. Violent temptations, by which the soul is set on fire of hell, are the darts which Satan shoots at us. Faith is the shield with which we must quench these fiery darts, wherein we should receive them, and so render them ineffectual, that they may not hit us, or at least that they may not hurt us.[20]

2 Thessalonians 3:3

> But the Lord is faithful; he will strengthen you and guard you from the evil one.

Paul begins chapter 3 of his second letter to the Thessalonians with an appeal for prayer "that the word of the Lord may spread rapidly and be honored, just as it was with you" (v. 1). In addition, Paul asks his readers to pray that he and his companions be delivered from "wicked and evil people, for not all have faith" (v. 2).

Paul uses two adjectives to describe those attacking his ministry. "Wicked" is from the Greek *atopos* and means "out of place," "improper," "wrong-headed," or "perverse." These people behave in ways unbecoming of Christians. The second word Paul uses, "evil," is from the Greek *poneros*, which we already addressed in this chapter as a term meaning "bad," "evil," or "malicious."

Paul seems to have a particular group in mind, perhaps Jewish opponents of the gospel in Corinth (Acts 18:6ff). In any case, these wicked people do not appear to be Christians, for Paul follows his description of them with the phrase, "for not all have faith" (2 Thess. 3:2). That is, these opponents refuse to embrace the objective truths of the gospel message.

The apostle then turns his attention to the distressed Thessalonians, who continue to suffer persecution at the hands of their contemporaries (2 Thess. 1:4-6), with Satan as the instigator (1 Thess. 3:5; and see 2:18; 2 Thess. 2:9). Paul seeks to encourage them: "But the Lord is faithful; he will strengthen and guard you from the evil one" (2 Thess. 3:3). Paul contrasts the lack of faith found in opponents of the gospel with the steadfast faithfulness of God, who continues to strengthen and guard his people from Satan.

The ancient system of patronage is in view here, a system in which benefactors extend protection to their clients. In the present text, the Lord is viewed as protector in his faithfulness to persecuted Christians. As such, he strengthens them in the midst of trials and keeps them from falling. Gene Green comments:

> This promise is hardly meant to convey to the church that they will not suffer but rather affirms that in the midst of their sufferings their faithful Patron will strengthen them so that they will not fall. He will shield them from the ultimate shame of succumbing to the wiles of their adversary.[21]

"The evil one" translates an adjective (*tou ponerou*) that may be either masculine and personal (as the CSB and NIV translate), or neuter as a general reference to evil (as in the KJV and RSV). Some commentators believe "evil" rather than "the evil one" is the preferred understanding as Paul addresses various manifestations of evil already afflicting the church.[22]

However, it seems that Paul is writing about the diabolical work of a person in opposition to the Lord and his church. The early church referred to Satan as *ho poneros*, "the evil one" (Matt. 6:13; Eph. 6:16). In addition, Paul used personal language to describe the activities of Satan as a present-day hinderer of his work (1 Thess. 2:18), a tempter seeking to undercut the faith of the church (1 Thess. 3:5), and a future enemy with which to be reckoned (2 Thess. 2:9). A personal "evil one" is the antithesis of a personal Lord (*kyrios*).

In the end, despite the evil one's unceasing ploys, the Lord's faithfulness assures us that suffering has meaning (2 Thess. 1:4-5), that God deals harshly with those who persecute his people (2 Thess. 1:6-10), and that our future is secure in Christ (2 Thess. 1:11-12; 3:4-5).

1 John 2:12-14

> I am writing to you, little children, since your sins have been forgiven on account of his name. I am writing to you, fathers, because you have come to know the one who is from the beginning. I am writing to you, young men, because you have conquered the evil one. I have written to you, children, because you have come to know the Father. I have written to you, fathers, because you have come to know the one who is from the beginning. I have written to you, young men, because you are strong, God's word remains in you, and you have conquered the evil one.

John addresses three groups of people in these verses: children, fathers, and young men. Augustine believed, as do other commentators, that the three groups represent three stages of spiritual pilgrimage. The children are newborn babes in Christ. The young men are more developed Christians engaging successfully in spiritual warfare. And the fathers are the most mature believers, deep in spiritual knowledge and experience.

While this is a possible reading, it seems better to view "children" as all of John's readers, and "young men" and "fathers" as those who may be distinguished by age within the church.

Based on the author's consistent use of "children" to mean *all* his readers (1 John 2:1, 12, 14, 18, 28; 3:7, 18; 4:4; 5:21), we may conclude that John's application of "children" in these verses encompasses men and women of all ages and is not a reference to youngsters or the spiritually immature. This reflects John's affection for his readers, along with his own more senior standing in relation to them.

Next, "fathers" should be seen as older people, not exclusively men, and not necessarily those who are spiritually advanced. The fact that some readers are addressed as "fathers" and "young men" reflects a first-century way of speaking, but it does not exclude females in the audience.

There is only one other place in the New Testament where believers are called fathers. In 1 Timothy 5:1, Paul tells the young pastor, Timothy, how to relate to older men in the church at Ephesus: "Don't rebuke an older man, but exhort him as a father ..." The designation "father" clearly means an older man, but there is no indication he is more spiritually mature than his pastor.

Finally, "young men" should be understood as younger people, not just men, and not necessarily the spiritually immature. The word for "young men" (Gr. *neaniskos*) is found only in 1 John 2:13-14 in all of John's writings. It does occur nine times in the Synoptic Gospels and Acts, where it consistently refers to younger people. And if we return to Paul's first letter to Timothy, the apostle urges the young pastor to treat "younger men as brothers" (1 Tim. 5:1). In context, "younger men" are those closer to Timothy's age.

Now that we understand the audience to whom John is writing, we may rightly ask why he twice commends his younger readers for having "conquered the evil one." Clearly, Satan, not evil in general, is in John's mind. He seems to be addressing the men and women on the front lines of Christ's kingdom – younger and perhaps middle-aged people raising families, engaging the marketplace, and assuming leadership positions in the church as it advances into enemy territory. Their victory over the evil one is rooted in their faith in Christ and the power of God's Word.

Why are they strong? Because the Word of God lives (Gr. *menei*, literally "remains") in them. Unlike the antichrists who oppose the Son of God, the "young men" are from God, and the one who is in them (God) is greater than the one who is in the world (Satan; see 1 John 4:4). Further, they have been born of God, which ensures their ultimate victory over the world (1 John 5:4).

Finally, God protects the young men so the evil one cannot touch them (1 John 5:18). Believers' victory over the evil one is assured because the Father abides in them, Christ protects them, and the Holy Spirit empowers them. The young men's faith in the triune God brings victory that overcomes the world – and overcomes the one who presently holds the world in sway (1 John 5:19).

Before moving on, we should note how John twice uses the phrase "have conquered the evil one." The phrase translated "have conquered" draws from the Greek *nikao*, which means "to carry off the victory," "overcome," or "prevail." As A. T. Robertson notes, "The Greek tense shows a permanent victory after conflict."[23] Faith in Jesus and his finished work on the cross secures our victory over sin and death because Christ has decisively routed and irreversibly defeated the evil one.

1 John 3:11-12

> For this is the message you have heard from the beginning: We should love one another, unlike Cain, who was of the evil one and murdered his brother. And why did he murder him? Because his deeds were evil, and his brother's were righteous.

John repeatedly states that true followers of Jesus love one another – so much so that this differentiates us from unbelievers (cf. 1 John 2:7-11; 3:11-18; 4:7-21; 5:1-4). This message does not originate with John, for Jesus taught the same truth: "I give you a new command: Love one another. Just as I have loved you, you are also to love one another. By this everyone will know that you are my disciples, if you love one another" (John 13:34-35).

Now, John sets this command against the backdrop of a dark event in human history: the story of Cain. John has in mind Genesis 4, where we read the account of Cain and Abel, the sons of Adam and Eve. Both sons offer sacrifices to God. Abel, a shepherd, brings the firstborn of his flock and their fat portions to the Lord. Cain, a farmer, presents some of the land's produce.

The Lord accepts Abel's offering but rejects Cain's, a judgment that infuriates Cain. We can't be certain that Abel's offering is more pleasing to God because it is an animal sacrifice, for grain offerings later come to play an important role in the sacrificial system under the Mosaic Law. Rather, it seems Cain and Abel offer their sacrifices with totally different attitudes toward God and one another.

The Lord asks Cain, "Why are you furious? And why do you look despondent? If you do what is right, won't you be accepted? But if you do not do what is right, sin is crouching at the door. Its desire is for you, but you must rule over it" (vv. 6-7). These verses infer that Cain's offering is rejected, not because of its contents, but because Cain's heart is evil.

John's reference to Cain as "of the evil one" has no parallel in the Genesis account. However, in some Jewish texts, the murder of Abel is regarded as a satanically inspired act.[24] Philo, a first-century Jewish philosopher, portrays Cain as a man enslaved to self-love.[25] In the Targums,[26] Cain reportedly boasts, "There is no judgment, there is no Judge, there is no other world, there is no gift of good reward for the just and no punishment for the wicked."[27] Surely, Cain reflects the evil one's arrogance and malicious attitude toward others.

Reflecting on Genesis 4, the writer of Hebrews notes, "By faith Abel offered to God a better sacrifice than Cain did. By faith he was approved as a righteous man, because God approved his gifts, and even though he is dead, he still speaks through his faith" (Heb. 11:4). In other words, what differentiates Abel from Cain is the former man's faith and the latter man's lack of it.

Unrepentant after the Lord's gentle rebuke, Cain urges his

brother to go out into the field with him. There, Cain attacks Abel and kills him. When the Lord inquires as to the whereabouts of Abel, Cain's infamous reply is, "Am I my brother's keeper?" (Gen. 4:9 KJV).

The Lord responds with a curse: "So now you are cursed, alienated from the ground that opened its mouth to receive your brother's blood you have shed. If you work the land, it will never again give you its yield. You will be a restless wanderer on the earth" (vv. 11-12).

Even so, the Lord places a mark on Cain to protect him, threatening vengeance seven times over to anyone who kills him. Cain goes out from the Lord's presence and lives in the land of Nod, east of Eden. His descendants are enumerated to the sixth generation. Gradually, they become so corrupt that God sends a deluge to prevent the final triumph of evil.

John perhaps draws the concept of Cain being "of the evil one" (Gr. *ek tou ponerou*) from Genesis 4:7, where God warns Cain that "sin is crouching at the door." As Daniel Akin observes, "The adjective *ponerou* ('evil') indicates the active exercise of evil in one's behavior. Cain demonstrated the defining actions of his spiritual father."[28] Cain drew his murderous inspiration from the evil one, the archetypal murderer from the very beginning (John 8:44).

In his description of the murder, John reveals Cain's diabolical nature when he uses the Greek word *esphazen*, which means "to slaughter, butcher" – literally, "to cut the throat."[29] This is killing for the sake of killing, with no remorse. It is taking another person's life for the sake of self-satisfaction and in the name of self-justification. And it begs the question: Why?

John answers: "Because his [Cain's] deeds were evil, and his brother's were righteous" (1 John 3:12). The brothers' deeds – Abel's sacrifice and Cain's murder of Abel – flow from their characters. Abel's reverent offering of a blood sacrifice provokes jealousy in Cain. Jealously descends into hatred, and hatred into murder.

In a sense, Cain murders his brother *before* he strikes him dead because Cain sets his mind to the evil task. This serves as a severe warning to us that our thoughts and attitudes, if unchecked, lead to all kinds of malice. It's the point Jesus drives home in the Sermon on the Mount when he teaches about murder and adultery (Matt. 5:21-30). In a nutshell, Cain murders Abel because wicked people hate righteousness in the same way that Satan hates God and God's people. Cain sides with the evil one and thus emulates his spiritual father.

In the end, Cain has no ground for complaint, just as Satan has no excuse for rebellion. If Cain does what is right, he and his sacrifice are accepted (Gen. 4:7). In the same way, the evil one had all the advantages of an anointed guardian cherub before his fall (Ezek. 28:14). Both are willingly disobedient. Both are shameless. Both are cast out.

In his short epistle, Jude writes of false teachers who have infiltrated the church: "Woe to them! For they have gone the way of Cain ..." (v. 11). Simply put, the way of Cain is the way of religion without faith. It is the way of pride, a man establishing his own righteousness and rejecting the righteousness of God that comes through faith in Christ. Warren Wiersbe writes, "Cain became a fugitive and tried to overcome his wretchedness by building a city and developing a civilization (Gen. 4:9ff). He ended up with everything a man could desire – everything except God, that is."[30]

Cain rejects God's way of salvation, though he is not ignorant of it. By clothing Adam and Eve with the skins of animals (Gen. 3:21), God makes it clear that the only way of forgiveness is shedding the blood of an innocent animal substitute. Cain would have none of it, preferring to approach the altar with the fruits of his own labor – and later, spilling the blood of an innocent human being.

Why does God reject Cain's offering? Because Cain's heart – like the heart of his spiritual father – is not right before God. Cain is the prototype of human wickedness. As such, Cain, and all those who mimic his attitude toward God and God's people, reflect the nature of the evil one, who was a murderer from the beginning.

1 John 5:18-19

> We know that everyone who has been born of God does not sin, but
> the one who is born of God keeps him, and the evil one does not
> touch him. We know that we are of God, and the whole world is
> under the sway of the evil one.

John notes *the evil one* twice in these verses, once to illustrate
believers' insulation from Satan, and once to explain the unbelieving
world's enslavement to his powers. The apostle also begins each of
these verses with the words "we know," bringing his epistle to a close
with summarizing statements. Finally, John uses the descriptor "born
of God" twice in verse 18, signifying different persons in each
reference.

Verse 18 begins with a curious statement: "We know that everyone
who has been born of God does not sin." This is almost identical to
John's earlier statement in 1 John 3:9: "Everyone who has been born of
God does not sin." The Greek literally reads "does not sin," but the
tense often carries with it a progressive meaning. That's why some
English translations render the phrase "cannot keep on sinning"
(ESV) or "cannot go on sinning" (NIV).

This seems to capture the writer's intent more accurately. John is
not advocating the view that a true follower of Jesus attains sinless
perfection in this earthly life, for earlier in the epistle he urges us to
confess our sins (1:9). Further, he reminds us that if we claim to be
sinless, we make God a liar (1:10).

Rather, John's use of the perfect participle for "born of God" (Gr.
gegennemenos) suggests a permanent relationship begun in the past
with continuing benefits from the new birth. One of these benefits is
the God-given ability not to fall into long-term, habitual sin. We sin,
of course, but sin does not enslave us because the indwelling Spirit
empowers us to conquer temptation, and because God always offers
an avenue of escape (1 Cor. 10:13). As John Stott notes, "The perfect
participle indicates that the new birth, far from being a transient
phase of religious experience, has a continuing result. He who has

been begotten (or born) of God remains his child with permanent privileges and obligations."[31]

John simply assures us that Christ finishes the good work he began in us (cf. Phil. 1:6). Having been regenerated, or "born of God," we are made new creatures in Christ (2 Cor. 5:17). Our desires are different. We seek to please God. The Holy Spirit continues his work of sanctification – conforming us to the image of Jesus. Having been delivered from Satan's kingdom and brought into the kingdom of God, we are freed from bondage to evil, and our lives should increasingly reflect the character of our Savior. Sin should be the exception, not the rule, in our lives.

But why is it that Christians – those "born of God" – do not continue in sin? The second half of verse 18 tells us: because "the one who is born of God keeps him, and the evil one does not touch him." Commentators are divided as to whether this second reference to one "born of God" refers to Christians or to Christ. While John often describes Christians as those who are born of God (1 John 2:29; 3:9; 4:7; 5:1, 4, 18), it seems better to understand Christ as the apostle's focus here.

Christians cannot keep themselves secure; that's the work of God. Further, followers of Jesus cannot resist the evil one in their own power. Jesus is the one who keeps his disciples safe. He says of his followers, whom he calls sheep, "I give them eternal life, and they will never perish. No one will snatch them out of my hand." And then he adds, "My Father, who has given them to me, is greater than all. No one is able to snatch them out of the Father's hand. I and the Father are one" (John 10:28-30).

In his high priestly prayer, Jesus tells the Father, "While I was with them, I was protecting them by your name that you have given me. I guarded them and not one of them is lost, except the son of destruction, so that the Scripture may be fulfilled" (John 17:12). The idea of believers being safe in the Lord is found in the writings of Peter and Jude as well (1 Pet. 1:5; Jude 24).

While it's true that Scripture generally does not refer to Jesus as "born of God," Jesus refers to himself as God's "only begotten Son"

(John 3:16 KJV, NASB 1995), "one and only Son" (CSB, NIV), or "only Son" (ESV). The Greek term is *monogenes* and is pivotal to an understanding of Jesus' divine nature and eternal relationship to the Father. James White explains how linguistic studies, and the discovery of ancient papyri in the Egyptian deserts within the last century, have clarified a proper understanding of this term:

> It was assumed that the term was made up of two parts: *monos*, which means "only," and *gennao*, which is a verb meaning "to beget, give birth to." The assumption was half correct. *Monogenes* does come from *monos* but not from *gennao*; rather, the second part of the word comes from a noun, *genos*, that means "kind" or "type." Therefore, *monogenes* means "one of a kind, unique" rather than "only begotten," and, accordingly, the term was used of an only son, a unique son. The importance for Christology is clear: No one can base a denial of the Son's eternal nature upon this term, for it does not refer to a "beginning" at all but instead describes the uniqueness of the object.[32]

Throughout his writings, John wants us to know that while Jesus is the Son of God, his Sonship is an eternal, one-of-a-kind relationship with God the Father. Believing sinners are "begotten" in the sense that we are born again, or made spiritually alive through the regenerating work of the Holy Spirit. Our sonship is through adoption; Christ's Sonship is by the very nature of his eternal relationship with the Father.

And so, Christ, who is "born of God" in a unique way as the eternal Son of God, keeps secure those who are "born of God" through the regenerating work of the Holy Spirit. The Spirit is our seal, or God's mark of ownership on us, and our guarantee of everlasting life (2 Cor. 1:22; Eph. 4:30). And there's more.

John writes that the evil one does not "touch" us. The Greek word rendered "touch" is *haptetai* and means "to fasten to, adhere to ... to fasten fire to a thing, kindle, set on fire." The evil one seeks to attach himself to us like fire to dry wood, thus doing us harm. But Christ does not permit Satan's fiery darts to torch those he has redeemed. The final chapter of this book explores how the full armor of God quenches the evil one's flaming arrows. Satan and his minions constantly bombard us with trials and temptations. Christ makes sure that the one who roams the earth like a lion (1 Pet. 5:8) is kept on a short chain.

In verse 18, John reminds us that *we know* everyone born of God does not continue in sin because Christ guards our hearts and shields us from the evil one's attacks. Then, in verse 19, the apostle tells us *we know* that we are of God (or "children of God" as in the NIV), in stark contrast to those in the world who are under the sway of the evil one. This is meant to assure us that God is our Father, and thus he sees us differently than those who reject his offer of adoption. The evil one can't touch God's children, but the whole world is helplessly under Satan's thumb. There are only two possible loyalties. Each person either is "of God" or "under the sway of the evil one."

In Chapter 12, we identify several ways Jesus and the New Testament writers apply the Greek word *kosmos*, often translated "world." In the context of John's epistle, it seems clear that *kosmos* identifies the world order alienated from God, in rebellion against him, and condemned for its godlessness. This is the world over which Satan rules.

Believers are *of* God, while unbelievers are, in a sense, *in* the evil one. That is, they are in his grip and under his control. Not only that, they are citizens of his kingdom and, unwittingly, captives in his dark domain. John does not depict non-Christians as yearning to be free of the evil one, or struggling against the chains that bind them. Rather, they seem quite satisfied to be prisoners, and quite unaware of the death penalty hanging over them. Satan not only takes them captive to do his will (2 Tim. 2:26), he blinds them to the reality of their enslaved condition (2 Cor. 4:4).

As one commentator puts it, the world is:

... dominated by the devil, who controls it with tyrannical authority, organizing and orchestrating its life and activities to express his own rebellion and hatred against God.... That is why the world's freedom is slavery, and the devil's offer of autonomy from God, which lies at the root of all sin, an allusion.[33]

Finally, John tells us the whole world is "under the sway" of the evil one. The NIV renders it "under the control," while the NASB says the whole world "lies in the power" of Satan. Everyone who has rejected God's gracious offer of salvation falls into this category, without exception. Satan's authority over them is absolute but not inevitable.

Christ came to seek and to save the lost (Luke 19:10). He invaded Satan's kingdom, breaking into the strong man's house and binding him so that the Son of Man might plunder the evil one's goods (Matt. 12:29). That means Jesus rescues sinners from the evil one's domain and brings them into the kingdom of light.

To be under the sway, under the control, or to lie in the power of the evil one derives from the Greek *keimai*, which means to lie like an infant or a corpse, set and situated beyond one's own control. Metaphorically, as John uses it here, it means to be held in subjection.

Truly, the evil one has his children under control. His empire is vast. His citizens willingly follow his lead. But their presumed autonomy is a deception. They may think, speak, and act according to their own desires, but the evil one pulls the strings behind the scenes and, as such, keeps the unbelieving world in a drunken and deadly stupor.

Summary

Key takeaways about *the evil one*:

(1) History records the names and deeds of many evil men and women, from Nero to Hitler. Yet behind them all is a personality who birthed evil and who inspires it in all people, especially those who willingly become his instruments of malice. Of course, we're talking about Satan, whom Scripture often calls *the evil one*.

(2) Evil is not so much the opposite of good as it is the *absence* of good, or the perversion of good. Just as darkness may only be described in contrast to light, evil is only understood in relation to good. And that's the rub, because all human beings, though made in the image of God, are evil. We all sin, and our sin separates us from an eternally and unequivocally good creator (Rom. 3:10, 23; 6:23).

(3) New Testament writers use a variety of Greek words to depict evil. Their meanings range from *wicked* to *wrong*, and from *malice* to *unclean*. The Greek term often used to describe Satan is *ho poneros* – the evil one; it conveys an ethical meaning related to a being who is wholly wicked.

(4) Numerous New Testament passages shed light on the evil one:

- Matthew 5:37 – Followers of Jesus are to be truthful at all times. If we resort to empty pledges and oaths, our words more accurately mirror those of the evil one than of the Lord.
- Matthew 6:13 – We are to pray for deliverance from the evil one, from whom all evil ultimately proceeds.
- Matthew 13:19 – Just as birds don't wait for the farmer to leave his field before snatching seeds from the footpaths, the evil one descends immediately on hardened hearts to keep them from truly hearing the gospel and thus being saved.
- Matthew 13:24-30, 37-43 – The kingdom of heaven and the evil one's kingdom exist simultaneously during this "present evil age" (Gal. 1:4). But a day of harvest, and separation of the wheat and weeds, is coming.
- John 17:15 – In his high priestly prayer, Jesus asks the Father to protect his disciples from the evil one. In addition, Jesus prays for his followers' unity and sanctification.
- Ephesians 6:16 – The evil one hurls a seemingly endless volley of temptations – "flaming arrows" – at us. To quench them, we must take up the shield of faith.

- 2 Thessalonians 3:3 – Despite the evil one's unceasing ploys, the Lord's faithfulness assures us that suffering has meaning, that God deals harshly with those who persecute his people, and that our future is secure in Christ.
- 1 John 2:12-14 – Faith in Jesus secures our victory over sin and death because Christ has decisively routed and irreversibly defeated the evil one.
- 1 John 3:11-12 – Cain murders Abel because wicked people hate righteousness in the same way that Satan hates God and God's people. Cain sides with the evil one and thus emulates his spiritual father.
- 1 John 5:18-19 – Having been delivered from the evil one's kingdom and brought into the kingdom of God, we are freed from bondage to evil, and our lives should increasingly reflect the character of our Savior.

(5) John tells us the whole world is "under the sway" of the evil one. That is, everyone who has rejected God's gracious offer of salvation falls into this category, without exception. Satan's authority over them is absolute – but it's not inevitable.

Questions for Personal or Group Study

1. In this chapter, we made the observation, "Evil is not so much the opposite of good as it is the *absence* of good, or the perversion of good." What are some examples of good things God has given us that we distort and thus make evil?

2. Consider the words of Jesus in Matthew 5:37: "But let your 'yes' mean 'yes,' and your 'no' mean 'no.' Anything more than this is from the evil one." How are Jesus' first-century listeners abusing the practice of taking oaths? Why do you think Jesus accuses Satan of being behind it all?

3. What do you think Jesus means when he instructs us to ask the Father, "And do not bring us into temptation, but deliver us from the evil one" (Matt. 6:13)? Does God really *lead* us into temptation? And if we truly pray for deliverance from Satan, why do we still fail so often in our battles with sin?

4. Jesus and the New Testament writers often refer to Satan as *the evil one*. What does this say about the devil's unique place in our sinful and fallen world? Put another way, why are demons and human beings called *evil*, but the term *evil one* is reserved for Satan alone?

5. In what way is the whole world "under the sway of the evil one" (1 John 5:19)? What does John mean by "world"?

BEELZEBUL: PRINCE OF DEMONS

When you think about crime bosses, whose name rises to the top? Perhaps your first impulse is to go with Vito Corleone. However, the character in Mario Puzo's *The Godfather* is mostly a composite figure based on real Mafia kingpins Frank Costello, Don Joe Profaci, and Carlo Gambino.[1] Besides, Vito Corleone fades into the shadows of his ascending son Michael, who eclipses his father at the top of the Corleone family and runs it with calculating brutality.

Well then, let's consider Vito Genovese, a real mobster who distinguished himself during Prohibition. Another good choice: Lucky Luciano, the father of modern organized crime. Or, take your pick of Al Capone, better known as "Scarface" and leader of the Valentine's Day Massacre; Bugsy Siegel, the Jewish-American mobster who helped put Las Vegas on the map; Carlo Gambino, who took over the Mangano family and renamed it after himself; John Gotti, also known as "The Teflon Don" until throat cancer took his life; or Vincent Louis Gigante, a heavyweight boxer who became a brutal mob enforcer. Any of these colorful characters might lay claim to being the most feared crime boss in the underworld.

But they all take a back seat to Salvatore Toto Riina, perhaps the most notorious mobster of all time. Born in Corleone, Sicily, Riina became boss of the Sicilian Mafia. During his criminal career, Riina personally murdered at least forty people and ordered hits on hundreds of others, including several anti-Mafia prosecutors. Long after his death in Parma Prison, just a day after his eighty-seventh birthday, Riina is considered the most dangerous mob boss ever.[2]

One common characteristic of these infamous men is their ability to lead. Leveraging their larger-than-life personalities, they ply persuasion, intimidation, and elimination to rise to the top of their organizations. In the process, they rally a host of like-minded criminals to carve out a kingdom in their chosen areas of interest – money laundering, bookmaking, drugs, prostitution, and a host of other lucrative enterprises.

These men are known mostly as incendiary leaders who seem as enthralled with the twisted means of their businesses as they are with the results. They lead fiercely loyal families in a dangerous world. And, in a certain way, they are flesh-and-blood images of a true underworld lord the Bible sometimes calls *Beelzebul*.

Beelzebul / Beelzebub

The name *Beelzebul* (or *Beelzeboul*, *Beelzebub*) appears seven times in the Gospels (Matt. 10:25; 12:24, 27; Mark 3:22; Luke 11:15, 18, 19), as well as in the pseudepigraphal *Testament of Solomon*. The etymology of *Beelzebul* is uncertain, although it might be traced to the Philistine god Baal-zebub, who was worshiped in Ekron. We get an indication of this in the Book of 2 Kings, where King Ahaziah incurs God's wrath after requesting an oracle from Baal-zebub:

> After Ahab's death, Moab rebelled against Israel. Ahaziah had fallen through the latticed window of his upstairs room in Samaria and was injured. So he sent messengers, instructing them, "Go inquire of *Baal-zebub, the god of Ekron*, whether I will recover from this injury."
>
> But the angel of the Lord said to Elijah the Tishbite, "Go and meet the messengers of the king of Samaria and say to them, 'Is it because there is no God in Israel that you are going to inquire of

Baal-zebub, the god of Ekron? Therefore, this is what the LORD says: You will not get up from your sickbed; you will certainly die.'" Then Elijah left.

The messengers returned to the king, who asked them, "Why have you come back?"

They replied, "A man came to meet us and said, 'Go back to the king who sent you and declare to him, "This is what the LORD says: Is it because there is no God in Israel that you're sending these men to inquire of *Baal-zebub, the god of Ekron*? Therefore, you will not get up from your sickbed; you will certainly die"'" (2 Kings 1:1-6, emphasis added).

In the pseudepigraphal *Testament of Solomon*, God sends Michael the archangel to give Solomon a ring with power over demons. Armed with the ring, Solomon subdues Beelzebul and other demons. The story doesn't end well for Solomon, however. He falls prey to beautiful women who lead him to sacrifice to Baal, Rapha, Moloch, and other gods, resulting in the departure of God's Spirit from Solomon (vv. 5, 12-16, 128-130).

The name *Baal-zebub,* used in 2 Kings 1, means "lord of the flies" and may be a derisive renaming of the Canaanite deity *Baal-zebul,* or "Baal (lord) the Prince." If that's true, Baal the Prince is unceremoniously recast as *lord of the flies.*[3] Even worse, as Leon Morris notes, "The Jews may have further corrupted this into ... 'lord of dung,' which would be a way of further insulting the heathen deity."[4]

Theodore Lewis notes that the etymology of *Beelzebul* has proceeded in other directions, as well. For example, some scholars connect *zebul* with a noun meaning "abode" or "dwelling," suggesting Beelzebul is master of the heavens and thus a chief rival to Yahweh. Perhaps this is why Jesus pointedly refers to himself as "the head of the house," pitting himself against Beelzebul and his domain in Matthew 10:25. Yet another view connects the name *Beelzebul* with the Aramaic *be el debaba,* which means "enemy" or "adversary," which might help explain the equation of Beelzebul with Satan.[5]

Whichever view is correct, the New Testament clearly identifies Beelzebul as Satan, the prince of demons. Jesus and the religious leaders who oppose him use the name *Beelzebul* as a synonym for Satan in numerous places in the Gospels. Let's briefly survey these Scripture passages.

Matthew 10:25

Jesus prepares his followers for persecution. He warns that he is sending the disciples out as sheep among wolves, so he urges them to be as shrewd as serpents and as innocent as doves. The Savior further predicts they will be handed over to local courts and flogged in the synagogues. Further, they are going to be brought before governors and kings for Messiah's sake. Family members will betray one another, even giving them up to death. Everyone will hate the disciples because of Jesus' name.

So, how does Jesus instruct his disciples to respond? "When they persecute you in one town, flee to another," he says. "For truly I tell you, you will not have gone through the towns of Israel before the Son of Man comes" (Matt. 10:23).

Then, Jesus teaches them:

> A disciple is not above his teacher, or a slave above his master. It is enough for a disciple to become like his teacher and a slave like his master. If they called the head of the house 'Beelzebul,' how much more the members of his household (Matt. 10:24-25)!

Clearly, Christ's opponents slander his disciples and attribute their good works to an evil source. If the religious leaders call Jesus *Beelzebul* (prince of demons), and accuse him of performing miracles in the power of the evil one, then ungodly men and women will reject the gospel message and accuse Christ's servants of demonically inspired mischief. As R. T. France observes, "The disciple who has the privilege of sharing Jesus' work and representing him must also expect to share his unpopularity."[6]

As noted earlier, Jesus' reference to himself as "the head of the house" may be a pointed contrast between himself, the true Lord, and Beelzebul, the falsely worshiped lord of heaven.

Matthew 12:24, 27

Jesus engages in recurring conflict with the Pharisees throughout Matthew 12. After Jesus' disciples are seen plucking and eating heads of grain on the Sabbath, the religious leaders scold Jesus for allowing his followers to "do what is not lawful to do on the Sabbath" (12:2). Jesus delivers a countercharge, accusing the Pharisees of condemning the innocent. And then he boldly proclaims his deity: "For the Son of Man is Lord of the Sabbath" (12:8).

Next, Jesus enters the synagogue, where he meets a man with a shriveled hand. The Pharisees test Jesus, asking, "Is it lawful to heal on the Sabbath?" (12:10). Jesus replies, "Who among you, if he had a sheep that fell into a pit on the Sabbath, wouldn't take hold of it and lift it out? A person is worth far more than a sheep; so it is lawful to do what is good on the Sabbath" (12:11-12). Then, Jesus heals the man's shriveled hand. This enrages the Pharisees, who depart the synagogue and plot to kill Jesus (12:13-14).

After a short respite, in which Jesus continues his healing ministry, the Pharisees deliver their strongest attack on the Savior:

> Then a demon-possessed man who was blind and unable to speak was brought to him. He healed him, so that the man could both speak and see. All the crowds were astounded and said, "Could this be the Son of David?"
>
> When the Pharisees heard this, they said, "This man drives out demons only by Beelzebul, the ruler of the demons."
>
> Knowing their thoughts, he told them, "Every kingdom divided against itself is headed for destruction, and no city or house divided against itself will stand. If Satan drives out Satan, he is divided against himself. How then will his kingdom stand? And if I drive out demons by Beelzebul, by whom do your sons drive them out? For

this reason they will be your judges. If I drive out demons by the Spirit of God, then the kingdom of God has come upon you" (Matt. 12:22-28).

Much is happening in this scene. First, notice that demonization may manifest itself in physical disabilities. This is not always the case, nor are all physical disabilities the result of demon possession. But it's clear in this instance that a demon successfully prevents his human victim from speaking and seeing. In response, Jesus *heals* the man. Matthew does not say an exorcism takes place, but no doubt he implies it when he records that the man is now able to both speak and see. Further, the Pharisees confirm that Jesus has driven out a demon.

Next, Jesus' miracle astonishes the crowds, who wonder aloud, "Could this be the Son of David?" Jesus is so unlike their messianic expectations. He does not present himself as a conquering king or a forceful military commander. In fact, just a few verses earlier, he exhorts the people not to make him known (12:16-21). And yet, he speaks and acts with divine authority. Thus, people are compelled to entertain the possibility that this man from Nazareth is the promised Messiah.

The Pharisees, however, are fully convinced Jesus is a pretender – a false prophet, a blasphemous self-promoter, a sorcerer, or perhaps even someone in league with Satan. They state their case clearly: "This man drives out demons only by Beelzebul, the ruler of the demons" (12:24). The religious leaders are certain that the only way Jesus can cast out demons is with a little help from the prince of demons. Put another way, the Pharisees accuse Jesus of being Satan's agent, claiming that Jesus performs extraordinary acts of exorcism only with Satan's permission and help.

Of course, this is a baseless charge, which Jesus masterfully exposes. He knows the Pharisees' thoughts – that their accusation is rooted, not in ignorance, but in unbelief, or even envy – so he counters them on two fronts. First, he states the obvious: "Every kingdom divided against itself is headed for destruction, and no city or house divided against itself will stand. If Satan drives out Satan, he is divided against himself. How then will his kingdom stand?" (12:25-26).

The Pharisees know, from history and personal observation, that kingdoms often crumble from within. Even smaller realms, such as cities and households, cannot withstand squabbling and factionalism. Perhaps some Pharisees are prompted to think about current battles their Jewish sect is having with the Sadducees, Herodians, and Zealots with respect to practicing their faith while under Roman occupation.

If they live long enough, they will see how residents of Jerusalem in AD 70 worsen the Roman siege of their fortified city as they engage in vicious infighting. And it's hard to dispute the truth that households are destroyed and reputations ruined when family members rise up against one another. Common wisdom shows that divided organizations come unraveled. The Pharisees are naïve if they think Satan is unaware of this truth.

Further, if Satan empowers Jesus to cast out demons, he's just handing his arch-enemy the combination to his vault. The evil one is enabling Jesus to dismantle an army of evil spirits and free human captives under Satan's power. Why would the ruler of demons wish for his own demise? Why would he pit one evil spirit against another? It is a patently absurd position. Jesus knows it. And, of course, the Pharisees know it, too.

But Jesus doesn't stop there. He offers a second line of attack: "And if I drive out demons by Beelzebul, by whom do your sons drive them out? For this reason they will be your judges" (12:27). The Pharisees have spoken in haste. They have not stopped to reflect that some of their own people perform exorcisms – a fact Josephus affirms and claims to have witnessed.[7] We even read about itinerant Jewish exorcists in the Book of Acts, including seven sons of Sceva, who carry on a dubious deliverance ministry (Acts 19:13-16).

In any case, the Pharisees would emphatically deny that Jewish exorcists are in league with the evil one. And yet, if supernatural authority is required to cast out demons, where are the Jewish exorcists getting their help? Obviously not from Satan.

Jesus leverages this well-known truth to place the Jewish exorcists over the Pharisees in judgment. These exorcists no doubt would testify to the fact that casting out demons is not a work of Satan. And they would rightly condemn the Pharisees for ascribing to Satan a work the exorcists know only comes from God.

Now, Jesus makes a final point: "If I drive out demons by the Spirit of God, then the kingdom of God has come upon you" (12:28). It's obvious that Satan cannot – or at least, would not – cast out his own minions, thus sabotaging his kingdom. And the Pharisees are not denying that a supernatural activity has taken place. The only question is the source of Jesus' power over demons. So, Jesus asks the Pharisees to consider that he drives out demons by the Holy Spirit. And with this divine activity, he demonstrates that the kingdom of God has arrived – a kingdom at odds with Satan's domain.

A Cautionary Tale

Perhaps that's why Jesus immediately follows this statement with a parable: "How can someone enter a strong man's house and steal his possessions unless he first ties up the strong man? Then he can plunder his house" (12:29). It's clear in this context that Satan is the strong man who possesses great treasure and power. But Jesus has come, not to serve the evil one, but to bind him and to plunder his goods.

The kingdom of heaven – that is, the rule of God – has come to earth, personified in King Jesus. He launches a frontal assault on the evil one's realm, overpowers Satan through kingdom miracles like healings and exorcisms, and frees those in the grip of the evil one. The miracles Jesus performs – miracles of creation, such as turning water into aged wine, and miracles of restoration, such as casting out demons and healing the sick – prove his deity and demonstrate the work of the Holy Spirit in him.

The Pharisees should be in awe of Jesus, as the crowds are. Yet, they have so hardened their hearts that they have passed the point of no return. Later, Jesus pronounces woes against the Pharisees and scribes, reminding them they are filling up the measure of their fathers' sins (Matt. 23:31-32). Jesus seems to be saying there is a limit to the mischief God graciously permits – a line in the sand, if you will. When a person, family, city, or nation crosses that line, God's mercy gives way to divine judgment.

We see it in the days of Noah, at Sodom, and in the defeat of both the northern and southern kingdoms of Israel. No doubt, the Pharisees who plot Jesus' death also have crossed that line. For this reason, they are hastening the day of judgment that falls on Israel in AD 70, when the Romans besiege Jerusalem, destroy the temple, kill more than one million Jews, and scatter the rest. It is a particularly pointed accusation that the Pharisees are guilty of an unpardonable sin – ascribing to Satan what only God can do.

Jesus then draws another line, and every person must find himself or herself on one side or the other. "Anyone who is not with me is against me," he says, "and anyone who does not gather with me scatters" (12:30). The Son of David indeed has come as a conquering king, but his enemy is not the Romans. Rather, Jesus has set his sights on a much more imposing foe. He has come to invade Satan's kingdom, conquer Beelzebul by his own blood, storm the gates of hades, and deliver those held prisoner in the evil one's lair.

Later, when Jesus asks his disciples who they say he is, Peter asserts, "You are the Messiah, the Son of the living God" (Matt. 16:16). Jesus confirms Peter's confession and then declares, "on this rock I will build my church, and the gates of Hades will not overpower it" (Matt. 16:18).

By "this rock," Jesus may be referring to Mount Hermon, the seat of ancient pagan practices and, in the Savior's day, considered the very gates of hades. In essence, Jesus declares war on the evil one and then almost immediately sets his sights on Jerusalem, where he endures the cross, only to rise triumphantly three days later. This is why Jesus came into the world, and he bids us join him – or oppose him. There is no neutral ground – no Switzerland, if you will – in the global war for human souls.

Where there can be no neutrality, our choices present serious consequences. Jesus offers forgiveness for "every sin and blasphemy," but not for "blasphemy against the Spirit" (12:31). It's not that other sins are petty and easily forgiven. All sins grieve the heart of God, and each sin demands the death penalty – a payment only an eternal being who has taken on sinless human flesh can pay.

When we agree with God that we have sinned, and when we repent and entrust our lives to Christ, we pass immediately and irrevocably from spiritual death to everlasting life (John 5:24). But the Pharisees' sin of blasphemy against the Holy Spirit – ascribing the Spirit's work to the prince of demons – fills up their measure of sin. The sin is unpardonable, not because God cannot forgive it, or because he would not forgive it if they truly repented. It is unpardonable because their blasphemy against the Spirit is damning evidence of hearts hardened beyond all remedy. They do not come to Christ because they will not come to Christ.

Put another way, in the context of this passage, sin against the Son of Man is rejection of the gospel, a violation that may be set right through repentance. However, sin against the Holy Spirit is full and final rejection of the gospel in that it denies the evident work of the three persons of the Trinity. It is conscious, willful, determined, and irreversible hardness of heart, for which there is no cure, only judgment.

The unpardonable sin, as Jesus depicts it here in Matthew's Gospel, cannot be committed today. It was a particular sin the Pharisees wrought against the triune God. They had rejected the testimony the Father had sent through the prophets. They sought to kill the eternal Son of God, who came in fulfillment of messianic prophecies. And they blasphemed the Holy Spirit by equating his divine power with demonic forces. Once the three persons of the Godhead are cast off, where else is one to go for salvation?

The Pharisees witness first-hand the Word who became flesh (John 1:14) and reject him. They deny the divine power of his miracles.

They cling to their corrupt legalism rather than embrace the Son of God, who came offering freedom. And they take their stand on the wrong side of the line, thinking they are doing the Lord's work when they cry out for the death of the Lamb of God.

At the same time, there is a sense in which a person in our day may commit an unpardonable sin. Though we do not see Jesus in the flesh – teaching, healing, and casting out demons – we have eyewitness testimony of his finished work on the cross. Further, all people have sufficient revelation of God in conscience and creation so that, one day, they stand before God without excuse (Rom. 1:20). To consciously, willfully, repeatedly reject the Son of God is to stand across the line from Jesus and refuse his gracious invitation to cross over. As one commentator puts it:

> When a person takes up a position like that of the Pharisees, when, not by way of misunderstanding but through hostility to what is good, that person calls good evil and, on the other hand makes evil his good, then that person has put himself in a state that prevents forgiveness.[8]

The Ruler of Demons

We should take note of the Pharisees' description of Beelzebul as "the ruler of the demons" (12:24). There is little doubt Satan commands a vast army of evil spirits. Jesus tells us hell has been prepared for "the devil and his angels" (Matt. 25:41), while other passages indicate that evil spirits operate in a hierarchy that is well-constructed and strategically led.

The word "ruler" is *archon* in Greek and means "commander," "chief," "prince," or "magistrate." In the New Testament, *archon* depicts several different types of rulers: rulers over nations (Matt. 20:25; Acts 4:26); religious leaders (Matt. 9:18, 23; 23:13; Acts 3:17); and city authorities (Acts 16:19).

But *archon* also refers to leaders in the demonic realm. In one of the passages we're currently studying (Matt. 12:22-28), Beelzebul is called the *archon* (prince, ruler) of demons (cf. Mark 3:22; Luke 11:15). Elsewhere, Satan is called *archon* of this world. Consider:

John 12:31. After Jesus predicts his crucifixion and the Father speaks from heaven, the Son of Man declares:

> "Now is the judgment of this world. Now the *ruler* [Gr. *archon*] of this world will be cast out. As for me, if I am lifted up from the earth I will draw all people to myself." He said this to indicate what kind of death he was about to die (12:31-33, emphasis added).

John 14:30. Throughout John 14, Jesus promises to send "another Counselor" like himself – the Holy Spirit, who will be with, and in, his disciples (14:16-17). He then describes the marvelous manner in which the Father and Son will make their home with those who love Jesus (14:18-21, 23). And he assures the disciples that the Father will send the Holy Spirit in Jesus' name to teach them all things and remind them of everything Jesus has told them (14:26).

Finally, Jesus promises his followers peace and urges them to not let their hearts be troubled (14:27). He goes on to say:

> You have heard me tell you, "I am going away and I am coming to you." If you loved me, you would rejoice that I am going to the Father, because the Father is greater than I. I have told you now before it happens so that when it does happen you may believe. I will not talk with you much longer, because the *ruler* [Gr. *archon*] of the world is coming. He has no power over me. On the contrary, so that the world may know that I love the Father, I do as the Father commanded me (14:28-31, emphasis added).

John 16:11. Jesus tells his disciples to brace for future persecution, while assuring them of assistance from the coming Holy Spirit who, through their faithful proclamations, convicts the unbelieving world of sin, righteousness, and judgment, "because the *ruler* [Gr. *archon*] of this world has been judged" (emphasis added).

Ephesians 2:2. Paul reminds his readers that, prior to conversion, they "walked according to the ways of this world, according to the *ruler* [Gr. *archon*] of the power of the air, the spirit now working in the disobedient" (emphasis added). Paul also writes about the evil one's "domain of darkness" where he and evil spirits are at work (Col. 1:13). Satan not only commands a worldly domain; he rules a demonic host that resides in the spiritual realm. We more fully explore Satan as the ruler of this world in Chapter 12.

Even though human, demonic, and Satanic authorities threaten the gospel, we should take heart. Jesus reigns as the *archon* of all the kings of the earth. As John declares to the seven churches in Asia Minor, Jesus Christ is "the faithful witness, the firstborn from the dead and the *ruler* [Gr. *archon*] of the kings of the earth" (Rev. 1:5, emphasis added).

Jesus' encounters with the Pharisees in Matthew 12 show a common understanding of Beelzebul, or Satan, as ruler over a vast spiritual realm. He has a kingdom, and he engages a phalanx of evil spirits to enslave people in sin and sickness. Unlike Jewish exorcists of the first century, who go through elaborate ceremonies in their sometimes-successful efforts to expel demons from people, Jesus commands demons with the same verbal authority he exercised in the creation of the universe.

Without exception, evil spirits know Jesus, revile him, and fear him. When Jesus casts them out, whether into a herd of pigs or off to desert places, they obey – and they understand that they, along with their prince, are destined for the lake of fire and sulfur (Matt. 25:41; Rev. 20:10).

Mark 3:22

Mark 3:20-30 runs parallel to Matthew 12:22-28 but provides added details:

> Jesus entered a house, and the crowd gathered again so that they were not even able to eat. When his family heard this, they set out to restrain him, because they said, "He's out of his mind."

The scribes who had come down from Jerusalem said, "He is possessed by *Beelzebul*," and, "He drives out demons by *the ruler of the demons*."

So he summoned them and spoke to them in parables: "How can Satan drive out Satan? If a kingdom is divided against itself, that kingdom cannot stand. If a house is divided against itself, that house cannot stand. And if Satan opposes himself and is divided, he cannot stand but is finished. But no one can enter a strong man's house and plunder his possessions unless he first ties up the strong man. Then he can plunder his house.

"Truly I tell you, people will be forgiven for all sins and whatever blasphemies they utter. But whoever blasphemes against the Holy Spirit never has forgiveness, but is guilty of an eternal sin" – because they were saying, "He has an unclean spirit" (emphasis added).

Mark introduces Jesus' family into the story. It's troubling to read that members of his own household think he's insane and seek to restrain him. Even worse, scribes from Jerusalem have a crueler diagnosis. They blurt out their belief that Beelzebul possesses Jesus and empowers him to drive out demons. This is similar to the charge of the Pharisees in Matthew 12, but with the twisted addition that the evil one has assumed complete control over Jesus.

Jesus responds with the same parables Matthew records about a house divided against itself and the plundering of a strong man's house. And he makes it clear that ascribing the work of the Holy Spirit to Satan is unpardonable because it reveals the hardened and unrepentant hearts of many religious leaders.

Luke 11:15, 18, 19

Luke's account of the same story (Matt. 12:22-28; Mark 3:20-30) mentions only that the demon has made the man mute, not blind as well. Further, Luke doesn't pin the blasphemous accusations specifically on the scribes or Pharisees, but simply writes, "some of them said …" Further, he adds, "And others, as a test, were demanding a sign from heaven." Note the account in context:

> Now he was driving out a demon that was mute. When the demon came out, the man who had been mute spoke, and the crowds were amazed. But some of them said, "He drives out demons by *Beelzebul, the ruler of the demons*." And others, as a test, were demanding of him a sign from heaven.
>
> Knowing their thoughts, he told them, "Every kingdom divided against itself is headed for destruction, and a house divided against itself falls. If Satan also is divided against himself, how will his kingdom stand? For you say I drive out demons by *Beelzebul*. And if I drive out demons by *Beelzebul*, by whom do your sons drive them out? For this reason they will be your judges. If I drive out demons by the finger of God, then the kingdom of God has come upon you. When a strong man, fully armed, guards his estate, his possessions are secure. But when one stronger than he attacks and overpowers him, he takes from him all his weapons he trusted in, and divides up his plunder. Anyone who is not with me is against me, and anyone who does not gather with me scatters (Luke 11:14-23, emphasis added).

Luke further identifies the "strong man" as one who is fully armed, while the "stronger" one takes away his weapons and divides his plunder. This indicates the nature of the spiritual battle taking place in the unseen realm. Satan has his schemes (Eph. 6:11), disguises (2 Cor. 11:14), and a voracious appetite (1 Pet. 5:8). He also commands a host of well-armed, organized demons who engage in guerilla warfare for the hearts and minds of human beings made to be God's imagers. We are defenseless in our own strength. But as the apostle Paul states:

> … the weapons of our warfare are not of the flesh, but are powerful through God for the demolition of strongholds. We demolish arguments and every proud thing that is raised up against the

knowledge of God, and we take every thought captive to obey Christ
(2 Cor. 10:4-5).

Paul further urges us to put on the full armor of God so we may
resist the devil and take our stand. The Lord gives us the belt of truth;
the breastplate of righteousness; sandaled feet that swiftly carry the
gospel; the shield of faith that enables us to extinguish the flaming
arrows of the evil one; the helmet of salvation; and the sword of the
Spirit, which is the Word of God. With these, we are to pray in the
Spirit at all times and stay alert (Eph. 6:10-18).

The battle is long, requiring perseverance. Satan's army attacks
and counter-attacks with relentless fervor and seemingly
unstoppable power. But Christ has overcome Satan and his worldly
realm, and we may take comfort in knowing that a victorious
outcome is never in doubt because our Savior has overcome the
world (John 16:33).

Prince Charming

Satan indeed leads a horde of evil spirits (Matt. 25:41; Rev. 12:9). He is
a formidable foe, equipped with great intelligence and supernatural
power. Further, he commands a well-organized force that scouts
human beings, waits, and attacks at opportune times. The Gospels
and the Book of Acts describe these beings as "unclean spirits"
about twenty times, and as "demons" about fifty times. Jesus
confirms the conventional Jewish belief in his day that Satan –
whom the scribes and Pharisees call *Beelzebul* – rules these evil
spirits.

Humans are never commanded in Scripture to rebuke Satan or
demons. Even Michael the archangel defers to the Lord (Jude 9). But
we *are* instructed to submit ourselves to God and resist the evil one
(Jas. 4:7). This is because we know Jesus has won the battle, having
overcome the evil one through his sinless life, death, burial, and
resurrection. We resist when we are fully clothed in the armor of
God. And even when the evil one's attacks have worn down our

resistance to temptation, we find the Lord has made an avenue for our escape (1 Cor. 10:13).

Beelzebul is a prince indeed – perhaps even a Prince Charming when he's at his masquerading best. He reigns over a kingdom, and he rules loyal subjects who inhabit the spiritual realm. In addition, he has enslaved countless human beings, holding them captive to do his will (2 Tim. 2:26).

Thankfully, the ultimate *archon*, the Lord Jesus Christ, has invaded Beelzebul's kingdom and disarmed him. Now, Jesus is actively plundering the evil one's goods, setting captives free, and making adopted children of those formerly in bondage to sin and destined for a common eternity with their prince in the lake of fire.

Summary

Key takeaways about *Beelzebul*, prince of demons:

(1) While the etymology of *Beelzebul* is uncertain, possibly traced to the Philistine god Baal-zebub, the New Testament clearly identifies Beelzebul as Satan, prince of demons. Jesus, and the religious leaders who oppose Jesus, use the name *Beelzebul* as a synonym for Satan in numerous places in the Gospels.

(2) Jesus prepares his followers for persecution. If the religious leaders call Jesus *Beelzebul* (prince of demons), and accuse him of performing miracles in the power of the evil one, then ungodly men and women will reject the gospel message and accuse Christ's servants of demonically inspired mischief (Matt. 10:24-25).

(3) As Jesus makes clear throughout his recurring battles with religious leaders, the Son of David indeed has come as a conquering king, but his enemy is not the Romans. Rather, Jesus has set his sights on a much more imposing foe. He has come to invade Satan's kingdom, to conquer Beelzebul by Jesus' own blood, to storm the gates of hades, and to deliver those held prisoner in the evil one's lair.

(4) Blasphemy against the Holy Spirit is unpardonable, not because God cannot forgive it, or because he would not forgive it if people truly repented. It is unpardonable because blasphemy against

232 | ROB PHILLIPS

the Spirit is damning evidence of hearts hardened beyond all remedy. The Pharisees in Jesus' day do not come to Christ because they will not come to Christ.

(5) Jesus' encounters with the Pharisees in Matthew 12 show a common understanding of Beelzebul as ruler over a vast spiritual realm. The evil one has a kingdom, and he engages a phalanx of evil spirits to enslave people in sin and sickness. Unlike Jewish exorcists of the first century, who go through elaborate ceremonies in their sometimes-successful efforts to expel demons from people, Jesus commands demons with the same verbal authority he exercised in the creation of the universe.

(6) In a parallel to Matthew 12, Mark 3 introduces Jesus' family, as well as scribes, into the story. Members of Jesus' own household think he's insane. But the scribes have a crueler diagnosis. They blurt out their belief that Beelzebul possesses Jesus and empowers him to drive out demons. This is similar to the charge of the Pharisees in Matthew 12, but with the twisted addition that the evil one has assumed complete control over Jesus.

(7) Jesus has invaded Beelzebul's kingdom and disarmed him. Now, Jesus is actively plundering the evil one's goods, setting captives free, and making adopted children of those formerly in bondage to sin.

Questions for Personal or Group Study

1. Jesus and the religious leaders of his day use the name *Beelzebul* in reference to Satan. What are the Old Testament roots of this name (2 Kings 1:1-6)? Why did ancient Jews distort the name to mean "lord of the flies" or "lord of dung"?
2. Read Matthew 10:24-25. How does Jesus employ the name *Beelzebul* to prepare his disciples for persecution?
3. Why do you think the religious leaders of Jesus' day accuse him of casting out demons by Beelzebul, the ruler

of the demons (see Matt. 12:22-28)? How does Jesus expose their hypocrisy?

4. In several New Testament passages (e.g., Matt. 12:24; Mark 3:22; Luke 11:15; John 12:31), Beelzebul is called an *archon* (prince, ruler). Over whom or what does Satan rule?

5. Are followers of Jesus ever commanded to rebuke Beelzebul? How did Michael the archangel deal with the evil one in their dispute over the body of Moses (Jude 9)? What is a proper Christian response to attacks of the evil one (Jas. 4:7; cf. 1 Cor. 10:13)?

Paul's singular use of Belial may be a stern warning to the Corinthians to separate themselves from the crafty false teachers who, under the influence of Satan, proclaim "another Jesus," "a different spirit," and "a different gospel" (2 Cor. 11:4).

11

BELIAL

Satan is called *Belial* (or *Beliar*) on only one occasion in the New Testament. As Paul instructs the Corinthians to separate themselves from unbelievers, he asks a series of rhetorical questions:

> For what partnership is there between righteousness and lawlessness? Or what fellowship does light have with darkness? What agreement does Christ have with *Belial*? Or what does a believer have in common with an unbeliever? And what agreement does the temple of God have with idols (2 Cor. 6:14-16, emphasis added)?

The answer to all of these questions, of course, is "none whatsoever." Paul contrasts the holiness of Christ with the wickedness of Satan. He also draws a sharp distinction between the expected behavior of Christians and followers of the evil one. But does Scripture provide us with other clues as to the identity of Belial?

The Hebrew word *beliyya'al* occurs twenty-seven times in the Old Testament – never as a proper name for Satan, although there is an implied connection between *beliyya'al* and the underworld.

In Psalm 18:4-6, *beliyya'al* (translated "torrents of destruction" in the CSB and "floods of ungodly men" in the KJV) is united with *death* and *sheol* to form three great enemies of God's people. Perhaps that's why some commentators refer to "sons of Belial," like the rapists and murderers at Gibeah, as "hellions" or "a gang of local hell raisers" (Judg. 19:22).

Meanwhile, the Dead Sea Scrolls and other ancient materials depict Belial as the leader of the forces of darkness.[1] In fact, *Belial* is the most frequently used title of the leader of the sons of darkness in the Qumran manuscripts.[2] He also graces the pages of many pseudepigraphal works. In the *Testament of Judah*, for example, Belial will be cast into the fire to burn forever (25:3; cf. Rev. 20:10).

Nothing Profitable

Belial comes from the Hebrew word for "wickedness" (*bly'l*) and is associated with the concept of worthlessness. *Beli* means "without" and *ya'al* means "profit;" thus, the wicked produce nothing profitable. Some interpreters derive *Belial* from a Hebrew verb, *bala*, which means "to swallow up" or "engulf." In this regard, the word is connected with *sheol*, the abode of the dead, which swallows up the departed.

Throughout the Old Testament, *beliyya'al* is used mostly to describe those engaging in serious crimes against Israel's religious or social order. For example, *beliyya'al* depicts the heart of those who refuse to lend money in a sabbatical year (Deut. 15:9), and those who counsel against Yahweh (Nah. 1:11).[3]

There's more. "Children of Belial" entice the Israelites to serve other gods (Deut. 13:13 KJV). "Sons of Belial" demand homosexual sex from a house guest in Gibeah, then rape and murder his concubine (Judg. 19:22-28 KJV). "Men of Belial" refuse to share the spoils of battle with those who stayed behind (1 Sam. 30:22 KJV). When Eli's sons abuse the sanctuary, they are considered "sons of Belial" who do not know the Lord (1 Sam. 2:12-25 KJV). Other English translations use "scoundrels," "worthless men," "wicked men," "base men," or "troublemakers" to describe those associated with Belial.

In a pledge of integrity, King David declares, "I will not let anything worthless (Heb. *dbr bly'l*) guide me" (Ps. 101:3). Specifically, he rejects deceit, slander, and lying – actions specifically associated with Satan elsewhere in Scripture.

In Psalm 41:8-9, David connects Belial with "a vile disease" (NIV) and betrayal. Jesus quotes verse 9 as a prophecy about Judas, whom the devil entices to raise his heel against the Messiah: "I'm not speaking about all of you; I know those I have chosen. But the Scripture must be fulfilled: The one who eats my bread has raised his heel against me" (John 13:18). Even so, the Old Testament connection between Belial and Satan is mostly implied rather than explicit.

However, in pseudepigraphal literature and the Qumran texts,[4] Belial is well attested as the proper name of the devil. Examples include *Testament of Levi* 18:4; War Scroll (1QM); and Thanksgiving Scroll (1QH). Peter Bolt explains:

> Here an ongoing struggle between good and evil is represented mythically as a battle on high between the angel Michael and Belial. The present age is the time of Belial's rule, and he is the leader of the people opposed to God. After a momentous struggle, God will bring about the permanent annihilation of Belial and all his forces of evil, human and angelic.[5]

Meet Mastemah

The pseudepigraphal and Qumran texts also introduce us to the name *Mastemah* for Satan/Belial. The Hebrew *mstmh* occurs twice in Hosea 9:7-8, meaning "hostility," but nowhere else in the Old Testament. However, the pseudepigraphal Book of Jubilees depicts Mastemah as the prince of evil spirits sent to trouble human beings (Jub. 10:8, 11). New Testament writers never use Mastemah as a name for Satan, although "hostility" is associated with the evil one's activities (e.g., John 8:39-44; 1 John 2:12-14, 3:10-12; cf. Rev. 12:12, 17).

So, why does Paul use *Belial* in his warning to the Corinthians? It's possible that he's not making a personal reference to Satan, but expressing a concern that the Corinthians avoid false teachers. Clearly, he contrasts righteousness and lawlessness, light and darkness, and the temple of God and idols. The contrast between Christ and Belial could be understood as one between the holiness of Christ and the wickedness of false teachers.

However, if Paul *does* have Satan in mind, he connects Belial with lawlessness, darkness, unbelief, and idolatry – worthless traits the "super apostles," who have infiltrated the church, exhibit. Paul exposes these "super apostles" as "false apostles, deceitful workers, disguising themselves as apostles of Christ." They disguise themselves as ministers of righteousness because Satan "disguises himself as an angel of light" (2 Cor. 11:5, 13-15).

So, Paul's singular use of *Belial* may be a stern warning to the Corinthians to separate themselves from the crafty false teachers who, under the influence of Satan, proclaim "another Jesus," "a different spirit," and "a different gospel" (2 Cor. 11:4).

Summary

Key takeaways about *Belial*:

(1) Satan is called *Belial* on only one occasion in the New Testament (2 Cor. 6:15). Paul contrasts the holiness of Christ with the wickedness of Satan. He also draws a sharp distinction between the expected behavior of Christians and followers of the evil one.

(2) *Belial* comes from the Hebrew word for "wickedness" (*bly'l*) and is associated with the concept of worthlessness. *Beli* means "without" and *ya'al* means "profit;" thus, the wicked produce nothing profitable. This certainly is consistent with the nature of the evil one.

(3) Throughout the Old Testament, *Belial* (Heb. *beliyya'al*) is used mostly to describe those engaging in serious crimes against Israel's religious or social order. However, in pseudepigraphal literature and the Qumran texts, *Belial* is well attested as the proper name of the devil.

(4) Paul's singular use of *Belial* in 2 Corinthians 6:15 may be a stern warning to the Corinthians to separate themselves from the crafty

false teachers who, under the influence of Satan, proclaim "another Jesus," "a different spirit," and "a different gospel" (2 Cor. 11:4).

Questions for Personal or Group Study

1. Read 2 Corinthians 6:14-16. With whom does Paul compare *Belial*? And what clues does Paul give us that *Belial* is Satan?

2. What are some ways the Old Testament ties the Hebrew word *beliyya'al* to the underworld? For example, consider Deuteronomy 13:13; Judges 19:22-28; and Psalm 18:4-6.

3. Why do you think Paul uses *Belial* in his warning to the Corinthians (2 Cor. 6:14-16; see also 2 Cor. 11:5, 13-15)?

Satan is an evil, controlling ruler who commands the hearts of unbelievers. He is the god of this age and the ruler of the power of the air.

12

RULER OF THIS WORLD

It's good to be sultan. Just ask Hassanal Bolkiah, who rules the Nation of Brunei, one of the world's few absolute monarchies. The sultan is among the richest persons on the planet. Since 1967, he has presided over a tiny state that boasts an exceptionally high standard of living, thanks to substantial oil and gas reserves.

The sultan and his subjects pay no taxes. In addition to his role as sultan, Bolkiah is the prime minister, head of the defense and finance ministries, a general in the armed forces, an honorary admiral in the Royal Navy, and inspector-general of police. He lives in the largest palace in the world, the Istana Nurul Iman, which features 1,788 rooms.[1] Perhaps most notably, he owns one of the longest names known to modern-day monarchs: Sultan Haji Hassanal Bolkiah Mu'izzaddin Waddaulah ibni Al-Marhum Sultan Haji Omar 'Ali Saifuddien Sa'adul Khairi Waddien Sultan and Yangdi-Pertuan of Brunei Darussalam Jones (okay, fine, I tossed in *Jones*).[2]

While the sultan has a lot going for him, he can't hold a candle to another monarch who is far richer, more powerful, and more influential, whose kingdom can't be confined to national boundaries, and who has ruled over his subjects far longer than the sultan's half-century of dominance. Scripture reveals his many names, including Satan, the devil, the evil one, Beelzebul, and the ruler of this world.

In this chapter, we explore how Jesus and the New Testament writers brand Satan *the ruler of the world, the ruler of this world, the god of this age,* and *the ruler of the power of the air.* Our main focus is on the words of Jesus in three passages in the Gospel of John.

John 12:31

Jesus is preparing Philip and Andrew for the Messiah's imminent death. "The hour has come for the Son of Man to be glorified," he says. "Truly I tell you, unless a grain of wheat falls to the ground and dies, it remains by itself. But if it dies, it produces much fruit" (John 12:23-24). Soon after, Jesus confesses, "Now my soul is troubled. What should I say – Father, save me from this hour? But that is why I came to this hour. Father, glorify your name" (vv. 27-28).

The Father speaks from heaven, "I have glorified it, and I will glorify it again" (v. 28). A crowd has gathered. Hearing the voice, some think it is thunder. Others believe an angel has spoken.

Jesus responds, "This voice came, not for me, but for you. Now is the judgment of this world. Now *the ruler of this world* will be cast out. As for me, if I am lifted up from the earth I will draw all people to myself" (vv. 30-32, emphasis added). He says this to indicate the type of death he faces: crucifixion.

Jesus clearly has Satan in mind when he refers to "the ruler of this world." To better understand what Jesus means in this passage, and in future references to the evil one, we should take a moment to explore the terms *ruler* and *world.*

Ruler

The word *ruler* in John 12:31 comes from the Greek *archon*, which is sometimes translated "prince," "chief," or "magistrate." It means "a first in rank or power." In the New Testament, *archon* depicts several different kinds of rulers: rulers over nations (Matt. 20:25; Acts 4:26); rulers of synagogues, as well as other Jewish leaders (Matt. 9:18, 23; 23:13; Acts 3:17); and city authorities (Acts 16:19).

At the same time, New Testament writers employ *archon* to describe rulers in the unseen realm. For example, Beelzebul is called the *archon* (prince, ruler) of demons (Matt. 12:24; Mark 3:22; Luke 11:15). And, Jesus calls Satan the *archon* of this world (John 12:31; 16:11; cf. Eph. 2:2).

So, if Jesus and the New Testament writers acknowledge Satan as one with authority over this world, what do they mean by *world*?

World

The English word *world* in the New Testament usually is a translation of the Greek *kosmos*, which means "that which is ordered or arranged." It's where we get the English term *cosmetics*.[3] It is related to a verb that means "to set in order," or "to adorn, decorate." As William Mounce explains, "In classical Greek and the LXX [Septuagint, or the Greek translation of the Old Testament], *kosmos* communicated the idea of order and adornment, and from this it developed into the basic term for the cosmos or the universe."[4]

New Testament writers employ *kosmos* nearly two hundred times in a variety of ways. First, *kosmos* refers to the universe, which God designed and created to have order. In his address on Mars Hill, Paul notes, "The God who made the world [*kosmos*] and everything in it – he is Lord of heaven and earth – does not live in shrines made by hands" (Acts 17:24). And in his high priestly prayer, Jesus tells the Father, "I want those you have given me to be with me where I am, so that they will see my glory, which you have given me because you loved me before the world's [*kosmos*] foundation" (John 17:24).

Second, *kosmos* describes the planet Earth. It is mankind's dwelling place as contrasted with heaven. After Jesus feeds five thousand, the people marvel at this miracle and remark, "This truly is the Prophet who is to come into the world [*kosmos*]" (John 6:14).

Later, Jesus invites his disciples to accompany him to Judea as he works his way toward the home of his recently deceased friend, Lazarus. When the disciples remind him that the Jews in Judea just tried to stone him, Jesus replies, "Aren't there twelve hours in a day? If anyone walks during the day, he doesn't stumble, because he sees the light of this world [*kosmos*]" (John 11:9).

Third, *kosmos* depicts all humanity. In what is perhaps Jesus' most memorable statement, he says:

> "For God loved the world [*kosmos*] in this way: He gave his one and only Son, so that everyone who believes in him will not perish but have eternal life. For God did not send his Son into the world [*kosmos*] to condemn the world [*kosmos*], but to save the world [*kosmos*] through him" (John 3:16-17).

Paul writes this about the apostles' mistreatment:

> Up to the present hour we are both hungry and thirsty; we are poorly clothed, roughly treated, homeless; we labor, working with our own hands. When we are reviled, we bless; when we are persecuted, we endure it; when we are slandered, we respond graciously. Even now, we are like the scum of the earth [*kosmos*], like everyone's garbage (1 Cor. 4:11-13).

Fourth, *kosmos* summarizes the totality of human existence in this present life, with all its experiences, possessions, and emotions. Jesus uses *kosmos* in this way as he challenges his disciples to deny themselves:

> "If anyone wants to follow after me, let him deny himself, take up his cross, and follow me. For whoever wants to save his life will lose it, but whoever loses his life because of me will find it. For what will it benefit someone if he gains the whole world [*kosmos*] yet loses his life? Or what will anyone give in exchange for his life? For the Son of Man is going to come with his angels in the glory of his Father, and

then he will reward each according to what he has done. Truly I tell you, there are some standing here who will not taste death until they see the Son of Man coming in his kingdom" (Matt. 16:24-28).

Paul uses *kosmos* in a similar way in his discussion of the impact of marriage on service to the Lord:

The unmarried man is concerned about the things of the Lord – how he may please the Lord. But the married man is concerned about the things of the world [*kosmos*] – how he may please his wife – and his interests are divided. The unmarried woman or virgin is concerned about the things of the Lord, so that she may be holy both in body and in spirit. But the married woman is concerned about the things of the world [*kosmos*] – how she may please her husband. I am saying this for your own benefit, not to put a restraint on you, but to promote what is proper and so that you may be devoted to the Lord without distraction (1 Cor. 7:32-35).

Finally, *kosmos* identifies the world order alienated from God, in rebellion against him, and condemned for its godlessness. This is the world over which Satan rules, according to Jesus and the New Testament writers. In a blunt discussion with Israel's leaders, Jesus distinguishes "this world" from the heavenly realm. He tells them, "You are from below ... I am from above. You are of this world [*kosmos*]; I am not of this world [*kosmos*]. Therefore I told you that you will die in your sins. For if you do not believe that I am he, you will die in your sins" (John 8:23-24).

The apostle Paul writes about the folly of human wisdom as expressed in this world system: "For the wisdom of this world [*kosmos*] is foolishness with God, since it is written, He catches the wise in their craftiness; and again, The Lord knows that the reasonings of the wise are futile" (1 Cor. 3:19-20). Paul further instructs Christians to exercise church discipline when a professing Christian lives like a citizen of Satan's world:

I wrote to you in a letter not to associate with sexually immoral people. I did not mean the immoral people of this world [*kosmos*] or the greedy and swindlers or idolaters; otherwise you would have to leave the world [*kosmos*]. But actually, I wrote you not to associate with anyone who claims to be a brother or sister and is sexually immoral or greedy, an idolater or verbally abusive, a drunkard or a swindler. Do not even eat with such a person. For what business is it of mine to judge outsiders? Don't you judge those who are inside? God judges outsiders. Remove the evil person from among you (1 Cor. 5:9-13).

There is little doubt that Satan rules over this broken world system, as both Jesus and Paul make clear. Further, in his first epistle, John tells us "the whole *world* is under the sway of the evil one" (1 John 5:19, emphasis added).

These and other Scripture verses help define the tension in which Christians live. We are not of this world. That is, followers of Jesus are citizens of his kingdom, not Satan's crumbling empire. Even so, we must live for a time as resident aliens in the evil one's sinful and fallen domain.

This means, for one thing, to live faithfully is to be hated, as Jesus explains: "If the world hates you, understand that it hated me before it hated you. If you were of the world, the world would love you as its own. However, because you are not of the world, but I have chosen you out of it, the world hates you" (John 15:18-20).

This truth surfaces again in Jesus' high priestly prayer to the Father, in which Jesus refers to the world (*kosmos*) multiple times:

"I have given them your word. The world hated them because they are not of the world, just as I am not of the world. I am not praying that you take them out of the world but that you protect them from the evil one. They are not of the world, just as I am not of the world. Sanctify them by the truth; your word is truth. As you sent me into the world, I also have sent them into the world. I sanctify myself for them, so that they also may be sanctified by the truth" (John 17:14-19).

Dead to the World

There are several other truths related to believers' relationship with the world. First, we are to regard ourselves as dead to the world. That is, we understand the inherently evil nature of Satan's domain and separate ourselves from it. As Paul writes, "The world has been crucified to me through the cross, and I to the world" (Gal. 6:14). James adds, "Pure and undefiled religion before God the Father is this: to look after orphans and widows in their distress and to keep oneself unstained from the world" (Jas. 1:27).

Second, we must not ride the fence between this world and the world to come. In light of eternity, we cannot possess dual citizenship. Whoever wants to be a friend of this world makes himself or herself an enemy of God (Jas. 4:4).

Third, our love reveals our loyalties. As John writes:

> Do not love the world or the things in the world. If anyone loves the world, the love of the Father is not in him. For everything in the world – the lust of the flesh, the lust of the eyes, and the pride in one's possessions – is not from the Father, but is from the world (1 John 2:15-16).

Finally, we are encouraged to take the long view. The sinful and fallen world in which we live is passing away, but the person devoted to Christ remains forever (1 John 2:17). Our focus should not be on what we temporarily experience with our five senses, but on what is unseen and eternal (2 Cor. 4:18).

Jesus does not dispute Satan's claim of authority over this world. During the wilderness temptations, the evil one takes Jesus to a high mountain and shows him all the kingdoms of the world and their splendor. "I will give you all these things if you will fall down and worship me," Satan promises (Matt. 4:8).

Jesus does not challenge the evil one's ability to deliver on his promise – to regale the Son of Man with wealth and fame. Instead, Jesus cuts to the heart of Satan's temptation – the evil one's motivation to exalt himself before the second Adam and thus ruin God's plan of redemption. To the devil's alluring pledge, Jesus replies, "Go away, Satan! For it is written: Worship the Lord your God, and serve only him" (Matt. 4:10).

Satan departs, but only for a time (Luke 4:13).

Taken together, Jesus' words to his disciples – "the ruler of this world will be cast out" – now become clear. Our Savior acknowledges the evil one as a ruling authority, one whose *world* is an ordered rebellion against the Creator. It is a powerful system that attracts fallen human beings through "the lust of the flesh, the lust of the eyes, and the pride in one's possessions" (1 John 2:16). However, Satan's rebellion is temporary and destined for failure. His place, long ago prepared, welcomes him one future day with torment forever and ever (Matt. 25:41; Rev. 20:10).

It should be noted that two other Greek words sometimes are translated "world" in the New Testament. One is *oikoumene*, which means "inhabited world," and the other is *aion*, which refers to an age or period of time.[5]

John 14:30

Jesus calls Satan "the ruler of the world" in John 14. The Savior tells his disciples:

> "Peace I leave with you. My peace I give to you. I do not give to you as the world gives. Don't let your heart be troubled or fearful. You have heard me tell you, 'I am going away and I am coming to you.' If you loved me, you would rejoice that I am going to the Father, because the Father is greater than I. I have told you now before it happens so that when it does happen you may believe. I will not talk with you much longer, because *the ruler of the world* is coming. He has no power over me. On the contrary, so that the world may know that I love the Father, I do as the Father commanded me. Get up; let's leave this place" (John 14:27-31, emphasis added).

Jesus' followers are troubled because he has repeatedly announced his imminent departure (John 14:2-4, 12, 18-19). They are worried, despite the Lord's assurances they will do even greater works than he has done. He promises to answer their prayers and send another Comforter, the Holy Spirit, to be *with* them and *in* them (vv. 12-17). Jesus also pledges to bequeath them peace – not a hollow worldly peace but an enduring one.

Indeed, the world is powerless to give peace because sinful and fallen people are unable to overcome their own pride, greed, hatred, malice, and fear. But the transcendent peace Jesus promises comes through his pending death, in which he absorbs the sins of mankind and introduces the promised messianic peace in a way no one thought possible.

The Romans maintained *Pax Romana* through the sword, and many Jewish people expected the Messiah to wield even greater military and political clout. But instead, through his humble obedience to the Father, Jesus brings a deeper, more stable, more lasting tranquility – first, to the hearts of believers, and ultimately to the entire world.

Jesus gently rebukes his followers, telling them if they truly loved him, they would rejoice in his return to the Father. His departure ensures they will be with him forever.

And then, Jesus makes a statement that often is misunderstood, or even is twisted to deny his deity: "the Father is greater than I." The tension comes when John clearly proclaims Jesus' equality with God (John 1:1, 18; 5:16-18; 10:30; 20:28), while at the same time revealing Jesus' obedience to the Father and his dependence upon him (John 4:34; 5:19-30; 8:29; 12:48-49).

It is wrong to play one truth against the other. That is, it is wrong to say either that Jesus is human and therefore cannot be divine, or to say that Jesus is divine and therefore cannot be human. But the immediate context resolves this difficulty. Jesus' statement, "the Father is greater than I," cannot mean Jesus is not God, for he clearly claims deity throughout Scripture. Nor can it mean Jesus is a lesser god, for Jewish monotheism considered such thinking anathema.

So, how should we understand this hard saying? It seems best to connect "the Father is greater than I" with the main clause, "If you loved me, you would rejoice that I am going to the Father." D. A. Carson notes that if Jesus' disciples truly loved him, they would be glad he is returning to the Father – to the sphere where he belongs, to the glory he had with the Father before the world began, and to the place where the Father is undiminished in glory and unquestionably greater than the Son in his incarnate state. Carson further writes:

> To this point the disciples have responded emotionally entirely according to their perception of *their own* gain or loss. If they had loved Jesus, they would have perceived that his departure to his own "home" was *his* gain and rejoiced with him at the prospect. As it is, their grief is an index of their self-centeredness.[6]

All of this serves as a backdrop for Jesus' statement, "the ruler of this world is coming" (John 14:30). No doubt, the disciples understand this as a reference to Satan, whom Jesus acknowledges as the leader of the *kosmos* alienated from God and in rebellion against him. But in what way is Satan coming?

The evil one often works directly in his own behalf, as in the garden of Eden with Eve (Gen. 3:1-7) and in the wilderness with Jesus (Matt. 4:1-11; Luke 4:1-13). Quite often, however, Satan employs demonic or human agents to do his bidding. We see this throughout Scripture as demons harass people and, in some cases, cause illnesses (e.g., Mark 1:21-27; 9:14-29; Luke 8:26-39; Eph. 6:12; 1 Tim. 4:1-2).

At the same time, Satan occasionally uses people to exercise his authority in the world. For example, Jesus tells unbelieving Jews they are of their father, the devil, and therefore want to carry out his desires (John 8:42-47). In the context of the passage currently under study (John 14:27-31), Jesus has Judas Iscariot in mind as the agent of Satan's work.

Whatever role Judas plays in the death of Jesus, Satan is the one pulling the strings. Recall what Jesus tells the disciples in John 6:70,

"Didn't I choose you, the Twelve? Yet one of you is a devil." John explains, "He was referring to Judas, Simon Iscariot's son, one of the Twelve, because he was going to betray him" (v. 71).

That becomes even more clear when Jesus and the disciples observe the Passover meal on the evening before Jesus' death. After Jesus washes the disciples' feet and promises blessings for those who follow his example, he states:

> "I'm not speaking about all of you; I know those I have chosen. But the Scripture must be fulfilled: The one who eats my bread has raised his heel against me. I am telling you now before it happens, so that when it does happen you will believe that I am he. Truly I tell you, whoever receives anyone I send receives me, and the one who receives me receives him who sent me" (John 13:18-20; cf. Ps. 41:9).

Immediately after this, Jesus is troubled in his spirit and says, "Truly I tell you, one of you will betray me" (John 13:21).

The disciples are stunned. They look at one another in confusion as to which of the Twelve is the betrayer. Peter urges John to get more details. So, John leans back against Jesus and asks, "Lord, who is it?" (v. 25).

Jesus replies, "He's the one I give the piece of bread to after I have dipped it."

Then, Jesus dips the bread and offers it to Judas Iscariot (v. 26). After Judas eats the morsel of food, John records, "Satan entered him." Jesus tells Judas, "What you're doing, do quickly" (v. 27).

This is a rare biblical instance of Satan entering, or taking complete control of, a human being. Demons often control persons in what we commonly call *demon possession*, but what is more accurately translated *demonization*. That is, demons don't actually own human beings – only God possesses saved people as his adopted children, and only Satan owns lost people and enslaves them in darkness – but demons can and do enter human spirits and exert varying degrees of control over them.

In the case of Judas Iscariot, Satan already owns him in that Judas is not a true follower of Jesus. However, rather than influence Judas through temptation – the lust of the flesh, the lust of the eyes, and the pride in one's possessions (1 John 2:16) – he now commands Judas' thoughts and deeds from within.

There is one other possible satanic proprietorship in Scripture. Paul warns about a coming *man of lawlessness*, whom we know more commonly as the antichrist. The apostle describes him as one who "opposes and exalts himself above every so-called god or object of worship, so that he sits in God's temple, *proclaiming that he himself is God*" (2 Thess. 2:4, emphasis added). As Jesus is God incarnate, Satan comes as the ultimate counterfeit Christ, inhabiting the spirit of a willing human deceiver and proclaiming himself God in human flesh. While Paul does not say the evil one *enters* or *possesses* the man of lawlessness, it appears Satan controls the antichrist in much the same way he controlled Judas Iscariot.

Through Judas, Satan attains his goal of Jesus' betrayal, which leads to the Savior's arrest, condemnation, and crucifixion. Yet the evil one is self-deceived, as Jesus makes clear. He tells his disciples that the ruler of the world "has no power over me. On the contrary, so that the world may know that I love the Father, I do as the Father commanded me" (John 14:30-31). Jesus' words recall a Jewish idiom frequently used in legal contexts. When Jesus says Satan has no power over him, it means the evil one has no claim on Jesus, nothing with which to legitimately condemn him.[7]

How true this is. Jesus is not of this world (John 8:23), nor has he ever sinned (John 8:46). Satan could only wield power over Jesus if there were justifiable charges to be leveled against him. There are none. This is the clearest case in history of a frivolous lawsuit.

And Jesus wants his disciples to understand this. Far from a defeat at the hands of Satan and his human agent, Judas, Jesus' imminent death is the fulfillment of God's eternal plan. Jesus came into this world – both the physical realm and the evil system under Satan's control – to die (John 18:36; 1 Tim. 1:15; 1 John 4:10; Rev. 13:8). He lays down the challenge to Satan in the foothills of Mount Hermon, declaring that his church is about to storm the gates of hades. Then, he sets his eyes on Jerusalem, where he is to suffer, die, and rise from the dead (Matt. 16:13-23).

All of this is according to God's determined plan and foreknowledge (Acts 2:22 ff.). Jesus' obedience to the Father flows out of love for him. This love and obedience are supremely displayed in Jesus' willingness to lay down his life (John 10:17-18). And Jesus challenges his disciples to model the same love and obedience with respect to him as they keep his commandments (John 14:15, 21, 23).

As John MacArthur notes:

> Jesus came to earth, of course, to reveal God to mankind. He came to teach truth. He came to fulfill the Law. He came to offer His kingdom. He came to show us how to live. He came to reveal God's love. He came to bring peace. He came to heal the sick. He came to minister to the needy.
>
> But all those reasons are incidental to His ultimate purpose. He could have done them all without being born as a human. He could have simply appeared – like the angel of the Lord often did in the Old Testament – and accomplished everything in the list above, without actually becoming a man. But He had one more reason for coming: He came to die.[8]

The ruler of this world is coming to carry out his murderous schemes through Judas Iscariot, and through the Jewish leaders to whom Jesus is betrayed. Because of this, Jesus' time with his disciples is short. Yet, this is not a defeat for the Son of Man. Quite the contrary. The evil one has no power over the sinless Son of God, who voluntarily lays down his life, only to take it up again on the third day after his crucifixion. Jesus' death on the cross displays God's love for the world (John 3:16; Rom. 5:8) and Jesus' special love for believers (John 15:13; Gal. 2:20). But it's more than that. It's a declaration to the world of Jesus' supreme love for his Father.

As Rodney Whitacre notes, "The cross is both God's judgment and his evangelism, and both are expressions of his love."[9]

John 16:11

John 16:7-11 reads:

> "Nevertheless, I am telling you the truth. It is for your benefit that I go away, because if I don't go away the Counselor will not come to you. If I go, I will send him to you. When he comes, he will convict the world about sin, righteousness, and judgment: About sin, because they do not believe in me; about righteousness, because I am going to the Father and you will no longer see me; and about judgment, because *the ruler of this world* has been judged" (emphasis added).

This is the third time in John's Gospel that Jesus refers to Satan either as "the ruler of the world" or "the ruler of this world." Jesus is preparing the disciples for his departure and the inevitable persecution of the saints to come. At the same time, Jesus tells his followers it is to their advantage that he goes away. This is because Jesus' ascension follows his finished work of redemption – that is, his death, burial, and resurrection. Further, when Jesus sits down at the Father's right hand, he serves as our great high priest, mediator, and intercessor.

But it gets even better. Jesus promises to send "another Counselor" like himself. The Holy Spirit, untethered to a physical body as Jesus is in the Incarnation, will be both *with* and *in* Jesus' followers. In many respects, we might see the Holy Spirit as the divine agent of everlasting life. Both the Father and Jesus send him, and his work is wonderfully comprehensive.

For example, the Spirit *regenerates* believing sinners, making us spiritually alive. He *indwells* our human spirits, which now serve as the holy of holies for God's Shekinah glory. He *seals* us, or places God's mark of ownership on us. He is the Spirit of *adoption*, ensuring that newborn babes in Christ are welcomed into God's family. He *sanctifies* us, or sets us apart and begins the lifelong process of conforming us to the image of Christ. He helps us pray. He gives us spiritual gifts to employ in service to the Lord. And he does much more. So, Jesus promises the Spirit to encourage his followers. He ensures them they are not to be left as orphans.

At the same time, Jesus describes the Holy Spirit's future work in the unbelieving world. In the immediate context, Jesus may be referring to unbelieving Jews in general, and to unbelieving Jewish leaders in particular. Up to now, Jesus certainly has warned the religious elite about their sins and the dire consequences of persistent unbelief (John 8:21, 24; 9:41; 15:22, 24; 19:11). In one particularly pointed statement, Jesus says, "Therefore I told you that you will die in your sins. For if you do not believe that I am he, you will die in your sins" (John 8:24).

But taking a wider view, Jesus' words apply to all unbelievers. Specifically, Jesus cites three ways the coming Spirit is to *convict* unbelievers. The Greek verb *elencho* occurs eighteen times in the New Testament. It may mean "to convict," "to put to proof," "to test," "to lay bare, expose," "to refute," "to reprove, rebuke," or "to chastise," among other meanings.[10] Primarily, however, *elencho* has to do with showing people their sin and calling them to repentance.[11] As D. A. Carson notes:

> In common with other New Testament usages, *elencho* means "to convict (the world)" in the personal sense, *i.e.* not arguing the case for the world's objective guilt before God at the final Great Assize [final judgment], but shaming the world and convincing it of its own guilt, thus calling it to repentance.[12]

Just as Jesus has exposed the world's evil in its rejection of him (John 15:18-25), the Spirit is to continue this work, initially through the disciples' witness (John 15:26-27). The Spirit's purpose is to drive people to the liberating truth of the gospel of Jesus Christ, and thus to glorify him (John 16:14). Rather than a mournful event, Jesus' imminent departure is a glorious affair because it comes after he has completed the work he came to do through his death, burial, and resurrection. Then, seated at the Father's right hand, Jesus and the Father send the Spirit to extend Jesus' earthly ministry in remarkable ways the disciples cannot yet grasp.

Jesus explains that the Spirit is sent to convict the unbelieving world about sin, righteousness, and judgment. First, about sin "because they do not believe in me" (John 16:9). If people did believe in Jesus, they would embrace his truthful statements about himself, realize their guilt, and turn to him for salvation. But instead, their unbelief produces condemnation (John 3:18, 36), along with a blinding ignorance of their peril. As Gerald Borchert puts it:

> The idea of sin here is not merely conceived in terms of a listing of erroneous acts but of the fundamental act of choosing another god. Such an act of rejection means that one stands above God in the way in which Adam and Eve first rebelled against God in the Garden.[13]

So, the Holy Spirit graciously but firmly presses the point of unbelievers' willful rejection of the Son of God as their only remedy for sin. He seeks to confront men and women with their inescapable guilt so they will turn to Jesus and seek his mercy.

Second, the Holy Spirit convicts the unbelieving world of righteousness "because I [Jesus] am going to the Father and you will no longer see me" (John 16:10). It may seem odd at first glance that the Spirit convicts unrighteous people of *their* righteousness. But that's precisely the point. Just as the prophet Isaiah tells his Judean brothers and sisters their "righteous acts" are like a soiled menstruous cloth ("polluted garment," Isa. 64:6), the Spirit draws a sharp contrast between human righteousness and Christ's righteousness. Human righteousness cannot pay the sin debt we owe God, nor is it sufficient to curry God's favor.

There is plenty of manmade righteousness in Jesus' day, and the Lord spends considerable time exposing it for the fraud that it is. Rather than embrace Jesus as Messiah, the religious leaders seek to kill him (John 7:19). Further, there are many places in the New Testament where the world's righteousness is shown to fall short of God's perfect standard (Matt. 5:20; Rom. 10:3; Phil. 3:6-9; Tit. 3:5). The Spirit's mission is to expose human righteousness for what it is – an affront to God – and thus to point people to the perfect righteousness of Christ, in which believing sinners may be clothed.

The Spirit carries on this work because Jesus is returning to the Father. One of Jesus' most significant ministries is exposing the unbelieving world's self-righteousness. As the light of the world, he chases darkness away wherever he goes (John 3:19-21; 7:7; 15:22, 24). But who is to continue this work when Jesus returns to the Father? The Holy Spirit, of course, primarily through the testimony of Jesus' followers, whom the Spirit inhabits and empowers.

One of the most common acts of self-righteousness the world offers today goes something like this:

> I believe in God and do my best to live a good life. I love my spouse and my children. I work hard. I pay my taxes. I go to church and even put some of my hard-earned money in the offering plate. I give to charitable causes. I do my civic duty. I'm a good neighbor. I'm not saying I'm perfect, but on balance, I think the good Lord would agree that I'm all right.

To which the Holy Spirit whispers forcefully, "No! You're not all right. You're pretentious. You're self-righteous. You're deceived. And you're in grave danger."

Which leads to the third way the Holy Spirit convicts the unbelieving world. He convicts the world of judgment "because the ruler of this world has been judged" (John 16:11). The NIV renders it, "because the prince of this world now stands condemned." The world's sense of judgment is wrong because the world itself is sinful and fallen.

Further, the world's morally perverse judgment hinges on the one who is a liar from the beginning. If Satan stands condemned by the triumph of the cross, "the false judgment of those who follow in his train is doubly exposed. The need for conviction of this false judgment is all the more urgent; the world is condemned already and in desperate need to learn of its plight."[14]

Jesus' opponents condemn him as a Sabbath breaker, a false prophet, and a satanically empowered miracle worker. But the Holy Spirit reveals that it is the evil one who stands condemned at Jesus' glorification. This judgment, in turn, condemns the unbelieving world, for unbelievers have the devil as their father (John 8:44).

So, Satan stands condemned through the victorious work of Christ and the convincing testimony of the Holy Spirit. No doubt, Satan is severely diminished today. He has been cast out of heaven, and now he's confined to ruling the unseen realm and prowling the earth (1 Pet. 5:8). While there is a significant gap between the time of Satan's condemnation and his formal sentencing, the day is coming when the ruler of this world is cast into the lake of fire (Matt. 25:41; Rev. 20:10).

The Holy Spirit reveals the truth that Satan's condemnation is an accomplished fact. The evil one's punishment in hell is certain. And for those who side with him and his failed kingdom, they, too, face an eternity apart from the Prince of Peace. Instead, they suffer forever with the prince of this world. As Colin Kruse writes, "The prince of this world, the distorter of true judgment, stands condemned, and the role of the Counsellor will be to prove wrong those of the world who likewise distort true judgment, particularly in relation to Jesus."[15]

Just as Jesus promised to rescue believing sinners from the domain of darkness, the Holy Spirit confirms this gracious work. For unbelievers to be redeemed, the Holy Spirit must convict them of the sin of unbelief, the futility of self-righteousness, and the perilous future condemnation they share with the prince of this world. The purpose of the Spirit's convicting work is to shake unbelievers from their comfortable stupor.

Further, it is to confront them with the inescapable truth that faith in Jesus alone brings forgiveness of sin, transfers Christ's perfect righteousness to their account, and rescues them from an eternity in outer darkness, where the ruler of this world doesn't just stand condemned, but is actually damned. John's visions, captured in the Book of Revelation, portray not only the great power of evil and its seductive ways (Rev. 12:3-4; 13:1-18; 17:1-14), but its clear and final defeat (Rev. 14:17-20; 19:11-21; 20:7-10).

Before moving on, we should note that the apostle John addresses the subject of Satan as the ruler of this world in the conclusion of his first epistle:

> We know that everyone who has been born of God does not sin, but the one who is born of God keeps him, and the evil one does not touch him. We know that we are of God, and *the whole world is under the sway of the evil one.* And we know that the Son of God has come and has given us understanding so that we may know the true one. We are in the true one – that is, in his Son, Jesus Christ. He is the true God and eternal life (1 John 5:18-20, emphasis added).

John contrasts the security of believers with the perilous state of everyone else. The individual "who has been born of God" – brought from spiritual death into spiritual life through the finished work of Christ and the regeneration of the Holy Spirit – does not continue in habitual sinful practices. That's because "the one who is born of God" (a unique reference to Jesus; see Chapter 9) keeps him from returning to the evil one's domain of darkness.

This doesn't mean Christians are exempt from temptation, or even from satanic and demonic attacks. However, the evil one and his minions operate under the sovereignty of God. Satan could not touch Job without God's permission (Job 1:11-12; 2:3-6).

Ancient Judaism recognized that Satan needed God's consent to test God's people, and that God rejected Satan's accusations against God's own people. As Craig Keener notes:

> Judaism acknowledged that all the nations except themselves were under the dominion of Satan and his angels. The source of this idea

is not hard to fathom; nearly all Gentiles worshiped idols, and most also practiced sexual immorality and other sins.[16]

The difference between true believers and everyone else is that the former belong to God, while the latter are under the control of – literally "lie in" – the evil one. John's use of "the world" represents human society under the power of Satan and at war with God and his people.

We should grasp a subtle distinction in this passage. Believers are *of* God, born into his kingdom and adopted as his children. Meanwhile, unbelievers are *in* the evil one – that is, in his grip and under his control. There are only two possible states of existence. Every person either is *of God* or *under the sway of the evil one*. There is no middle ground.

As John Stott notes, "It is not pictured as struggling vigorously to be free but as quietly lying, perhaps even unconsciously asleep, in the embrace of Satan. The evil one does not 'touch' the Christian, but the world is helplessly in his grasp."[17]

Paul's Teaching

The apostle Paul makes at least two direct references to Satan's authority over the world (2 Cor. 4:3-4; Eph. 2:1-2). In his second letter to the Corinthians, Paul notes:

> But if our gospel is veiled, it is veiled to those who are perishing. In their case, *the god of this age* has blinded the minds of the unbelievers to keep them from seeing the light of the gospel of the glory of Christ, who is the image of God (2 Cor. 4:3-4, emphasis added).

Throughout the church age, Bible interpreters have disagreed about the identity of *the god of this age*. Most of us are inclined immediately to understand this as a reference to Satan. After all, Paul writes about the evil one in other parts of this letter. For example, the apostle urges his readers to forgive and welcome back a believer under church discipline, noting that Satan's schemes include unforgiveness, which enables him to take advantage of Christians (2 Cor. 2:11). Later, Paul warns that Satan disguises himself as an angel of light (11:14). And finally, Paul shares a personal experience in which a "messenger of Satan" is sent to keep him from sliding into the sin of self-exaltation (2 Cor. 12:7). So, it seems natural to understand *the god of this age* as Satan.

However, early church fathers Cyril of Jerusalem and Ambrosiaster believed Paul was writing about God. Their argument was simple: Only God is truly sovereign over this age (the Greek word is *aion*, which may be translated "age" or "era"). Cyril and Ambrosiaster argued that if Satan is called "god" (Greek *theos*) in 2 Corinthians 4, and Jesus is called "God" (*theos*) elsewhere in the New Testament (John 1:1-3, 17-18; Tit. 1:3-4), then the passages in John and Titus cannot refer to Jesus as the true God. In other words, if Satan is *theos* and Jesus is *theos*, there is nothing uniquely divine about the Son of God.[18]

Understanding *the god of this age* as God is not as far-fetched as one might imagine. Note what Paul writes to the Romans about the work of God in hardening certain people's hearts:

> What then? Israel did not find what it was looking for, but the elect did find it. The rest were hardened, as it is written, God gave them a spirit of stupor, eyes that cannot see and ears that cannot hear, to this day.... I don't want you to be ignorant of this mystery, brothers and sisters, so that you will not be conceited: A partial hardening has come upon Israel until the fullness of the Gentiles has come in (Rom. 11:7-8, 25; cf. Isa. 6:9-10).

God rules supremely over all authorities and domains. In the process, he accomplishes his divine purposes, which may include leveraging satanic, demonic, and human rebellion.

Even so, these two passages – Romans 11 and 2 Corinthians 4 – do not appear to be directly related. Further, if we see how Paul uses the

262 | ROB PHILLIPS

word *theos* in other passages, it should become clear that he means to identify Satan, not God, as the god of this age. For example, concerning enemies of the cross, Paul writes, "Their end is destruction; *their god is their stomach*; their glory is in their shame; and they are focused on earthly things" (Phil. 3:19). In addition, Paul says pagans offer sacrifices to other gods (*theoi*), who in fact are demons (1 Cor. 10:19-20).

What's more, in the second of Paul's direct references to Satan and his command over the world, we detect a similar context to that of 2 Corinthians 4:

> And you were dead in your trespasses and sins in which you previously lived according to the ways of this world, according to *the ruler of the power of the air*, the spirit now working in the disobedient (Eph. 2:1-2, emphasis added).

Taken together, these Pauline passages seem to describe an evil, controlling ruler who commands the hearts of unbelievers. So, Satan is the better candidate for *the god of this age* (2 Cor. 4:4). This is consistent with Paul's depiction of Satan as *the ruler of the power of the air* (Eph. 2:2).

Age and Air

But what do the terms *this age* and *the air* mean in a New Testament context? Let's look a little closer.

The Greek word for age (*aion*) sometimes is translated "world," but more properly it depicts the temporal aspects of the world. It can refer to time without end, or eternity (Rom. 1:25; 2 Cor. 11:31; Phil. 4:20). However, *aion* often is used to describe shorter periods of time, especially the present age. Satan is the god of this age (2 Cor. 4:4). And the cares of this age/world (*aion*) choke the word of the gospel as it grows (Matt. 13:22).

The expression *this age* often is set against the age to come (Matt. 12:32; Eph. 1:21; Heb. 6:5). Christians are warned not to be conformed to this age (Rom. 12:2), but to live sensible, righteous, and godly lives (Tit. 2:12). Demetrius deserts Paul because he is in love with this present age (2 Tim. 4:10). In contrast, Jesus promises to be with his followers "to the end of the age" (Matt. 28:20).

So, it seems best to understand *this age* as a limited time in which Satan rules over a kingdom in opposition to the eternal kingdom of God. Put another way, Satan's rule is restricted in scope and in time. He commands a vast empire, but one that neither endures nor challenges the sovereignty of Almighty God.

As for the meaning of *the air*, we are told that Satan is *the ruler of the power of the air* (Eph. 2:2). This is sometimes rendered "the prince of the power of the air" (KJV, ESV, NASB); "the prince that ruleth in the air" (GNV); "the commander of the powers in the unseen world" (NLT); "the ruler of the spiritual powers in space" (GNT); and "the ruler of the kingdom of the air" (NIV).

The word *air* may be translated "foggy atmosphere," indicating the darkness Satan prefers to the light. But the entire phrase could simply mean that the evil one commands those principalities and powers that operate in the unseen realm.[19] It was commonly believed that evil spirits dominated the lowest realm of the heavens, known as the atmospheric realm, far below the stellar heavens and the highest heaven, where God sits enthroned. "Air" was the usual term for atmospheric heaven.[20]

In the New Testament, the air (Greek *aer*) is the realm of the demonic. The Greeks thought of the "lower air" to be impure and therefore the domain of evil spirits.[21] A. T. Robertson notes, "'Air' was used by the ancients for the lower and denser atmosphere, and another word for the higher and rarer. Satan is here [Eph. 2:2] pictured as ruler of the demons and other agencies of evil, 'the prince of this world' (John 16:11)."[22]

Interestingly, Paul writes in 1 Thessalonians 4:17 that we are to be caught up in future resurrection to meet the Lord in the air (Greek *aera*), perhaps giving us a preview of a crushing blow to the realm the evil one presently rules.

Scorched Earth

Satan rules a vast empire that includes evil spirits, fallen human beings, and a worldly system in opposition to God. He directs his world with all the panache of a formerly anointed cherub, complete with lies, deceit, creaturely delights, false promises, and incessant appeals to the lust of the flesh, the lust of the eyes, and the pride in one's possessions. His kingdom is in direct opposition to God, God's kingdom, and God's people.

While the ruler of this world cannot win – Christ already has defeated him through the Son of Man's sinless life and finished work on the cross – he wages war as if convinced he still can vanquish his creator. And he carries on a scorched-earth policy in the hope there is nothing left for the redeemed sons of God to enjoy. That, of course, is a fool's pursuit, for when Christ returns, he purges this fallen world of sin and its stain, and thus makes everything new (Rev. 21:5).

Summary

Key takeaways about *the ruler of this world*:

(1) Jesus and the New Testament writers brand Satan *the ruler of the world*, *the ruler of this world*, *the god of this age*, and *the ruler of the power of the air*. Jesus sheds a great deal of light on the subject in key passages in the Gospel of John.

(2) The Greek word *archon* often is translated "ruler," "prince," "chief," or "magistrate." It means "a first in rank or power." *Archon* may depict different kinds of human rulers, or rulers in the unseen realm. For example, Jesus calls Beelzebul the *archon* (prince, ruler) of demons, as well as the *archon* of this world.

(3) The English word *world* in the New Testament usually is a translation of the Greek *kosmos*, which means "that which is ordered or arranged." New Testament writers employ *kosmos* nearly two hundred times in a variety of ways to mean: (a) the universe; (b) the planet Earth; (c) all humanity; (d) the totality of human existence in this present life; and (e) the world order alienated from God, in

rebellion against him, and condemned for its godlessness – this is the world over which Satan rules.

(4) As Christians, we are to regard ourselves as dead to the world. That is, we understand the inherently evil nature of Satan's domain and separate ourselves from it. As Paul writes, "The world has been crucified to me through the cross, and I to the world" (Gal. 6:14).

(5) As the ruler of this world, Satan may work directly in his own behalf, as in the garden of Eden with Eve and in the wilderness with Jesus. Quite often, however, Satan employs demonic or human agents to do his bidding. Nowhere is this demonstrated more powerfully than in Satan's complete control over Judas Iscariot, who betrays Jesus.

(6) Jesus tells his disciples the ruler of this world "has no power over me" (John 14:30). These words recall a Jewish idiom frequently used in legal contexts. When Jesus says Satan has no power over him, he means the evil one has no claim on Jesus, nothing with which to legitimately condemn him.

(7) We should grasp a subtle distinction in 1 John 5:18-20. Believers are *of* God, born into his kingdom and adopted as his children. Meanwhile, unbelievers are *in* the evil one – that is, in his grip and under his control. There are only two possible states of existence. Every person either is *of God* or *under the sway of the evil one*. There is no middle ground.

(8) The apostle Paul describes Satan as an evil, controlling ruler who commands the hearts of unbelievers. He is *the god of this age* (2 Cor. 4:4) and *the ruler of the power of the air* (Eph. 2:2).

Questions for Personal or Group Study

1. What are some different meanings of the Greek word *kosmos* – translated "world" – in the New Testament? How is Satan's world distinct from the rest?
2. In what ways does Satan exercise his authority as *the ruler of this world*?

3. How should Christians relate to the fallen world in which we live, knowing that Satan rules over it?

4. Read John 16:7-11. What does Jesus mean when he says "the ruler of the world has been judged"? If Satan's judgment already has occurred, why does he continue to rule his kingdom?

5. What ultimately becomes of Satan's world? When does this happen?

13

THE DESTROYER

W ho was the most destructive human monster in the last hundred years? Adolf Hitler may be the first that comes to mind. He plunged dozens of nations into a global war that decimated cities, enslaved nations, targeted Jews and other minorities, and resulted in fifteen million combat fatalities and forty-five million civilian deaths.[1]

Joseph Stalin matched Hitler stride for stride in brutality and nearly kept pace in the body count, racking up an estimated twenty million civilian deaths in labor camps, forced collectivization, famine, and executions between 1927 and 1953.[2]

Not to be outdone, China's Mao Zedong – an admirer of Stalin – preyed voraciously on his own countrymen. At the end of his Cultural Revolution, Great Leap Forward (also known as the Great Leap Famine), and a variety of purges, Chairman Mao authorized an estimated forty-five million Chinese deaths.[3]

Hitler, Stalin, and Mao are etched in history, not for their lofty visions of a new world order, or their intoxicating rhetoric, or their sheer force of will, but for the magnitude of destruction they imposed – in large measure on their own people and property.

As horrifying as these tyrants are, they are little more than pale projections of the ultimate destroyer: the evil one, who prowls the earth like a roaring lion (1 Pet. 5:8). From the beginning, Satan has distinguished himself as a destroyer. He invades the serenity of the garden, where God and humans meet for intimate fellowship. He wrecks man's relationship with God, with one another, and with the created order. The whole world lies barren and wanting today because of him.

Satan's thirst for destruction is perpetually unquenched. Where new followers of Jesus blossom, the destroyer seeks to stunt their growth. Where marriages flourish, he seeks to sabotage the covenants of faithfulness. Where healthy churches emerge, he seeks to infect their leaders with pride and pettiness.

The destroyer is the antithesis of God, who created everything very good – including Satan. And yet the evil one has risen up in opposition to the Lord. He wants to take God's place as the central focus of human worship. He wants to devastate as many lives as possible, for they reflect the image of God. He wants to demolish the institutions God has established – marriage, family, community, nation, church – because they shape God's good purposes for us.

The destroyer vies for sovereignty in a world he did not create. And if he can't have the world, he plans to destroy it – to poison it through deception, hatred, hostility, arrogance, and death. Of all the names for the evil one, *the destroyer* perhaps best captures his purpose in an ongoing rebellion against the Creator. He simply carries out a scorched-earth policy against God and against those made in God's image.

Nowhere does the Bible explicitly call Satan *the destroyer*, with the possible exception of Revelation 9:11, which we examine shortly. Even so, Satan cuts a wide swath of ruin from the very beginning. While Augustine and others commonly refer to what happened in the garden as "the Fall," Jacques Ellul more recently cast it as "the Rupture," in which God's created order was split asunder.[4] As Frank Thielman notes, "from the time of the woman's encounter with the deceitful serpent in the garden, Satan has been on a rampage against

God's people."[5] Perhaps Graham Cole captures it best when he describes Satan as "the malevolent spoiler."[6]

Let's begin with the apostle John's description of Apollyon – the destroyer – in Revelation 9, and then widen our study to additional New Testament passages, most notably John 10:10 and 1 Peter 5:8.

Revelation 9:1-11

The fifth angel blew his trumpet, and I saw a star that had fallen from heaven to earth. The key for the shaft to the abyss was given to him. He opened the shaft to the abyss, and smoke came up out of the shaft like smoke from a great furnace so that the sun and the air were darkened by the smoke from the shaft. Then locusts came out of the smoke on to the earth, and power was given to them like the power that scorpions have on the earth. They were told not to harm the grass of the earth, or any green plant, or any tree, but only those people who do not have God's seal on their foreheads. They were not permitted to kill them but were to torment them for five months; their torment is like the torment caused by a scorpion when it stings someone. In those days people will seek death and will not find it; they will long to die, but death will flee from them.

The appearance of the locusts was like horses prepared for battle. Something like golden crowns was on their heads; their faces were like human faces; they had hair like women's hair; their teeth were like lions' teeth; they had chests like iron breastplates; the sound of their wings was like the sound of many chariots with horses rushing into battle; and they had tails with stingers like scorpions, so that with their tails they had the power to harm people for five months. They had as their king the angel of the abyss; his name in Hebrew is *Abaddon*, and in Greek he has the name *Apollyon* (emphasis added).

The Hebrew *Abaddon* means "destruction," and the Greek *Apollyon* may be rendered "destroyer." Bible commentators differ as to whether Apollyon is Satan, a powerful demon under Satan's control, a personification of the abode of evil spirits, or someone else.

Peter Bolt observes, "Most theologians agree that the Destroyer and king is the devil, the prince of demons. The name accords well with Satan's role of introducing death into the world and with the fact that Jesus called him a murderer."[7] J. I. Packer is one leading theologian who holds this view.[8]

Other Bible commentators, like Merrill Unger, distinguish Apollyon from Satan. They argue that Apollyon is a great demon ruler and an underling of the evil one.[9] Still others argue that Apollyon is the personification of the abode of evil spirits, in much the same way death and hades are personified in Revelation 20:14. Louis Sweet notes:

> Since Apollyon is a personification he is not to be identified with Satan or with any other being to whom historical existence and definite characteristics are ascribed. He is the central figure in an ideal picture of evil forces represented as originating in the world of lost spirits and allowed to operate destructively in human life.[10]

In support of this view, *The Lexham Bible Dictionary* adds:

> The Old Testament personifies Abaddon, making it synonymous with insatiability (Prov. 27:20). Job describes it as having a voice (Job 28:22). Abaddon is mysterious – only God understands it (Job 26:6; Prov. 15:11), and God is not praised there (Ps. 88:11).[11]

John Bunyan's *The Pilgrim's Progress* features Apollyon as the most formidable foe that Christian, the story's protagonist, encounters. By deception and force, Apollyon tries to turn Christian back to the City of Destruction from which he has come. While Bunyan's work is allegorical, it links to the historic reality of a cosmic battle for human souls, and Apollyon figures prominently in both.

Finally, some commentators suggest the name *Apollyon* is a play on *Apollo*, the Greek god of death and pestilence, of whom locusts were a symbol. Roman emperors Caligula, Nero, and Domitian reportedly claimed to be incarnations of Apollo. Therefore, it's possible John may be taking a veiled stab at the Roman emperors who fancied themselves gods but proved to be evil incarnate.

While each of these views has merit, it seems best to see the "star that had fallen from heaven to earth" in Revelation 9:1, and the "angel of the abyss" (*Abaddon, Apollyon*) in verse 11, as the same figure, most likely Satan. Christ has defeated Satan through his finished work on the cross (1 John 3:8). He has foreseen Satan falling from heaven (Luke 10:18), and now he directs the evil one's fall (Rev. 9:1).

Christ holds the keys of death and hades (Rev. 1:18). And now he begins to execute judgment on the ruler of this world, who already stands condemned (John 16:11). Satan does not go quietly. Under Christ's sovereign permission, *Abaddon* takes the key to the shaft of the abyss and releases a demonic hoard that torments the world's unbelievers. As G. K. Beale notes, "Neither Satan nor his evil servants can any longer unleash the forces of hell on earth unless they are given power to do so by the resurrected Christ."[12]

Even if Apollyon is not another name for Satan, this destroyer most certainly works in concert with the evil one to wreak havoc on the earth. John's purpose is not so much to identify Apollyon as to foretell a dark period in human history when imprisoned spirits are set free.

Sheol, Death, and Grave

Keeping Revelation 9:11 in view, let's consider a number of Old Testament passages from which John may have drawn. The Hebrew *Abaddon* occurs six times in the Old Testament. In five of these passages, the word is combined either with *sheol*, *death*, or *the grave* in such a way as to indicate moral distinctions in the realm of the dead. Note these passages, which feature italics for emphasis:

Job 26:5-6 - The departed spirits tremble beneath the waters and all that inhabit them. *Sheol* is naked before God, and *Abaddon* has no covering.

Job 28:22 - *Abaddon* and *Death* say, "We have heard news of it [wisdom] with our ears."

Psalm 88:11 - Will your faithful love be declared in *the grave*, your faithfulness in *Abaddon*?

Proverbs 15:11 - *Sheol* and *Abaddon* lie open before the Lord – how much more, human hearts.

Proverbs 27:20 - *Sheol* and *Abaddon* are never satisfied, and people's eyes are never satisfied.

The sixth Old Testament reference does not pair Abaddon with another term of the afterlife, but it conveys the same message:

Job 31:12 - For it [sin] is a fire that consumes down to *Abaddon*; it would destroy my entire harvest.

So, in the Old Testament, *Abaddon* means a place of utter ruin, death, desolation, or destruction.[13]

The apostle John may be drawing from these Old Testament verses to depict an underworld haunt of evil spirits. Satan, or a powerful ruler under his authority, rules over it as king. John seems to be describing a personal being, for the apostle describes him as "king," "angel of the abyss," "his," and "he" (Rev. 9:11).

The evil forces Abaddon marshals are described as locusts, but with additional images implying power and destructiveness. Yet, they carry out their wicked deeds within the boundaries God has set for them. They are permitted only to torment – not kill – those who lack the seal of God on their foreheads. Further, they are prevented from harming the grass, green plants, and trees. Finally, the clock is ticking as they have only five months to do their worst.

Other Destroyers

We should note that, besides Abaddon, the Bible speaks of other destroyers – divine, human, and animal. For example, Samson is depicted as the destroyer of the Philistines' land (Judg. 16:24). Evil King Ahab calls the prophet Elijah the one who ruins Israel (1 Kings 18:17). The king of Babylon – perhaps with a double reference to a king and the evil one behind him – is the destroyer of nations (Isa. 14:12). And God vows to repay the Israelites for years of damage that destroying locusts have wrought (Joel 2:25).

We could cite other references, but it's interesting that Old Testament writers tend not to distinguish between what God causes and what he permits – that is, between primary and secondary causes. In some cases, the destroyer that God sends may actually be the preincarnate Christ, appearing as the angel of the LORD. This may be the case in Exodus 12, where *the destroyer* passes over Israelite homes whose doorposts display blood from the Passover lamb (Exod. 12:21-23). In this event, the destroyer acts exactly as Yahweh promised to act himself (Exod. 12:12-13).

We find another example of the preincarnate Christ as destroyer in 2 Samuel 24 and 1 Chronicles 21. King David orders a census, for which he is punished. The Lord sends a plague that kills seventy thousand Israelites. The one delivering the plague is a destroying angel, "the angel of the LORD," who stands between heaven and earth with a drawn sword.

The image of "the angel of the LORD" wielding a sword is seen elsewhere in Scripture. This angel confronts Balaam, the rogue prophet for hire (Num. 22:23, 31). The angel further appears to Joshua as commander of the Lord's army (Josh. 5:13-15). And he lights up the sky in the last days as the returning "KING OF KINGS AND LORD OF LORDS," a sharp sword protruding from his mouth (Rev. 19:11-16).

The destroying role of the angel of the LORD is further implied in

2 Kings 19:35-36 and Isaiah 37:36-37, as the angel kills 185,000 Assyrians in a single night. Last, we should note an Old Testament reference to "the destroyer" in the Book of Hebrews: "By faith he [Moses] instituted the Passover and the sprinkling of the blood, so that the destroyer of the firstborn might not touch the Israelites" (Heb. 11:28).

If the preincarnate Christ sometimes is depicted as the destroyer, this by no means lets Satan off the hook. When Yahweh sends a destroyer, he does so with a purpose: to judge, separate the holy from the profane, deliver a message, or save his people. His actions always are holy, just, and consistent with his omniscience. Whether the Lord demands the lives of seventy thousand Israelites, or destroys "the man of lawlessness" with the breath of his mouth (2 Thess. 2:3, 8), he always serves as the righteous judge.

In stark contrast, Satan destroys for the sheer delight of demolition. His motives oblige him to counter God – to blaspheme his name, reject his authority, resist his decrees, corrupt his good works, poison his waters, sow tares in his wheat fields, blur the lines between holy and profane, twist the truth, and murder the innocents. All the while, Satan conducts a scorched-earth policy, knowing full well he has suffered defeat, yet refusing to concede a single inch of his shrinking kingdom.

The evil one is the first – and last – destroyer. His ambush of Adam and Eve resulted in the great rupture – separating people from God and from one another, and bringing a curse on the cosmos that continues causing it to groan beneath the weight of sin (Rom. 8:22). But the promised seed of woman serves notice to the evil one that his rebel days are numbered (Gen. 3:15).

The preincarnate Christ proves to be the consummate destroyer across the pages of the Old Testament. He judges evil, wipes out armies that oppose his covenant people, fights as commander of the Lord's army, sends arrogant earthly kings retreating with their tails between their legs, and chastens his own people. One day, the returning Christ finally destroys those who destroy the earth (Rev. 11:18), as well as the destroyer (Apollyon) himself.

John 10:7-10

Jesus said again, "Truly I tell you, I am the gate for the sheep. All who came before me are thieves and robbers, but the sheep didn't listen to them. I am the gate. If anyone enters by me, he will be saved and will come in and go out and find pasture. *A thief comes only to steal and kill and destroy.* I have come so that they may have life and have it in abundance (emphasis added).

Jesus weaves the language of ancient Near Eastern shepherds into this teaching. In particular, he plies the imagery of the gate, the shepherd, and the sheep to emphasize the security found only in him, and the dangers posed by those who seek to savage the flock.

Verse 10 is key because Satan often is understood as the *thief* to whom Jesus refers. While the evil one certainly steals, kills, and destroys, Jesus has set his sights on Israel's false prophets and religious elites. In John 10:1, for example, he declares, "Truly I tell you, anyone who doesn't enter the sheep pen by the gate but climbs in some other way is a thief and a robber." This likely is a reference to the religious leaders of Jesus' day, for whom the Savior reserves his strongest rebukes in Matthew 23, issuing a string of woes for scribes and Pharisees he calls "hypocrites," "blind guides," "blind fools," "blind people," "snakes," and "brood of vipers." He tells them, "How can you escape being condemned to hell?" (Matt. 23:33).

In John 10:8, Jesus says, "All who came before are thieves and robbers." He is not referring to faithful Old Testament leaders like Moses, Isaiah, and Daniel. Rather, he hints at despotic leaders throughout Israel's history, as well as messianic pretenders who promise the people freedom but lead them into war, suffering, and slavery. "The freedom Jesus wins for his people will be achieved not by sword and shield, but by a cross. If large crowds are taken up with pretenders, the real sheep do not listen to them."[14]

Jesus also may be referring to Old Testament passages like Jeremiah 23 and Ezekiel 34, in which the prophets pronounce judgment on Israel's leaders for their failure to care for the people. In addition, Jesus may have in mind messianic pretenders (cf. Matt. 24:24; Mark 13:22), or more likely the Jews who treated the man born blind so callously (John 19:13-14). Sheep don't listen to shepherds like this because the sheep don't recognize the corrupt shepherds' voices.

Jesus follows this by saying, "I am the gate. If anyone enters by me, he will be saved and will come in and go out and find pasture. A thief comes only to steal and kill and destroy. I have come so that they may have life and have it in abundance" (John 10:9-10).

It seems clear that Jesus is setting himself against the corrupt leaders in Israel's past, and the "blind guides" of his own day. These are thieves and robbers who scale the rock walls and claw through the thorns to get to the sheep. But as the good shepherd, Jesus protects and feeds his sheep, calls them by name, and lays down his life for them.

While Satan does not appear to be the thief to whom Jesus refers, the evil one no doubt positions himself in the background, inciting rebellion, fostering deception, and scattering the flock that Jesus promises to make as one. Jesus' reference to "other sheep" (John 10:16) most likely refers to Gentiles, whom God has always planned to be a part of the redemption story. D. A. Carson notes:

> Jesus the gate is the sole means by which the sheep may enter the safety of the fold or the luxurious forage of the pasture. The thought is akin to 14:6: "I am the way and the truth and the life. No one comes to the Father except through me." While the thief comes only to steal and kill and destroy, Jesus comes that they may have life, and have it to the full. This is a proverbial way of insisting that there is only one means of receiving eternal life ... only one source of knowledge of God, only one fount of spiritual nourishment, only one basis for spiritual security – Jesus alone.[15]

The images of Jesus as the good shepherd, the gate, and the one who knows his sheep are best understood in the context of Middle Eastern shepherding. The sheep pen typically is a round or square enclosure with high stone walls, topped with briars to keep wild animals out. There is a single opening, where the shepherd serves as the "gate" or "door," even to the point of sleeping in the doorway at night, thus functioning as the only way in or out of the sheep pen.

The Greek word translated "gate" is *thyra*, meaning "door." Jesus portrays himself as the shepherd who makes himself the sealer of the sheep pen, the one who provides security for the sheep within and who threatens violence to anyone or anything aiming to harm the flock.

When Jesus tells his listeners he has come to give them life "in abundance," the Greek *perisson* means "that which goes way beyond necessity." John wants his readers to know that the gift of Jesus, and the eternal life he brings, are beyond our wildest dreams.

But delivering life to the fullest comes at a price, as Jesus explains in John 10:11: "I am the good shepherd. The good shepherd lays down his life for the sheep." As Colin Kruse notes:

> A shepherd would rarely, if ever, actually die in protection of his sheep (to do so would leave the sheep defenseless). Jesus was extending the imagery beyond its normal limits and pointing forward to the time when he would, in fact, lay down his life for the sake of the people.[16]

So, John 10:10 almost certainly is not a direct reference to Satan. However, the corrupt leaders of ancient times, and the self-righteous religious leaders of Jesus' day, act in a manner consistent with the deeds of their father, the devil. They steal, kill, and destroy because they pattern their lives after a supernatural prototype for whom destruction comes naturally.

1 Peter 5:6-9

> Humble yourselves, therefore, under the mighty hand of God, so that he may exalt you at the proper time, casting all your cares on

him, because he cares about you. Be sober-minded, be alert. Your
adversary the devil is prowling around like a roaring lion, looking
for anyone he can devour. Resist him, firm in the faith, knowing that
the same kind of sufferings are being experienced by your fellow
believers throughout the world.

Peter is no stranger to the wiles of the devil. As he concludes his
first epistle, Peter urges believers suffering persecution to humble
themselves (5:6). Peter knows, as does the apostle Paul, that pride,
especially among leaders, plays into the hands of the evil one (cf.
1 Tim. 3:6-7). In addition, Peter encourages his readers to cast their
cares on God, fully confident the Lord understands their trials and
cares deeply for them. As they humble themselves before God and
trust him to take vengeance on their persecutors, the Lord exalts
them when the time is right – perhaps in this life, and most certainly
when they stand before him at the judgment seat of Christ (cf. Rom.
14:10; 2 Cor. 5:10).

Peter then exhorts his fellow believers to be sober-minded and
alert because their common adversary – the devil – prowls around
like a lion, looking for anyone he can devour. Peter writes out of
painful personal experience. Let's briefly recount two such occasions.

Matthew 16

Jesus has taken his disciples to Caesarea Philippi. There, in the
foothills of Mount Hermon, at a place historically known for its
paganism – even the very gates of hades – Jesus asks his disciples who
people say he is. The disciples offer several replies: John the Baptist,
Elijah, Jeremiah, or one of the prophets. But then Jesus asks directly,
"But you [plural] ... who do you say that I am?" (Matt. 16:15).

Peter steps forward and boldly proclaims, "You are the Messiah,
the Son of the living God" (v. 16).

Jesus acknowledges Peter's truthful declaration, which is not
Peter's own but the Father's revelation from heaven. Jesus goes on:
"And I also say to you that you are Peter, and on this rock I will build

my church, and the gates of Hades will not overpower it" (v. 18). While there is much debate about the identity of the rock upon which Christ builds his church,[17] it is clear that Peter's truthful revelation about Jesus is the heart of the gospel message.

This is a high point in the apostle's ministry, yet his boldness soon gives way to arrogance:

> From then on Jesus began to point out to his disciples that it was necessary for him to go to Jerusalem and suffer many things from the elders, chief priests, and scribes, be killed, and be raised the third day. Peter took him aside and began to rebuke him, "Oh no, Lord! This will never happen to you!"
>
> Jesus turned and told Peter, "Get behind me, *Satan*! You are a hindrance to me because you're not thinking about God's concerns but human concerns" (Matt. 16:21-23, emphasis added).

The very reason Jesus comes to earth as Messiah is to lay down his life. Now that Peter has properly identified Jesus, the Lord sets his sights on Jerusalem, where he must exchange his sinless life for our redemption. Thinking the Messiah's immediate mission is to assume King David's throne, Peter puffs up with pride and presumes to scold the Son of God.

Jesus quickly turns from commendation to condemnation, referring to Peter as "Satan" (Greek *Satanas*). Whether Jesus is simply calling Peter an adversary, or identifying him with the evil one, it is a stinging rebuke. And, as Peter crafts the closing lines of his first epistle, there's little doubt he remembers how quickly he dropped his guard and switched from an advocate to an adversary of the Lord.

Matthew 26 / Luke 22

Perhaps Peter also recalls the night before Jesus is crucified. The apostles have celebrated the Passover with Jesus, who sadly relays to them, "Tonight all of you will fall away because of me, for it is written: I will strike the shepherd, and the sheep of the flock will be scattered. But after I have risen, I will go ahead of you to Galilee" (Matt. 26:31-32).

Characteristically impulsive, Peter tells Jesus, "Even if everyone falls away because of you, I will never fall away" (v. 33).

"Truly I tell you," Jesus says to Peter, "tonight, before the rooster crows, you will deny me three times" (v. 34).

"Even if I have to die with you," Peter boasts, "I will never deny you." All the disciples say the same thing (v. 35).

Luke records an additional comment in his Gospel. Jesus tells Peter, "Simon, Simon, look out. Satan has asked to sift you like wheat. But I have prayed for you that your faith may not fail. And you, when you have turned back, strengthen your brothers" (Luke 22:31-32).

Peter does indeed deny three times that he knows Jesus (Luke 22:54-62). Evidently, God has granted Satan permission to savage Peter with temptation, and to scatter the disciples (the "you" in "sift you like wheat" is plural in the Greek). For a moment after Peter's third denial, Jesus and Peter briefly lock eyes. Peter is deeply convicted and rushes outside, weeping.

But Peter rebounds. Jesus prays for him, and Peter is a humbler and more teachable servant when he encounters Jesus on the beach after the resurrection (John 21:15-21). Just as Peter has denied Jesus three times, he now humbly affirms his love for the Lord three times, even refusing to use the word *agapao* – God's kind of love – in expressing his love of Jesus; instead, he uses *phileo*, more commonly applied as friendly affection.

All this is to say that Peter knows first-hand the perils of dropping one's guard in the presence of the evil one. So, in 1 Peter 5:8, he strongly urges his readers to be sober-minded and alert. Just as a prowling lion often pounces on the weak, the straggler, the wanderer, and the inattentive, Satan most easily devours those who are lifted up with pride, or who wage spiritual battles in fleshly strength, or who drift into apathy.

In 1 Peter 5:5, the apostle quotes from the Septuagint version of Proverbs 3:34, urging his readers to clothe themselves with humility toward one another. That's because "God resists the proud but gives grace to the humble." He immediately follows with the exhortation, "Humble yourselves, therefore, under the mighty hand of God, so that he may exalt you at the proper time, casting all your cares on him, because he cares about you" (vv. 6-7). The idea of clothing ourselves with humility may be a reference to Jesus in the upper room on the night of Passover, when the Lord wraps a towel around his waist and washes the disciples' feet (John 13:1-17).

Peter understands that worry is a form of pride. When anxiety fills our minds, we are convinced we must solve our own problems in our own strength. This gives Satan a foothold in our thoughts, where he leverages pride into a pantheon of idols: distrust, fear, judgmentalism, and greed, to name a few. But when we cast our worries on God, we acknowledge his sovereignty. In addition, we trustingly carry out our roles as adopted children of the King. Peter's anxiety about Jesus' imminent death was a form of pride that led him to scold the Son of God and to arrogantly insist he would never let Jesus down. As a result, Satan grinds him to powder.

So, Peter exhorts his readers with two imperatives: be sober-minded, and be alert. "Sober-minded" comes from the Greek *nepho* and may be rendered "calm and collected in spirit." Peter uses the same verb in 1 Peter 1:13 and 4:7. In both contexts, he addresses the need for clear thinking since the return of Christ is imminent.

"Alert" translates the Greek verb *gregoreo* and means "to watch," "give strict attention to," or "be vigilant." This word also is used in eschatological contexts (e.g., Matt. 24:42-43; 25:13). As Thomas Schreiner notes, "Believers must remain vigilant and alert until the very end because the devil seeks to destroy their faith. The devil inflicts persecution on believers so that they will deny Christ and lose their eschatological reward."[18]

When Peter describes the evil one as "your adversary," he uses the Greek *antidikos*. This is the only time this term is used in Scripture to portray Satan. The Greek *anti* means "against," and *diko* means "lawsuit." Strictly speaking, the evil one is a prosecuting attorney, which harkens back to the adversary (Heb. *satan*) in Zechariah 3:1-2. Many scholars believe this accuser to be Satan, who stands in the heavenly assembly and makes his case against Joshua the high priest. Of course, the Lord rebukes Satan in that heavenly exchange. Peter may have this Old Testament encounter in mind as he warns us about Satan's trash-talking skills.

Prowling, Roaring, Ravaging

Peter depicts Satan as a prowling, roaring, and voracious lion, seeking "anyone he can devour." First, he prowls around (*peripateo* – to make one's way; to make due use of opportunities). This harkens back to Job 1:7 and 2:2, in which the Lord asks *the satan* where he has come from. "From roaming through the earth," the adversary replies, "and walking around on it." According to Marvin Vincent, the word *peripateo* gave identity to a sect of Greek philosophers known as *Peripatetics*, who walked around while teaching or disputing.[19] Satan is the consummate *Peripatetic* – always on the move, and always looking for a fight.

Next, Satan roars. The particular Greek word *oruomenos* is used only here in the New Testament. It describes the howl of a beast in fierce hunger. His purpose is to produce fear in our hearts. In the context of 1 Peter, the evil one uses persecution – verbal and social abuse at the hands of Greco-Roman neighbors, who ostracize Christians because they no longer participate in their pagan practices (1 Pet. 4:3-4) – to scare believers back into their previous lifestyles. In stark contrast to God, who tenderly cares for his children, the evil one stalks and terrifies believers in order to devour their confidence in God and thus lose rewards they are storing up in heaven.

Finally, Satan is a ravaging lion. The apostle John refers to Jesus as "the Lion" for his courage (Rev. 5:5). In contrast, Satan is "a roaring lion" because of his fierceness. One is the true Lion of Judah, while the other is a counterfeit. One comes to deliver, the other to devour. One comes to conquer, the other to crush. One comes to defend, the other to decimate. One comes to restore, the other to carry out a scorched-earth policy before he is caged and declawed. One is to be celebrated, the other to be feared. One ultimately is to be worshiped, the other to be tormented night and day forever (Rev. 20:10).

Drinking Down

Peter notes that the evil one, like a ferocious lion, seeks to "devour." The Greek word Peter uses here is *katapino*, which means "to drink down, swallow, destroy." New Testament writers use the term in a variety of ways. When Jesus calls the scribes and Pharisees "blind guides," he accuses them of straining out a gnat but *gulping down* a camel (Matt. 23:24). Paul looks forward to the day when death is *swallowed up* in victory at the resurrection of the just (1 Cor. 15:54). Paul further urges Corinthian believers to forgive a repentant sinner, lest he be "*overwhelmed* by excessive grief" (2 Cor. 2:7).

The writer of Hebrews remembers that when the Egyptians sought to cross the Red Sea on dry ground, they were *drowned* (Heb. 11:29). And in his vision of the woman, the child, and the dragon, John sees that the earth helps the woman (Israel) as she escapes the flood waters the dragon has spewed in her path: "The earth opened its mouth and *swallowed up* the river that the dragon had spewed from his mouth" (Rev. 12:16). No doubt, in Peter's reference to Satan, we see a desire to completely consume those who follow Jesus, especially those who remain faithful in persecution.

The earth is Satan's domain. As such, he roams it freely, moving from place to place. And believers, who are in this world but not of it (cf. John 17:14-15), are vulnerable prey. As David Walls and Max Anders note:

> Peter envisions the devil as a cunning and evil personal being who has the ability to attack Christians and to disrupt the life and unity of the church.... He is the master of ingenious strategies, and his tactics must not be allowed to catch us unaware.[20]

But how, exactly, do we see evidence of Satan's destructive work in people's lives? The New Testament reveals certain human characteristics that Satan and demons may prompt:

(1) bizarre or violently irrational evil behavior, especially in opposition to the gospel or to Christians (Mark 1:24; 5:2-5; 9:18; Acts 16:16-18; Rev. 2:10);

(2) malicious slander and falsehood in speech (John 8:44; 1 John 4:1-3);

(3) increasing bondage to self-destructive behavior (Mark 5:5; 9:20);

(4) stubborn advocacy of false doctrine (1 John 4:1-6);

(5) the sudden and unexplained onslaughts of emotions, such as fear, hatred, depression, anxiety, violent anger, etc., which are both contrary to God's will and inappropriate in one's situation (note the "flaming arrows of the evil one" in Eph. 6:16);

(6) deep spiritual evil, which God gifts some Christians to discern (1 Cor. 12:10).[21]

Satan Targets our Temples

Satan seeks not only to destroy our spiritual lives – our confidence in the Lord, our testimonies, our spiritual disciplines – but our physical lives as well. Warren Wiersbe points out that Satan targets our bodies for a number of reasons.

First, our bodies are *temples* where God resides (1 Cor. 6:19-20; Phil. 1:20; 1 Pet. 2:9). "This means when Satan attacks your body, he is attacking the one means God has for revealing his grace and love to a lost world. Creation reveals the power, wisdom, and glory of God; but Christians reveal the grace and love of God."[22]

Second, our bodies are God's *tools* (Rom. 6:12-13). Just as he employed the natural abilities of Noah to build an ark, and the skills of Bezalel and Oholiab to construct the tabernacle, the Lord uses our bodies as his hands and feet to carry out the Great Commission.

"Just as God the Son had to take on a body to accomplish his work on earth, so the Holy Spirit needs our bodies," writes Wiersbe. The members of your bodies are tools in the Spirit's hands to help build the church here on earth. We should never minimize the stewardship of our bodies. "The Christian who is careless about his health or safety is playing right into the hands of the destroyer."[23]

Third, our bodies are God's *treasury* (2 Cor. 4:7; 1 Tim. 6:20; 2 Tim. 1:14; 2:2). When God saved us, he put the treasure of eternal life within our bodies. We have the very life of God in us. "God did not give you this great treasure simply to protect it – an earthen vessel is not the safest place for a treasure! He gave you this treasure that he might *invest it* through you in the lives of others."[24]

Finally, our bodies are God's *testing ground* (Rom. 12:1; 1 Cor. 9:27). Satan can rob us of our rewards by attacking our bodies and getting us to break the rules of conduct God has set for us. The athletic imagery Paul uses in writing to the Corinthians serves as a backdrop for Christian living.

In the Isthmian Games in Corinth, athletes not only had to be talented and fit; they had to keep the rules or be disqualified. "It is not a matter of salvation, but of rewards for faithful service," writes Wiersbe. "The athlete did not lose his citizenship if he broke the rules; he only forfeited his reward, a shameful experience indeed."[25]

While our souls and spirits are of everlasting value to God, so are our bodies. We must be sober-minded and alert to the destroyer's attacks on our physical beings as well as our spiritual lives. That's one reason Peter challenges believers, who are "living as exiles dispersed abroad" (1 Pet. 1:1), to *resist* the evil one and remain "firm in the faith" (1 Pet. 5:9).

Resist is a strong term. The Greek *anthistemi* means "to set one's self against," "to withstand" or "oppose." Luke uses this word to describe Elymas' resistance to the gospel that Paul and Barnabas preached; he *opposed* them (Acts 13:8). Paul uses *anthistemi* to relay his face-to-face opposition to Peter at Antioch (Gal. 2:11). He also applies this term to the resistance of Jannes and Jambres against Moses (2 Tim. 3:8), and to Alexander the coppersmith's response to Paul – "he strongly opposed our words" (2 Tim. 4:15). James tells Christians to "submit to God. *Resist* the devil, and he will flee from you" (Jas. 4:7, emphasis added). So, our resistance to the devil should not be passive. Instead, Peter urges us to engage actively against our most dangerous foe.

Peter's encouragement to stand "firm in the faith" (1 Pet. 5:9) reminds us that we do not wage war against the evil one on our own. Rather, our feet are planted on holy ground, for the Spirit of God who dwells in us goes wherever we go. Further, we are given powerful spiritual weapons for battle, enabling us to demolish arguments raised against the knowledge of God (2 Cor. 10:3-5). The Lord also equips us for spiritual warfare with Christian armor (Eph. 6:11-18). Last, as we engage the evil one in the colosseum of spiritual warfare, we should be encouraged that our audience is "a large cloud of witnesses surrounding us" (Heb. 12:1) – heroes who, by faith:

> conquered kingdoms, administered justice, obtained promises, shut the mouths of lions, quenched the raging of fire, escaped the edge of the sword, gained strength in weakness, became mighty in battle, and put foreign armies to flight. Women received their dead, raised to life again. Other people were tortured, not accepting release, so that they might gain a better resurrection. Others experienced mockings and scourgings, as well as bonds and imprisonment. They were stoned, they were sawed in two, they died by the sword, they wandered about in sheepskins, in goatskins, destitute, afflicted, and mistreated. The world was not worthy of them. They wandered in deserts and on mountains, hiding in caves and holes in the ground. All these were approved through their faith, but they did not receive what was promised, since God had provided something better for us, so that they would not be made perfect without us (Heb. 11:33-40).

Marvin Vincent notes that the Greek word rendered "firm" is *stereos* and might better be translated "steadfast." This conveys the sense of *"compactness, compact solidarity,* and is appropriate, since a number of individuals are addressed and exhorted to withstand the onset of Satan as one compacted body."[26]

This may help strengthen our understanding of what it means to stand firm. God has chosen us according to the foreknowledge of God the Father (1 Pet. 1:2); sanctified us through the Holy Spirit (1:2); sprinkled us with the blood of Jesus Christ (1:2); given us new birth into a living hope through the resurrection of Jesus (1:3); provided us with an imperishable inheritance (1:4); guarded us by his power (1:5); is building individual believers into a corporate spiritual house, a holy priesthood (2:5); has declared us a chosen race, a royal priesthood, a holy nation, and a people for his possession (2:9); has called us out of darkness into his marvelous light (2:9); and so much more.

The Consummate Destroyer

Saddam Hussein knew the war was over. The Iraqi dictator had failed in his effort to occupy Kuwait. And if he couldn't have the country, he wasn't about to let anyone else benefit from its riches. As a U.S.-led coalition of forces drove out the last of Hussein's troops, he sent mercenaries to blow up more than six hundred producing oil wells in Kuwait. The result: towering infernos that took fire-fighting specialists seven months to extinguish.

Long after the 1991 Persian Gulf War ended, the Gulf was awash in poisonous smoke, ash, and soot. Literal lakes of oil formed. Black rain fell. Livestock breathing misty, dark air died from blackened lungs.

Hussein's scorched-earth policy ultimately failed. After U.S. troops invaded Iraq in 2003, soldiers found the defeated dictator hiding in a "spider hole." An Iraqi court convicted Hussein of crimes against humanity and unceremoniously hanged him late in 2006.

Hussein was a chronic destroyer. He had engaged in a bloody stalemate with Iran, tried foolishly to take Kuwait, brutalized his own people, and purged his leadership team. He eliminated anyone he could not trust, or any person he even suspected. He exalted himself at the expense of all others.

This tyrant was perhaps the last of the twentieth century's most brutal dictators, carrying his deeds into a new millennium. Like Hitler, Stalin, and Mao who preceded him, Hussein lived and died defiantly – and destructively. But none of these men holds a proverbial candle to the ultimate destroyer.

From the beginning, Satan has fought for sovereignty over a world he did not create. And if he can't have it, he plans to destroy it – to poison it through deception, hatred, hostility, arrogance, and death. Of all the names for the evil one, *the destroyer* perhaps best captures his purpose in the ongoing rebellion against God. He simply wages a no-holds-barred, battle-to-the-death campaign against God, and against those made in God's image.

There is no doubt that the evil one is the consummate destroyer. From the garden of Eden to the day he is cast into the lake of fire, Satan plows a wide and indiscriminate path of discord, pain, sorrow, violence, hatred, distrust, arrogance, bitterness, division, doubt, and idolatry everywhere he goes. While it's true that Scripture nowhere explicitly calls Satan *the destroyer*, it is an apt descriptor of the one who takes everything good and ruins it.

We are called to resist the evil one, standing firm in God, who created us and redeemed us. As the world's tyrants pass from the scene, they have a court date before the great white throne. And like the unseen destroyer, their sentence is in the lake of fire and sulfur (Rev. 20:10).

For Christians facing persecution, like so many first-century followers of Jesus, we are called to persevere. Justice for oppressors is guaranteed – if not now, then at the return of Christ. And reward for faithful believers is certain – perhaps not in this life, but most certainly at the *bema*, where Christ places imperishable crowns on our heads. Even better, he repeats the seven most blessed words every Christian longs to hear: "Well done, thou good and faithful servant" (Matt. 25:21 KJV).

Summary

Key takeaways about *the destroyer*:

(1) As *the destroyer*, Satan vies for sovereignty in a world he did not create. And if he can't have the world, he plans to destroy it – to poison it through deception, hatred, hostility, arrogance, and death. He simply carries out a scorched-earth policy against God and against those made in God's image.

(2) In Revelation 9:1-11, *Abaddon* is thought by some scholars to be either Satan, a powerful demon under Satan's authority, a personification of the abode of evil spirits, or a reference to wicked Roman emperors. While we take the position that Abaddon *is* Satan, John's purpose is not so much to identify Apollyon as to foretell a dark period in human history when imprisoned spirits are set free.

(3) Appearing six times in the Old Testament, *Abaddon* means a place of utter ruin, death, desolation, or destruction. So, in Revelation 9, John may be drawing from these Old Testament verses to depict an underworld haunt of evil spirits. And yet, John seems to identify a person who rules over the underworld, referring to him as "king" and "angel of the abyss."

(4) The Bible speaks of other destroyers besides Satan: Samson, Elijah, the king of Babylon, and even the preincarnate Christ (the angel of the LORD). But Satan is unique in that he destroys for the sheer delight of demolition. He conducts a scorched-earth policy, knowing full well he has suffered defeat, yet refusing to concede an inch of his shrinking kingdom.

(5) John 10:10 almost certainly is not a direct reference to Satan. However, the corrupt leaders of ancient times, and the self-righteous religious leaders of Jesus' day, act in a manner consistent with the deeds of their father, the devil. They steal, kill, and destroy because they pattern their lives after a supernatural prototype for whom destruction comes naturally.

(6) Jesus and Satan are contrasting *lions* in Scripture. One is the true Lion of Judah, while the other is a counterfeit. One comes to deliver, the other to devour. One comes to conquer, the other to

crush. One comes to defend, the other to decimate. One comes to restore, the other to wreak havoc on the earth before he is caged and declawed. One is to be celebrated, the other to be feared. One ultimately is to be worshiped, the other to be tormented night and day forever.

(7) Peter writes out of painful experience – trying to prevent Jesus from going to the cross, and denying Jesus three times – when he exhorts us to be sober-minded and alert in our encounters with Satan. The evil one prowls around like a lion, looking for someone to devour.

Questions for Personal or Group Study

1. Nowhere does the Bible explicitly call Satan *the destroyer*, with the possible exception of Revelation 9:11. Even so, based on the whole of Scripture, why do you think *the destroyer* is a fitting title for the evil one?
2. Read Revelation 9:1-11. What are several different views about the identity of *Abaddon*? Which view do you prefer, and why?
3. How is *Abaddon* linked to *sheol*, *death*, and *the grave* in the Old Testament? How might John be drawing from Old Testament imagery to depict an underworld haunt of evil spirits, complete with a ruler over them?
4. The Bible actually speaks of many destroyers, both human and divine. Who are some of these figures? Consider Exodus 12:21-23; Judges 16:24; and Isaiah 14:12.
5. Jesus speaks of a thief who steals, kills, and destroys (John 10:10). Who is this thief?

THE ONE FOR WHOM HELL IS PREPARED

T he Souza-Baranowski Correctional Center in Massachusetts is well into its third decade of operation and has yet to report a single breakout. The SBCC, as insiders call it, has earned its reputation as the most technologically advanced and secure prison in the world – even more secure than Russia's notorious Black Dolphin Prison, or the ADX prison in Colorado, dubbed the "Alcatraz of the Rockies."

Roughly six hundred corrections officers guard Souza-Baranowski's fifteen hundred prisoners. But just to be sure, the omniscient eye of a robotic overlord carefully monitors every inch of the facility. More than forty graphic-interfaced computer terminals drive a keyless system that controls every aspect of the prison, from doors to the water supply. If that's not enough, three hundred and seventy high-definition cameras record everything at all times. Plus, a taut-wire fence and microwave detection system guard the perimeter.

If you think you can simply snip a few wires or pull the plug on the entire system, think again. SBCC is one of the only U.S. prisons designed to run entirely on solar and hydroelectric power. Oh, and for anyone trying the old-school method of digging out, the prison was built using the highest-strength concrete and tool-resistant steel available. Hollywood blockbuster *Escape Plan* to the contrary, not even Arnold Schwarzenegger and Sylvester Stallone could bust out of this place.[1]

A prison of this stature isn't built overnight. It requires careful planning, thorough research, an advanced grasp of the sciences, and special insight into the minds of the world's most diabolical criminals. For most inmates, SBCC is their final venue; once inside, their fate is sealed.

Imagine the far greater mind of God that designed and built *gehenna*, the everlasting lake of fire and sulfur prepared for the devil and his angels (Matt. 25:41), and a place into which they are cast to be tormented day and night forever (Rev. 20:10). This inescapable prison, which the world's unbelievers share (Rev. 20:15), is both a fascinating and terrifying place.

Satan may rule a kingdom of evil spirits and rebellious people today. He may even prowl the earth like an uncaged lion. But he lays no claim to hell. And despite common beliefs that the evil one welcomes willing sinners into a never-ending fraternity kegger beyond the grave, hell is the final stop on Satan's long descent into ruin. There, in the presence of God and his holy angels, the party ends. The evil one gets his comeuppance and forever loses his freedom.

In many snapshots of Satan throughout the Bible, it may appear he is an unbeatable foe. He entices the first man and woman to sin, thus plunging the human race into a cataclysmic fall, and placing the created order under a curse. He openly accuses God's servants of unworthiness. He destroys Job's property, kills his family, takes away his health, and turns his wife against him. He tries wiping out the Israelites so there is no chosen people through whom Messiah comes, and then he inspires King Herod to try killing the newborn king in Bethlehem. He harasses Jesus and the apostles, causes serious illnesses, controls Jesus' betrayer, spreads spiritual blindness, deceives many, divides the church, prowls the earth like a lion, and leads an all-out blitz against Christ and his church in the last days. At times, we may wonder when all of this ends.

But end it does. God's judgments have spanned human history. They begin in the expulsion of Adam and Eve from the garden (Gen. 3), and they end at a great white throne (Rev. 20). The Day of the Lord is coming, an event the Old Testament prophets and New Testament writers repeatedly warn us about (e.g., Isa. 2:6-22; Amos 5:18-19; Rom. 2:1-3). Jesus emphatically tells us a day is coming when all people are resurrected and judged, resulting in everlasting life or never-ending damnation (John 5:28-29).

But human beings are not the only ones to receive final judgment. Jesus makes it clear that a place is prepared for the evil one and his minions. A day has been set when Christ judges Satan and banishes him forever into the lake of fire. So, let's consider Satan's final date with destiny as we explore key passages of Scripture, most notably Matthew 25:31-46 and Revelation 20:1-3, 10.

The Eternal Fire: Matthew 25:31-46

In Matthew 24-25, Jesus is on the Mount of Olives with his disciples, responding to their questions about the future destruction of the temple and the end of the age. He closes out the so-called Olivet Discourse with the parable of the sheep and goats, revealing the preparation of a final place of judgment for Satan, evil spirits, and unbelievers. A key verse reads: "Then he [the Son of Man] will also say to those on the left, 'Depart from me, you who are cursed, into the eternal fire prepared for the devil and his angels!'" (Matt. 25:41).

The central theme of this parable is that Christ separates believers from unbelievers at his return. Jesus also makes it clear that all angelic and human rebels are banished from his presence. This passage deals with human works, not as a condition of salvation, but as evidence of one's regard for the Son of Man. Consider the full text:

> When the Son of Man comes in his glory, and all the angels with him, then he will sit on his glorious throne. All the nations will be gathered before him, and he will separate them one from another, just as a shepherd separates the sheep from the goats. He will put

the sheep on his right and the goats on the left. Then the King will say to those on his right, "Come, you who are blessed by my Father; inherit the kingdom prepared for you from the foundation of the world.

"For I was hungry and you gave me something to eat; I was thirsty and you gave me something to drink; I was a stranger and you took me in; I was naked and you clothed me; I was sick and you took care of me; I was in prison and you visited me."

Then the righteous will answer him, "Lord, when did we see you hungry and feed you, or thirsty and give you something to drink? When did we see you a stranger and take you in, or without clothes and clothe you? When did we see you sick, or in prison, and visit you?"

And the King will answer them, "Truly I tell you, whatever you did for one of the least of these brothers and sisters of mine, you did for me."

Then he will also say to those on the left, "Depart from me, you who are cursed, into the eternal fire prepared for the devil and his angels! For I was hungry and you gave me nothing to eat; I was thirsty and you gave me nothing to drink; I was a stranger and you didn't take me in; I was naked and you didn't clothe me, sick and in prison and you didn't take care of me."

Then they too will answer, "Lord, when did we see you hungry, or thirsty, or a stranger, or without clothes, or sick, or in prison, and not help you?"

Then he will answer them, "Truly I tell you, whatever you did not do for one of the least of these, you did not do for me."

And they will go away into eternal punishment, but the righteous into eternal life (Matt. 25:31-46).

There is considerable disagreement among Bible commentators as to *when* this judgment takes place and *who* it involves as sheep and goats. Some interpreters believe this parable is a general description of the final judgment of all people – a summary of both the judgment seat of Christ for believers (Rom. 14:10; 2 Cor. 5:10) and the great white throne judgment for unbelievers (Rev. 20:11-15), even though a thousand years or more may separate them.

Others believe this parable teaches a particular judgment for those who survive the great tribulation and witness the return of Christ. This view is based, in part, on the fact that there is no mention of resurrection prior to this judgment.

Further complicating the picture is how one understands the word "nations" in verse 32. It could be interpreted "Gentiles," or as representatives of the world's sovereign nations, or as individuals alive at the time of Christ's glorious appearing.

Key Truths from This Parable

Whatever view one takes of the *when* and *who* of this parable, we may glean several key truths from Jesus' teaching about the sheep and goats:

First, this judgment occurs after the personal, visible, physical return of Christ with his angels. It's also after Jesus is seated on his "glorious throne" (v. 31). New Testament writers use a variety of terms to describe this event. The king's coming is his *parousia* (1 Thess. 4:15), a term used in the first century to describe a dignitary's visit to a certain place. Christ's return also is his *epiphaneia*, or visible appearance (1 Tim. 6:14), as well as his *apocalypsis*, or unveiling (1 Pet. 4:13). The return of the king is nothing less than the Day of the Lord (1 Cor. 1:8). And while Christ's return is a celebrated event that all Christians eagerly anticipate, it also is a time of fearful judgment.

Second, there is a separation of sheep and goats. Jesus employs this analogy to depict believers and unbelievers. Sheep and goats often graze together, as his listeners know. It takes the trained eye of a shepherd to separate them at the time of shearing. Sheep symbolize mildness, simplicity, innocence – the qualities of one completely dependent upon the shepherd for protection and care. They also are more highly valued because of their wool. Jesus refers to himself as a shepherd who faithfully separates the sheep from the goats.

Jesus knows who belongs to him and who does not. "My sheep

296 | ROB PHILLIPS

hear My voice, I know them, and they follow Me," he says in John 10:27. Further, he willingly lays down his life for his sheep (John 10:11). There are many other references to God/Christ as the shepherd and to his followers as sheep (see Ps. 23:1; 80:1; Zech. 13:7; Matt. 26:31; John 10:14, 16; Heb. 13:20; 1 Pet. 2:25; 5:4). In this parable, Jesus plainly teaches that a time is coming when those who are of his flock enjoy the benefits of his kingdom, while those who have rejected him are rejected themselves.

Unlike sheep, goats are naturally quarrelsome and selfish – a stark contrast that highlights the profane and impure character of unbelievers. Goats also are associated with demonology and evil.

Knowing his sheep as distinct from the goats, Jesus sets the two apart, placing the sheep at his right hand and the goats at his left. In ancient times, the right hand is the place of honor. It denotes special privilege and authority. Jesus often is depicted at the right hand of the Father in heaven (e.g., Matt. 26:64; Rom. 8:34; Col. 3:1; Heb. 12:2). In contrast, the left is a place of dishonor, "the side of ill omen."[2]

Third, both the sheep and goats seem surprised at the rationale for their judgment: how they treated "the least of these brothers and sisters of mine" (v. 40). We know from Jesus' own words that eternal life is received by faith and not by works (John 5:24). So, what Jesus seems to be saying is that the way his sheep treat God's children demonstrates they truly know him. Meanwhile, the neglect with which the goats regard the same people reveals their disdain for the Great Shepherd.

When Jesus makes the treatment of "the least of these" a personal matter, both the sheep and goats protest. "Lord, when did we see you hungry and feed you, or thirsty and give you something to drink?" the sheep ask in amazement. "When did we see you a stranger and take you in, or without clothes and clothe you? When did we see you sick, or in prison, and visit you?" (vv. 37-39).

The king responds, "Truly I tell you, whatever you did for one of the least of these brothers and sisters of mine, you did for me" (v. 40).

The righteous are amazed – not that Jesus says they acted out of love for him, but that he reveals himself as the personal object of their deeds. The wicked are shocked for the same reason. Their personal neglect of God's people exposes their contempt for God himself. We should note that commentators generally understand "the least of these" to refer either to Christ's followers, who humbly obey him and often suffer persecution as a result, or to anyone in need. In either case, the test is the way people standing in judgment treat those the world regards as insignificant.

Fourth, distinct places are prepared for the sheep and goats. Jesus tells the sheep, "Come, you who are blessed by my Father; inherit the kingdom prepared for you from the foundation of the world" (v. 34). God's kingdom – that is, his reign, or authority to rule – has always existed and must be entered into by faith.

Christ has known his sheep from eternity past and has "prepared" a special place of honor for them. This honor is bestowed when the kingdom of the world becomes "the kingdom of our Lord and of his Christ, and he will reign forever and ever" (Rev. 11:15). God's kingdom is not an afterthought. Its citizens are elect from eternity past. After Christ's return, Satan, sin, and death are fully and finally banished, and Christ makes everything new in the new heavens and new earth (2 Pet. 3:10-13; Rev. 21-22; cf. Isa. 65:17).

As for the goats, Jesus says, "Depart from me, you who are cursed, into the eternal fire prepared for the devil and his angels" (v. 41). In contrast to the sheep, who are welcomed into Christ's kingdom, the goats are banished to a singular place prepared for Satan and evil spirits.

The idea of banishment is consistent in New Testament teachings about those who reject Christ. Jesus calls false prophets "lawbreakers," declares that he never knew them, and commands them to depart from him (Matt. 7:23). Paul writes of the day when Christ "takes vengeance with flaming fire on those who don't know God and on those who don't obey the gospel of our Lord Jesus. They will pay the penalty of eternal destruction from the Lord's presence and from his glorious strength ..." (2 Thess. 1:8-9). And at the great white throne judgment, the Judge throws the wicked into the lake of fire (Rev. 20:15).

298 | ROB PHILLIPS

Note in Jesus' words to the goats that hell is a place "prepared for the devil and his angels." Put another way, Jesus does not tell the goats that hell is prepared for *them*, but for another race of beings – rebellious angels. There is no hint of redemption for the evil one and his angelic cronies. Christ did not come in the likeness of sinful and fallen angels, but in the likeness of sinful and fallen people. Salvation is God's exclusive gift to humans, a gift denied to the evil one and fallen angels.

Nevertheless, those who reject Christ occupy the same place of everlasting punishment as Satan. Just as saints enjoy everlasting life in the presence of the triune God and God's holy angels, unbelievers experience banishment to hell, along with "the god of this age" (2 Cor. 4:4) and his angelic minions. Unbelievers do not care for heirs of the kingdom because they have no regard for the king. And so, by their choice, the goats depart into eternal fire.

Fifth, this judgment is final and everlasting. The sheep gladly accept eternal life as the ultimate act of God's grace. The goats, however, depart in stunned silence to hell. There is no higher court to which they may appeal. No second chances. No calls for clemency. No end to the consequences of their sin; that is, no annihilation, and no universal salvation. Just the stark reality of eternity in outer – and utter – darkness.[3]

We have invested a good deal of time in this parable to show that Jesus clearly teaches a final judgment, as well as a final destination, for all people. God has prepared a place of blessing for those who submit willingly to his Son's kingship. It's a place of rest, peace, security, and joy in the presence of the triune God, his holy angels, and other heavenly beings. At the same time, those who reject the Lord's gracious provision for their sin, and who rebel against his kingship, are cast into a place not prepared for them, but a place where they nevertheless suffer the same fate as the ones for whom hell is created: Satan and evil spirits. Together, they all go to a place of "eternal punishment," while the redeemed enjoy "eternal life."

But Why *Eternal*?

We should clarify that only God is truly eternal. That is, only the uncreated Father, Son, and Holy Spirit share the unique attribute of being without beginning or end. So, in what sense are we to understand the final destinies of the sheep, goats, Satan, and evil spirits as *eternal*?

The Greek word rendered "eternal" in this passage is *aionios*, which generally means "without beginning or end, that which always has been and always will be."[4] In some contexts, *aionios* may be rendered "without beginning" or "without end, never to cease, everlasting." R. T. France says the word "may convey either the sense of 'going on forever' or that of 'belonging to the age to come.'"[5]

Since these places of blessing and punishment are "prepared," they must have come into existence; that is, God must have created them. Surely, the earthly kingdom in which the sheep enjoy everlasting life, and into which God brings his heavenly throne, is created (and ultimately renovated; cf. 2 Pet. 3:10-13). So, the concept of "eternal life" means not only "without end;" it also signifies a *quality* of life as we enjoy unbroken fellowship with the one who truly is eternal.

Many Scriptures address the qualitative nature of eternal life with Christ. Jesus' words in John 5:24 are one example: "Truly I tell you, anyone who hears my word and believes him who sent me *has eternal life* and will not come under judgment but has passed from death to life" (emphasis added). Believing sinners receive eternal life now, as a present reality, passing from spiritual death into new life in Christ. As Paul puts it, "For you died, and your life is hidden with Christ in God" (Col. 3:3).

This is eternal life in the qualitative sense. Followers of Jesus do not become eternally existing beings; only God is without beginning or end. But because we have entered into a covenant relationship with the Son of God, his eternal life is bound to ours. And thus, as long as Jesus lives, we live, too (John 14:19).

But there's more. This qualitative aspect of eternal life is permanent and non-revocable, thus everlasting. That is, those who receive eternal life through faith in Jesus enjoy the never-ending benefits of our covenant relationship with him. We look forward to the new heavens and new earth, where we enjoy face-to-face fellowship with our creator for all eternity.

Perhaps there is a similar sense in which Satan, evil spirits, and wicked people enter into both qualitative and quantitative "eternal punishment." God certainly foreknows their banishment to the lake of fire, and they stand condemned today (John 3:18; 16:11). Just as believers are foreknown, elected, and predestined outside of time – one might say in "eternity past" – so Satan, evil spirits, and unbelievers are foreknown as those who reject God and thus choose eternity apart from him.

Wicked angels and unbelieving people live today as renegades, outside the intimate fellowship that believers in Christ and holy angels enjoy with God. Thus, they presently reap everlasting punishment in a qualitative sense. They experience never-ending punishment, in the quantitative sense, when they are cast into outer darkness after final judgment. So, their "eternal punishment" is foreknown, determined, experienced now in spiritual darkness, and without end.

Finally, when we think of the fires of hell, we should not disconnect them from the presence of God. Remember that God often is associated with fire throughout Scripture. He appears to Moses in a burning bush (Exod. 3). His presence radiates through the pillar of fire and cloud during the Israelites' forty years in the desert. He comes down on Mount Sinai in fire (Exod. 19:18). The writer of Hebrews depicts him as a "consuming fire" (Heb. 12:29). John's vision of heaven shows the seven spirits – or seven-fold Spirit – blazing like fire before the throne in heaven (Rev. 4:5). Further, John sees those who worship the beast being tormented with fire and sulfur in the sight of the holy angels and in the sight of the Lamb (Rev. 14:10).

The fires with which God is associated provide holy angels and believing sinners with light, warmth, protection, and guidance. These same fires torment rebellious angels and unrepentant sinners. In some respects, the blazing brilliance of hellfire is the backside of heaven's Shekinah glory. It continuously reveals the holiness of God and perpetually sears the blackened hearts of the damned. The fires of heaven and hell are not two distinct fires. They share the same divine source but have very different effects on the righteous and the wicked.

The Abyss: Revelation 20:1-3

Before Satan is cast into the lake of fire to be tormented forever, Revelation 20:1-3 details a thousand-year imprisonment:

> Then I saw an angel coming down from heaven holding the key to the abyss and a great chain in his hand. He seized the dragon, that ancient serpent who is the devil and Satan, and bound him for a thousand years. He threw him into the abyss, closed it, and put a seal on it so that he would no longer deceive the nations until the thousand years were completed. After that, he must be released for a short time.

The Greek word *abyssos*, rendered "abyss," "pit," or "bottomless pit" in many English translations, occurs nine times in the New Testament. In most occurrences, it refers to a place of temporary confinement for certain evil spirits. For example, in Jesus' encounter with "Legion," the demons who possess this Gerasene man beg Jesus not to banish them to the abyss – no doubt a place evil spirits fear (Luke 8:31).

Later, both Peter and Jude refer to a place where particularly nasty evil spirits are kept in reserve for judgment. Peter uses the Greek *tartaroo* (transliterated "Tartarus" in 2 Pet. 2:4 HCSB), and Jude describes it as a place where certain rebellious spirits are kept in "eternal chains in deep darkness" (Jude 6). In the Book of Revelation, demonic "locusts" and a murderous beast emerge from the abyss, and Satan is cast there for a time (Rev. 9:1-11; 11:7; 20:1-3). The only exception seems to be Romans 10:7, in which Paul uses *abyss* as a synonym for the grave (or perhaps the underworld), contrasting Jesus' descent into it with the Savior's ascension into heaven.[6]

Note several characteristics of the abyss. First, it is under God's sovereign control. An angel must be given the key for the shaft to the abyss, for the angel has no authority to open it on his own (Rev. 9:1; 20:1). The beast upon whom the "Mother of Prostitutes" rides comes up from the abyss, only to go to destruction (Rev. 17:5, 8). Demons fear the abyss and seek to avoid it, although Jesus has the final say (Luke 8:31). And Satan is seized, bound, and thrown into the abyss for a thousand years – a sentence he cannot appeal or shorten (Rev. 20:1-3).

We also may note the relative unimportance of Satan in these verses. It is not the Father, the exalted Son of God, or the Holy Spirit who deals with the evil one. Rather, an unnamed angel is dispatched to lock Satan in the abyss.

Second, the abyss is a place of confinement. Like Satan, evil spirits seem to desire freedom to prowl the earth (1 Pet. 5:8). They crave autonomy – independence from God, and both the ability and opportunity to oppose him. In the abyss, however, they are kept under lock and key. Jude describes it as a place where some evil spirits are "kept in eternal chains in deep darkness" (Jude 6). No doubt, the expression "chains" is used figuratively since evil spirits are non-corporeal beings and physical chains cannot bind them. Nevertheless, they are imprisoned, and God, who is spirit (John 4:24), knows full well how to keep spirits he created in their place.

We should note, as well, the significance of the seal the angel places on the abyss. It is "a surer seal to keep him [Satan] from getting out than [Satan's] seal over Jesus in the tomb of Joseph, which was burst on the resurrection morn."[7]

Third, the abyss is a place of temporary punishment. Satan is kept there for a thousand years, only to be cast into the lake of fire to be tormented night and day forever (Rev. 20:10). Like *hades*, the abode of the dead where the wicked go between physical death and final judgment, the abyss is imprisonment, with no parole, for evil spirits. Ultimately, both "death" and "Hades" are cast into the lake of fire, for they are temporary states of punishment and are no longer needed after final judgment (cf. Rev. 20:14).

Similarly, once Satan, evil spirits, and wicked people are cast into hell, the abyss serves no further purpose. Though temporary, the abyss is a place of genuine punishment, for confinement prevents Satan and evil spirits from carrying out their wicked campaign against God and God's people.

Fourth, the abyss is intended for Satan and evil spirits, not people. The departed spirits of human beings reside in a temporary place called *sheol* in the Old Testament and *hades* in the New Testament. Of course, followers of Jesus go directly into his presence in heaven upon physical death, where they await resurrection, glorification, and everlasting life in the new heavens and new earth (2 Cor. 5:1-10; Phil. 1:21-24; 2 Pet. 3:10-13; Rev. 21-22). But nowhere in Scripture are people described as being in the abyss.

Death and hades, which John personifies in Revelation 20:14, clearly impact all humanity. But believers should take heart. The risen Christ holds the keys of death and hades (Rev. 1:18) and ultimately casts them both into the lake of fire (Rev. 20:14).

Finally, the abyss is a reverse image of heaven. Just as "Every good and perfect gift is from above, coming down from the Father of lights" (Jas. 1:17), the abyss spews nothing but wickedness from below. As Walter Elwell and Barry Beitzel point out:

> This is in keeping with the metaphor and the picture throughout Revelation in which the Dragon and the Beast attempt to duplicate the power and glory reserved for God alone. Just as heaven is a source of all that is worthwhile, the bottomless pit is the source of all that is evil.[8]

The Millennium

If the abyss is a real but temporary place in which Satan is bound, we might also ask whether the thousand-year period of his imprisonment should be understood literally or figuratively. The thousand years, or *millennium*, of Revelation 20 is a much-debated period of time. There are at least four major views:

Historic premillennialists believe the church will endure a period of tribulation before Christ returns to resurrect his church and reign on earth for a thousand years. This view is called "historic" because some early church fathers, such as Justin Martyr and Irenaeus, embraced it. For our purposes, it's important to note that Satan is seen as bound at the beginning of the millennium and released for a short time at the end of it, before being cast into the lake of fire (Rev. 20:7-10). So, Satan's binding is *future*.

Dispensationalists also argue for a thousand-year reign of Christ on earth. Before this occurs, however, Christ resurrects and snatches away his church in an event known as *the rapture*. This sets off seven years of tribulation on earth, with Satan working through his primary human agents, the antichrist and false prophet, to foment great persecution of Jews and Gentiles who come to faith in Christ. At the end of the tribulation, Christ returns and binds Satan for a thousand years, releasing him briefly at the end before casting him into the lake of fire. As in historic premillennialism, Satan's binding is *future*.

Amillennialists understand the thousand years in figurative terms. They see the millennium as the present day, with Christ reigning from heaven. He returns one future day to resurrect and judge all people. Meanwhile, Satan is bound – and has been bound since Christ's first coming – in that he may deceive individuals but not nations. Satan's binding is *present*, and it ends with the future return of Christ, who casts Satan into hell.

Postmillennialists believe the "thousand years" constitute a lengthy period of enormous blessing that precedes the second coming of Christ. Satan has been bound since the Incarnation, and he remains so, except for a brief period just prior to Christ's return. Like amillennialists, postmillennialists hold that Satan remains active as a tempter to individuals, but he may not deceive the nations. Satan's binding, therefore, is *present*.

While these four views differ in how they understand what the

Book of Revelation teaches about the millennium and the binding of Satan, they all agree in a future, personal, glorious return of Jesus. They also agree that Christ binds, or will bind, Satan to limit his global influence. And, they agree Satan ultimately is cast into the lake of fire prepared for him and evil spirits (Matt. 25:41).

Whether Satan is presently bound, or is bound at some future date, Revelation 20:7 records that he is "released from his prison." Immediately, the unreformed tyrant returns to his life of crime, deceiving the nations so that a large number of followers – "like the sand of the sea" – rally behind him to surround "the encampment of the saints" (vv. 8-9). It is an ill-advised and short-lived rebellion, as the apostle John records:

> Then fire came down from heaven and consumed them. The devil who deceived them was thrown into the lake of fire and sulfur where the beast and the false prophet are, and they will be tormented day and night forever and ever (vv. 9-10).

The phrase "forever and ever" may be translated "into the ages of the ages." We might compare it with Jesus' words in Matthew 25:46 concerning the sheep and goats: "And they [goats] will go away into *eternal* punishment, but the righteous into *eternal* life." As we noted earlier, the English word "eternal" translates the Greek *aionios*; the same word is used convey the idea of "forever and ever" in Revelation 20:10.

Some may argue that hell is a temporary place of punishment – leading ultimately to redemption or annihilation, and thus opening the door to a second chance beyond the grave. There's another side to that coin. If the "eternal punishment" Jesus describes in the parable of the sheep and goats ends in annihilation, then "eternal life" just might not be eternal, either. But the writings of John, as well as other texts, argue against such a view. Further, the writer of Hebrews makes it abundantly clear that judgment, not a do-over, awaits all people after death (Heb. 9:27).

The conditional view of eternal life leads to even greater

concerns. Think about it: If Adam and Eve fell into sin despite living in the perfect environment of Eden, couldn't glorified humans fall into sin and find themselves disqualified from the new heavens and earth? If so, the whole doctrine of eternal punishment vs. eternal life comes unraveled. So, it seems best to take the words of Jesus and John at face value regarding "eternal punishment" and the torment that lasts "forever and ever."

Kendall Easley makes a key point as we struggle with the chronology of Satan's rise and fall as depicted in the Book of Revelation: "However we interpret the binding of Satan in Revelation 20, we must never lose the essential New Testament teaching that his primary defeat was in the death and resurrection of Jesus, and his ultimate defeat is already certain."[9]

The evil one's temporary imprisonment in the abyss in some ways mirrors the intermediate confinement of wicked people in hades. When unbelievers die physically, their spirits depart to hades, where they are held until their future resurrection and arraignment before the great white throne (Rev. 20:11-15). Upon their conviction in final judgment, Christ banishes them to the lake of fire.

Similarly, Satan experiences an intermediate state when imprisoned in the abyss. After a thousand years, he is released for a short time, proving his impenitent nature through immediate rebellion. Swiftly and decisively, he is cast into hell to be tormented night and day forever and ever. So, Satan and the wicked follow a similar pattern: rebellion, imprisonment, arraignment, conviction, sentencing.

As Christ is the second Adam, freeing his followers from the bonds of death and hades, Satan is the prototype of wicked humans, experiencing temporary confinement in the underworld before being cast eternally, and irrevocably, into the lake of fire.

The Lake of Fire and Sulfur: Revelation 20:10

> The devil who deceived them was thrown into the lake of fire and sulfur where the beast and the false prophet are, and they will be tormented day and night forever and ever (Rev. 20:10).

In this verse, John describes Satan's ultimate destination as "the lake of fire and sulfur." In Matthew 25:41, Jesus calls it "the eternal fire prepared for the devil and his angels." Jesus and the New Testament writers also describe this place as "outer darkness," "eternal punishment," and "the second death." But there is an even more descriptive term for this place: *gehenna*, or hell.

While the Hebrew *sheol* and the Greek *hades* generally depict the temporary abode of the dead, *gehenna* and its associated terms describe a place of everlasting future punishment, not only for Satan and evil spirits, but also for those whose names are not written in the book of life (Rev. 20:15).

The noun *gehenna* is derived from the Valley of Hinnom. Located southwest of Jerusalem, this steep, rocky valley is the scene of human sacrifices to pagan deities (2 Kings 23:10; 2 Chron. 28:3; 33:6). A particular part of the valley is called Tophet, which means "fire-stove," where Israelite children are burned as offerings to the false gods Moloch and Baal. Jeremiah declares it the "Valley of Slaughter" (Jer. 7:31-34). To the Jewish mind, the images of fire and destruction become appropriate representations of the eventual fate of idol worshipers.

Jesus seizes rabbinic language connected with gehenna, such as "unquenchable fire" and "never-dying worms" (cf. Isa. 66:24), to impress upon his listeners that their choices in this life have everlasting consequences. In fact, of the twelve uses of *gehenna* in the New Testament, eleven come from the lips of the Messiah. The lone exception is James, who writes that the tongue "sets the course of life on fire, and is itself set on fire by hell (*gehenna*)" (Jas. 3:6).

It's probable that Jesus uses *gehenna* on only four occasions: in the

Sermon on the Mount (Matt. 5:22, 29, 30); in warning the disciples not to fear men (Matt. 10:28; Luke 12:5); in a discourse on relationships (Matt. 18:9; Mark 9:43, 45, 47); and in his denunciation of the scribes and Pharisees (Matt. 23:15, 33). Traditionally, these passages are understood to speak of final judgment, with Jesus using images from everyday life to warn about a place of everlasting punishment.

We should note that some commentators see Jesus speaking in more limited terms. Steve Gregg, in *All You Want to Know About Hell*, argues that Jesus may have used *gehenna* literally to warn first-century Jews that they are about to suffer fiery judgment at the hands of the Romans for their rejection of the Messiah – a judgment that falls hard on Jerusalem and its inhabitants in AD 70.[10]

This is not to deny the existence of hell as a place of everlasting separation from God, since other texts speak of resurrection, final judgment, and fiery punishment for the wicked. But it is to encourage us to carefully consider the context of each passage of Scripture so we do not glean more from a text than is warranted.

It's also important to understand *who* and *what* are cast into the lake of fire. The beast and the false prophet are tossed there (Rev. 19:20). So is Satan (Rev. 20:10), as is anyone whose name is not found written in the book of life (Rev. 20:15); this includes cowards, unbelievers, the vile, murderers, the sexually immoral, sorcerers, idolaters, and all liars – meaning the unrepentant wicked (Rev. 21:8; cf. 1 Cor. 6:9-10; Gal. 5:19-21; Eph. 5:5). Ultimately, death and hades also are banished to hell, since there is no longer any need for physical death or a temporary spiritual existence in the underworld (Rev. 20:14).

John describes Satan's torment as enduring "day and night forever and ever." This phrase may be considered metaphorically as "without intermission" or "unceasingly." As surely as Christ's kingdom is "forever and ever" (Rev. 11:15), so is the length of Satan's punishment. The same divine fire that comes down from heaven in judgment of wicked people now engulfs the ultimate rebel (cf. 2 Kings 1:10, 12; Rev. 20:9).

The fires of hell devour, but do not annihilate, wicked humans and evil spirits. For unbelieving people, hell transforms the temporary consequences of sin, such as physical death and disembodiment in hades, into permanent and unalterable punishments such as the second death, darkness, and separation from the intimacy God offers all people through his Son's finished work on the cross.

As the apostle Paul writes, those who don't know God and those who do not obey the gospel "pay the penalty of eternal destruction from the Lord's presence ..." (2 Thess. 1:9). Perhaps this divine act of judgment is the first step in what Peter describes as God's work of creating new heavens and a new earth. He first purges sin and its stain from the created order, and then restores the earth, skies, and outer space to their former pristine condition (2 Pet. 3:10-13; Rev. 21-22).

Is Hellfire Literal?

We might ask: When Jesus and the New Testament writers depict hell, are we to take the lake of fire literally or figuratively? Godly scholars stand on both sides of the debate. Charles Spurgeon, for example, spoke of hell's fire as real:

> Now, do not begin telling me that that is metaphorical fire: who cares for that? If a man were to threaten to give me a metaphorical blow on the head, I should care very little about it; he would be welcome to give me as many as he pleased. And what say the wicked? "We do not care about metaphorical fires." But they are real, sir – yes, as real as yourself. There is a real fire in hell, as truly as you have now a real body – a fire exactly like that which we have on earth in everything except this – that it will not consume, though it will torture you. You have seen the asbestos lying in the fire red hot, but when you take it out it is unconsumed. So your body will be prepared by God in such a way that it will burn forever without being consumed; it will lie, not as you consider, in metaphorical fire, but in actual flame.[11]

William Crockett expresses a different view, one shared by such theologians as John Calvin and J. I. Packer:

> Christians should never be faced with this kind of embarrassment – the Bible does not support a literal view of a burning abyss. Hellfire and brimstone are not literal depictions of hell's fictions, but figurative expressions warning the wicked of impending doom.[12]

Theologian Charles Hodge adds:

> There seems no more reason for supposing that the fire spoken of in Scripture is to be a literal fire, than that the worm that never dies is literally a worm. The devil and his angels who are to suffer the vengeance of eternal fire, and whose doom the finally impenitent are to share, have no material bodies to be acted upon by elemental fire.[13]

Wicked humans, however, *do* possess material bodies following their resurrection. So the fires of hell, whether literal or figurative, are designed to inflict torment on the whole person.

It may help to remember that the Bible uses fire metaphorically many times. Daniel sees the throne of God in heaven as "flaming fire; its wheels were blazing fire" (Dan. 7:9). James describes the tongue as an appendage that "sets the course of life on fire, and is itself set on fire by hell" (Jas. 3:6). So, it may be that the Bible's depiction of hell in such graphic terms is God's way of explaining an indescribable place in language we can understand. Whether literal or metaphorical, the fires of hell are to be avoided at all costs, and the blood of Jesus is to be pleaded for forgiveness of sins while there is yet time.

Is Hell Forever?

Do hell's inhabitants experience suffering without end?

Anglican cleric John Stott, who wrote the influential book *Basic*

Christianity, found the idea of eternal suffering in hell so repugnant that he rejected it in favor of annihilationism.

Those who embrace the idea of body and soul ceasing to exist after a time of punishment in hell point out that the "fire" and "worms" to which Jesus refers in Matthew 10:28 are indeed eternal, but the body and soul are destroyed: "Don't fear those who kill the body but are not able to kill the soul; rather, fear him who is able to *destroy* both soul and body in hell" (emphasis added).

Consider two observations. First, the rabbinic understanding of these terms is that the bodies and souls of the wicked are eternal, not just the fires and worms.[14]

Second, the term "destroy" in Matthew 10:28 does not mean annihilated. As *Thayer's Greek-English Lexicon* defines the word *apollumi*, it means "to be delivered up to eternal misery." In every instance where the word *apollumi* is found in the New Testament, something other than annihilation is described.[15] For example, people do not pass into nonexistence when they are "dying of hunger" (Luke 15:17), and wineskins don't vanish into thin air when they burst and "are ruined" (Matt. 9:17). In each of these instances, New Testament writers use the term *apollumi*.

While rejecting annihilationism, other Christian leaders favor the idea of suffering in the afterlife as a prerequisite for heaven. This may be in hell, or in an intermediate state such as purgatory. Augustine, sometimes wrongly called "the father of purgatory," was never completely convinced of the need for purging sins after death. Nevertheless, he conceded the possibility. He once wrote:

> Of those who suffer temporary punishments after death, all are not doomed to those everlasting pains which are to follow that judgment; for to some ... what is not remitted in this world is remitted in the next, that is, they are not punished with the eternal punishment of the world to come.[16]

Put another way, Augustine seemed to believe there may be real, but temporary, punishment for those destined for heaven. Meanwhile, eternal punishment is reserved for the unsaved.

Even so, Jesus' teachings on "outer darkness," "eternal fire," and "eternal punishment" seem to support the concept of gehenna as a place of conscious, everlasting separation from God. There is no scriptural provision for temporal post-mortem punishment to pay off the debt owed an eternally holy God. Nor does there appear to be a temporary state of suffering for the adopted sons and daughters of God.

The apostle Paul describes heaven – not purgatory, nor time in hell followed by heaven – as the intermediate state between death and resurrection for the follower of Jesus. In 2 Corinthians 5, Paul describes two mutually exclusive states for Christians. While we are here on earth in our bodies, we are absent from the Lord. And when we are "away from the body," we are "at home with the Lord" (5:8).

If there is an interim step between death and heaven, the Bible makes no mention of it, and we would do well to rest in the plainly stated promises of God's Word. For those who die in the Lord, heaven can't wait, nor should it. At the same time, Scripture offers no false hope for the unbeliever – no second chance. As the writer of Hebrews makes clear, "it is appointed for people to die once – and after this, judgment" (Heb. 9:27).

The Goodness of Hell

Hell is an awful prospect for anyone. C. S. Lewis once shuddered at the concept of hell: "There is no doctrine which I would more willingly remove from Christianity than this, if it lay in my power."[17]

But let's consider for a moment that the notion of a loving God and the doctrine of hell are perfectly compatible. There is nothing of one that cancels out the other. Jesus speaks frequently on hell and alludes to it in parables. He tells some religious leaders they are headed for hell. He warns his listeners against this place where the worm does not die and the fires are not quenched. He refers to hell as "outer darkness." And he says hell was prepared for Satan and evil spirits, yet he makes it clear that many people are going to spend eternity there.

So, in what possible way is hell good?

First, hell is good because it is a place God prepared for the one who wrecked the goodness of creation – and the very goodness of beings made to be his imagers. The Greek word rendered "prepared" in Matthew 25:41 is *hetoimazo*. It means to make the necessary preparations, or to get everything ready. The term is drawn from the oriental custom of sending servants ahead of kings on their journeys to level the roads and make them passable. So, with hell, the Lord has made everything ready for the god of this age – the king of a corrupt and rebellious kingdom – to end his journey in outer darkness.

Second, hell is good because it affirms God's justice. If God only had the attributes of benevolence and mercy, hell would be an unreasonable reading of Scripture. But God is infinitely holy and perfectly just. To sin against him offends his very nature. Human beasts like Hitler, Stalin, and Pol Pot are responsible for the slaughter of millions of people whose lives ended in starvation, torture, human experimentation, or execution. How can the mere death of these tyrants by any means satisfy divine justice, let alone human justice?

If we accept the doctrine of universalism, we must admit that Osama bin Laden and Mother Teresa are feasting at the same banquet table. At the same time, if we embrace the dogma of annihilation, we struggle to explain how temporal suffering in the afterlife pays an eternal debt. Without the existence of hell, life indeed is cruel and life's creator is eternally unjust.

Third, hell is good because it affirms free will. While we may debate whether humans have libertarian free will or simply make decisions within predetermined boundaries, there is little question among Christians that God allows us to make choices for which he holds us accountable. In a world where God refuses to grant humans real choices, there is no freedom to love God.

If we view life fatalistically, God is a cruel puppet master who manipulates us before discarding us like broken toys. But the biblical concept of hell carries with it the clear teaching that people choose to spend eternity apart from Christ. As C. S. Lewis so poignantly penned, "[T]he doors of Hell are locked on the inside."[18] Without hell, our choices have no real meaning or lasting consequences.

Fourth, hell is good because it implies heaven. Many atheists attack the idea that a good God would send people to hell for eternity as payment for temporal sins. But they tend not to criticize the idea of a God – if he could possibly exist – who welcomes people into eternal bliss merely for being the recipients of his grace.

Freud argued that heaven is a product of wishful thinking. But if that's so, how does one explain the fact that many religions embracing heaven also have clear doctrines of hell? We are invited to join God in this life, and in the life to come, by his grace through faith. We may reject him and enter eternity on our own terms, but we cannot take God with us or it would cease to be hell.

While it is troubling to consider eternity in "outer darkness," the Bible is clear that hell is a place people choose to live independently of God – forever. We do not see the rich man repent of his sin after finding himself in torment in hades (Luke 16:19-31), nor do we see those before the great white throne asking to be nearer to Jesus (Rev. 20:11-15). Indeed, the blasphemers and unrepentant in Revelation hide themselves from the presence of God, preferring death under a deluge of rocks to life in the light of Christ (Rev. 6:15-17).

A final caution: When we say hell is good, we do not mean to gloat over those who enter eternity without Christ, no matter how wicked they may be. The Lord himself does not delight in the judgment of the ungodly. Rather, he took the human condition so seriously that he sent his Son to save us from ourselves.

Could Satan Be Saved?

Scripture is clear that Satan's eternal destiny is the unrelenting lake of fire. It is the place into which the antichrist, the false prophet, and all unbelievers are cast as well. It does not appear there is any reversal of fortune for those in hell. Nevertheless, some in the early church took a different view.

Clement of Alexandria, for example, thought there was hope for the devil based on God's limitless mercy. Clement's pupil, Origen, took it a step further. He argued for *apocatastasis*, or the idea that all things made by God return to him. He once wrote, "We believe that the goodness of God through Christ will restore his entire creation to one end, even his enemies being conquered and subdued."[19] In Origen's view, everyone – including Satan, evil spirits, and the most wicked humans – ultimately submit to God's sovereignty and are saved. Thus, Satan ceases to be evil and has his angelic nature restored.

Origen's view never gained much traction. Jerome and Augustine countered it. And the Council of Constantinople II in AD 553 anathematized the idea that the demonic could revert to the angelic in nature.[20] Graham Cole summarizes, "The darkness won't extinguish the light. The destiny of the darkness is its destruction. Fallen angels will experience the eternal fire. The devil may be the prince of this world. Be that as it may, in the next he has no kingdom."[21]

Satan cannot be *saved* – that is, restored to angelic holiness – for at least three reasons:

First, God has decreed that Satan will not be saved. The Lord has prepared the fires of hell for Satan and rebellious angels, who are cast into hell to be tormented night and day forever and ever – an unceasing suffering. Scripture offers no salvation to humans beyond the grave, or to Satan at any point after his rebellion. The biblical account is straightforward. The evil one rebelled, God prepared the lake of fire for him, and in the end God casts him into this place of unrelenting torment.

Second, Satan would refuse salvation if offered. Satan's rebellion, committed in the perfection of the created order, and done with superior knowledge, wisdom, and power, was such that it is irrevocable. Nothing in Scripture hints at the possibility of Satan seeing the error of his ways and repenting. He knows his time is short, yet rather than repent – as humans facing their own mortality are urged to do – he turns up the heat to wreak as much havoc as possible on God's reputation and God's people. After a thousand years in the abyss, Satan is neither contrite nor converted. His first act is not to repent, but to lead a global rebellion.

Third, there is no provision for salvation for Satan and fallen angels. Jesus did not come in the likeness of sinful angels, but in the likeness of sinful human beings. Forgiveness of sins, eternal life, adoption as children of God, and much more are reserved only for those whose salvation was secured in the sinless life, death, burial, and resurrection of Jesus, the God-Man. As the writer of Hebrews notes:

> Now since the children have flesh and blood in common, Jesus also shared in these, so that through his death he might destroy the one holding the power of death – that is, the devil – and free those who were held in slavery all their lives by the fear of death. For it is clear that he does not reach out to help angels, but to help Abraham's offspring. Therefore, he had to be like his brothers and sisters in every way, so that he could become a merciful and faithful high priest in matters pertaining to God, to make atonement for the sins of the people (Heb. 2:14-17).

A Real Place

Jesus is clear that *gehenna* – hell, the lake of fire and sulfur, outer darkness – is a real place prepared for Satan and evil spirits. It is a place of separation, darkness, torment, hopelessness, and regret (but not remorse). And yet it is a place fully within the scope of God's omnipresence, for Satan and demons are tormented in the presence of God and his holy angels, as are the wicked followers of the beast (Rev. 14:10).

God designed hell as a final destination for Satan and rebellious angels. There is no hope of redemption for them. Not now. Not ever. But there is hope for sinful and fallen human beings. Christ came in the likeness of sinful humans, adding full humanity to his deity, and living a sinless life so he could offer it up to the Father as an acceptable substitute for us.

Christ's eternal life pays an eternal debt we owe an eternally offended God. Jesus' death took the place of ours. His resurrection secured the keys of death and hades so that he is the firstfruits of the righteous dead (1 Cor. 15:20-23); we have his promise of future resurrection and glorification.

Every person lives forever. But where, and how, are the key questions. And these questions are answered in our response to the most important question Jesus ever posed: "Who do you say that I am?" (Matt. 16:15). Many people answer wrongly today. They regard Jesus as a good man, a prophet, or perhaps even a god. But it's not good enough to have a high opinion of Jesus. We must answer as Peter did: "You are the Messiah, the Son of the living God" (Matt. 16:16).

If we read chapters 12 and 20 of Revelation together, we gain a concise history of the evil one: (1) The dragon begins in the heavens (12:3); (2) he tries unsuccessfully to destroy Christ at his incarnation (12:4); (3) he is thrown to the earth for a season and deceives the nations (12:12); (4) he is cast into the abyss for a thousand years (20:3); (5) he is released for a short time and proceeds at once to deceive the nations (20:8); finally, (6) he is thrown into the lake of fire and sulfur to be tormented forever (20:10).[22]

The same holy fire that lights the way for Israelites crossing the desert, that resides in the Holy of Holies above the mercy seat, and that blazes in the human spirits of the redeemed, finally engulfs Satan, evil spirits, and human unbelievers. The holiness of God warms; it also burns.

Summary

Key takeaways about *the one for whom hell is prepared*:

(1) Satan may rule a kingdom of evil spirits and rebellious people today. He may even prowl the earth like an uncaged lion. But he lays no claim to hell, the final stop on Satan's long descent into ruin.

There, in the presence of God and his holy angels, the evil one gets his comeuppance and forever loses his freedom.

(2) The central theme of Jesus' parable of the sheep and goats (Matt. 25:31-46) is that Christ separates believers from unbelievers at his return. Jesus also makes it clear that all angelic and human rebels are banished from his presence. This passage deals with human works, not as a condition of salvation, but as evidence of one's regard for the Son of Man.

(3) Jesus says hell is a place "prepared for the devil and his angels" (Matt. 25:41). Put another way, Jesus does not tell the goats that hell is prepared for *them*, but for another race of beings – rebellious angels. Salvation is God's exclusive gift to humans, a gift denied to the evil one and fallen angels. Nevertheless, those who reject Christ necessarily occupy the same place of everlasting punishment as Satan.

(4) The fires with which God is associated in Scripture provide holy angels and believing sinners with light, warmth, protection, and guidance. These same fires torment rebellious angels and unrepentant sinners. In some respects, the blazing brilliance of hellfire is the backside of heaven's Shekinah glory. It continuously reveals the holiness of God and perpetually sears the blackened hearts of the damned.

(5) Before Satan is cast into the lake of fire to be tormented forever, he is sent for a time to the *abyss*, a place of temporary imprisonment where the evil one and certain demons are kept under lock and key. Incarceration doesn't reform Satan. After a thousand years he's released, and immediately he leads a final rebellion against God and God's people.

(6) While the Hebrew *sheol* and the Greek *hades* generally depict the temporary abode of the dead, *gehenna* and its associated terms describe a place of everlasting future punishment, not only for Satan and evil spirits, but also for those whose names are not written in the book of life.

(7) Are the fires of hell literal or figurative? Godly scholars stand on both sides of the debate. Whether literal or metaphorical,

however, the fires of hell are to be avoided at all costs, and the blood of Jesus is to be pleaded for forgiveness of sins while there is yet time.

(8) Universalism and annihilationism are two errant views of divine justice. If we accept the doctrine of universalism, we must admit that Osama bin Laden and Mother Teresa are feasting at the same banquet table. At the same time, if we embrace the dogma of annihilation, we struggle to explain how temporal suffering in the afterlife pays an eternal debt. Without the existence of hell, life indeed is cruel and life's creator is eternally unjust.

(9) Despite the views of some in the early church, Satan cannot be *saved* – that is, restored to angelic holiness – for at least three reasons: (a) God has decreed that Satan will not be saved; (b) Satan would refuse salvation if offered; and (c) there is no provision for salvation for Satan and fallen angels.

Questions for Personal or Group Study

1. If Jesus says hell is prepared for "the devil and his angels," why does he send people there?
2. What key truths about final judgment may we glean from Jesus' parable of the sheep and goats (Matt. 25:31-46)?
3. In what ways are "eternal life" and "eternal punishment" both qualitative and quantitative? That is, how do these terms describe a present reality, as well as a length of time?
4. Do you think the fires of hell are literal or figurative? Why?
5. In what ways is hell good?

Christ is our commander in chief, and we are his foot soldiers, fitted for battle.

ENGAGING THE EVIL ONE

Throughout this study, we have explored various names and titles for the archenemy of mankind. Satan stands defiantly against God and God's creatures. He appears as a beautiful and seductive "burning one" in Genesis 3. Then, across the pages of Scripture, we see his story unfold in nightmarish fashion as he slanders God, engages in hand-to-hand combat in the heavenly realms, and seeks to ruin the very beings God created as his imagers – namely, you and me.

Often, the evil one is successful. But he wages war in a shrinking theater. First thrown out of heaven, then cast to earth, then confined to the abyss, he finally is banished to the lake of fire, a place God specifically prepares for him and his spirit saboteurs.

At every diabolical turn, the evil one finds himself set back on his heels. First, in the wake of Adam and Eve's fall, Yahweh promises his human creatures a redeemer – the seed of woman – who is to crush the evil one's head, although at great personal cost (Gen. 3:15). Next, God bars humans from the tree of life so they won't be bound eternally in a fallen state (Gen. 3:22-24).

When Satan tries to wipe out the Jewish people, reduce their population, or even kill their anointed one, God intervenes. When the evil one tries to get Job to curse God, God places limits on how far Satan can go (Job 1:12; 2:6). When Satan steps forth in the divine council to accuse the high priest of unworthiness, the angel of the LORD becomes Joshua's advocate, forgiving his sins and dressing him in fresh clothes (Zech. 3:1-5).

When the tempter tries to catch Jesus at a vulnerable point during his earthly ministry, the Son of God plies Scripture to beat back the assault (Matt. 4:1-11; Luke 4:1-13). And when the destroyer thinks he has put an end to the Son of Man on the cross, Jesus conquers Satan, sin, and death through his physical resurrection.

In every case, God proves superior to this powerful and intelligent creature. Even the holy angels must battle Satan and his minions in the heavenlies, emerging victoriously after pitched battles (Dan. 10:1-21; Rev. 12:7-12).

Satan is most successful, it seems, bringing the fight to the weakest line of defense – human beings. He woos Eve into disobedience, and she in turn convinces Adam to defy God, plunging humanity and the created order into chaos (Gen. 3). Satan evidently gets Abram and Sarai to speed up God's timetable for a promised son. This results in sexual relations with an Egyptian slave, who bears a son that becomes a perpetual thorn in Israel's side (Gen. 16).

Later, Satan poisons the community of Israelites with grumbling and idolatry as they wander from Egypt to the Promised Land. He counsels the kings of Israel and Judah to abandon God and embrace idols. He gets Peter to rebuke Jesus for mentioning the necessity of the cross (Matt. 16:21-23). Then, he goads Peter to deny Jesus three times, and later to compromise on ethnic conciliation in the church (Luke 22:54-62; Gal. 2:11-16).

The evil one takes control of Judas Iscariot and, later, the antichrist (Luke 22:3; John 13:27; 2 Thess. 2:9-10; Rev. 13:2, 4). He gets Ananias and Sapphira to tell a white lie about a property transaction, resulting in a serious challenge to the integrity of the early church – not to mention their deaths (Acts 5:1-11). He continues today to prowl the earth like a ravenous lion, seeking whom he may devour (1 Pet.

5:8). He never rests, plying his subtle crafts of doubt, despair, and defiance.

But just as the Lord promises not to leave us as orphans (John 14:18), he vows to help us engage in battle against the evil one. After ascending into heaven, Jesus sends the Holy Spirit as the down payment on our future home in glory. Further, the Spirit intercedes for us, helps us pray, indwells us, sanctifies us, confirms we are God's children, and helps us discern between the true promises of God and the counterfeit guarantees of Satan.

Further, the New Testament tells us God has equipped us to wage war with Satan. Perhaps no other passage makes this as clear as Ephesians 6:10-20, where the apostle Paul exhorts us to "put on the full armor of God" so we can "stand against the schemes of the devil" (vv. 11-12). Let's look at this passage in context and then briefly survey the full armor God supplies to his followers.

The Full Armor of God

Ephesians 6:10-20 reads:

> Finally, be strengthened by the Lord and by his vast strength. Put on the full armor of God so that you can stand against the schemes of the devil. For our struggle is not against flesh and blood, but against the rulers, against the authorities, against the cosmic powers of this darkness, against evil, spiritual forces in the heavens. For this reason take up the full armor of God, so that you may be able to resist in the evil day, and having prepared everything, to take your stand. Stand, therefore, with truth like a belt around your waist, righteousness like armor on your chest, and your feet sandaled with readiness for the gospel of peace. In every situation take up the shield of faith with which you can extinguish all the flaming arrows of the evil one. Take the helmet of salvation and the sword of the Spirit – which is the word of God. Pray at all times in the Spirit with every prayer and request, and stay alert with all perseverance and intercession for all the saints. Pray also for me, that the message may be given to me

when I open my mouth to make known with boldness the mystery of the gospel. For this I am an ambassador in chains. Pray that I might be bold enough to speak about it as I should.

Paul urges Christians to "be strengthened by the Lord and by his vast strength," and then to put on "the full armor of God" (vv. 10-11). Everything about this passage leans into Christ. He is our strength. He supplies the armor. His protection enables us to stand, resist, take up, persevere, and emerge victoriously from a battle waged in the unseen realm.

Christ provides all this, but we must appropriate it by faith. The full armor of God is essential because the evil one has more than a quiver of arrows. He employs many different weapons, all designed to lay us out and thus render us useless – or worse, a hindrance to the kingdom – on the battlefield. And he leads a powerful army of demonic foot soldiers.

The full armor (Greek: *panoplia*) is the sum total of all the pieces – from helmet to sandals, and from shield to sword. *Panoplia* appears in only one other place outside Ephesians 6. Luke records a parable of Jesus as he responds to false accusations that he casts out demons by Beelzebul, the ruler of demons:

> When a strong man, fully armed, guards his estate, his possessions are secure. But when one stronger than he attacks and overpowers him, he takes from him all his weapons (*panoplia*) he trusted in, and divides up his plunder. Anyone who is not with me is against me, and anyone who does not gather with me scatters (Luke 11:21-23).

In this parable, Jesus likens Satan to a fully armed strong man. But "one stronger than he" (Jesus) invades Satan's kingdom and renders the evil one's armor and weapons inoperable. As a result, Jesus is not in league with Satan, as Israel's religious leaders allege. Rather, he is at war with the evil one and plunders his goods, rescuing lost sinners from the domain of darkness and delivering them into the kingdom of God. We should note, however, that Satan is well equipped to engage in battle with us. Thus, it is essential that we heed Paul's urging to put on the *panoplia* of God.

We may think of the armor of God in two ways. First, as aspects of God's character. The Old Testament sometimes depicts God as a warrior. In Israel's song of deliverance, Moses declares, "The LORD is a warrior; the LORD is his name" (Exod. 15:3). In messianic passages, Isaiah sometimes refers to the coming savior in military terms:

> ... but he will judge the poor righteously and execute justice for the oppressed of the land. He will strike the land with a scepter from his mouth, and he will kill the wicked with a command from his lips. Righteousness will be a belt around his hips; faithfulness will be a belt around his waist (Isa. 11:4-5).

In other places, Isaiah depicts the Lord as a defender of justice: "He put on righteousness as body armor, and a helmet of salvation on his head; he put on garments of vengeance for clothing, and he wrapped himself in zeal as in a cloak" (Isa. 59:17).

In other words, God's attributes, such as righteousness, are revealed to us as pieces of armor the divine warrior wears to carry out vengeance against the wicked and thus deliver his people. God is spirit, of course, and doesn't wear physical armor. Yet some biblical writers use the imagery of an armor-clad soldier to show us that the Lord always stands ready to defend us.

We might consider, for example, several places in the Old Testament where the angel of the LORD – the preincarnate Christ – is decked out as a warrior. He confronts Balaam, the prophet-for-hire, with a drawn sword in his hand (Num. 22:22-35). He appears to Joshua as commander of the LORD'S army (Josh. 5:13-15). He stands between heaven and earth wielding a sword over Jerusalem (1 Chron. 21:9-30). He is the LORD of Armies seated on his throne (Isa. 6:1-13; cf. John 12:37-41). And he rides a blazing, cherubim-propelled chariot-throne across the skies (Ezek. 1:1-28).

All of this is to say, in some respects, that the full armor of God depicts his divine attributes. When we engage in spiritual warfare, we are to "put on the Lord Jesus Christ" (Rom. 13:14; cf. Gal. 3:27). Putting on Christ means allowing his divine attributes to shield us and to arm us. It means following him in discipleship and letting him conform our lives to the image of Jesus (Rom. 8:29). It means relying fully on our righteous standing before God in Christ (Rom. 3:22; 1 Cor. 1:30; 2 Cor. 5:21). And it means abiding in Jesus and living to please him. As one writer notes, "We are clothed in Christ when we become so closely united with Jesus that others see Him and not us."[1] This is one way of seeing the full armor of God.

But another way is to understand the *panoplia* as God's individually crafted armor for us. Just as young David discovered he could not successfully engage in battle with Goliath while wearing King Saul's armor, we should understand that the armor God supplies is not one-size-fits-all. We need our own breastplate, sandals, helmet, shield, and sword, which God fits for our personalities, measure of faith, and spiritual gifts. Christ is our commander in chief, and we are his foot soldiers, fitted for battle.

Paul makes it clear this battle is not in the physical realm, for "our struggle is not against flesh and blood, but against the rulers, against the authorities, against the cosmic powers of this darkness, against evil, spiritual forces in the heavens" (Eph. 6:11-12). Ultimately, our enemies are not false teachers, pagans, or persecutors of Christians, no matter how aggressively they oppose the gospel. Rather, we do battle in the spiritual realm.

Paul lays out a hierarchy of evil spirits under Satan's command without providing a detailed organizational chart. But that is not his primary concern. He wants us to know these demonic underlings engage in tactics suited to their diabolical skills. Therefore, we must be fully armed in order to stand against the devil's schemes.

Walter Liefield writes:

> While it may be difficult to identify and distinguish between the specific powers named here [Eph. 6:11-12], the point is clearly made that whatever supernatural forces there may be in this universe, Christ has gained victory over them and so may we. To recognize

that is not to diminish the immense spiritual force they represent. Were that the case, there would be no need for the armor and there would be no occasion for the battle.[2]

The devil's "schemes" (Gr. *methodeia*) suggest deceit, craft, and trickery. Paul uses the same term in Ephesians 4:14 to describe "human cunning with cleverness in the *techniques* of deceit" (emphasis added). The apostle also warns the church at Corinth about Satan's means of deception through counterfeit teachers:

> For such people are false apostles, deceitful workers, disguising themselves as apostles of Christ. And no wonder! For Satan disguises himself as an angel of light. So it is no great surprise if his servants also disguise themselves as servants of righteousness. Their end will be according to their works (2 Cor. 11:13-15).

While our struggle as Christians is not against flesh and blood, victory in the spiritual realm requires that the eternal Son of God take on human form. And this he does, as the writer of Hebrews attests: "Now since the children have flesh and blood in common, Jesus also shared in these, so that through his death he might destroy the one holding the power of death – that is, the devil" (Heb. 2:14).

Because of Christ's victory over the evil one, we may take our stand – that is, maintain our ground, hold fast, neither yielding nor fleeing – as we are clad in the full armor of God. In the ancient form of hand-to-hand combat pictured here, the first duty of soldiers forming a line is to stand side by side, with large rectangular shields forming a wall of defense. As one commentator puts it, "the present picture is not of a march, or of an assault, but of the holding of the fortress of the soul and of the Church for the heavenly King."[3]

Noting Paul's exhortation in Ephesians 6 to "stand" and "take your stand," Liefield writes:

> There is no need, then, for Christians to accomplish what has already been done. Instead we must resist the attempts of Satan

both to retake territory no longer his and to defame Christ and his kingdom by causing us to fail. To *stand* is neither static nor passive, but the active accomplishment of our present task.[4]

The Pieces of Armor

Now, let's turn our attention to the individual pieces of armor. The order in which they are described generally is the order in which soldiers put them on.

Truth Like a Belt

While many modern translations refer to "truth like a belt" (CSB) or "the belt of truth" (ESV, NIV), the KJV renders it, "having your loins girt about with truth." Similarly, the NASB 1995 says, "having girded your loins with truth." The latter understanding may be more to the point.

Ancient warriors and athletes, like other people of the time, wore loose-fitting clothing, which needed to be gathered and secured before any physical activity could ensue. This was done in different ways and for different purposes (see 2 Kings 4:29; Luke 12:35-36; John 13:4-5). The metaphor of girding is used in Scripture because it describes the need to prepare oneself for the spiritual work ahead.

It's interesting to note that the Passover was eaten with the loins girded and shoes on the feet, indicating a readiness to move at the Lord's command (Exod. 12:11). Isaiah writes that "faithfulness" (*truth* in the Septuagint) is the belt around Messiah's waist (Isa. 11:5).

A warrior may secure his clothing in a number of ways. For example, he may wear a foundational piece beneath his armor, then strap on an exterior belt or sash, or simply gather the loose folds of his robes. Whatever method the soldier employs, the belt is not, strictly speaking, part of the armor. But girding is essential for the soldier to both wear his armor and have full mobility in battle.

There are two ways in which truth is part of God's armor. First, it is the truth of God's Word as opposed to the lies of Satan, who is the father of lies (John 8:44). Jesus says, "You will know the truth, and the truth will set you free" (John 8:32). The great truths of the Bible – the love of the triune God, the redemptive work of Christ, salvation by grace alone through faith alone in Christ, and others – set us free from Satan's lies.

Jesus is truth incarnate (John 14:6), and truth is the enemy of the evil one. While Satan often tells outright lies – "No! You will certainly not die" (Gen. 3:4) – he more often twists the truth so we feel at ease with falsehood and thus are caught off guard. Deception is high on the list of sins God considers an abomination. A "lying tongue" is "detestable to him" (Prov. 6:16-17).

Second, girding our loins means making a personal commitment to the truth – living lives of uprightness, sincerity, integrity, and a good conscience (2 Cor. 1:12; 1 Tim. 1:5, 18-19; 3:9). Putting on the belt of truth in this regard ensures that all the rest of our armor stays in place.

Without truth, there is no trustworthy revelation of God, no real Jesus, no gospel message, no future resurrection, no day of reckoning, no hell, no new heavens and earth, no hope for a sinful and dying world. If we do not gird our loins with the belt of truth, our armor tilts, our shield becomes heavy, and our sword dangles out of reach.

Righteousness Like Armor on Your Chest

Many English translations refer to this as "the breastplate of righteousness" (e.g., ESV, KJV, NIV, NASB). For Roman soldiers in the first century, standard armor featured the *lorica segmentata*, or segmented armor. It consisted of strips of iron joined together with hooks or straps. It covered the chest and shoulders, affording good protection from spears, arrows, and swords.[5] No doubt, the *lorica segmentata* was designed to protect a soldier's core, basically from the neck to the navel, where the ribs end. An arrow to the heart or a dagger to the liver could bring swift and certain death.

The righteousness with which we are clothed is not our own. None of us is righteous in ourselves; indeed, we are rotten to the core

(Rom. 3:10). Rather, it is Christ's perfect righteousness that guards our hearts. His sinlessness is imputed to us, resulting in justification. And there's more. The Holy Spirit – who has made us spiritually alive, taken up residence in our human spirits, and set us apart as adopted children of the Father – seals us by placing God's crest on our armor, signifying that our place in his kingdom is secure as we engage in battle under his command.

Satan seeks to convince us that our own righteousness is sufficient. He whispers that we may need Jesus for the big issues, but there's no reason to sweat the small stuff. The evil one's compelling appeal to our pride, fleshly desires, past victories, or current status in ministry is meant to convince us that Christ's righteousness is supreme but not supremely necessary. However, the Bible says, "Guard your heart above all else, for it is the source of life" (Prov. 4:23).

That may be a reason some commentators, like John Calvin, believe the breastplate is not necessarily the righteousness of Christ imputed to us (Rom. 3:21-22), but the believer's loyalty in action to the Lord's commands.[6] Perhaps the apostle Paul has both perspectives in view here. He uses the same Greek word for "armor on your chest" (*thoraka*) in Ephesians 6:14 as he does for "armor of faith and love" in 1 Thessalonians 5:8: "But since we belong to the day, let us be self-controlled and put on the armor of faith and love, and a helmet of the hope of salvation." Whether it is Christ's righteousness imputed to us, or our faithful response to Christ's commands – or both – the armor is intended to guard our hearts.

Feet Sandaled with Readiness for the Gospel of Peace

Paul likely has *caligae* in mind. These are tough but light open-toe sandals that extend partly up the leg, with nail-studded soles for traction. Rather than don heavy boots used in long marches, soldiers could wear *caligae* in hand-to-hand combat to ensure solid footing and ease of movement. Defenders were known to litter the ground with sharp objects designed to puncture feet, so a soldier's sandals offered further protection as he advanced toward enemy lines. Healthy feet were essential to the soldier's dual role of warrior and ambassador as he advanced the *Pax Romana*, or Roman peace.

This warrior-ambassador role describes Christian soldiers as well. While engaging the evil one in spiritual combat, we carry the gospel banner of peace for a lost world to see. Our feet must be swift and sure as we deliver the light of the gospel of the glory of Christ (2 Cor. 4:4). Declaring a message of hope for God's people, the prophet Isaiah writes: "How beautiful on the mountains are the feet of the herald, who proclaims peace, who brings news of good things, who proclaims salvation, who says to Zion, 'Your God reigns!'" (Isa. 52:7). The apostle Paul quotes this passage, tying it to the glorious task of those who proclaim the gospel (Rom. 10:14-15).

The Lord provides our sure-footedness, as biblical writers attest. In a message brimming with imagery of armor and battles, King David declares, "God is my strong refuge; he makes my way perfect. He makes my feet like the feet of a deer and sets me securely on the heights" (2 Sam. 22:33-34). And the prophet Habakkuk writes of his confidence in God: "The LORD my Lord is my strength; he makes my feet like those of a deer and enables me to walk on mountain heights!" (Hab. 3:19).

Meanwhile, Satan sets snares for our feet and places obstacles between us and those who desperately need the gospel message. He sows tares in Jesus' wheat fields; these are false professors of the Christian faith who threaten the purity of the church and the clarity of its message (Matt. 13:24-30, 36-43). He blinds the minds of unbelievers to the truth of the gospel (2 Cor. 4:4). He makes the gospel sound foolish (1 Cor. 2:14). He fashions "another gospel" that people embrace too easily (leading to false assurance) or pursue too vigorously (leading to a desperate and never-ending quest for works-based rest).

Further, the evil one cranks out false doctrines like universalism and annihilationism so heaven is cheapened and hell is less frightening. He adds rituals, ceremonies, and sacraments to the gospel so it appeals to our self-righteousness. He foments legalism so that people despair of ever finding true Sabbath rest in Jesus. He substitutes sincerity for genuine faith, offering many false paths to God. He takes unbelievers captive and manipulates them (2 Tim. 2:26). He befriends unbelievers, thus making them enemies of God (Rom. 5:10; Col. 1:21; Jas. 4:4). And he does much more.

Since the Lord has entrusted his followers with the gospel, we are to be ready at all times to give a reason for the hope that is in us (1 Pet. 3:15). We do this by walking in the footsteps of Jesus, as the apostle John writes, "The one who says he remains in him should walk just as he walked" (1 John 2:6).

The Shield of Faith

The shield is a movable piece of armor the soldier wields to deflect spears, arrows, and other projectiles. In the first century, Roman soldiers used three types of shields. The most famous, known as the *scutum*, was large (four feet by two and a half feet) and either rectangular or oval, designed to protect a soldier from chest to knees. The *scutum* also was concave, allowing the shield to provide greater protection of a soldier's flanks. Next was the *parma*, a round shield typically thirty-six inches across and used while fighting on horseback. Third, the *clipeus* was round or oval shaped, which legions used in concert with the *scutum*. The *clipeus* replaced the *scutum* as the standard shield of the Roman soldier by the third century.[7]

Paul employs the Greek word *thyreos* for "shield." It derives from *thyra*, the Greek word for door, and envisions the Roman *scutum*. Marching side by side, holding up these large door-like shields – sometimes over their heads – Roman soldiers could move effectively against a well-armed enemy. This is an apt description of how followers of Jesus advance the gospel, working in unison to deliver Christ's offer of peace in hostile territory.

Paul says the shield of faith enables us to extinguish the flaming arrows of the evil one. Flaming arrows are a double threat. They penetrate armor with their sharp tips, and their flames burn the skin or set ablaze any flammable protective gear. The shield, therefore, is the first line of personal defense, as is the believer's faith. Our trust in God – our complete confidence in him and his promises – enables us to withstand a barrage of Satan's fiery darts.

The evil one's flaming arrows are fired from many directions and at many angles. Essentially, they are his attempts to undercut our confidence in the Lord and thus stop our advance. For example, Satan may introduce doubts into a believer's thoughts: Am I really secure in my salvation? Can I fully trust God, even when I can't hear his voice? If God is with me, why am I failing? If God is good, why does evil seem to be winning? Who am I to think God should care for me among seven billion other people living on this spinning rock in a remote corner of the universe? Does my faith really make any difference?

If we begin to doubt God, we may stumble beneath the weight of the very shield given to protect us. Doubt is but one of Satan's fiery darts. Others include fear, anxiety, persecution, pride, envy, greed, impurity, judgmentalism, and self-reliance. These temptations are designed to get our attention off God and onto ourselves, or even to focus on our own abilities and thus relinquish our trust in the Lord. They fly in unexpectantly, piercing, and hot.

Just as flaming arrows produce puncture wounds and fast-spreading fires, so doubts, fears, anxieties, and other temptations may stop us in our tracks. A wounded soldier may become inwardly focused, attending to an urgent need to stop the bleeding or smother the fire. In a similar way, when Satan's fiery darts get past our shield of faith, they may lead us to be more consumed with the cares of this world than with the kingdom of God.

But we should take heart. As King David writes, "My shield is God Most High, who saves the upright in heart" (Ps. 7:10, NIV). Put another way, the shield isn't ours to fashion; it's God's to give. And in one sense, God himself is the shield. Further, he grants us saving faith that becomes an implement of spiritual protection. In ancient times, a shield often was covered with leather and presoaked in water to extinguish arrows dipped in tar and set on fire. Our shield of faith – the Lord himself and the measure of faith he gives us – ensures that while Satan's fiery darts may injure, they cannot kill.

Faith is not something we conjure up. It is God's gift to us. And he gives each of us a measure, or degree, of faith (Rom. 12:3). So it's not a matter of how much ability we have to trust in God; it's fully investing the faith God has given us in him. As we place every aspect of our lives in God's hands, we find our measure of faith growing until it becomes a *scutum*, protecting us from chest to knees.

As Marvin Vincent writes, "Faith, in doing away with dependence on self, takes away fuel for the dart. It creates sensitiveness to holy influences by which the power of temptation is neutralized. It enlists the direct aid of God."[8]

The Helmet of Salvation

The helmet, of course, protects the head. This is perhaps the most vital part of our bodies since it is the seat of thought and the core of action. In the first century, Roman soldiers wore helmets called *galeae*. These were fashioned out of bronze or iron, with leather or linen padding, hinged flaps to protect the jaws, a flange in back to shield the neck, and a crest of colored horsehair on top. Each helmet typically weighed 1.3 pounds. Some were fitted with visors to protect the face.

Like a helmet, salvation – deliverance from Satan, sin, and death through a covenant relationship with Christ – is our most vital possession. The gift of everlasting life encompasses all that God has done, is doing, and will do for us. It stretches from eternity past in foreknowledge, election, and predestination into the present in regeneration, justification, and sanctification, and out into eternity future in glorification. Salvation is a finished work with ongoing benefits. Paul makes this clear in Romans 8:29-30 as he lays out the *golden chain of redemption*:

> For those he foreknew he also predestined to be conformed to the
> image of his Son, so that he would be the firstborn among many

brothers and sisters. And those he predestined, he also called; and those he called, he also justified; and those he justified, he also glorified.

Note that Paul lists even our future glorification in the past tense. That's because it's an accomplished work. The Lord's salvation is unstoppable. It truly is the helmet in the full armor of God.

Even so, Satan seeks to bash our skulls. He knows he cannot reclaim those whom Jesus has plundered from the strong man's house (Matt. 12:29). He cannot kill those Christ has given everlasting life (John 14:19). He cannot erase what God has written in heaven (Luke 10:20). But he can swing his weapons wildly for our heads in hopes of causing a spiritual concussion that rattles our confidence in Christ.

He may wield persecution so we "curse God and die" (Job 2:9). He may flank us with enticements to sin so we ruin our testimonies and dishonor the name of Jesus. He may sucker-punch us with false doctrines or promises of prosperity. Or he may bludgeon us with doubts so we sink to the ground in despair. Our salvation, like a helmet, remains secure, but we have been spiritually diminished in our capacity to engage in battle with the evil one.

Though Satan may buffet us in many ways, Paul wants us to know that the helmet of salvation is God's irrevocable gift. It keeps us from the mortal blow of sin, and it protects us from the power of sin as we look forward to the day Christ delivers us from the very presence of sin. Perhaps that's one reason Paul writes these words of encouragement to the Thessalonians:

> But since we belong to the day, let us be self-controlled and put on the armor of faith and love, and a helmet of the hope of salvation. For God did not appoint us to wrath, but to obtain salvation through our Lord Jesus Christ, who died for us, so that whether we are awake or asleep, we may live together with him (1 Thess. 5:8-10).

As King David writes in his prayer for deliverance, "Lord, my

Lord, my strong Savior, you shield my head on the day of battle" (Ps. 140:7).

The Sword of the Spirit – Which is the Word of God

This is the only offensive weapon listed in the armor of God, although, admittedly, shields could be wielded to bludgeon enemies. Paul uses the Greek word *machaira* for "sword." This is a small sword or dagger, with either a curved or straight blade, designed to kill animals and engage in close combat. It is the type of sword Jesus' enemies carry when they come to arrest him in the garden of Gethsemane (Matt. 26:47). It is distinguished from the *rhomphaia*, a long, broad cutlass. In John's visions of Jesus in the Book of Revelation, he sees the glorified Lord with a two-edged *rhomphaia* protruding from his mouth, a symbol of his authoritative voice (Rev. 1:16; 2:12, 16; 19:15, 21).

As *rhomphaia* depicts the spoken words of Jesus, Paul uses *machaira* to describe the written Word of God. In Ephesians 6, he instructs us to take "the sword (*machaira*) of the Spirit – which is the word of God" (v. 17). Elsewhere, the author of Hebrews writes, "For the word of God is living and effective and sharper than any double-edged sword (*machaira*), penetrating as far as the separation of soul and spirit, joints and marrow. It is able to judge the thoughts and intentions of the heart" (Heb. 4:12).

When Satan presses near, we are to brandish the sword of the Spirit – the inspired, inerrant, infallible, and sufficient Word of God – to drive him to retreat. When Jesus is severely tested in the wilderness, he plies Scripture to send the evil one away (Matt. 4:1-11; Luke 4:1-13).

The Bible is the Spirit's sword because he is the primary agent through whom the Scriptures came to us. That is, the Spirit inspired the human writers who penned the very words of God (2 Sam. 23:2; 2 Tim. 3:16; Heb. 3:7-11; 9:8; 10:15-17; 1 Pet. 1:10-12). Peter writes, "Above all, you know this: No prophecy of Scripture comes from the prophet's own interpretation, because no prophecy ever came by the will of man; instead, men spoke from God as they were carried along by the Holy Spirit" (2 Pet. 1:20-21).[9]

As one commentary expresses it, the two-edged sword cuts both ways, striking some with conviction and others with condemnation. It is in the mouth of Christ (Isa. 49:2) and in the hand of his saints (Ps. 149:6). Christ's use of this sword in the temptation is our pattern of how we are to wield it against Satan. "There is no armor specified for the back, but only for the front of the body, implying that we must never turn our back to the foe; our only safety is in resisting ceaselessly."[10]

The sword of the Spirit wounds the evil one, laying bare his lies and separating truth from falsehood. But we must remain on guard, for a wounded lion may return to his prey. Even Jesus, after sending the tempter away in the wilderness, finds relief only "for a time" (Luke 4:13). It takes the return of the glorified Christ to dispense with the serpent, who is cast into the lake of fire and sulfur to be tormented day and night forever and ever (Rev. 20:10). Until then, followers of Jesus are to keep the sword of the Spirit close at hand.

Pray at All Times

Paul follows his teaching on the full armor of God with these words, "Pray at all times in the Spirit with every prayer and request, and stay alert with all perseverance and intercession for all the saints" (Eph. 6:18). We should always keep in mind that the armor is God's, the gospel is God's, and the mission is God's. Prayer is the deliberate means of clothing ourselves in God's provision. It acknowledges the Lord as our commander in chief and enables us to hear his voice over the din of raucous spiritual warfare. Just as our Savior provides us with suitable armor to engage the enemy in the unseen realm, he grants us prayer as a means of clear and constant communication throughout the battle.

The Holy Spirit is our helper in prayer. He lives in us – specifically in our human spirits, the holy of holies of our bodily temples (1 Cor. 3:16; 6:19). He is the Spirit of adoption, enabling us to call God our *Abba*, or Papa (Rom. 8:15-16; Gal. 4:6). He empowers us to pray and intercedes on our behalf, as Paul writes in Romans 8:26-27:

> In the same way the Spirit also helps us in our weakness, because we do not know what to pray for as we should, but the Spirit himself intercedes for us with inexpressible groanings. And he who searches our hearts knows the mind of the Spirit, because he intercedes for the saints according to the will of God.

As one commentary sums it up, "Even when you are clothed with the armor of God, you need to bathe it all in prayer. Prayer brings you into communion and fellowship with God so that His armor can protect you."[11]

In Ephesians 6, Paul paints a vivid portrait of the Christian soldier. The apostle covers his canvas with bold brushstrokes that reveal the severity of spiritual warfare and the necessity of being fully armed. Just as the Old Testament portrays God in his armor – a mighty warrior slaying the enemies of his people – so the New Testament tells us that followers of Jesus must put on the full armor of God so we may stand against the evil one's schemes.

Summary

Key takeaways about *engaging the evil one*:

(1) Satan is the archenemy of mankind. Although he often is successful in his campaign against God's people, he wages war in a shrinking theater. First thrown out of heaven, then cast to earth, then confined to the abyss, he finally is banished to the lake of fire, a place God specifically prepares for him and his spirit saboteurs.

(2) The New Testament tells us God has equipped us to wage war with Satan. Perhaps no other passage makes this as clear as Ephesians 6:10-20, where the apostle Paul exhorts us to "put on the full armor of God" so we can "stand against the schemes of the devil" (v. 11).

(3) We may think of the armor of God in two ways. First, as aspects

of God's character. God's attributes, such as righteousness, are revealed to us as pieces of armor the divine warrior wears to carry out vengeance against the wicked and thus deliver his people. But another way to think of the full armor of God is to understand it as God's individually tailored battle accouterments for us.

(4) Because of Christ's victory over the evil one, we may take our stand – that is, maintain our ground, hold fast, neither yielding nor fleeing – as we are clad in the full armor of God. What's more, we stand together as followers of Christ. In the ancient form of hand-to-hand combat, the first duty of soldiers forming a line is to stand side by side, with large rectangular shields forming a wall of defense.

(5) The apostle Paul urges Christians to put on "the full armor of God" (Eph. 6:11), which includes:

- Truth like a belt – a personal commitment to Jesus, who is the truth, and to his word.
- Righteousness like armor – Christ's perfect righteousness, which guards our hearts.
- Feet sandaled with readiness – so we may carry the gospel banner of peace for a lost world to see.
- The shield of faith – our complete confidence in God and his promises, which enables us to withstand a barrage of Satan's flaming arrows.
- The helmet of salvation – our deliverance from Satan, sin, and death through a covenant relationship with Christ.
- The sword of the Spirit – the inspired, inerrant, infallible, and sufficient Word of God.

(6) Prayer is the deliberate means of clothing ourselves in God's armor. It acknowledges the Lord as our commander in chief and enables us to hear his voice over the din of raucous spiritual warfare. Just as our Savior provides us with suitable armor to engage the enemy in the unseen realm, he grants us prayer as a means of clear and constant communication throughout the battle.

Questions for Personal or Group Study

1. What are several events recorded in Scripture in which Satan played a major role?
2. How does God equip Christians to engage in spiritual warfare?
3. Provide a short description of each piece in the armor of God (Eph. 6:10-20):

     (a) Truth like a belt
     (b) Righteousness like armor
     (c) Feet sandaled with readiness
     (d) Shield of faith
     (e) Helmet of salvation
     (f) Sword of the Spirit

4. Which piece of armor is the only offensive weapon? How may we use it effectively?
5. Why do you think Paul completes his teaching on the armor of God with the command, "Pray at all times"?

APPENDIX 1: ALL OCCURRENCES OF SATAN AND THE DEVIL IN THE NEW TESTAMENT

(CHRISTIAN STANDARD BIBLE)

References by Name / Title Only

Description	Passage	Quotation / Comment
Satan	Matt. 4:10	Jesus says, "Go away, Satan!"
Satan (2x)	Matt. 12:26	"If Satan drives out Satan, he is divided against himself ..." (cf. Mark 3:23, 26; Luke 11:18).
Satan	Matt. 16:23	Jesus says to Peter, "Get behind me, Satan!" (cf. Mark 8:33).
Satan (3x)	Mark 3:23, 26	"How can Satan drive out Satan?" ... "if Satan opposes himself" (cf. Matt. 12:26; Luke 11:18).
Satan	Mark 8:33	Jesus says to Peter, "Get behind me, Satan!" (cf. Matt. 16:23).
Satan	Luke 11:18	"If Satan also is divided against himself" (cf. Matt. 12:26; Mark 3:23, 26).
Satan	1 Tim. 5:15	Some younger widows have turned away to follow Satan.
Satan / the devil	Rev. 12:9	He is "the great dragon ... the ancient serpent, who is called the devil and Satan ...".
Satan / the devil	Rev. 20:2	An angel "seized the dragon, that ancient serpent who is the devil and Satan."

References by Actions (alphabetically)

Description	Passage	Quotation / Comment
Afflicts	Rev. 2:10	The devil is about to afflict some believers in Smyrna by throwing them into prison.
Binds	Luke 13:16	Jesus says, "Satan has bound this woman ..." (for 18 years).
Captures	2 Tim. 2:26	The devil has taken opponents of the gospel "captive to do his will."
Chastens	1 Tim. 1:20	Paul has delivered Hymenaeus and Alexander "to Satan, so that they may be taught not to blaspheme."
Deceives	Rev. 12:9	Satan "deceives the whole world ..."
	Rev. 20:7-10	After 1,000 years, Satan is released from the abyss and goes out to deceive the nations.
Destroys	1 Cor. 5:5	Regarding an open sinner, Paul tells the Corinthians to "hand that one over to Satan for the destruction of the flesh, so that his spirit may be saved in the day of the Lord."
Disguises	2 Cor. 11:14	"For Satan disguises himself as an angel of light."
Disputes	Jude 9	The devil disputes with Michael over the body of Moses.

References by Actions (alphabetically) pt. 2

Description	Passage	Quotation / Comment
Enters Judas	Luke 22:3	"Then Satan entered Judas ..."
	John 13:27	"Satan entered him (Judas)." (cf. John 6:70 – Jesus calls Judas "a devil").
Fills hearts to lie	Acts 5:3	Peter asks Ananias, "why has Satan filled your heart to lie to the Holy Spirit ...?"
Has children	John 8:44	Jesus says certain Jews "are of your father the devil."
	Acts 13:10	Calls Elymas the sorcerer, "you son of the devil."
	1 John 3:10	The "devil's children" do not do what is right; especially, they don't love their brothers and sisters.
Has followers	1 Tim. 5:15	"For some [younger widows] have already turned away to follow Satan."
Has power	Acts 26:18	Jesus is sending Paul to the Gentiles so they may turn "from the power of Satan to God."
	Heb. 2:14	Through his death, Jesus destroys "the one holding the power of death – that is, the devil ..."
Has secrets	Rev. 2:24	Some unbelievers at Thyatira hold "the so-called secrets of Satan."
Has a synagogue	Rev. 2:9; 3:9	Unbelieving Jews are a /the "synagogue of Satan."

References by Actions (alphabetically) pt. 3

Description	Passage	Quotation / Comment
Hinders	1 Thess. 2:18	"So we wanted to come to you – even I, Paul, time and again – but Satan hindered us."
Is conceited	1 Tim. 3:6	Paul warns against new converts serving as deacons, for they "might become conceited and incur the same condemnation as the devil."
Is an opportunist	Eph. 4:27	Paul instructs the Ephesians not to go to bed angry, for this gives "the devil an opportunity."
Is a tyrant	Acts 10:38	Peter tells how Jesus "went about doing good and healing all who were under the tyranny of the devil."
Plants sinful ideas	John 13:2	"Now when it was time for supper, the devil had already put it into the heart of Judas, Simon Iscariot's son, to betray him."
Prowls	1 Pet. 5:8	"Your adversary the devil is prowling around like a roaring lion, looking for anyone he can devour."
Schemes	Eph. 6:11	The full armor of God protects us against "the schemes of the devil" (cf. 2 Cor. 2:11).

References by Actions (alphabetically) pt. 4

Description	Passage	Quotation / Comment
Sets traps	1 Tim. 3:7	Deacons must have good reputations with those outside the church; otherwise, they may "fall into disgrace and the devil's trap."
	2 Tim. 2:26	God may grant opponents of the gospel repentance so they may "come to their senses and escape the trap of the devil ..."
Sifts	Luke 22:31	Jesus says to Peter, "Satan has asked to sift you like wheat."
Sins	1 John 3:8	"The one who commits sin is of the devil, for the devil has sinned from the beginning."
Sits enthroned	Rev. 2:13	Pergamum is "where Satan's throne is."
Sows	Matt. 13:39	Parable of wheat and weeds. Enemy who sows the bad seeds is the devil.
Takes advantage	2 Cor. 2:11	Paul urges the Corinthians to forgive a repentant sinner among them "so that we may not be taken advantage of by Satan. For we are not ignorant of his schemes."
Takes away	Mark 4:15	"Satan comes and takes away the word ..."
	Luke 8:12	"The devil comes and takes away the word ..."

References by Actions (alphabetically) pt. 5

Description	Passage	Quotation / Comment
Tempts believers	1 Cor. 7:5	Paul urges couples not to refrain from sexual intimacy for too long; "otherwise, Satan may tempt you because of your lack of self-control."
Tempts Jesus	Matt. 4:1-11	"Satan" named 4 times; "the devil," once; "the tempter," once.
	Mark 1:13	"Satan" named once.
	Luke 4:1-13	"The devil" named 4 times.
Torments	2 Cor. 12:7	To keep Paul from pride, God grants that a "messenger of Satan" be given to the apostle to "torment" him.
Works (evil)	2 Thess. 2:9-11	"The coming of the lawless one is based on Satan's working, with all kinds of false miracles, signs, and wonders, and with every wicked deception ..."

References to Destiny (alphabetically)

Description	Passage	Quotation / Comment
Bound / imprisoned	Rev. 20:2	An angel seizes the dragon, the ancient serpent who is the devil and Satan, and throws him into the abyss for 1,000 years.
	Rev. 20:7	"When the thousand years are completed, Satan will be released from his prison."
Crushed	Rom. 16:20	"The God of peace will soon crush Satan under your feet."
Falls	Luke 10:18	Jesus tells the 72, "I watched Satan fall from heaven like lightning."
Flees	Jas. 4:7	"Resist the devil, and he will flee from you."
	Matt. 4:11	Satan leaves Jesus after failing to successfully tempt him.
	Luke 4:13	Satan departs "for a time" after failing to successfully tempt Jesus.
Thrown out of heaven	Rev. 12:9-12	Michael the archangel defeats Satan and casts him to earth; now, the earth should beware, for the devil has come down with great fury.
Torment in eternal fire	Matt. 25:41	God prepared the eternal fire for the devil and his angels.
	Rev. 20:10	The devil who deceived the whole earth is "thrown into the lake of fire and sulfur" to be tormented day and night forever and ever.

APPENDIX 2: ALL REFERENCES TO SATAN IN THE NEW TESTAMENT

(CHRISTIAN STANDARD BIBLE)

References to Satan

Passage	Name(s)	Brief Description
Matt. 4:1-11	The devil (4x); the tempter; Satan	Satan tempts Jesus in the wilderness immediately after his baptism (cf. Mark 1:12-13; Luke 4:1-13).
Matt. 6:13	The evil one (or "evil" or "the evil")	In the Lord's Prayer (or Model Prayer), Jesus instructs his disciples to pray for deliverance from the evil one.
Matt. 9:32-34	The ruler of the demons	Jesus heals a mute man who is demon-possessed. But the Pharisees who witness the miracle accuse Jesus of casting out demons by the ruler of the demons (Satan).
Matt. 10:25	Beelzebul	Jesus tells the twelve, "If they [opponents of Christ] called the head of the house 'Beelzebul,' how much more the members of his household!"
Matt. 12:22-32	Beelzebul (2x); the ruler of the demons; Satan (2x); the strong man (2x)	Jesus heals a demon-possessed man who is blind and mute. The Pharisees accuse Jesus of casting out demons by Beelzebul. Jesus calls such false accusations blasphemy against the Holy Spirit, who empowers Jesus to perform such miracles. In fact, by his miracles, Jesus demonstrates that the kingdom of heaven has come and that Satan, the strong man, is bound (cf. Mark 3:20-30; Luke 11:14-23).

References to Satan, pt. 2

Passage	Name(s)	Brief Description
Matt. 13:19	The evil one	Explaining the parable of the sower, Jesus says Satan snatches away the word sown in the hardened heart (cf. Mark 4:15; Luke 8:12).
Matt. 13:38-39	The evil one; the devil	Explaining the parable of the wheat and tares, Jesus refers to unbelievers as children of the evil one, who sowed them in the world.
Matt. 16:23	Satan	Jesus tells Peter, "Get behind me, Satan!" after Peter rebukes Jesus for announcing his pending suffering and death (cf. Mark 8:33).
Matt. 25:41	The devil	Jesus declares that hell is prepared for "the devil and his angels."
Mark 1:12-13	Satan	The Spirit drives Jesus into the wilderness, where Satan tempts him for 40 days (cf. Matt. 4:1-11; Luke 4:1-13).
Mark 3:20-30	Beelzebul; the ruler of the demons; Satan (3x); strong man (2x)	The scribes accuse Jesus of driving out demons by Beelzebul, the ruler of the demons. Jesus calls such false accusations blasphemy against the Holy Spirit, who empowers Jesus to perform such miracles. In fact, by his miracles, Jesus demonstrates that Satan (the strong man) is bound (cf. Matt. 12:22-32; Luke 11:14-23).

References to Satan, pt. 3

Passage	Name(s)	Brief Description
Mark 4:15	Satan	Explaining the parable of the sower, Jesus says Satan snatches away the word sown in the hardened heart (cf. Matt. 13:19; Luke 8:12).
Mark 8:33	Satan	Jesus tells Peter, "Get behind me, Satan!" after Peter rebukes Jesus for announcing his pending suffering and death (cf. Matt. 16:23).
Luke 4:1-13	The devil (4x)	The devil tempts Jesus in the wilderness immediately after Jesus' baptism (cf. Matt. 4:1-11; Mark 1:12-13).
Luke 8:12	The devil	Explaining the parable of the sower, Jesus says Satan snatches away the word sown in the hardened heart (cf. Matt. 13:19 – "evil one"; Mark 4:15 – "Satan").
Luke 10:17-20	Satan; the enemy	After sending out 72 (or 70) disciples to proclaim the gospel in the towns to which Jesus is traveling, Jesus receives them back. They report that "even the demons submit to us in your name." Jesus says he watched Satan fall from heaven like lightning. He has given the disciples authority to trample on snakes and scorpions – likely a reference to evil spirits – and over all the power of the enemy. Yet, they are to rejoice not so much in this, but that their names are written in heaven.

References to Satan, pt. 4

Passage	Name(s)	Brief Description
Luke 11:14-23	Beelzebul (3x); the ruler of the demons; Satan; strong man	Jesus drives a demon out of a mute man, amazing the crowds but prompting some to accuse Jesus of casting out demons by the ruler of the demons (Beelzebul). Jesus counters that a house divided against itself (Satan vs. demons) cannot stand. Further, by his miracles, Jesus demonstrates that the kingdom of heaven has come and that Satan, the strong man, is overcome and his goods are plundered (cf. Matt. 12:22-32; Mark 3:20-30).
Luke 13:10-17	Satan	Jesus heals a woman "disabled by a spirit" for more than 18 years. The leader of the synagogue is indignant, claiming that such work should not be done on the Sabbath. In Jesus' rebuke of the leader, he acknowledges that "Satan" has bound this woman.
Luke 22:3-4	Satan	Satan enters Judas Iscariot, who then discusses with the chief priests and temple police how he can hand Jesus over to them (cf. John 13:27).
Luke 22:31	Satan	Jesus tells Peter that Satan has asked to sift him (Peter) like wheat.
John 8:38-44	Your father (4x); the devil; a murderer; a liar; the father of lies	Jesus tells Jews who want to kill him that their (spiritual) father is the devil, who is a murderer, a liar, and the father of lies.

References to Satan, pt. 5

Passage	Name(s)	Brief Description
John 12:31	The ruler of this world	The Father speaks from heaven. Jesus tells those who hear the voice that it is for him as he prepares for crucifixion. "Now is the judgment of this world," Jesus says. "Now the ruler of this world will be cast out."
John 13:2	The devil	At the time of the Passover meal, the devil already has put the notion of betraying Jesus into Judas' heart.
John 13:27	Satan	After Judas eats a piece of bread Jesus has given him at the Passover meal, Satan enters Judas (cf. Luke 22:3-4).
John 14:30	The ruler of this world	Jesus tells his followers, "the ruler of this world is coming" (perhaps in the person of Judas Iscariot to betray Jesus). Even so, "He has no power over me."
Acts 5:3	Satan	Peter confronts Ananias and says, "Why has Satan filled your heart to lie to the Holy Spirit and keep back part of the proceeds of the land?" Ananias and his wife Sapphira had sold a plot of land and claimed to bring the full amount as an offering, though they secretly kept back part for themselves (vv. 1-11).
Acts 10:38	The devil	In Cornelius' house, Peter preaches Jesus, "who went about doing good and healing all who were under the tyranny of the devil."

References to Satan, pt. 6

Passage	Name(s)	Brief Description
Acts 13:10	The devil	Paul confronts a Jewish false prophet named Bar-Jesus, or Elymas. He calls the sorcerer "son of the devil and enemy of all that is right."
Acts 26:18	Satan	Paul testifies before Agrippa to the words of Jesus, "I am sending you to them [Gentiles] ... so that they may turn from darkness to light and from the power of Satan to God ..."
Rom. 8:38-39	Powers	Nothing separates believers from the love of God, not even "powers" (Gr. *dynamis*), sometimes used of supernatural powers like Satan and demons.
Rom. 16:20	Satan	Paul tells the Romans, "The God of peace will soon crush Satan under your feet."
1 Cor. 2:6-8	Rulers (2x)	The "rulers of this age ... are coming to nothing." Their wisdom is not God's wisdom. If they had known God's wisdom, they would not have crucified the Lord of glory. These rulers are humans, but Paul could also be referring to human governments and authorities, as well as Satan and evil spirits.
1 Cor. 5:5	Satan	Paul instructs the Corinthians regarding an immoral person in the church: "hand that one over to Satan for the destruction of the flesh."

References to Satan, pt. 7

Passage	Name(s)	Brief Description
1 Cor. 7:5	Satan	Paul warns the Corinthians about husbands and wives depriving each other of sexual intimacy. If they do deprive one another, "Satan may tempt you because of your lack of self-control."
1 Cor. 15:24	Rule; authority; power	After Christ returns, he hands over the kingdom to God the Father, when he abolishes "all rule and all authority and power." This could be a reference to earthly powers, Satan and demonic powers, or both. In any case, they are called "all enemies" in v. 25, and they are placed under Christ's feet.
2 Cor. 2:10-11	Satan	Paul tells the Corinthians that forgiveness among Christians is essential in order to avoid being taken advantage of by Satan.
2 Cor. 4:4	The god of this age	Satan, "the god of this age," blinds the minds of unbelievers to keep them from seeing the light of the gospel.
2 Cor. 6:15	Belial	In arguing for holy living, Paul asks, "What agreement does Christ have with Belial? Or what does a believer have in common with an unbeliever?"
2 Cor. 11:3	Serpent	Paul tells the Corinthians, "But I fear that, as the serpent deceived Eve by his cunning, your minds may be seduced from a sincere and pure devotion to Christ."

References to Satan, pt. 8

Passage	Name(s)	Brief Description
2 Cor. 11:14	Satan	We should not be surprised that Satan "disguises himself as an angel of light."
2 Cor. 12:7	Satan	Describing a particular affliction to prevent self-exaltation, Paul writes that "a thorn in the flesh was given to me, a messenger of Satan to torment me ..."
Eph. 1:21	Ruler; authority; power; dominion	Christ is seated in the heavens, "far above every ruler and authority, power and dominion." Likely, Paul's reference includes Satan, evil spirits, holy angels, and earthly authorities.
Eph. 2:2	The ruler of the power of the air; the spirit now working in the disobedient	Paul writes that Christians formerly walked "according to the ways of this world, according to the ruler of the power of the air, the spirit now working in the disobedient" – a reference to Satan.
Eph. 4:27	The devil	Paul instructs Christians not to let anger overtake us – not to let the sun go down on our anger, for this gives the devil an opportunity (a foothold; beachhead) to control us.

References to Satan, pt. 9

Passage	Name(s)	Brief Description
Eph. 6:11-16	The devil; the evil one; (rulers; authorities; cosmic powers of darkness; evil, spiritual forces in the heavens)	Christians are to put on the full armor of God so we may stand against "the schemes of the devil" (v. 11). Our struggle is not against flesh and blood but against "the rulers, against the authorities, against the cosmic powers of this darkness, against evil, spiritual forces in the heavens" (v. 12). Among the pieces of our spiritual armor is the shield of faith with which we may "extinguish all the flaming arrows of the evil one" (v. 16).
Col. 1:16	Thrones; dominions; rulers; authorities	Jesus created everything, both visible and invisible, including thrones, dominions, rulers, and authorities – references to hierarchies of earthly and angelic/demonic forces. Satan could be included in this reference.
Col. 2:10	Ruler; authority	Paul warns the Colossians against "philosophy and empty deceit" (v. 8). He reminds them that Christ is the fullness of deity in human flesh (v. 9), and that Jesus is "the head over every ruler and authority," whether human or angelic/demonic; this could include Satan.
Col. 2:15	Rulers; authorities	In his finished work on the cross, Christ "disarmed the rulers and authorities and disgraced them publicly." While this could include Jewish and Roman authorities, it more likely depicts evil spirits under the authority of Satan.

References to Satan, pt. 10

Passage	Name(s)	Brief Description
1 Thess. 2:18	Satan	Paul writes that Satan hindered both him and his fellow laborers from returning to Thessalonica.
1 Thess. 3:5	The tempter	Paul sends Timothy to believers at Thessalonica to find out about their faith, "fearing that the tempter had tempted you and that our labor might be for nothing."
2 Thess. 2:9	Satan	The coming of "the lawless one" is based on Satan's working, with every kind of (false) miracle and wicked deception.
2 Thess. 3:3	The evil one	Paul reminds the Thessalonians that the Lord is faithful: "he will strengthen you and guard you from the evil one."
1 Tim. 1:20	Satan	Paul writes to Timothy that he has delivered Hymenaeus and Alexander to Satan so they may be taught not to blaspheme.
1 Tim. 3:6-7	The devil (2x)	A new convert should not be an overseer because he may become conceited and thus incur the same condemnation as the devil. Further, an overseer must have a good reputation among those outside the church. Otherwise, he may fall into disgrace and the devil's trap.

References to Satan, pt. 11

Passage	Name(s)	Brief Description
1 Tim. 5:14	The adversary	In his instructions to Timothy about widows, Paul urges younger widows to marry, have children, and manage their households (rather than take a widow's pledge only to renounce it later and engage in idleness). Paul wants to give the adversary no opportunity to make an accusation against the widow or the church in its ministry to widows.
1 Tim. 5:15	Satan	Paul notes that some younger widows have already turned away to follow Satan.
2 Tim. 2:26	The devil	Timothy is to instruct his opponents with gentleness in the hopes that God grants them repentance, leading them to the knowledge of the truth. "Then they may come to their senses and escape the trap of the devil, who has taken them captive to do his will."
Heb. 2:14	The devil	Through his death, Jesus destroyed "the one holding the power of death – that is, the devil."
Jas. 4:7	The devil	James urges his readers to "submit to God. Resist the devil, and he will flee from you."
1 Pet. 3:22	Authorities; powers	Among those over whom Christ reigns in heaven are "authorities" and "powers," which could include evil spirits under Satan's command.

References to Satan, pt. 12

Passage	Name(s)	Brief Description
1 Pet. 5:8	Adversary; the devil	Peter urges his readers to be sober-minded and alert, because the adversary, the devil, prowls around like a lion, looking for anyone he can devour.
1 John 2:13-14	The evil one (2x)	Twice, John writes that the young men have "conquered the evil one."
1 John 3:8-10	The devil (4x)	The one who commits/practices sin is "of the devil, for the devil has sinned from the beginning." The Son of God was revealed to "destroy the devil's works." The "devil's children" become obvious by their practice of sin.
1 John 3:12	The evil one	Cain was of "the evil one and murdered his brother."
1 John 5:18	The evil one	The evil one doesn't touch the one who is "born of God." This could be a reference to Jesus, who keeps the believer from Satan; a reference to fellow believers, who pray for and encourage the believer; or a reference to the believer himself/herself as he/she obeys God's commands.
1 John 5:19	The evil one	The whole world is under the sway of the evil one.

References to Satan, pt. 13

Passage	Name(s)	Brief Description
Jude 9	The devil	When Michael the archangel disputes with the devil over the body of Moses, he does not dare bring a slanderous accusation against him but says, "The Lord rebuke you!"
Rev. 2:9	Satan	Those falsely claiming to be Jews in Smyrna are "a synagogue of Satan."
Rev. 2:10	The devil	The devil is about to throw some believers at Smyrna into prison.
Rev. 2:13	Satan (2x)	Satan's throne is in Pergamum, where he lives.
Rev. 2:24	Satan	The faithful in Thyatira do not hold to the false teachings of Jezebel and thus haven't known the "so-called secrets of Satan."
Rev. 3:9	Satan	Jesus tells the church at Thyatira: "I will make those from the synagogue of Satan, who claim to be Jews and are not, but are lying – I will make them come and bow down at your feet ..."
Rev. 9:1	Star	When the fifth angel blows his trumpet, John sees a star that has fallen from heaven to earth. The key to the shaft to the abyss is given to him. Some commentators see this star as Satan. Others identify the star as a fallen angel (perhaps Abaddon), or as a holy angel fulfilling God's purpose.

References to Satan, pt. 14

Passage	Name(s)	Brief Description
Rev. 9:11	The angel of the abyss; Abaddon; Apollyon	The locusts have as their king the angel of the abyss. His name in Hebrew is Abaddon, and in Greek is Apollyon. Some commentators identify this angel as Satan. However, it's possible he is one of Satan's underlings, a destroying demon and one of the "rulers," "authorities," and "powers" mentioned in Eph. 6:12.
Rev. 11:7	Beast	A beast "that comes up out of the abyss" kills the two faithful witnesses of Christ. While this likely is the beast of Rev. 13 – a wicked human – he is strongly connected with Satanic and demonic power.
Rev. 12:3-4	Great fiery red dragon; dragon	John sees a great fiery red dragon with seven heads and 10 horns, with crowns on its seven heads. Its tail sweeps a third of the stars in heaven and hurls them to earth. The dragon stands in front of the woman (Israel) about to give birth so that he might devour the child.

References to Satan, pt. 15

Passage	Name(s)	Brief Description
Rev. 12:7-12	Dragon (2x); great dragon; ancient serpent; the devil (2x); Satan; the one who deceives the whole world; the accuser of our brothers and sisters	Michael the archangel and his angels defeat the dragon and his angels in a battle in heaven. Satan and his angels are thrown down to earth, resulting in great joy in heaven but woe on the earth and sea. The devil is furious because he knows his time is short.
Rev. 12:13-17	Dragon (3x); serpent (2x)	Thrown down to earth, the dragon persecutes the woman (Israel). God providentially rescues the woman from the serpent's presence and nourishes her in the wilderness. The serpent spews water in the wilderness in an effort to drown the woman, but the earth comes to her aid. Furious, the dragon leaves the woman in order to wage war against "the rest of her offspring – those who keep the commands of God and hold firmly to the testimony about Jesus."
Rev. 12:18 – 13:4	Dragon (3x)	The dragon stands on the sand of the sea as a beast comes up out of the sea. The dragon gives this beast his power, throne, and great authority. The whole earth worships the dragon because he has given authority to the beast.

References to Satan, pt. 16

Passage	Name(s)	Brief Description
Rev. 13:11	Dragon	Another beast (like the beast from the sea) comes up out of the earth. It has two horns like a lamb but speaks "like a dragon."
Rev. 16:13	Dragon	Unclean spirits like frogs come out of the mouth of the dragon, the beast, and the false prophet.
Rev. 17:3-18	Beast (9x); king	John sees a woman sitting on a scarlet beast covered with blasphemous names; he has seven heads and 10 horns. He is about to come up from the abyss and go to destruction. He wages war against the Lamb but is defeated. He hates the woman (prostitute) and makes her desolate; this is in accordance with God's plan. While this likely is the beast of Rev. 13 – a wicked human who is called a king (17:11) – he is strongly connected with Satanic and demonic power (cf. Rev. 11:7).
Rev. 19:19-20	Beast (2x)	The beast of Rev. 13 is thrown alive into the lake of fire and sulfur. While this likely is a wicked human being, he is strongly connected with Satan and demonic power (cf. Rev. 11:7; 13; 17:3-18).
Rev. 20:1-2	Dragon; ancient serpent; the devil; Satan	An angel comes down from heaven, seizes the dragon, throws him into the abyss, and binds him for 1,000 years. During this time, the dragon may not deceive the nations.

References to Satan, pt. 17

Passage	Name(s)	Brief Description
Rev. 20:4	Beast	The souls of Christian martyrs who had not worshiped the beast or his image come to life and reign with Christ for 1,000 years. While the beast likely is a wicked human, he is strongly connected with Satanic and demonic power (cf. Rev. 11:7; 13; 17:3-18; 19:19-20).
Rev. 20:7-10	Satan; the devil	After the 1,000 years are completed, Satan is released from his prison. He deceives the nations and gathers them for a final battle against "the encampment of the saints, the beloved city." Fire comes down from heaven and consumes them. The devil is thrown into the lake of fire and sulfur, where the beast and the false prophet are, to be tormented night and day forever.

APPENDIX 3: ALL REFERENCES TO EVIL SPIRITS IN THE NEW TESTAMENT

(CHRISTIAN STANDARD BIBLE)

References to Evil Spirits

Passage	Name(s)	Brief Description
Matt. 7:22	Demons	On judgment day, some false prophets claim to have driven out demons. Nevertheless, Jesus tells them, "I never knew you. Depart from me, you lawbreakers!" (v. 23).
Matt. 8:16	Demon-possessed; spirits	At Capernaum, Jesus drives evil spirits out of people described as demon-possessed. He does so "with a word" (cf. Mark 1:32-34; Luke 4:41).
Matt. 8:28-34	Demon-possessed (2x); demons	Two demon-possessed men in the region of the Gerasenes come out of the tombs to meet Jesus. They acknowledge Jesus as the Son of God, and the demons beg Jesus to inhabit a nearby herd of swine. Jesus grants permission. When the demons enter the pigs, the entire herd plunges down a steep ravine into the sea (cf. Mark 5:1-20; Luke 8:26-39).
Matt. 9:32-34	Demon-possessed; demon; demons; ruler of the demons	Jesus heals a mute man who is demon-possessed. But the Pharisees who witness the miracle accuse Jesus of casting out demons by the ruler of the demons (Satan).
Matt. 10:1-15	Unclean spirits; demons	Jesus gives the twelve authority over unclean spirits. He commands them to go to "the lost sheep of the house of Israel" (v. 6), proclaiming the kingdom of heaven, healing the sick, raising the dead, cleansing the lepers, and driving out demons (cf. Mark 6:7-13; Luke 9:1-6).

References to Evil Spirits, pt. 2

Passage	Name(s)	Brief Description
Matt. 12:22-32	Demon-possessed; demons (3x)	Jesus heals a demon-possessed man who is blind and mute. The Pharisees accuse Jesus of casting out demons by Beelzebul. Jesus calls such false accusations blasphemy against the Holy Spirit, who empowers Jesus to perform such miracles. In fact, by his miracles, Jesus demonstrates that the kingdom of heaven has come and that Satan, the strong man, is bound (cf. Mark 3:20-30; Luke 11:14-23).
Matt. 12:43-45	Unclean spirit; spirits	Jesus tells a parable of an unclean spirit who leaves a man but later returns with seven spirits more wicked than himself to inhabit an empty "house." This speaks of Israel, which has rightly abandoned idolatry but replaced it with empty ritual (cf. Luke 11:24-26).
Matt. 15:21-28	Demon	A Canaanite woman pleads with Jesus to heal her daughter, who is vexed with a demon. Jesus marvels at her faith and grants her request (cf. Mark 7:24-30).
Matt. 17:14-20	Demon	Jesus casts a demon out of a sick child after Jesus' disciples are unable to do it (cf. Mark 9:14-29; Luke 9:37-43).
Matt. 25:41	His (the devil's) angels	Jesus declares that hell is prepared for the devil and his angels.
Mark 1:21-28	Unclean spirit(s) (3x)	Jesus casts out an unclean spirit in the synagogue in Capernaum (cf. Luke 4:31-37).

References to Evil Spirits, pt. 3

Passage	Name(s)	Brief Description
Mark 1:32-34	Demon-possessed; demons (2x)	Jesus drives out many demons in Capernaum and does not permit the demons to speak because they know him (cf. Matt. 8:16; Luke 4:41).
Mark 1:39	Demons	Jesus goes into all Galilee, preaching in the synagogues and casting out demons.
Mark 3:11-12	Unclean spirits	Whenever unclean spirits see Jesus, they fall down before him and cry out, "You are the Son of God!" He strongly warns them not to make him known.
Mark 3:13-15	Demons	Jesus calls 12 apostles and gives them the authority to drive out demons.
Mark 3:20-30	Demons; unclean spirit	Scribes from Jerusalem accuse Jesus of driving out demons by the ruler of the demons (Beelzebul). Jesus counters that a house divided against itself cannot stand. He also warns against blasphemy of the Holy Spirit, who empowers Jesus to perform miracles, because the scribes say he has an unclean spirit (cf. Matt. 12:22-32; Luke 11:14-23).

References to Evil Spirits, pt. 4

Passage	Name(s)	Brief Description
Mark 5:1-20	Unclean spirit (2x); Legion; demons; unclean spirits; demon-possessed (3x)	A demon-possessed man in the region of the Gerasenes comes out of the tombs to meet Jesus. He identifies himself as Legion, for many demons possess him. He acknowledges Jesus as the Son of Most High God, and the demons beg Jesus to let them inhabit a nearby herd of swine rather than be sent out of the region. Jesus grants permission. When the demons enter the pigs, the entire herd plunges down a steep ravine into the sea (cf. Matt. 8:28-34; Luke 8:26-39).
Mark 6:7-13	Unclean spirits; demons	Jesus summons the twelve and sends them out in pairs, giving them authority over unclean spirits (cf. Matt. 10:1-15; Mark 3:13-15; Luke 9:1-6).
Mark 7:24-30	Unclean spirit; demon (3x)	Jesus casts an unclean spirit out of the daughter of a Syrophoenician woman (cf. Matt. 15:21-28).
Mark 9:14-29	Spirit (2x); unclean spirit; mute and deaf spirit	Jesus casts an unclean spirit out of a sick child after Jesus' disciples are unable to do it (cf. Matt. 17:14-20; Luke 9:37-43).
Mark 9:38-41	Demons	The apostle John reports seeing a man drive out demons, but the man does not follow the disciples. Jesus instructs him to leave the man alone, saying, "Whoever is not against us is for us" (cf. Luke 9:49-50).

References to Evil Spirits, pt. 5

Passage	Name(s)	Brief Description
Mark 16:9	Demons	After his resurrection, Jesus appears first to Mary Magdalene, from whom he had driven seven demons.
Mark 16:17-18	Demons	Jesus says driving out demons is one of the signs of those who believe in him.
Luke 4:31-37	Unclean demonic spirit; demon; unclean spirits	Jesus casts an unclean spirit out of a man in the synagogue at Capernaum (cf. Mark 1:21-28).
Luke 4:41	Demons	Jesus casts demons out of many people at Capernaum. The demons declare, "You are the Son of God!" (cf. Matt. 8:16; Mark 1:32-34).
Luke 6:18	Unclean spirits	Jesus makes well those tormented by unclean spirits.
Luke 7:21	Evil spirits	Jesus heals many people of evil spirits.
Luke 7:33	Demon	Jesus says, "For John the Baptist did not come eating bread or drinking wine, and you say, 'He has a demon!'"
Luke 8:2	Evil spirits; demons	Traveling with Jesus and the twelve from one town and village to another are some women that Jesus has healed of evil spirits and sicknesses, including Mary Magdalene, who had seven demons.

References to Evil Spirits, pt. 6

Passage	Name(s)	Brief Description
Luke 8:26-39	Demon-possessed (2x); unclean spirit; demon; Legion; demons (5x)	A demon-possessed man in the region of the Gerasenes comes out of the tombs to meet Jesus. He identifies himself as Legion, for many demons possess him. He acknowledges Jesus as the Son of Most High God, and the demons beg Jesus to let them inhabit a nearby herd of swine rather than be sent to the abyss. Jesus grants permission. When the demons enter the pigs, the entire herd plunges down a steep ravine into the sea (cf. Matt. 8:28-34; Mark 5:1-20).
Luke 9:1-6	Demons	Jesus summons the twelve and gives them authority over all the demons and to heal diseases. He sends them to proclaim the kingdom of God and to heal the sick (cf. Matt. 10:1-15; Mark 6:7-13).
Luke 9:37-43	Spirit; demon; unclean spirit	Jesus casts an unclean spirit out of a sick child after Jesus' disciples are unable to do it (cf. Matt. 17:14-20; Mark 9:14-29).
Luke 9:49-50	Demons	John tells Jesus about someone casting out demons. This person isn't one of the disciples. Jesus says not to stop the man "because whoever is not against you is for you" (cf. Mark 9:38-41).

References to Evil Spirits, pt. 7

Passage	Name(s)	Brief Description
Luke 10:17-20	Demons; snakes and scorpions; spirits	After sending out 72 (or 70) disciples to proclaim the gospel in the towns to which Jesus is traveling, Jesus receives them back. They report that "even the demons submit to us in your name." Jesus says he watched Satan fall from heaven like lightning. He has given the disciples authority to trample on snakes and scorpions – likely a reference to evil spirits – and over all the power of the enemy. Yet, they are to rejoice not so much in this, but that their names are written in heaven.
Luke 11:14-23	Demon (2x); demons (3x)	Jesus drives a demon out of a mute man, amazing the crowds but prompting some to accuse Jesus of casting out demons by the ruler of the demons (Beelzebul). Jesus counters that a house divided against itself (Satan vs. demons) cannot stand. Further, by his miracles, Jesus demonstrates that the kingdom of heaven has come and that Satan, the strong man, is overcome and his goods are plundered (cf. Matt. 12:22-32; Mark 3:20-30).
Luke 11:24-26	Unclean spirit; spirits (evil)	Jesus tells a parable of an unclean spirit who leaves a man but later returns with seven spirits more evil than himself to inhabit an empty "house." This speaks of Israel, which has rightly abandoned idolatry but replaced it with empty ritual (cf. Matt. 12:43-45).

References to Evil Spirits, pt. 8

Passage	Name(s)	Brief Description
Luke 13:10-12	Spirit	Jesus heals a woman "disabled by a spirit" for more than 18 years. The leader of the synagogue is indignant, claiming that such work should not be done on the Sabbath. In Jesus' rebuke of the leader, he acknowledges that "Satan" has bound this woman (vv. 14-17).
Luke 13:31-33	Demons	Some Pharisees warn Jesus to flee because Herod wants to kill him. Jesus responds, "Go tell that fox, 'Look, I am driving out demons and performing healings ...'"
John 6:70-71	A devil	Jesus tells his disciples that one of the twelve is a devil, referring to Judas Iscariot, who would betray Jesus.
John 7:20	Demon	The crowds in Jerusalem accuse Jesus of having a demon because he asks why they are trying to kill him.
John 8:48-52	Demon (3x)	The Jews seeking to kill Jesus accuse him of being a Samaritan and having a demon. This is because Jesus claims to be from God and thus holds the keys to everlasting life.
John 10:19-21	Demon (2x); demon-possessed	The Jews are divided about Jesus. Many claim he has a demon and is crazy. Others say he does not speak like someone demon-possessed; can a demon open the eyes of the blind?

References to Evil Spirits, pt. 9

Passage	Name(s)	Brief Description
Acts 5:16	Unclean spirits	Among the many apostolic signs and wonders being performed by Peter and others is the healing of those tormented by unclean spirits.
Acts 8:7	Unclean spirits	Philip performs signs in Samaria, including the casting out of unclean spirits from people who are possessed.
Acts 16:16-18	A spirit; the spirit	Paul casts a fortune-telling spirit out of a woman in Philippi.
Acts 19:11-12	Evil spirits	At Ephesus, God performs miraculous signs through Paul. Even facecloths or aprons that have touched his skin are brought to the sick. As a result, diseases leave people and evil spirits come out.
Acts 19:13-17	Evil spirits; evil spirit (2x)	Some itinerant Jewish exorcists attempt to cast out evil spirits in the name of "the Jesus that Paul preaches." Seven sons of Sceva, a Jewish high priest, attempt this as well, but an evil spirit overpowers them and drives them away naked.
Romans 8:38	Rulers; powers	Nothing separates believers from the love of God, not even "rulers" (Gr. *archai*, sometimes used of demons) and "powers" (Gr. *dynamis*, sometimes used of supernatural powers like Satan and demons).

References to Evil Spirits, pt. 10

Passage	Name(s)	Brief Description
1 Cor. 2:6-8	Rulers (2x)	The "rulers of this age … are coming to nothing." Their wisdom is not God's wisdom. If they had known God's wisdom, they would not have crucified the Lord of glory. These rulers are humans, but Paul could also be referring to human governments and authorities, as well as Satan and evil spirits.
1 Cor. 10:21-22	Demons (4x)	In warning against idolatry, Paul writes that those who sacrifice to idols "sacrifice to demons and not to God." He goes on to contrast the Lord's Supper with "the cup of demons" and "the table of demons," implying that demons are behind the idols worshiped by the Corinthians.
1 Cor. 15:24	Rule; authority; power	After Christ returns, he hands over the kingdom to God the Father, when he abolishes "all rule and all authority and power." This could be a reference to earthly powers, demonic powers, or both. In any case, they are called "all enemies" in v. 25, and they are placed under Christ's feet.
2 Cor. 12:7	A messenger of Satan	Perhaps (but by no means certain) Paul refers to an evil spirit – "a messenger of Satan" – sent to afflict him to prevent him from self-exaltation.

References to Evil Spirits, pt. 11

Passage	Name(s)	Brief Description
Eph. 1:21	Ruler; authority; power; dominion	Christ is seated in the heavens, "far above every ruler and authority, power and dominion." Likely, Paul's reference includes Satan, evil spirits, holy angels, and earthly authorities.
Eph. 6:11-16	The rulers; authorities; cosmic powers of darkness; evil, spiritual forces in the heavens	This includes Satan and evil spirits. Paul instructs Christians to put on the full armor of God so we may stand against "the schemes of the devil" (v. 11). Our struggle is not against flesh and blood but against "the rulers, against the authorities, against the cosmic powers of this darkness, against evil, spiritual forces in the heavens" (v. 12). Among the pieces of our spiritual armor is the shield of faith with which we may "extinguish all the flaming arrows of the evil one" (v. 16).
Col. 1:16	Thrones; dominions; rulers; authorities	Jesus created everything, both visible and invisible, including thrones, dominions, rulers, and authorities – references to hierarchies of earthly and angelic/demonic forces.
Col. 2:10	Ruler; authority	Paul warns the Colossians against "philosophy and empty deceit" (v. 8). He reminds them that Christ is the fullness of deity in human flesh (v. 9), and that Jesus is "the head over every ruler and authority," whether human or angelic/demonic.

References to Evil Spirits, pt. 12

Passage	Name(s)	Brief Description
Col. 2:15	Rulers; authorities	In his finished work on the cross, Christ "disarmed the rulers and authorities and disgraced them publicly." While this could include Jewish and Roman authorities, it more likely depicts evil spirits under the authority of Satan.
1 Tim. 4:1	Deceitful spirits; demons	Paul warns that "in later times" some will depart from the faith, heeding "deceitful spirits and the teachings of demons."
Jas. 2:19	Demons	Even demons believe that God is one – and they shudder.
Jas. 3:15	Demonic	Wisdom rooted in bitter envy and selfish ambition is "earthly, unspiritual, demonic."
1 Pet. 3:19	Spirits in prison	Some commentators believe Peter is referring to certain demons confined to the abyss (cf. Jude 6; 2 Pet. 2:4; Rev. 9:1-12, 14-15; Gen. 6:1-4).
1 Pet. 3:22	Authorities; powers	Among those over whom Christ reigns in heaven are "authorities" and "powers," which could include evil spirits.
2 Pet. 2:4	Angels	"God didn't spare the angels who sinned but cast them into hell and delivered them in chains of utter darkness to be kept for judgment." This could be a reference to certain demons confined to the abyss (cf. Jude 6; Rev. 9:1-12, 14-15; Gen. 6:1-4).

References to Evil Spirits, pt. 13

Passage	Name(s)	Brief Description
2 Pet. 2:10	Glorious ones	The "bold, arrogant" false teachers to whom Peter refers are not afraid to slander the "glorious ones" – quite possibly a reference to demons, especially in light of verse 11, in which Peter says holy angels do not mock or disregard the glorious ones. It seems the false teachers mock, or laugh at, the idea that their sensuous ways open them up to demonic influence.
1 John 4:1-6	Spirit (5x); spirits	These references to spirits likely are not references to evil spirits but rather may be interpreted in two senses: (1) John uses the word "spirit" to refer to false teachers who claim divine gifting for service; and (2) John uses "spirit" or "spirits" to identify an attitude that is in opposition to truth.
Jude 6	Angels	Angels who did not keep their own position, but abandoned their proper dwelling, are being kept in eternal chains in deep darkness for judgment. This could be a reference to certain demons confined to the abyss (cf. 2 Pet. 2:4; Rev. 9:1-12, 14-15; Gen. 6:1-4).
Jude 8	Glorious ones	False teachers in Jude's day "slander glorious ones," a possible reference to demons. See entry for 2 Pet. 2:10 above.

References to Evil Spirits, pt. 14

Passage	Name(s)	Brief Description
Rev. 9:1	Star	When the fifth angel blows his trumpet, John sees a star that has fallen from heaven to earth. The key to the shaft to the abyss is given to him. Some commentators see this star as a fallen angel (perhaps Abaddon). Others identify the star as Satan, or as a holy angel fulfilling God's purpose.
Rev. 9:3-10	Locusts (2x)	Locusts emerge from the abyss. They are given power to torment those on earth who do not have God's seal on their foreheads. They appear as horses prepared for battle, with golden crowns on their heads, human faces, hair like women's hair, teeth like lions' teeth, chests like iron breastplates, wings that produce substantial sound, and tails with stingers like scorpions. They are prevented from killing their prey but may torment them for five months.
Rev. 9:11	The angel of the abyss; Abaddon; Apollyon	The locusts have as their king the angel of the abyss. His name in Hebrew is Abaddon, and in Greek is Apollyon. Possibly, he is one of Satan's underlings, a destroying demon and one of the "rulers," "authorities," and "powers" mentioned in Eph. 6:12. Some commentators, however, identify this angel as Satan.
Rev. 9:13-19	Angels (2x)	Four angels bound at the Euphrates River are released to kill one-third of the human race. It appears that these angels command a demonic army described as 200 million mounted troops. The horses release plagues of fire, smoke, and sulfur.

References to Evil Spirits, pt. 15

Passage	Name(s)	Brief Description
Rev. 9:20	Demons	Despite the plagues of Rev. 9:18-19, the survivors refuse to repent of their "works," which includes worshiping demons.
Rev. 11:7	Beast	A beast "that comes up out of the abyss" kills the two faithful witnesses of Christ. While this likely is the beast of Rev. 13 – a wicked human – he is strongly connected with Satanic and demonic power (cf. Rev. 17:3, 7-8).
Rev. 12:7-12	Angels	Michael the archangel and his angels defeat the dragon and his angels in a battle in heaven. Satan and his angels are thrown down to earth, resulting in great joy in heaven but woe on the earth and sea.
Rev. 16:13-14	Unclean spirits; demonic spirits	Three unclean spirits like frogs come from the dragon's mouth, the beast's mouth, and the false prophet's mouth. They are demonic spirits performing signs, and they travel to the kings of the whole world to assemble them for the battle of Armageddon.

References to Evil Spirits, pt. 16

Passage	Name(s)	Brief Description
Rev. 17:3-18	Beast (9x); king	John sees a woman sitting on a scarlet beast covered with blasphemous names; he has seven heads and 10 horns. He is about to come up from the abyss and go to destruction. He wages war against the Lamb but is defeated. He hates the woman (prostitute) and makes her desolate; this is in accordance with God's plan. While this likely is the beast of Rev. 13 – a wicked human who is called a king (17:11) – he is strongly connected with Satanic and demonic power (cf. Rev. 11:7).
Rev. 18:2-3	Demons; unclean spirit	An angel announces the fall of Babylon the Great, which has become a home for demons and a haunt for every unclean spirit.
Rev. 19:19-20	Beast (2x)	The beast of Rev. 13 is thrown alive into the lake of fire and sulfur. While this likely is a wicked human being, he is strongly connected with Satanic and demonic power (cf. Rev. 11:7; 13; 17:3-18).
Rev. 20:4	Beast	The souls of Christian martyrs who had not worshiped the beast or his image come to life and reign with Christ for 1,000 years. While the beast likely is a wicked human, he is strongly connected with Satanic and demonic power (cf. Rev. 11:7; 13; 17:3-18; 19:19-20).

ENDNOTES

Introduction

1. "Top Names Over the Last 100 Years," https://www.ssa.gov/oact/babynames/decades/century.html.
2. Shel Silverstein, "A Boy Named Sue," performed by Johnny Cash.

Chapter 1 – Anointed Guardian Cherub

1. D. G. Hewitt, "From Hero to Zero: 20 of the Biggest Falls from Grace in History," https://historycollection.co/from-hero-to-zero-20-of-the-biggest-falls-from-grace-in-history/.
2. CSB Study Bible (Nashville, TN: Holman Bible Publishers, 2017), 1063, note on Isa. 14:3-4.
3. Origen, *On First Principles*, 1.5.5.
4. CSB Study Bible, 1063, note on Isa. 14:12.
5. See *Corpus Christianorum*, Series Latina (Turnhout, Belgium: Brepols, 1953), 73:168-169.

6. John R. Gilhooly, *40 Questions About Angels, Demons, and Spiritual Warfare* (Grand Rapids, MI: Kregel Academic, 2018), 107.

7. Gilhooly, 106-107.

8. Gilhooly, 107.

9. Gilhooly, 108.

10. CSB Apologetics Study Bible (Nashville, TN: Holman Bible Publishers, 2017), 1013, note on Ezek. 28:1.

11. Kenneth D. Boa and Robert M. Bowman Jr., *Sense & Nonsense about Angels & Demons* (Grand Rapids, MI: Zondervan, 207), 117-118.

12. *Ibid.*

13. Victor Harold Matthews, Mark W. Chavalas, and John H. Walton, *The IVP Bible Background Commentary: Old Testament,* electronic ed. (Downers Grove, IL: InterVarsity Press, 2000), Ezek. 28:14-16.

14. See G. K. Beale, "Adam as the First Priest in Eden as the Garden Temple," https://sbts-wordpress-uploads.s3. amazonaws.com/equip/uploads/2018/10/SBJT-22.2-Adam-as-Priest-Beale.pdf.

15. Michael S. Heiser summarizes this view and rebuts it in *The Unseen Realm: Recovering the Supernatural Worldview of the Bible* (Bellingham, WA: Lexham Press, 2015), 77-82.

16. C. Fred Dickason, *Angels: Elect & Evil* (Chicago: Moody Press, 1975, 1995), 136.

17. Graham A. Cole, *Against the Darkness: the Doctrine of Angels, Satan, and Demons* (Wheaton, IL: Crossway, 2019), 92.

18. Charles H. Dyer, "Ezekiel," *The Bible Knowledge Commentary: An Exposition of the Scriptures*, ed. J. F. Walvoord and R. B. Zuck, Vol. 1 (Wheaton, IL: Victor Books, 1985), 1283-1284.

19. *Ibid.*

20. Lamar Eugene Cooper, *Ezekiel*, Vol. 17, The New American

Commentary (Nashville, TN: Broadman & Holman Publishers, 1994), 264-270.

21. Michael S. Heiser, *Supernatural: What the Bible Teaches about the Unseen World – And Why It Matters* (Bellingham, WA: Lexham Press, 2015), 38.

22. Heiser, *Supernatural*, 38-39.

23. Heiser, *The Unseen Realm*, 91.

24. For more on the connection between Genesis 3, Isaiah 14, and Ezekiel 28, see Heiser, *The Unseen Realm*, 73-91.

25. John Piper, "Where Did Satan's First Desire for Evil Come From? An Interview with John Piper," https://desiringgod.org/interviews/where-did-satans-first-desire-for-evil-come-from.

26. Bodie Hodge, "What about Satan and the Origin of Evil?" *Answers in Genesis*, https://answersingenesis.org/angels-and-demons/satan/what-about-satan-and-the-origin-of-evil/.

27. "Satan's Sin," Evangelical Lutheran Synod, https://els.org/resources/answers/satans-sin/.

28. William D. Mounce, *Interlinear for the Rest of Us: The Reverse Interlinear for New Testament Word Studies* (Grand Rapids, MI: Zondervan, 2006), 903.

Chapter 2 – Serpent / Dragon – Part 1

1. "9 Powerful Snakes from History and Mythology," https://history.com/news/snake-symbol-history-mythology.

2. "Krak's Dragon," https://dragons.fandom.com/wiki/Krak%27s_Dragon. There are many versions of this story. The oldest version, from the 13th century, has the king's sons killing the dragon, with the eldest son then murdering his brother in order to take full credit for slaying the beast.

3. According to Andrew Naselli, there are sixteen biblical words referring to serpents – eleven in the Hebrew Old Testament and five in the Greek New Testament. The

words are: (1) *efeh* – "snake," occurring three times (Job 20:16; Isa. 30:6; 59:5); (2) *liwyathan* – "Leviathan, sea monster," occurring six times (Job 3:8; 40:25; Ps. 74:14; 104:26; Isa. 27:1 [2x]); (3) *nahash* – "snake," occurring thirty-one times (Gen. 3:1, 2, 4, 13, 14; 49:17; Exod. 4:3; 7:15; Num. 21:6, 7, 9 [3x]; Deut. 8:15; 2 Kings 18:4; Job 26:13; Ps. 58:5; 140:4; Prov. 23:32; 30:19; Eccles. 10:8, 11; Isa. 14:29; 27:1 [2x]; 65:25; Jer. 8:17; 46:22; Amos 5:19; 9:3; Mic. 7:17); (4) *pethen* – "horned viper," occurring six times (Deut. 32:33; Job 20:14, 16; Ps. 58:5; 91:13; Isa. 11:8); (5) *tsefa* – "poisonous snake, viper," occurring once (Isa. 14:29); (6) *tsifoni* – "poisonous snake, viper," occurring four times (Prov. 23:32; Isa. 11:8; 59:5; Jer. 8:17); (7) *akhshuv* – "poisonous horned viper, or adder," occurring once (Ps. 140:4); (8) *rahab* – "mythical monster ... symbolic designation for Egypt," occurring seven times (Job 9:13; 26:12; Ps. 40:5; 87:4; 89:11; Isa. 30:7; 51:9); (9) *saraph* – "serpent ... burning one," occurring seven times (Num. 21:6, 8; Deut. 8:15; Isa. 6:2, 6; 14:29; 30:6); (10) *shephiphon* – "horned viper," occurring once (Gen. 49:17); (11) *tannin* – "sea monster/dragon, serpent, crocodile," occurring fourteen times (Gen. 1:21; Exod. 7:9, 10, 12; Deut. 32:33; Job 7:12; Ps. 74:13; 91:13; 148:7; Isa. 27:1; 51:9; Jer. 51:34; Ezek. 29:3; 32:2); (12) *aspis* – "asp, Egyptian cobra," occurring once (Rom. 3:13); (13) *drakon* – "dragon," occurring thirteen times (Rev. 12:3, 4, 7 [2x], 9, 13, 16, 17; 13:2, 4, 11; 16:13; 20:2); (14) *herpeton* – "reptile," occurring four times (Acts 10:12; 11:6; Rom. 1:23; Jas. 3:7); (15) *echidna* – "snake ... a poisonous one," occurring five times (Matt. 3:7; 12:34; 23:33; Luke 3:7; Acts 28:3); (16) *ophis* – "a limbless reptile, snake ... a person perceived as dangerous ... a symbolic figure," occurring thirteen times (Matt. 7:10; 10:16; 23:33; Luke 10:19; 11:11; John 3:14; 1 Cor. 10:9; 2 Cor. 11:3; Rev.

9:19; 12:9, 14, 15; 20:2 [also Mark 16:18]). From: *The Serpent and the Serpent Slayer* (Wheaton, IL: Crossway, 2020), 133-135. Definitions drawn from Ludwig Koehler, Walter Baumgartner, and Johann Jakob Stamm, *The Hebrew and Aramaic Lexicon of the Old Testament*, ed. and trans. M. E. J. Richardson, 2 vols. (Leiden: Brill, 1994); Walter Bauer et. al., eds., *A Greek-English Lexicon of the New Testament and Other Early Christian Literature*, 3rd ed. (Chicago: University of Chicago Press, 2000).

4. Interestingly, Pharaoh's crown is wreathed with an asp. Just as the eagle is the ensign of Rome, the serpent/dragon is the symbol of Egypt.

5. Sharon Beekmann and Peter G. Bolt, *Silencing Satan: Handbook of Biblical Demonology* (Eugene, OR: Wipf & Stock, 2012), 70.

6. Naselli, 18.

7. Justin Martyr, Irenaeus, and other church fathers believed Satan used the serpent in the garden. Augustine wrote that the devil spoke through the serpent. And Calvin taught that Satan used the serpent to seduce the first humans to "deprive God of his due honor and hurl man himself into ruin." From Beekmann and Bolt, 71.

8. Heiser, *The Unseen Realm*, 74.

9. *Ibid.*

10. Donald Grey Barnhouse, *Genesis: A Devotional Commentary* (Grand Rapids, MI: Zondervan, 1970), 22.

11. D. A. Carson, *The God Who Is There: Finding Your Place in God's Story* (Grand Rapids, MI: Baker, 2010), 37.

12. Beekmann and Bolt, 128.

13. CSB Apologetics Study Bible, 692 (note on Ps. 74:13-14).

14. John's description of the woman in Revelation 12 recalls Old Testament depictions of Israel (Gen. 37:9; Isa. 54:1; Mic. 4:9-10). But these do not exclude other images taken from the culture in John's day. As noted in the magazine *Tabletalk*, "Some pagan myths also involved a woman

giving birth to a god or an emperor who defeated a dragon. That the woman gives birth to Jesus in Revelation is a powerful message for first-century pagans – the great God or emperor whom you seek is actually Jesus, who was crucified and rose again from the dead. All others are merely pretenders." From "Michael Battles Satan," Nov. 12, 2020, 48.

15. J. Daniel Hays, J. Scott Duvall, C. Marvin Pate, *Dictionary of Biblical Prophecy and End Times* (Grand Rapids, MI: Zondervan, 2007), 125.

16. R. J. D. Utley, *Hope in Hard Times – The Final Curtain: Revelation*, Vol. 12, Study Guide Commentary Series (Marshall, TX: Bible Lessons International, 2001), 89-90.

17. Hays, Duvall, and Pate, 399.

18. For example, Robert Jamieson, A. R. Fausset, and David Brown, *Commentary Critical & Explanatory on the Whole Bible.*

19. For example, Matthew Henry, *Matthew Henry's Commentary on the Whole Bible: Complete and Unabridged in One Volume.*

20. For example, J. F. Walvoord and Roy B. Zuck, *The Bible Knowledge Commentary: An Exposition of the Scriptures*; Warren W. Wiersbe, *The Bible Exposition Commentary.*

Chapter 3 – Serpent / Dragon – Part 2

1. Kendell H. Easley, *Revelation*, Vol. 12, Holman New Testament Commentary (Nashville, TN: Broadman & Holman Publishers, 1998), 369-371.

2. Revelation 20 is the only place in Scripture that refers to one thousand years during which Satan is bound. Few time periods in the Bible have been written about with so much conviction – and debated with so much contention.

A number of Old Testament passages speak of a coming golden age on earth – an age when swords are beaten into plowshares and the lamb lies down with the lion, when justice reigns and people joyously ascend the temple mount in Jerusalem to worship the reigning Messiah. Further, the idea of a messianic reign is rooted in Jewish thought, with a wide range of corresponding years – forty, four hundred, a thousand, and so on. Some interpreters take the thousand years literally; others, figuratively. One view is that the number one thousand is the number ten cubed: Ten is the number of completeness, and three is the number of God; therefore, ten to the third power shows the perfect completion of the Lord's work in human history. Whatever one's view, we should keep in mind the certainty of Christ's return, the clear limits the Lord sets on the dragon's antics, and the inevitability of the dragon's final defeat as he is cast into the lake of fire.

3. "The Servant in Battle," *The Valley of Vision: A Collection of Puritan Prayers & Devotions* (Edinburgh, UK; Carlisle, PA: The Banner of Truth Trust, 1975), 328.

Chapter 4 – Satan / The Devil

1. "Lizzo sued for defamation after accusing delivery girl of stealing her food," *Independent*, Nov. 16, 2019, https://www. independent.co.uk/arts-entertainment/music/news/lizzo-postmates-delivery-food-stolen-sued-privacy-latest-a9205381.html.

2. "Elon Musk trial: Billionaire to face jury over 'pedo guy' tweet aimed at British cave rescuer," *Independent*, May 11, 2019, https://www.independent.co.uk/news/world/americas/elon-musk-trial-pedo-guy-tweet-defamation-vernon-unsworth-thai-cave-rescue-a9176071.html.

3. "Defamation by Instagram? The Game Slapped With Lawsuit from Baby Sitter," *The Hollywood Reporter*, July 25, 2018, https://www.hollywoodreporter.com/thr-esq/defamation-by-instagram-game-slapped-593230.

4. Norman L. Geisler and Douglas E. Potter, *The Doctrine of Angels & Demons* (Indian Trail, NC: Norm Geisler International Ministries, 2016), 28.

5. "Satan, devil," Eugene E. Carpenter and Philip W. Comfort, *Holman Treasury of Key Bible Words: 200 Greek and 200 Hebrew Words Defined and Explained* (Nashville, TN: Broadman & Holman Publishers, 2000), 386.

6. James Montgomery Boice, *Genesis: An Expositional Commentary*, Vol. 1, Genesis 1-11 (Grand Rapids, MI: Baker Books, 1982, 1998), 154.

7. M. G. Easton, *Easton's Bible Dictionary* (New York: Harper & Brothers, 1893).

8. For more on the angel of the LORD, see Rob Phillips, *Jesus Before Bethlehem: What Every Christian Should Know About the Angel of the LORD* (Jefferson City, MO: High Street Press, 2020).

9. 2 Sam. 24:1 identifies Yahweh, not Satan, as the one who incites King David to take a census. While there are several possible explanations for the apparent discrepancy between this verse and 1 Chron. 21:1, it seems best to understand this as an example of God using secondary causes – in this case, Satan – to carry out his will.

10. For a more thorough examination of Num. 22-24, 31, see Phillips, *Jesus Before Bethlehem*, 95-106.

11. *Mounce's Complete Expository Dictionary of Old & New Testament Words*, gen. ed. William D. Mounce (Grand Rapids, MI: Zondervan, 2006), 563.

12. Leon Morris, *Revelation: An Introduction and Commentary*, Vol. 20, Tyndale New Testament Commentaries (Downers Grove, IL: InterVarsity Press, 1987), 156-157.

13. There is some question as to whether the accuser in this

passage is Satan. The definite article precedes the name, thus: *the satan*. Therefore, some interpreters argue this figure is not the serpent of Gen. 3 and Rev. 12. Rather, he is an angelic accuser. For our purposes, we are pursuing *the satan* as the evil one, for his words and deeds seem consistent with those of Satan throughout Scripture.

14. Compare 2 Sam. 24:1, which says God (not Satan) stirred up David to number his troops. The same Hebrew word (*wayyaset*) is translated "incited" in 1 Chron. 21:1 and "stirred up" in 2 Sam. 24:1. We know God is not the author of evil and does not tempt anyone to sin (Jas. 1:13). As Eric Lyons explains, "The difference lies with the sense in which the word is used: Satan incited (or tempted – cf. 1 Thess. 3:5) David more directly, while God is spoken of as having incited David because he **allowed** such temptation to take place." From "Who Incited David to Number Israel?" https://apologticspress.org/apcontent.aspx?category=6&article=784.

15. Beekmann and Bolt, 115.

16. F. Duane Lindsey, "Zechariah," *The Bible Knowledge Commentary: An Exposition of the Scriptures*, ed. J. F. Walvoord and R. B. Zuck, Vol. 1 (Wheaton, IL: Victor Books, 1985), 1554.

17. G. Michael Butterworth, "Zechariah," *New Bible Commentary: 21st Century Edition*, ed. D. A. Carson et. al., 4th ed. (Leicester, England; Downers Grove, IL: InterVarsity Press, 1994), 869.

18. Robert James Utley, *Hope in Hard Times - The Final Curtain: Revelation*, Vol. 12, Study Guide Commentary Series (Marshall, TX: Bible Lessons International, 2001), 91.

19. Some argue that Satan still has access to the throne of God based on Job 1-2 and Zechariah 3, but these are Old Testament references. New Testament writers do not record Satan or his angels standing in God's presence after the resurrection of Christ. This doesn't prove Satan

lacks access to heaven today, but it casts doubt on the notion.

20. Heiser, *Supernatural*, 59-60.

Chapter 5 – Father of Lies

1. Lois Tverberg, "Eve's Error," En-Gedi Resource Center, https://engediresourcecenter.com/2015/07/03/eves-error/.
2. Tverberg, "Eve's Error."
3. Kurt Strassner, *Opening Up Genesis*, Opening Up Commentary (Leominster: Day One Publications, 2009), 32-39.
4. According to Alfred Edersheim, a teacher of languages and Warbutonian Lecturer at Lincoln's Inn (Oxford), there are at least 465 messianic references in the Old Testament. See John Ankerberg, John Weldon, and Walter C. Kaiser Jr., *The Case for Jesus the Messiah: Incredible Prophecies That Prove God Exists* (Chattanooga, TN: The John Ankerberg Evangelistic Association, 1989), 12.
5. Ankerberg, Weldon, and Kaiser, 24.
6. See Phillips, *Jesus Before Bethlehem*.
7. Boa and Bowman, 83.
8. Boa and Bowman, 87.
9. R. C. Sproul, "Satan the Proud and Powerful (Part 1)," https://ligonier.org/blog/satan-proud-and-powerful-part-1/.
10. Augustine of Hippo, "Lectures or Tractates on the Gospel According to St. John," *St. Augustine: Homilies on the Gospel of John, Homilies on the First Epistle of John, Soliloquies*, ed. Philip Schaff, trans. John Gibb and James Innes, Vol. 7, A Select Library of the Nicene and Post-Nicene Fathers of the Christian Church, First Series (New York: Christian Literature Company, 1888), 238-239.
11. D. A. Carson, *The Gospel According to John*, The Pillar New

Testament Commentary (Leicester, England; Grand
Rapids, MI: InterVarsity Press; W. B. Eerdmans, 1991), 353.
12. Henry, 1971-1972.
13. Rodney A. Whitacre, *John*, Vol. 4, The IVP New Testament
Commentary Series (Westmont, IL: IVP Academic, 1999),
223-228.
14. Henry, 1971-1972.
15. Beekmann and Bolt, 136.

Chapter 6 – Murderer

1. Caroline Davies and Mark Tran, "Teenager detained for 27
years for two 'brutal and sadistic' murders," *The Guardian*,
https://theguardian.com, April 29, 2016; Riley Paul Reese,
"10 of the Youngest Serial Killers in History," https://vocal.
media/criminal/10-of-the-youngest-serial-killers-in-
history.
2. The Hebrew word for "murder" in Exod. 20:13 is *ratsach*: to
dash in pieces; that is, to kill a human being, especially to
murder, slay, or assassinate.
3. *The Westminster Confession*, 5:4 (Edinburgh, UK; Carlisle,
PA: The Banner of Truth Trust, 2018), 28.
4. David Maxwell points out that the Greek in John 8:44
could read, "The devil is a liar and so is his father." The
"devil" in this case, metaphorically speaking, is Cain, who
imitates Satan by murdering his brother and then lying
about it. Maxwell also points to 1 John 3:12, in which the
apostle says Cain "was of the evil one," a statement that
essentially makes the evil one Cain's father. However, this
view seems to beg the questions: When did Cain see Satan
murder? And whom did Satan murder? See "The Devil Is
a Liar and So Is His Father: Why Greek Matters," https://
concordiatheology.org/2019/06/the-devil-is-a-liar-and-so-
is-his-father-why-greek-matters/.

5. https://blueletterbible.org/lang/Lexicon/Lexicon.cfm?sgrongs=H4191&t=KJV.

6. There is considerable debate between those who believe in a two-part division of human nature (material and immaterial) and those who believe in a three-part division (body, soul, and spirit). The difference is not as significant as it may appear, according to James Boice, who explains: "All the three-part division is intended to imply is that man is separated from the plant world, along with the animals, by virtue of possessing a distinct, self-conscious personality. He is separated from the animals by that which makes him aware of God. The soul is that with which man thinks, feels, reacts, and aspires. The spirit, or capacity for spirit, is that with which man prays. Man worships while animals do not." See *Genesis: An Expositional Commentary*, Vol. 1, 172.

7. Boice, 172.

8. Beekmann and Bolt, 145-146.

9. Boice, 173.

10. John R. W. Stott, *Basic Christianity* (Grand Rapids, MI: Eerdmans, 1958), 72, 75.

11. *Expository Dictionary of Bible Words*, ed. Stephen D. Renn (Peabody, MA: Hendrickson Publishers Marketing, LLC, 2005), 797.

12. John M. Frame, *Systematic Theology: An Introduction to Christian Belief* (Phillipsburg, NJ: P&R Publishing Company, 2013), 311.

Chapter 7 – Tempter

1. Boa and Bowman, 114.

2. Boa and Bowman, 115.

3. Matt. 4:1-11; Mark 1:12-13; Luke 4:1-13.

4. The Greek verb used in Matt. 4:1 is *anago*; in Luke 4:1, *ago*. Both mean "to lead up" or "to take one with."

5. Beekmann and Bolt, 132.

6. Beekmann and Bolt, 133.

7. Gene L. Green, *The Letters to the Thessalonians*, The Pillar New Testament Commentary (Grand Rapids, MI; Leicester, England: W. B. Eerdmans Pub., 2002), 164-165.

8. Tim Shenton, *Opening Up 1 Thessalonians*, Opening Up Commentary (Leominster: Day One Publications, 2006), 56-59.

9. Mounce, *Mounce's Complete Expository Dictionary of Old & New Testament Words*, 715.

10. *Ibid.*

11. Roger Barrier, "What is the Difference between Temptations, Trials, and Tests in the Bible?", https://www.crosswalk.com/church/pastors-or-leadership/ask-roger/what-is-the-difference-between-temptations-trials-and-tests-in-the-bible.html.

12. Juli Camarin, "Temptation vs. Testing, What's the Difference?", https://jcblog.net/hebrews/2/18/temptation-vs-testing-whats-the-difference.

13. Beekmann and Bolt, 131.

14. Craig Blomberg, *Matthew*, Vol. 22, The New American Commentary (Nashville: Broadman & Holman Publishers, 1992), 120.

15. Leon Morris, *The Gospel According to Matthew*, The Pillar New Testament Commentary (Grand Rapids, MI; Leicester, England: W. B. Eerdmans; InterVarsity Press, 1992), 148.

16. Mounce, *Mounce's Complete Expository Dictionary of Old & New Testament Words*, 715.

Chapter 8 – Deceiver

1. "Deceiver," https://merriam-webster.com/thesaurus/deceiver.
2. "Lexicon: Strong's H5377 – *nasha*," https://blueletterbible.org/lang/lexicon/lexicon.cfm?Strongs=H5377&t=KJV.
3. "Lexicon: Strong's G538 – *apatao*," https://www.blueletterbible.org/lang/lexicon/lexicon.cfm?Strongs=G538&t=KJV.
4. Mounce, *Mounce's Complete Expository Dictionary of Old & New Testament Words*, 161-162.
5. Beekmann and Bolt, 137.
6. Jared C. Wilson, *The Gospel According to Satan: Eight Lies About God That Sound Like the Truth* (Nashville, TN: Nelson Books, 2020), 53.
7. John Piper, "Satan's Ten Strategies Against You," https://desiringgod.org/articles/satans-ten-strategies-against-you.
8. R. C. Sproul defines a miracle as an "extraordinary work performed by the immediate power of God in the external perceivable world, which is an act against nature that only God can do." He further notes that there is no word for "miracle" in the original languages of Scripture. Our English term *miracle* translates Hebrew and Greek terms that are more literally rendered as "signs" or "wonders." This shows miracles are not merely to meet the physical needs of people but rather to point beyond themselves to authenticate a word from God. See "Are Miracles for Today?", https://ligonier.org/learn/devotionals/are-miracles-today/.
9. *Ibid*.
10. "What does the Bible say about demonic/satanic miracles?" https://gotquestions.net/Printer/demonic-satanic-miracles-PF.html.
11. "Who Really Is the Faithful and Discreet Slave?", https://

www.jw.org/en/library/magazines/w20130715/who-is-faithful-discreet-slave/.

12. David E. Garland, *2 Corinthians*, Vol. 29, The New American Commentary (Nashville, TN: Broadman & Holman Publishers, 1999), 129-132.

13. See b. 'Abod. Zar. 22b; b. Sabb. 145b-146a; b. Yebam. 103b; b. Sota 9b; 1 Enoch 69:5-6; 2 Enoch 31:6; Apoc. Abr. 23:5; 4 Macc. 18:7-8.

14. Garland, 462-464.

15. C. Hodge, *An Exposition of the Second Epistle to the Corinthians* (1859; reprint, Grand Rapids, MI: Baker, 1980), 253.

16. "Lexicon: Strong's G3835 – *panourgos*," https://blueletterbible.org/lang/lexicon/lexicon.cfm?Strongs=G3835.

17. "Lexicon: Strong's G3540 – *noema*," https://blueletterbible.org/lang/lexicon/lexicon.cfm?Strongs=G3540&t=KJV.

18. Paul Barnett, *The Message of 2 Corinthians: Power in Weakness*, The Bible Speaks Today (Leicester, England; Downers Grove, IL: InterVarsity Press, 1988), 164.

19. W. E. Vine, *Vine's Expository Dictionary of Old and New Testament Words*, Vol. 2: E-Li (Old Tappan, NJ: Fleming H. Revell Company, 1981), 80.

20. Garland, 485-487.

21. These passages do not contradict each other. God sovereignly allows Satan to do what the evil one wants – and King David to do what he himself wants (2 Sam. 24:10) – in order to teach David to trust God rather than the king's armies.

22. Donald Guthrie, *Pastoral Epistles: An Introduction and Commentary*, Vol. 14, Tyndale New Testament Commentaries (Downers Grove, IL: InterVarsity Press, 1990), 91.

23. *Ibid*.

24. "What Does It Mean that Women Will Be Saved through

Childbearing? (1 Timothy 2)", https://crossway.org/articles/
what-does-it-mean-that-women-will-be-saved-through-
childbearing-1-timothy-2/.

25. *Expository Dictionary of Bible Words: Word Studies for Key English Bible Words Based on the Hebrew and Greek Texts*, ed. Stephen D. Renn (Peabody, MA: Hendrickson Publishers Marketing, LLC, 2005), 1065-1066.

26. William Barclay, *The Revelation of John*, Vol. 2 (Saint Andrew Press, 1960; *Daily Bible Study*), n.p.

27. David B. Barrett, George T. Kurian, Todd M. Johnson, *World Christian Encyclopedia: A Comparative Survey of Churches and Religions in the Modern World* (New York: Oxford University Press, 2001), n.p.

28. Warren W. Wiersbe, *The Bible Exposition Commentary*, Vol. 2 (Wheaton, IL: Victor Books, 1996), 603-604.

Chapter 9 – Evil One

1. Akarsh Mehrotra, "15 of the Most Evil Men the World Has Ever Seen," https://www.scoopwhoop.com/world/most-evil-people/.

2. "7 Most Evil Women in History," https://www.goliath.com/random/7-most-evil-women-in-history/.

3. Morris, *The Gospel According to Matthew*, 122-125.

4. Craig S. Keener, *Matthew*, Vol. 1, The IVP New Testament Commentary Series (Downers Grove, IL: InterVarsity Press, 1997), Matt. 5:33.

5. Some later manuscripts add, "For yours is the kingdom and the power and the glory forever. Amen."

6. For example, the KJV, ESV, and NASB read, "deliver us from evil."

7. Blomberg, 118-121.

8. "Strong's Definition," https://www.blueletterbible.org/lang/lexicon/lexicon.cfm?strongs=G4920.

9. Morris, *The Gospel According to Matthew*, 345-346.

10. Blomberg, 218.

11. Fred H. Wight, *Manners and Customs of Bible Lands* (Chicago: Moody Press, 1953), n.p.

12. Boice, 154.

13. Carson, *The Gospel According to John*, 565.

14. *Ibid*.

15. Robert A. Morey, *Studies in the Atonement* (Las Vegas, NV: Christian Scholars Press, 2007), 292-293.

16. Henry, 2032.

17. Marvin Richardson Vincent, *Word Studies in the New Testament*, Vol. 3 (New York: Charles Scribner's Sons, 1887), 409-410.

18. Francis Foulkes, *Ephesians: An Introduction and Commentary*, Vol. 10, Tyndale House New Testament Commentaries (Downers Grove, IL: InterVarsity Press, 1989), 180-181.

19. William Gurnall, *The Christian in Complete Armour*, Vol. 1, cited in John R. W. Stott, *God's New Society: The Message of Ephesians*, The Bible Speaks Today (Downers Grove, IL: InterVarsity Press, 1979), 275-277.

20. Henry, 2319.

21. Green, *The Letters to the Thessalonians*, 337–339.

22. D. Michael Martin, *1, 2 Thessalonians*, Vol. 33, The New American Commentary (Nashville, TN: Broadman & Holman Publishers, 1995), 265–267.

23. A. T. Robertson, *Word Pictures in the New Testament* (Nashville, TN: Holman Bible Publishers, 2000), 640.

24. For example, note the second-century BC *T. Benjamin* 7:1-5 and the first- or second-century AD *Apocalypse of Abraham* 24:3-5, according to Colin G. Kruse in *The Letters of John*, The Pillar New Testament Commentary (Grand Rapids, MI; Leicester, England: W. B. Eerdmans Pub., 2000), 133-134.

25. *That the Worse Attacks the Better*, 32, 78, cited in Thomas R. Schreiner, *1, 2 Peter, Jude*, Vol. 37, The New American

Commentary: An Exegetical and Theological Exposition of Holy Scripture (Nashville, TN: B&H Publishing Group, 2003), 407.

26. Or Targumim: spoken paraphrases, explanations, and expansions of the Jewish Scriptures that rabbis give in the common language of the listeners, which in the first century is Aramaic.

27. *Pseudo-Jonathan and Neofiti*, cited in Schreiner, 462, specifically, "The Targumic Versions of Genesis 4:3-16: In *Post-Biblical Jewish Studies*, SJLA 8 (Leiden: Brill, 1975), 97-99, translated by G. Vermes.

28. Daniel L. Akin, *1, 2, 3 John*, Vol. 38, The New American Commentary (Nashville, TN: Broadman & Holman Publishers, 2001), 155.

29. Akin, 155.

30. Wiersbe, *The Bible Exposition Commentary*, Vol. 2, 554-555.

31. John R. W. Stott, *The Letters of John: An Introduction and Commentary*, Vol. 19, Tyndale New Testament Commentaries (Downers Grove, IL: InterVarsity Press, 1988), 191-194.

32. James R. White, *Scripture Alone: Exploring the Bible's Accuracy, Authority, and Authenticity* (Bloomington, MN: Bethany House Publishers, 2004), 186-187.

33. David Jackman, *The Message of John's Letters: Living in the Love of God*, The Bible Speaks Today (Leicester, England; Downers Grove, IL: InterVarsity Press, 1988), 169-170.

Chapter 10 – Beelzebul: Prince of Demons

1. Seth Ferranti, "Meet the Unconventional Mafia Boss Who Inspired 'Godfather' Don Corleone," https://www.vice.com/en_us/article/nekm3z/who-is-don-vito-corleone-godfather-based-on-frank-costello.

2. Aiden Mason, "The 20 Most Brutal Mob Bosses in

History," https://www.tvovermind.com/brutal-mob-bosses/.

3. Beekmann and Bolt, 121.
4. Morris, *The Gospel According to Matthew*, 259.
5. Theodore J. Lewis, "Beelzebul," ed. David Noel Freedman, *The Anchor Yale Bible Dictionary* (New York: Doubleday, 1992), 638-640.
6. R. T. France, *Matthew: An Introduction and Commentary*, Vol. 1, Tyndale New Testament Commentaries (Downers Grove, IL: InterVarsity Press, 1985), 189.
7. Titus Flavius Josephus, *History of the Jewish War* 7.185; *The Antiquities of the Jews* 8:45-49.
8. Morris, *The Gospel According to Matthew*, 259.

Chapter 11 – Belial

1. Theodore J. Lewis, "Belial," ed. David Noel Freedman, *The Anchor Yale Bible Dictionary* (New York: Doubleday, 1992), 654-656.
2. Justin W. Bass, "Belial," ed. John D. Berry et. al., *The Lexham Bible Dictionary* (Bellingham, WA: Lexham Press), 2016.
3. Beekmann and Bolt, 123.
4. Pseudepigraphal literature consists of Jewish writings ascribed to various biblical patriarchs and prophets but composed later, roughly within 200 years of Jesus' birth. Thus, they are considered *pseudepigraphal,* or "falsely attributed." The Qumran texts, also known as the Dead Sea Scrolls, are ancient Jewish religious manuscripts found in the 1940s and 1950s in the Qumran caves in the Judean desert, near the Dead Sea.
5. Beekmann and Bolt, 124.

Chapter 12 – Ruler of This World

1. "The world's longest-reigning monarchs," https://www.bbc.com/news/uk-37628230.

2. "Hassanal Bolkiah," https://en.wikipedia.org/wiki/Hassanal_Bolkiah.

3. Carpenter and Comfort, 425.

4. Mounce, *Mounce's Complete Expository Dictionary of Old & New Testament Words*, 808.

5. Much of our discussion of *the world* is drawn from Walter A. Elwell and Barry J. Beitzel, "World," *Baker Encyclopedia of the Bible* (Grand Rapids, MI: Baker Book House, 1988), 2163-2164.

6. Carson, *The Gospel According to John*, 505-509.

7. *Ibid.*

8. John MacArthur, "1 Timothy 1:15 – Jesus was Born to Die," https://covenantlifetampa.org/2017/12/1-timothy-115-jesus-was-born-to-die/.

9. Whitacre, 368-370.

10. Mounce, *Interlinear for the Rest of Us*, 823.

11. Carson, *The Gospel According to John*, 534-539. Besides John 16:8, the other uses of *elencho* are found in Matt. 18:15; Luke 3:19; John 3:20; 8:46; 1 Cor. 14:24; Eph. 5:11, 13; 1 Tim. 5:20; 2 Tim. 4:2; Tit. 1:9, 13; 2:15; Heb. 12:5; Jas. 2:9; Jude 15, 22; Rev. 3:19.

12. *Ibid.*

13. Gerald L. Borchert, *John 12-21,* Vol. 25B, The New American Commentary (Nashville, TN: Broadman & Holman Publishers, 2002), 164-167.

14. Carson, *The Gospel According to John*, 534-539.

15. Colin G. Kruse, *John: An Introduction and Commentary*, Vol. 4, Tyndale New Testament Commentaries (Downers

Grove, IL: InterVarsity Press, 2003), 324-327.

16. Craig S. Keener, *The IVP Bible Background Commentary: New Testament* (Downers Grove, IL: InterVarsity Press, 1993), 1 John 5:18-21.

17. John R. W. Stott, *The Letters of John*, 193-194.

18. Michael S. Heiser explains and counters this position in *The Bible Unfiltered: Approaching Scripture on Its Own Terms* (Bellingham, WA: Lexham Press, 2017), 181-184.

19. John R. W. Stott, *God's New Society: The Message of Ephesians*, The Bible Speaks Today (Downers Grove, IL: InterVarsity Press, 1979), 73-74.

20. Keener, *The IVP Bible Background Commentary*, Eph. 2:1-2.

21. Robert James Utley, *Paul Bound, the Gospel Unbound: Letters from Prison (Colossians, Ephesians and Philemon, Then Later, Philippians)*, Vol. 8, Study Guide Commentary Series (Marshall, TX: Bible Lessons International, 1997), 85.

22. Robertson, 471.

Chapter 13 – The Destroyer

1. "Research Starters: Worldwide Deaths in World War II," https://www.nationalww2museum.org/students-teachers/student-resources/research-starters/research-starters-worldwide-deaths-world-war.

2. Bill Keller, "Major Soviet Paper Says 20 Million Died As Victims of Stalin," *The New York Times*, Feb. 4, 1989, https://www.nytimes.com/1989/02/04/world/major-soviet-paper-says-20-million-died-as-victims-of-stalin.html.

3. Ian Johnson, "Who Killed More: Hitler, Stalin, or Mao?", *The New York Review of Books*, https://www.nybooks.com/daily/2018/02/05/who-killed-more-hitler-stalin-or-mao/.

4. Jacques Ellul, *The Humiliation of the Word* (Grand Rapids, MI: Eerdmans, 1985), chapter 7.

5. Frank Thielman, *Theology of the New Testament: A*

Canonical and Synthetic Approach (Grand Rapids, MI: Zondervan, 2005), 634.

6. Cole, chapter 4.

7. Beekmann and Bolt, 148.

8. J. I. Packer, *Concise Theology: A Guide to Historic Christian Beliefs* (Wheaton, IL: Tyndale, 1993), 69.

9. Merrill F. Unger, *Biblical Demonology: A Study of Spiritual Forces Today* (Grand Rapids, MI: Kregel, 1994), 73-74.

10. Louis Matthews Sweet, "Apollyon," ed. James Orr et. al., *The International Standard Bible Encyclopedia* (Chicago: The Howard-Severance Company, 1915), 201-202.

11. "Abaddon," ed. John D. Barry et. al., *The Lexham Bible Dictionary* (Bellingham, WA: Lexham Press, 2016).

12. G. K. Beale, *The Book of Revelation: A Commentary on the Greek Text*, The New International Greek Testament Commentary, eds. I. Howard Marshall and Donald A. Hagner (Grand Rapids, MI: Wm. B. Eerdmans Publishing Co., 1999), 493.

13. Elwell and Beitzel, "Abaddon," *Baker Encyclopedia of the Bible*, 4.

14. Carson, *The Gospel According to John*, 383-385.

15. *Ibid.*

16. Kruse, *John: An Introduction and Commentary*, 229-233.

17. The phrase "this rock" may be a reference to Mount Hermon, where ancient paganism locates the "gates of Hades." Thus, Jesus stands at the entrance to the underworld and picks a fight with the evil one, declaring that the church will prevail through the Savior's finished work on the cross. Michael Heiser has written extensively about this. For a summary, see *The Unseen Realm*, 281-287.

18. Schreiner, *1, 2 Peter, Jude*, Vol. 37, The New American Commentary, 238-246.

19. Marvin Richardson Vincent, *Word Studies in the New Testament*, Vol. 1 (New York: Charles Scribner's Sons, 1887), 667-670.

20. David Walls and Max Anders, *I & II Peter, I, II & III John, Jude*, Vol. 1, Holman New Testament Commentary (Nashville, TN: Broadman & Holman Publishers, 1999), 90-95.

21. Wayne A. Grudem, *1 Peter: An Introduction and Commentary*, Vol. 17, Tyndale House Commentaries (Downers Grove, IL: InterVarsity Press, 1988), 201-205.

22. Warren W. Wiersbe, *The Strategy of Satan: How to Detect and Defeat Him* (Carol Stream, IL: Tyndale House Publishers, Inc., 1979), 29.

23. Wiersbe, *The Strategy of Satan*, 30.

24. Wiersbe, *The Strategy of Satan*, 31.

25. Wiersbe, *The Strategy of Satan*, 32.

26. Vincent, *Word Studies in the New Testament*, Vol. 1, 667-670.

Chapter 14 – The One for Whom Hell Is Prepared

1. Quinn Myers, "5 Most Inescapable Prisons in the World," https://www.maxim.com/maxim-man/5-most-inescapable-prisons-world.

2. Morris, *The Gospel According to Matthew*, 633-641.

3. We should note that Jesus refers to the fires of hell as "eternal." The Greek word *aionios* means "without beginning or end, that which always has been and always will be," according to *Thayer's Greek Lexicon* (Blueletterbible.com). In some contexts, *aionios* may be rendered "without beginning" or "without end, never to cease, everlasting." R. T. France says the word "may convey either the sense of 'going on forever' or that of 'belonging to the age to come.' If it is the former, the reference might be either to a fire which never goes out because it is constantly fed with new fuel, even though the fuel does not last forever, or to an unending experience of burning for the *cursed*. It is clear therefore that the

terminology of this verse and of verse 46 [Matt. 25:46] does not by itself settle the issue between those who believe that hell consists of endless conscious torment and those who see it as annihilation. Whereas the 'kingdom' in v. 34 was prepared for the blessed, the fire here is not *prepared* for the cursed, but rather for *the devil and his angels*; the cursed are going to a fate that was not meant to be theirs." France, 357-362.

4. *Thayer's Greek Lexicon,* Blueletterbible.com.
5. France, 357-362.
6. In Rom. 10:7, Paul freely adapts Deut. 30:12-13, in which Moses contrasts going "up to heaven" with traveling "across the sea." The Israelites need to do neither, for the Lord's command is "certainly not too difficult or beyond your reach."
7. Robert Jamieson, A. R. Fausset, and David Brown, *Commentary Critical and Explanatory on the Whole Bible*, Vol. 2 (Oak Harbor, WA: Logos Research Systems, Inc., 1997), 598.
8. Elwell and Beitzel, "Bottomless Pit," *Baker Encyclopedia of the Bible*, 375.
9. Easley, 369-371.
10. Steve Gregg, *All You Want to Know About Hell: Three Christian Views of God's Final Solution to the Problem of Sin* (Nashville, TN: Thomas Nelson, 2013), 86-98.
11. C. H. Spurgeon, "The Resurrection of the Dead," *Spurgeon's Sermons*, Vol. 2, No. 66, Feb. 17, 1856.
12. William Crockett, *Four Views on Hell* (Grand Rapids, MI: Zondervan, 1996), 44.
13. Charles Hodge, *Systematic Theology*, Vol. 3 (Grand Rapids, MI: William B. Eerdmans Publishing Company, 1975), 868.
14. Robert A. Morey, *Death and the Afterlife* (Minneapolis, MN: Bethany House Publishers, 1984), 90.
15. *Ibid*.
16. Augustine, *City of God* 21:26.

17. C. S. Lewis, *The Problem of Pain*, cited in "Banished from Humanity: C. S. Lewis and the Doctrine of Hell" by Randy Alcorn, March 18, 2015, http://desiringgod.org/articles/banished-from-humanity.

18. Lewis, *The Problem of Pain*, cited in "Seeing Hell through the Reason and Imagination of C. S. Lewis" by Douglas Beyer, Jan. 1, 1998, http://discovery.org/a/507.

19. *On First Principles* 1.6.1. Origen felt he had scriptural support of *apocatastasis* in such New Testament passages as Acts 3:21; Rom. 5:17; 11:36; 1 Cor. 15:26-28; Phil. 2:10; and 1 John 4:8.

20. The substance of these paragraphs has been gleaned from Cole, *Against the Darkness*, 220.

21. Cole, 223.

22. Easley, 369-371.

Chapter 15 – Engaging the Evil One

1. "What does it mean to put on Christ in Romans 13:14?", https://gotquestions.org/put-on-Christ.html.

2. Walter L. Liefeld, *Ephesians*, Vol. 10, The IVP New Testament Commentary Series (Downers Grove, IL: InterVarsity Press, 1997), Eph 6:10.

3. H. C. G. Moule, *Commentary on Ephesians* (Cambridge: Cambridge Bible, 1884), n.p., quoted in Foulkes, *Ephesians: An Introduction and Commentary*, 175-185.

4. Liefeld, Eph 6:10.

5. "Armor," https://romanmilitary.net/tools/armor/.

6. Mentioned by Foulkes, 175-185.

7. Graham Land, "3 Kinds of Ancient Roman Shields," https://www.historyhit.com/kinds-of-ancient-roman-shields/.

8. Vincent, *Word Studies in the New Testament*, Vol. 3, 409-410.

9. For more on the collaborative work of the Father, Son, and

Holy Spirit in producing the written Word of God, see Rob Phillips, *What Every Christian Should Know About the Trinity* (Jefferson City, MO: High Street Press, 2019), 185-205.

10. Jamieson, Fausset, and Brown, 357-358.
11. "Armor of God: What is it?", https://bibleinfo.com.

ADDITIONAL RESOURCES

ORDER ADDITIONAL MATERIALS FROM HIGH STREET PRESS

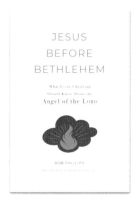

Jesus Before Bethlehem: What Every Christian Should Know About the Angel of the LORD

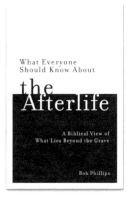

What Everyone Should Know About the Afterlife: A Biblical View of What Lies Beyond the Grave

What Every Christian Should Know About Salvation: Twelve Bible Terms That Describe God's Work of Redemption

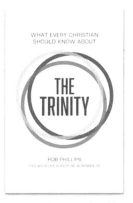

What Every Christian Should Know About the Trinity: How the Bible Reveals One God in Three Persons

Order these books and more through the retailers listed at our website:
highstreet.press/titles

The Apologist's Tool Kit: Resources to Help You Defend the Christian Faith

The Last Apologist: A Commentary on Jude for Defenders of the Christian Faith

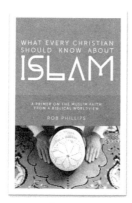

What Every Christian Should Know About Islam: A Primer on the Muslim Faith from a Biblical Worldview

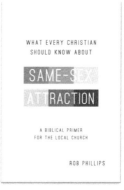

What Every Christian Should Know About Same-Sex Attraction: A Biblical Primer for the Local Church

Order these books and more through the retailers listed at our website:
highstreet.press/titles